THE BEST OF
LOS ANGELES

A DISCRIMINATING GUIDE

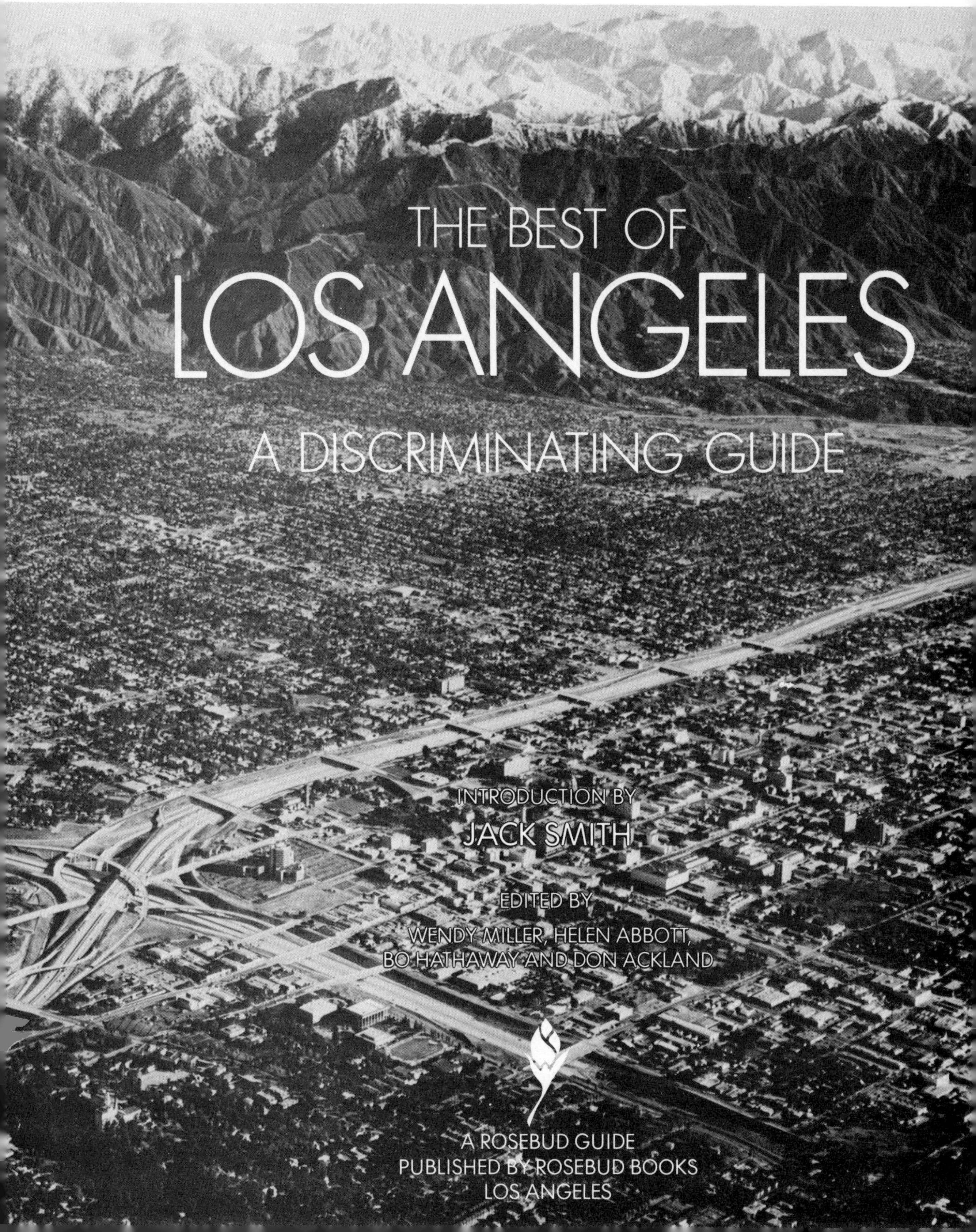

THE BEST OF
LOS ANGELES

A DISCRIMINATING GUIDE

INTRODUCTION BY

JACK SMITH

EDITED BY

WENDY MILLER, HELEN ABBOTT,
BO HATHAWAY AND DON ACKLAND

A ROSEBUD GUIDE
PUBLISHED BY ROSEBUD BOOKS
LOS ANGELES

For information contact Rosebud Books, 8777 Lookout
Mountain Avenue, Los Angeles, California 90046.

Jacket design by Laura LiPuma
Jacket photograph by Thomas P. Vinetz
Book design by Alex D'Anca

LIBRARY OF CONGRESS
CATALOG CARD NUMBER: 80-50656
Smith, Jack, et al.
The Best of Los Angeles
Los Angeles, Calif. : Rosebud Books, Inc
336 p.
8004   800305

Printed in the United States of America
ISBN 0-86558-001-4

This Rosebud Guide is dedicated to the
Pacific Ocean and the San Gabriel
Mountains, between whose graces
Los Angeles lives.

This guidebook is the product of many people's dedicated
efforts. Some contributed their special knowledge of the city,
others their skills and energy. We would like to thank: Ana
Austin, Brenda Austin, Richard Beale, Carol Bryson, Bob
Cato, Colin Clark, Faith Clark, Alex D'Anca, Claudia
Forman, Len Forman, Pattie Freeman, Rick Frey, Gilbert
Friedman, Jeff Kerns, Anita Keys, Roberta Kimmel, Annette
Kraus, Laura LiPuma, Curt Marvis, Katherine Miller, Sherry
Northridge, Chris Painter, Diana Peterson, Ave Pildas,
Bernard Schleifer, Marilyn Scott, Hildegard Shulman, Martin
Sweeney, Janice Gilbar Treadwell
and Gretchen Woelfle.

A special thanks to Sandy Pollock for suggesting the idea of
a comprehensive guide to Los Angeles. And most of all to
the fourteen authors and experts who labored beyond the
call of duty to make The Best of Los Angeles a reality,
and who patiently endured until their efforts found their
way into print.

Rosebud Books
Summer, 1980

CONTENTS

Hollywood Bowl.

Opening day of Union Station, April 1939.

Los Angeles International Airport.

READER'S NOTE

How to Use
The Best of Los Angeles:
A Discriminating Guide

Compiling this guidebook has been an immense endeavor, like charting the stars. Los Angeles is one of the largest and most diverse cities in the world. It's an international center of trade, technology, and entertainment, a place where the sun shines in June and in January. Its real estate ranks among the most desirable in the world, its people among the most interesting. The region is an explorer's dream. Nearly everything can be found here. Where else in these United States can you travel a few miles in any of several directions and find mountains, the ocean, the desert, forests, sunshine and snow. As Jack Smith says in his Introduction, "It is all make-believe and it is all real."

Fourteen of L.A.'s finest journalists, who make it their business to know the city, have profiled it, described it, dissected it, and put it back together for you with an added piece of their personality. Now, we are the first to admit that writers who live this intimately with a city of this complexity cannot be unbiased—who would want them to be?

These chapters are your special guidebook. If you're not one already, they will make you a fan of Los Angeles. And we hope you continue to follow our authors as they chronicle the city in such periodicals as the Los Angeles *Times*, the *Herald-Examiner*, *New West*, and *Los Angeles Magazine*.

Alfresco dining at the Farmer's Market during the late 1950s.

Because of the distances involved, jaunts around L.A. take a bit of planning. We recommend you call your destinations first to check current hours and prices. If you need help with directions through our throng of towns and streets, the Visitors Information Center, 628-3101, will be glad to assist.

Every attraction listed is worth a visit, but the very special places we have rated with **rosebuds**. One **rosebud** indicates an exceptional delight, two **rosebuds** are better yet and recommend it as the centerpiece of a trip, and three **rosebuds** highlight those finest places you should see if you're only in town for a few days. Entries marked with a † have been written by the Rosebud editors rather than the chapter author.

one ❧ means exceptional

two ❧❧ mean highlight of a trip

three ❧❧❧ mean the finest

The Best of Los Angeles: A Discriminating Guide will be revised regularly. In a city in which change is the only constant, new editions are mandatory. We would appreciate your comments, suggestions for revisions, and constructive criticisms. And don't hoard your favorite places. The world is to share; and especially in Los Angeles there is plenty to go around. Write us at 8777 Lookout Mountain Avenue, Los Angeles 90046.

And most of all, enjoy this stellar city.

THE EDITORS

The Brown Derby in 1936. The auto is one of the first V-8s introduced by Ford.

AN INTRODUCTION TO
THE BEST OF LOS ANGELES

by Jack Smith
LOS ANGELES TIMES

T he movie critic Pauline Kael once said that *Casablanca* shows how good a bad motion picture can be.

Los Angeles shows how good a bad city can be.

That is to say, Los Angeles is not a critical success. It has had almost universally bad reviews, going back all the way to Willard Huntington Wright, who complained in 1913 that "the lights go out at midnight," and H.L. Mencken, who observed after a visit in the 1920s that "the whole place stank of orange blossoms."

Since then Eastern journalists and pundits of various stripe have damned Los Angeles as an aesthetic, spiritual, and cultural waste-land. They come out in relays with their portable typewriters, their toothbrushes and their prejudices, and go home suntanned and rejuvenated—with their prejudices intact.

Nobody seems to like Los Angeles but the people. Almost everybody in the world wants to come and see Los Angeles; and when they do they come back to see it again—not only once, but twice, three times, the way they go back to see *Casablanca;* and finally a lot of them never go home again. That's how most of us got here.

How a city that has had such a bad press can be so boffo at the box office is not really hard to explain. The critics never actually see Los Angeles. They are like Herb Caen, the bard of San Francisco, who came to Los Angeles some years ago to write a piece about it but went home empty-handed. "I couldn't find it," he explained.

That was not entirely a joke. More than any other metropolis in the world, Los Angeles is hard to find. There is an *invisible* Los Angeles not easily discerned by strangers. It is known only to those who have lived here for a time, especially through a winter or two. It can not be observed simply by lunching in the Polo Lounge at the Beverly Hills Hotel or by taking a bus out Wilshire Boulevard past the La Brea Tar Pits. It is to be found only in such qualities as newness, freedom, space, variety, tolerance, opportunity, and optimism, and inescapably the weather.

There is of course a visible Los Angeles, but it is not easy to find either, because it is rather low-profile and scattered, and familiar only to the natives. For that reason Los Angeles is hard to photograph, and it has never been a best seller, I imagine, as a picture postcard. There is no way of making a single photograph of Los Angeles to show its drama and character, the way New York City can be photographed from the Brooklyn Bridge, or San Francisco from Alcatraz.

Being scattered and fragmented as it is by its spacious setting, and by the automobile and the freeways, much of Los Angeles remains unknown not only to tourists, but also to those who live here. Year-round residents tend to become fixed in orbits, and soon they have marked out a Los Angeles that would be as unfamiliar to several million other residents as Istanbul. There are hundreds of thousands of Angelenos who boast of never having been downtown;

The world-famous Grauman's Chinese Theatre in Hollywood. Embedded in cement are the footprints and handprints of over 150 celebrities.

there are other hundreds of thousands who have never wet their feet in the Pacific Ocean, much less explored the tidepools at Crescent Bay Beach, whose name they have never even heard. There are thousands of people in West Los Angeles who have never seen the Watts Towers and thousands in Watts who have never seen the County Museum of Art. They live like castaways on a Treasure Island without a map, ignorant of the treasures that lie just beyond their own immediate environs.

The Best of Los Angeles: A Discriminating Guide, more than any other book I have seen, provides such a map, one that describes the variety and attractions of this city. With vigor and zeal its authors have explored, discovered, and described the hundreds of cafes, beaches, boutiques, spas, museums, emporiums, theaters, homes, hotels, and watering holes that give Los Angeles its life and texture.

Los Angeles Hall. in the 1930s.

Although the listings are selective, with emphasis on quality rather than quantity, this guidebook is remarkably complete. It includes dozens of boutiques and restaurants and bars and other special places I have never even heard of, much less visited. And I am reconciled to the possibility that it has necessarily left out others that even its authors and editors have never heard of. But enough is enough. *The Best of Los Angeles* is like a panoramic photograph of the sky at night: it might not show all the stars in the heavens, but it shows the range and spaciousness of that sky and offers more to see and visit than anyone is likely to do in a lifetime.

I am sure my own orbit will be extended by some of the alluring places the authors have brought to light. Not every reader will be moved to follow Maurice Zolotow to *all* his favorite places,

Shopping on Olvera Street on a sunny day in 1939.

Jack Benny and Mary Livingstone at Union Station.

especially such esoteric shrines as Tyrone Power's tomb and the orphan home in which little Norma Jean Baker dreamed of becoming Marilyn Monroe. But some will, and someday I myself intend to follow him through that "lovely garden courtyard" to the apartment at the back where F. Scott Fitzgerald, off the booze, fought vainly to finish *The Last Tycoon* before his heart gave in. To each his own legend.

There is a quality of make-believe about Los Angeles that is invariably noted by its critics, but this too is an illusion. As Zolotow points out in his guide to the old Hollywood studios, the creation of make-believe takes skill, imagination, and hard work. The movies were not made by the waving of a wand, but by the labors of the most wonderful collection of tradesmen, artists, craftsmen, engineers, and lunatics who ever lived and worked together in one place.

It would have been impossible for this industry not to leave its mark on Los Angeles beyond the studios, and that is why, to this day, we find people living side by side in Italian villas, Spanish castles, Greek temples, Tudor mansions, Egyptian palaces, and Islamic mosques. But the houses are quite real. They have real plumbing and real fireplaces and real kitchens and bedrooms, for all their make-believe fronts; and the people who live in them are no less real than the people who live in rows of brownstones on Manhattan Island.

Almost everywhere in Los Angeles you will find a touch of this make-believe reality, this playfulness, this amiable pretense that one can be what one fancies oneself to be. In a place where the sun shines, and where there is no entrenched society, no standard taste, and no ancient rules, people are always at play, even when they build their restaurants, factories, and shelters. We live in French chateaux, and we dine out in Polynesian longhouses.

It is a quality that permeates this guidebook. Even the history, which is brief, lively, and respectful of the facts, sounds as if it might have been written about some imaginary Lotus Land where bands of romantic actors came to play at making history. We are told, for example, that the first English-speaking white man to take up residence in Los Angeles was a pirate who had been captured while he and his crew were marauding along the coast. He would of course have been hanged, but his skills and his charm won the hearts of his captors and he lived to marry the daughter of a prominent family and become an honored citizen. A perfect role for Errol Flynn.

What sets a city apart from an overgrown village is not so much its size as its possibilities. This is known to anyone who ever had a broken axle or a transmission failure in a highway town and had to hole up for a day or two while waiting for parts to come from civilization by Greyhound bus. It takes fifteen minutes to find the restaurant and the bar and the drug store (for a toothbrush and a paperback book), and there isn't anything else to find.

Like John Wellington Wells, Los Angeles is a dealer in magic and spells, and if anything anyone lacks, they will find it already in stacks—a cup in the shape of a duck at the Propinquity boutique (open late); great potato pancakes at Nate 'n Al's; glass animals and vases at the Glass Menagerie; custom sweatshirts at the Great American Sweatshirt Company; cutrate children's clothing at the Ridiculous Discount Shop; sexy slips and negligees at Trashy Lingerie; an antique print at Yesteryear, Ltd.; a piece of Lindy's New York cheesecake at La Difference (also try the pureed eggplant); shabu-shabu and yosenabe at A Thousand Cranes; carrot cakes at the Bubbles Baking Company; and at Cassell's Patio, one of the best hamburgers in Los Angeles, which means the world.

It is all make-believe and it is all real.

Clark Gable in The Daily News *office.*

As silly as it may seem to ask movie stars to imprint their hands and feet in wet cement, for posterity, it is not silly to the thousands who step down from buses in front of Grauman's Chinese Theater every day of the year to witness this phenomenon, this humble proof that the gods and goddesses of the screen, including the Invisible Man, are flesh and blood, and leave footprints on the earth, like everyone else.

Nowhere in the book is this oneness of make-believe and reality more graphically captured than in Zolotow's wanderings among the relics and symbols of Hollywood. Not only does he show us Schwab's drugstore, known the world over as the place where Lana Turner was discovered; he also shows us the Top Hat Malt Shop, across the street from Hollywood High School, where Lana Turner real!y *was* discovered. But the Top Hat Malt Shop isn't there anymore. Now which indeed is the proper shrine? The drug store where Miss Turner was *not* discovered, but which is still there? Or the malt shop where she *was* discovered, but which isn't there anymore? Which is the myth and which the reality?

He takes us to the Ravenswood on Rossmore and tells us it is not only owned by Mae West, but that Miss West resides in the penthouse suite. Mae West is real, and living, and resides in the penthouse of a concrete apartment building, in Hollywood, a place that is said to be only a state of mind.

I once interviewed Miss West in that apartment. The carpet and the walls and the furniture were white. The maid was in white, and Miss West, when she made her entrance, was in white lace and her face was white, and the only color in the room was the lovely chocolate of the maid's face and hands and the painted red lips and painted nails of Miss West. It seemed unreal.

That was many, many years ago, when Mae West was only sixty. And at this writing she is still there.

So much for the myth that Los Angeles is a myth.

It is as real as Treasure Island, and it remains to be explored. Here is the map.

June 8, 1889, opening day of the cable line at Spring and First.

A BRIEF HISTORY

by Bruce Henstell,
LOS ANGELES MAGAZINE
AND CALIFORNIA HISTORICAL SOCIETY

There must have been other suburbs besides Eden. Somewhere on Biblical freeways beyond or before that special place, there must have been other sites, but Eden is the one which got the publicity, and it is Eden we remember. So too Los Angeles. It is part, after all, of the state of California: a lush, beautiful land containing the magnetic hills of San Francisco and the fertile plains of the central valley. But it is Los Angeles which dominates California. It is Los Angeles which is the modern Eden.

Controversy surrounds the origins of the name "California." One charming version concerns a novel, *Las Sergas de Esplandián*, a kind of Renaissance science fiction, written around the year 1500. Its author, in fantasizing a siege upon the city of Constantinople, has the city saved by the wondrous appearance of Queen Calafia, empress of a race of black Amazons, residents of the far-away "Isla de California." From there the word seems to have entered into common use as a land far away, magical, and very wealthy, for the land of California was a land of gold.

The sixteenth century was the heyday of Spanish exploration of the New World. Cortes had found and plundered the Aztec cities of Mexico. From there, for the next two hundred years, the Spanish were to radiate out emissaries of exploration and settlement. At first their goal was the Seven Cities of Cíbola, cities constructed of gold, supposedly somewhere in the modern American southwest.

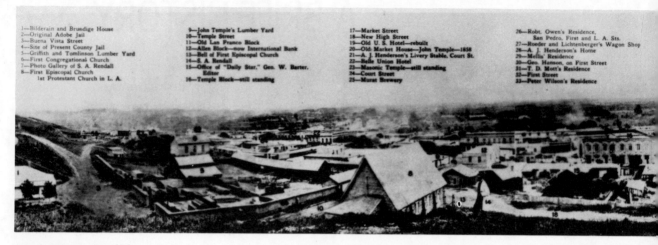

1—Bilderain and Brundige House
2—Original Adobe Jail
3—Buena Vista Street
4—Site of Present County Jail
5—Griffith and Tomlinson Lumber Yard
6—First Congregational Church
7—Photo Gallery of S. A. Rendall
8—First Episcopal Church
　　1st Protestant Church in L. A.

9—John Temple's Lumber Yard
10—Temple Street
11—Old Lan Franco Block
12—Allen Block—now International Bank
13—Bell of First Episcopal Church
14—S. A. Rendall
15—Office of "Daily Star," Geo. W. Barter, Editor
16—Temple Block—still standing

17—Market Street
18—New High Street
19—Old U. S. Hotel—rebuilt
20—Old Market House—John Temple—1858
21—A. J. Henderson's Livery Stable, Court St.
22—Belle Union Hotel
23—Masonic Temple—still standing
24—Court Street
25—Murat Brewery

26—Robt. Owen's Residence,
　　San Pedro, First and L. A. Sts.
27—Roeder and Lichtenberger's Wagon Shop
28—A. J. Henderson's Home
29—Mellis' Residence
30—Geo. Hanson, on First Street
31—T. D. Mott's Residence
32—First Street
33—Peter Wilson's Residence

Los Angeles in the 1870s when the census might have been taken with a single photograph.

Francisco Vásquez de Coronado tramped extensively through present-day Arizona and found the Seven Cities. They appeared golden alright, but only in the bright sun. In reality they were the mud and stone dwellings of cliff Indians—imposing, but not for their mineral wealth. Gradually the idea of unfound treasures passed from the Spanish agenda and instead the goal became the full exploration and settlement of the new lands north of Mexico, "Alta California."

In 1542 Juan Rodríguez Cabrillo sailed an elaborate expedition up to California. He found a small port which he named San Miguel, and landed at what we now call Catalina Island, San Pedro, Ventura, Point Conception, and Monterey.

In 1577 a freebooter named Francis Drake set sail from England, his official mission a guarded secret. But appropriation of Spanish wealth in the New World was not far from his mind. Once in the Pacific he raided the coast of Latin America and explored the coast of California, which he "discovered" and named New Albion.

Drake's expedition spurred the Spanish to tighten their control of the territory. In the early 1600s Sebastían Vizcaíno was dispatched to continue exploration and mapping. Vizcaíno had the habit, despite orders, of renaming places. Cabrillo's San Miguel now became San Diego, San Salvador Island Vizcaíno renamed Santa Catalina and a place called the Bay of Pines became Monterey, in honor of his voyage's sponsor, the Conde de Monterey.

Finally and decisively, in 1769 Don Gaspar de Portolá convinced the government of the Spanish New World to undertake an active policy of settlement. Portolá, a native of the New World, a soldier and civil servant, left for the north accompanied by Fray Junípero Serra. After a difficult overland march they reached San Diego which was proclaimed a royal presidio, or fort. Fray Serra set about establishing a chain of missions, each a day apart and con-

CHRONOLOGY

SEPTEMBER, 1542: *Juan Rodríguez Cabrillo becomes the first white man to set foot in California, landing in San Miguel (San Diego).*

JULY, 1769: *Don Gaspar de Portolá, two friars, twenty-seven soldiers, seven Catalonians, fifteen Christian Indians, and eight or nine muleteers, make camp by the side of a river they call the Porciúncula. It is a very pleasant spot for camping and it subsequently becomes Los Angeles.*

nected by a road he called "El Camino Real," the King's Highway.

Struggling north, Portolá's army, "wholly prostrate, some half-disabled, others on foot, without strength," according to the expedition's excellent diarist Fray Juan Crespí, a few days later entered "a spacious valley, well-grown with cottonwoods and alders, among which ran a beautiful river from the north-northwest. . . . Toward the north-northeast there is another river bed which forms a spacious watercourse, but we found it dry. . . . We halted not very far from the river, which we named Porciúncula." Here they set up camp, near a small Indian village. The natives brought them corn and tobacco. Portolá and his band had become the first of their race to spend a night in downtown Los Angeles.

Their camp, near the village the Indians called Yang-Na, was somewhere around Commercial and Alameda streets. Crespí called it "a pleasant place." The Porciúncula is now the Los Angeles River.

In 1771 a mission was opened nearby at San Gabriel. In 1777 Felipe de Neve became governor of Alta California with the intent of erecting a string of civil pueblos to complement the missions. The first was San José. In 1781 it was Los Angeles' turn.

The plan called for twenty-four families to be recruited in Mexico and resettled near where Portolá had camped. They were expected to be sober, industrious types with skills enough to sustain a small community. The government would supply a measure of money, animals, and land. Alas, only twelve families could be rounded up. Contrary to later romantic myth, they were hardly the caballero type. Indeed, they were barely as sober and not nearly as industrious as the government had hoped. Only poor people who despaired of their lives in Mexico were about to undertake so arduous a journey into a very great nowhere. Eleven families, including some black or mulato, eventually reached the selected location. On September 4, 1781, city building began. Despite

SEPTEMBER 8, 1771: *Mission San Gabriel Arcangel, the fourth Spanish mission in California, is formally founded, on the banks of Rio San Miguel, also known as Rio de los Temblores, the river of the earthquakes.*

SEPTEMBER 4, 1781: *According to the instructions of Governor of Alta California Felipe de Neve, El Pueblo de Nuestra Señora la Reina de los Angeles de Porciúncula is founded. Later generations find it expedient to call the place simply "Los Angeles" or "Los." The names of the city's settlers, a ragtag band recruited in northern Mexico, are not immortalized by the contemporary Los Angeles nor does any plaque mark the spot of the founding of the city.*

another romantic myth, it was without much ceremony. More likely these first few citizens quickly set about providing themselves with shelter and food, and the fewer formalities the better. The Indians of Yang-Na now found themselves to be living in something called El Pueblo de Nuestra Señora la Reina de los Angeles de Porciúncula (The Town of Our Lady the Queen of the Angels by the Porciúncula), a name with about as many letters as the new town had people.

Nothing in the pueblo's first half-century put the world on notice that it was destined to become a great city. The Indians were herded into the missions under the benign if authoritarian hand of the fathers. In time soldiers retired from garrison duty, remained, were granted huge tracts of land called ranchos, and settled into peaceful lives of cattle raising. Remote from Mexico, remoter still from Spain, Alta California followed its own course. The residents thought of themselves as Californios: more genteel, more hospitable, more sophisticated than many in the empire.

The dusty pueblo, however, became something of a sink for the more undesirable elements. A visitor wrote of town life, "The pueblo of Nuestra Señora contains a population of one thousand five hundred souls, and is the noted abode of the lowest drunkards and gamblers in the country. This den of thieves is situated . . . in one of the loveliest and most fertile districts of California."

DECEMBER 8, 1822: *The Church on the Plaza of Los Angeles is dedicated.*

MARCH 26, 1825: *California officially becomes part of the Republic of Mexico.*

JANUARY 21, 1836: *By government decree, Los Angeles is raised from the status of a pueblo (town), to that of a ciudad (city).*

Little here was ever new. The world turned, but elsewhere. In 1825 Alta California ceased being Spanish and became part of the new Republic of Mexico. It hardly mattered.

Then, in 1826, an event of historic importance occurred. Joseph Chapman was an American, a sailor with a pirate band which had burned Monterey and then marauded its way down the coast. Near Santa Barbara the Californios trapped Chapman ashore. Had the roles been reversed with Chapman Spanish and his captors American he might well have been summarily hanged. Instead Chapman was taken to Los Angeles and put on probation. He became a valued member of the community owing to his mechanical skills, eventually marrying into a prominent family and gaining the acceptance of all. He was the first speaker of English to take up permanent residence in Los Angeles.

Chapman represented the beginning of what was to become a flood. Next came the mountain men, hardy trappers who forged their way across the deserts and mountains surrounding the city as had the Spanish one and two hundred years before. They were not looked upon with great favor. Sylvester and James Pettie, father and son, journeyed to California from Kentucky only to have the governor imprison them. Sylvester died in captivity. But James Pettie was offered an extraordinary deal. It was found he had a knowledge of innoculation. At the time a smallpox epidemic raged. Pettie was offered his freedom providing he innoculated the citizens, especially the Indians, against the disease. He agreed and with the imposing title of "Surgeon Extraordinary to His Excellency, The Governor of California," Pettie faithfully executed his part of the deal.

Chapman, the Petties, the fabled mountain man Jedediah Smith and others were followed by yet another sort of American: the Yankee. Abel Stearns was one. He arrived in Los Angeles, adopted the Spanish language and the Catholic Church and in time became Don Abel, one of the more respected members of the community and the owner of vast tracts of land. He fell in love with Arcadia Bandini, the fourteen-year-old daughter of a prestigious family, and married her. It was a spring-autumn affair: Stearns was then in his fifties. His wife's first name lives on in a suburb of the city. Pliny Fiske Temple, of Temple Street fame, was another. The Spanish could never quite get the hang of "Pliny Fiske" and P.F. Temple took the nom de plume of Francisco, becoming F.P.F. Temple or simply Don Juan Temple. He, too, embraced the Church and the heart of the daughter of a Californio grandee and became in time one of the city's pioneer bankers.

Despite the respectability of these newcomers, the infusion of an American strain into Los Angeles did not pass without trepidation. Governor Pío Pico wrote: "We find ourselves suddenly threatened by hordes of Yankee immigrants . . . whose progress we cannot arrest. . . . They are cultivating farms, establishing vineyards, erecting sawmills, sawing up lumber, building workshops, and doing a thousand other things which seem natural to them." A clash of cultures was forming: the industrious eager-beaver Americans pitted against the ancient, settled Spanish who viewed life with as much an eye to its style as to the amount of lumber sawed or crops raised.

On the other hand, the Californios often chaffed at the insensitivity which their own government, hundreds of miles away in Mexico City, showed to Upper California. The remote province was hardly garrisoned in force, and it became clear that sooner or later it would cleave off from Mexico.

Lookout Mountain in 1910.

Its future was problematic. Americans in the East saw domination of the entire continent as part of their "manifest destiny." Some in California favored an independent republic, following the example of Texas. The British were still interested, and some Californios wanted the region to become a colony of that empire. Added to the brew was the presence in the state, presumably on a scientific expedition, of the quixotic General John C. Fremont, the "Pathfinder." He did his best to encourage the Californians to do their worst. In 1846 a short-lived "Bear Flag" republic of California was declared. Then war between the United States and Mexico broke out. The Bear Flaggers were sworn into the American army and an American fleet, conveniently nearby, seized the capital at Monterey.

In the midst of the war Los Angeles was taken without opposition. The Americans now made a critical mistake. A young officer was

JULY 22, 1847: *A commission charged with investigating the irregularity of Los Angeles streets professes itself stunned: "Your commissions could not be but amazed seeing the disorder and the manner how the streets run. More particularly the street which leads to the cemetery, whose width is out of proportion to its length, and whose aspect offends the sense of the beautiful which should prevail in the city."*

1851: Rancho La Brea. Originally two rooms of adobe built by John Thompson who sold the property to Arthur Gilmore. Gilmore and his son, Earl, expanded and renovated the structure. Completed in about 1947, the building stands in the parking lot of the Farmer's Market.

FEBRUARY 2, 1848: *The treaty of peace between the United States and Mexico, ending the Mexican War, is signed. Los Angeles, for better or worse, is hereafter American.*

placed in command of the town, which was fine with the Angelenos as long as the new master respected local tradition. But the young American officer was rude and the Californios of Los Angeles did not like rudeness. Patriotism, laced with wine, emerged, and Los Angeles rose in belated resistance, sealing the Americans off on Fort Moore hill, in the present Civic Center. The Americans were invited to surrender, outnumbered as they were, and with good sense they agreed. Their punishment was to be shown the city's door and invited never to return. They did return, however, and with reinforcements. Again they were defeated, this time by the aggressive mounted tactics of the Californio vaqueros, or cowboys, and the Los Angeles artillery, which consisted of one four-pound cannon dragged along by a rope and nicknamed "The Old Woman's Gun." But the Americans regrouped and attacked again, this time defeating the Angelenos in what was called the Battle of the Mesa.

On January 10, 1848, the American flag was raised for the second and last time in Los Angeles. In February California became a territory of the United States and in 1850 a state. Not much, however, changed in Los Angeles: the language and laws were still Spanish; the customs those of the Californios. They were tolerant but looked with some suspicion upon the Americans, all spit and polish and business. An American band was assigned to the plaza and each day at sunset offered a concert. The Californios understood music and appreciated a people who played it. Links were forged which perhaps were more important than those written in distant cities upon the parchment of treaties.

In the 1850s and 1860s new immigrants appeared in the now American city of Los Angeles; many were German Jews, all of whom learned Spanish before English. Forms changed: the Spanish *ayuntamiento* became the city's common council and the *alcalde* was now called the mayor. But seated on the council in this period was one member who spoke only Spanish, one only French, with the rest bilingual—giving the city a hint of the cosmopolitan flavor it would develop in a much later period. It wasn't until 1851 that the first child of two American parents was born in the city. The local newspaper was *La Estrella de Los Angeles*, the *Star*, which published in both Spanish and English. Things went on very much as they had before.

Then gold was discovered in northern California. Many passing through to the gold fields quartered briefly in Los Angeles, contributing to its reputation as a hellhole. The crowds in the north generated a demand for even the scrawny Southern California cattle which heretofore had little value save for their hides. These were boom times for the Californios, providing they could keep their land.

In the transition to American rule, Congress set up a lands commission to review the ancient Spanish and Mexican land grants and certify titles. The commission was, in the end, to prove disastrous to the grandees of Southern California. First, the commission sat in San Francisco, conducting its investigations from afar. The dons of old Los Angeles, many of whom were hardly fluent in English, found themselves having to hire strange creatures called lawyers, and found themselves plunged into a mire of American legalisms. The Californios were not a people for legalisms. The land they lived upon, was so vast, their relationships with their neighbors so secure, that few bothered with details that enterprising Yankees considered essential. Grants of land were often phrased in metaphoric fashion; boundary markers such as the old oak down by the river and the big rock on top of the hill had often over the years simply vanished.

The boom years for cattle were followed by three years of drought in the 1860s which once and forever ruined the cattle industry. The land claims actions dragged on and on. Many of the Californios were forced to put up their land to pay their legal fees and were presented with the irony of having gained a title only to lose it to their American lawyers.

Worse still was the fate of the Indians. Forced to the bottom of the social order, they deteriorated rapidly. A vicious trade developed. Indians were employed as unskilled labor in the vineyards

APRIL 4, 1850: *The state legislature passes the act of incorporation for Los Angeles.*

APRIL 15, 1851: *John Gregg Nichols is born. He is the first child of two American parents born in Los Angeles. (Congratulations: in 1852 his father is elected mayor.)*

JULY 18, 1851: *On a motion by John O. Wheeler, city councilman, city policemen are henceforth to wear a ribbon reading, in both English and Spanish: "City Police, organized by the Common Council of Los Angeles, July 12, 1851."*

surrounding Los Angeles. They were paid on Fridays, their wages supplemented with a bottle of aguire, the local, and potent, brandy. Soon they would be seen drunk on Calle de los Negros, Los Angeles' then skid row. They would eventually be arrested and dried out and on Monday auctioned off to vineyard owners willing to pay their fines for public intoxication in exchange for their week's labor. The Indians of Los Angeles, whose wicker huts and gentle lifestyle form part of the education of every grammar school child in the city today, were driven nearly to extinction. Of their culture little remained.

In 1858 Los Angeles was linked to San Francisco and St. Louis by the Butterfield stage. In 1859 Don Juan Temple built an office block which housed the first city hall. In 1860 Los Angeles and San Francisco were joined by telegraph.

Immigration continued although hardly in overflowing numbers. Many new arrivals were from the southern states. El Monte was a hotbed of pro-slavery sympathy. When the Civil War came there was talk of Los Angeles declaring for the Confederacy. But just talk; the city was solidly Democratic and probably strongly Confederate, but the Angelenos of the day favored talk over action.

No boom times were enjoyed except for the excitement of being the base of the U.S. Camel Corps. At war's end Los Angeles was still somewhat notorious. Hardly a day passed in which a dead body or two did not turn up: when a day without such a reminder of the city's frontier nature did arrive it was news indeed. It had not been so long before that the city's new religious divines had, almost to a man, abandoned the place to Satan. As one remarked: "To preach week after week to empty benches is certainly not encouraging, but when in addition . . . a minister has to contend against a torrent of vice and immorality which obliterates all traces of the Christian sabbath; when he is compelled to endure the blasphemous denunciations of his divine mission, to live where society is disorganized, religion scoffed at, where violence runs riot, and even life itself is unsafe—such condition of affairs may suit some men, but it is not calculated for the peaceful labors of one who follows unobtrusively the foot-steps of the meek and lowly Savior."

Still the lovely natural setting and potential of the land made the city very special. "It was a grand country," a contemporary wrote, "and one could get along with less than in any other part of the United States and still be respectable and fat."

By the 1870s Los Angeles was looking more like an American town. It had a number of new faces, Easterners convinced the place had a great future. Los Angeles had even made the Eastern newspapers, albeit in an ignominious manner. In 1871 a race riot had broken out—a mob of whites turned against the city's small Chinese community for an imagined infraction. Nineteen Chinese were lynched. One of the few to emerge from these sad events with any dignity

was a young policeman, Emil Harris, who had tried to stand against the crowd. Harris later became the city's first, and only, Jewish chief of police.

Frontier justice was a fact of life. One city mayor stayed a lynch mob only by promising that if the courts, seated far away in Northern California, did not dispatch prompt justice, he would himself resign and lead a mob. And when the courts were slow he in fact did resign and lead the mob. He was re-elected to office almost immediately.

But there was other, and better, publicity about this strange new place. Charles Nordoff, a young journalist, wrote a book which received wide attention in the East. *California for Health, Profit and Residence* sparked new interest in Southern California. Then silver and lead were discovered in the mountains north and east of the city, and Los Angeles benefited in being the terminal for this trade.

A railroad was constructed linking downtown and what passed for the city's harbor at San Pedro. A cathedral, St. Vibiana's, was built. The common council ordered all homes and businesses in the city to adopt street numbers. The Merced was opened as the city's first structure built specifically as a theater. The official inauguration had to be delayed until a troupe of actors could arrive by ship from

July 4, 1871: The first civic parade in Los Angeles. The flower-festooned horse-drawn fire wagon is being led by the traditional marching band at Main, north of Temple.

JULY 31, 1873: *The first Los Angeles Chamber of Commerce is organized.*

AUGUST 8, 1873: *The city's first synagogue is dedicated at Fort (Broadway), between Second and Third streets.*

San Francisco. Ice, made by machine, was introduced. The first fire department, the first synagogue, and the first library were opened. And Angelenos began to think about the transcontinental railroad.

It was clear in late nineteenth-century America that the railroad would decide the fate of every would-be city. A railroad meant prosperity or at least the promise of prosperity. The absence of one meant the future was indeed bleak.

The Southern Pacific, after its parent company united with the Union Pacific at Promontory Point, Utah in 1869, was now lustily building south from its headquarters in San Francisco, through the great central valley. As it progressed it struck "bargains" with towns in its path or, if the bargain was not satisfactory to the railroad, it simply built around the town or founded a new one. Only two cities in the valley declined the railroad's offer and survived.

Los Angeles, with a population of 5,000 in 1870 and 10,000 in 1880, knew it had no compelling reason to be selected the Southern Pacific's southern terminus, or the western terminus of a second, southern, transcontinental route. There was, by way of competition, San Diego, approximately the same size, with the same boosters, the same respectable growth of late, and possessed of a magnificent harbor.

The Southern Pacific was willing to build into Los Angeles provided the city give it some incentive to do so. The incentive the railroad had in mind included a sizeable number of acres downtown, free of charge, upon which to build a terminal. And the S.P. wanted control of the short line which connected L.A. with San Pedro and this, too, free of charge. To boot, the railroad wanted a cash subsidy of five percent of the county's assessed valuation.

JULY 1, 1877: The U.S. Signal Corps opens the city's first weather bureau.

NOVEMBER 25, 1877: City council changes the name of Lovers Lane to Date Street. (There's a moral here.)

Needless to say there were more than a few in town who were willing to tell the railroad exactly what it could do with its rails. Calmer heads prevailed. However extortionary the railroad's terms, to decline meant the inevitable decay of the city. By a vote of the people, they were accepted. In 1876 rail transportation with the East via San Francisco was opened. The introduction of service was but the beginning of a protracted feud between the city and the octopus in which little love was lost on either side. It would take until the early twentieth century before the political control the railroad exercised over the city could be broken.

Not surprisingly the city rejoiced when a second rail line was laid in the mid-1880s. The coming of the Santa Fe offered competition to the Southern Pacific. At first spectacular competition. The Santa Fe had not long begun service when a furious rate war broke out. Fares to the East were cut in half and then cut again. No sooner would the S.P. post a price than the Santa Fe would undercut it and vice versa. In the midst of the confusion the Santa Fe undercut its own price.

1885: The construction of the Los Angeles and San Gabriel Valley Railroad.

1889: The Cahuenga Valley Railroad.

FEBRUARY 8, 1881: *City council outlaws the sale of opium in the city.*

SEPTEMBER 5, 1881: *The hundredth anniversary of the city is celebrated. Alas, it is the wrong day. The correct date is September 4, but a local historian made a mistake.*

NOVEMBER 29, 1885: *The first Santa Fe train enters the city via the Southern Pacific's tracks from Colton.*

There were those who suspected that the rate war was a bit of promotion. Regardless, it had its effect. For the coming of the Santa Fe to Los Angeles launched a boom little short of volcanic. Here at last was proof of what the boosters had long insisted: Los Angeles would be discovered and when it was discovered it would grow.

The way had been prepared for this boom by publicity. It was an event of major importance when, in 1884, California citrus, rushed to a fair at New Orleans by the for-the-moment cooperative railroad, bested that from Florida. Los Angeles' reputation as a place for growing the most amazing variety of fruits and vegetables was established.

And the climate and land seemed equally spectacular when applied to humans. The climate was heralded as the miracle cure in an age fascinated with miracle cures. It was an age endlessly affected by chronic ailments, if the profusion of patent medicines is any indication.

The city took notice, then, in 1885 when the usually dull summer months became no longer dull. In normal times the tourists fled the imagined horrors of a summer in semitropical Los Angeles. Yet now they stayed. And in the winter they came in increasing droves, by the trainload. Boarding houses in town filled up. Housing was at a premium. Everybody was looking for a place to live or at least land to own. Boom. The word was on everybody's lips. A mania of speculation took hold. Everything was suddenly for sale at a price higher than what it had sold for yesterday, and it could reasonably be expected to sell for still more tomorrow. So it went for the next few years while the city's population shot up fivefold.

Professional boomers made their appearance. Politely they were real estate men, less politely they were hucksters and con men with one finger on the public's pulse and the others firmly on its pocketbook. Whole cities were laid out overnight; bleak, arid land in actuality, they were pictured as busy metropolises in colorful advertisements. Few bothered to view the land they intended to purchase. At one point the vast emptiness east of Los Angeles, all the way out to the Mojave Desert, was platted for development: would-be, maybe, about-to-be new cities.

The methods used in promotion were colorful to say the least. One new town was Gladstone: its selling point was that William Gladstone, then prime minister of England, had been given a deed. One wonders what happened to Disraeli. Hotels were thrown up overnight on the site of a new city, to convince potential buyers the developers meant business. Often the hotel was the only building the town would ever see. Building materials were dumped on lots as if purchasers had already begun construction. Oranges were tied to Joshua trees on desert acreage which was then sold as orchards.

"If a new townsite," recorded one who saw it all, "was situated in a river wash or a stony canyon, the sand and boulders were boosted as building material . . . if the townsite was out on the desert, it was boosted as a natural health resort . . . if the townsite was situated in a swamp . . . a fictitious harbor was boosted." James Guinn, a historian of the boom, described one townsite as being "most easily accessible by means of balloon, and was as secure from hostile invasion as the homes of the cliff dwellers. Its principal resource . . . was a view—a view of the Mojave desert." A second town nearby "was a city of greater resources . . . being located higher up on the mountain it had a more extended view of the desert." One broadside describing a new town situated on the San Gabriel River showed a mighty steamboat chugging upstream. At that point the San Gabriel runs underground.

But perhaps the comment which sums up the often incredible heights attained during the boom is that laid to J.S. Slauson whose name remains with us upon a major boulevard. Slauson platted a new town. When it was pointed out the land selected was sand and hardly inviting, Slauson replied: "If it's not good for a town it isn't good for anything."

In 1887 the boom broke. Not burst, but merely broke. Speculators suffered, but Los Angeles was no South Seas Bubble, which, after flourishing briefly in the limelight, exploded and was forgotten. The doldrums set in, but Los Angeles remained.

From 11,000 in 1880, Los Angeles grew to more than 50,000 by 1890. Now began perhaps the most pacific and beautiful days the city was ever to know. Growth was slower, but the city did grow. And it began to take a thoroughly modern form. Street lights were installed featuring the marvel of the age—electricity. Actual sidewalks of concrete began to replace dust and mudholes. The Grand Opera House, as fine a theater as a city could want, was opened. A symphony orchestra was begun, one of only a few in America.

A professional fire department was created, the police department reorganized. Charity Street was renamed Grand Avenue: the residents didn't like the thought of "living on Charity." Banks opened, and a new courthouse, the grandest one west of Denver, was constructed at the corner of Temple Street and Broadway. Edward Doheny discovered oil at the corner of Second Street and Glendale. It seems tar, or brea as it was known to the Spanish, had long bubbled up in various parts of the city. Now a new business was established, one destined to reach gushing proportions in the new century.

A fiesta was held yearly and the city decked itself out in flowers for the occasion. It lampooned the boom days it had survived and celebrated the promise which yet remained. New theaters opened; street railways appeared upon which residents could travel far and wide, even to Mt. Lowe beyond the "crown city" of Pasadena, Los Angeles' great competitor for cultural dominance. The Mt. Lowe

JANUARY 20, 1887: *There's a land boom on. On this day sales reach a total of $1,679,945, a new high.*

NOVEMBER 4, 1892: *With a pick and shovel, Edward L. Doheny begins prospecting for oil at the corner of Second Street and Glendale. He finds it.*

JANUARY 26, 1894: *The Vegetarian Society of Southern California, a branch of the Vegetarian Society of America in Philadelphia, is founded.*

MAY 5, 1895: *The Los Angeles and Pasadena electric railway, built by pioneer transportation man Moses Sherman, opens.*

1897: Cahuenga Pass connecting Hollywood and the San Fernando Valley.

DECEMBER 16, 1896: *Colonel Griffith J. Griffith presents the city with land for the park which bears his name.*

APRIL 26 AND 27, 1899: *Work begins on the harbor at San Pedro. A two-day celebration is the first order of business.*

line provided a magical ride on narrow-gauge tracks up to what appeared to be the top of the world at which point one found a tavern.

Colonel Griffith J. Griffith gave the city a huge tract of land for a park. But perhaps the surest sign of how far and how fast the city had come was the creation of a Pioneers' Club to reminisce about the old days. Historian Guinn wrote: "Never before or since has the Angel City been so beautiful as she was in the closing years of the first century.

In these halcyon days preceding 1900, Los Angeles triumphed in a fateful inter-city war. The issue was the construction of a harbor capable of meeting the demands of the modern day. The one at San Pedro was a poor excuse, not much more than a shallow mudflat. Ships had to be off-loaded at sea and their cargo taken in on smaller boats.

Some had suggested moving the harbor elsewhere. Ballona, now Playa del Rey, was briefly a candidate, as was Redondo Beach. The major alternative was Santa Monica; the reason was, again, the Southern Pacific railroad.

If San Pedro were developed as a harbor it would be one over which the Southern Pacific would not exercise monopoly control. At Santa Monica, the railroad did have such control and soon erected a pier, ran a rail line out, and began calling it Port Los Angeles. Businessmen realized that if federal funds for a harbor were applied to

Santa Monica and not San Pedro, they would once again be putting themselves within the grasp of the octopus, the omniverous railroad.

The battle waged through the halls of Congress where the city was blessed by having, as senator, Southern Californian Stephen White, a brilliant lawyer and, it turned out, a skillful political tactician. The battles of this war were the proceedings of no less than three independent panels of experts appointed by Congress to determine whether San Pedro or Santa Monica would make the better harbor. Each time San Pedro was the choice, and each time the railroad used its power to block any appropriation.

Even after the railroad was defeated and the money given to San Pedro, the railroad succeeded in delaying the start of construction. Finally, in early 1899, President William McKinley stood at his desk in Washington and pressed a button which was to start the mechanism for dumping the first rocks for the new breakwater. The device failed to operate and anxious Angelenos scampered onto the boat and began tossing the stones in by hand.

Circa 1903: Colonel Griffith J. Griffith.

A festival followed. The city knew a canal would someday be built across Central America and would provide quick sea access to the

1891: "Crown City," Pasadena, and the Tournament of Roses.

21

THE BEST OF LOS ANGELES IN COLOR

Los Angeles is a city of color.

The hues are at times neon of dayglow brassy. At other times they are as subtle as the tints of vegetation, sunsets, or the changing seasons. The variety and contrasts are endless and exciting.

The city of Los Angeles blends magically into a vast and varied landscape of natural colors and shapes. More than any other great city, Los Angeles is a part of the geography that shaped and holds it.

Here is a city where the old and the new meet and embrace. History does not struggle to be recognized; it is preserved and lovingly reflected in the very design of the city itself. Los Angeles is western and Spanish and essentially American. It is adventurous, growing, exciting, and brimming with life.

The best of American culture can be seen here—a culture that accommodates differences and choices, opportunity and enchantment. Here one will find Chinatown and little Tokyo, Chicano festivals and Hollywood premieres, fast food and haute cuisine. Here too people dress in the most sophisticated fashions or the simplest; they build adobe, ranch style homes and mountain side chateaux, high-rise city condominiums and beach cottages. They make music as different as classical and new wave, and everything in between. In a city where entertainment is the main business, anything can happen. The arts flourish and mingle in surprising ways.

Downtown Los Angeles is a study in contrasts—City Hall, once the city's tallest structure, the spind-ly palms and the modest stucco apartments.

Los Angeles at night from Griffith Park.

Touring Topics published by the Automobile Club of Southern California from 1909 to 1933.

The face of the revitalized Los Angeles—the Pacific Design Center at the intersection of Melrose and San Vicente.

*Built in 1893 with "no expense spared." Ironwork from France, the woodwork by outstanding craftsmen.
At times threatened, but now lovingly preserved—the Bradbury Building, downtown Los Angeles.*

Venice Beach.

*Jogging through the coral trees
on San Vicente Boulevard.*

Nestled in Arroyo Seco, USC battles Michigan in another classic confrontation at the granddaddy of all bowls, the Rose Bowl.

Historic Chinatown, located in the 900 block of North Broadway, is a colorful center of long-standing Los Angeles traditions.

In Venice, the Ocean Front Walk, the choice is yours—sun, water, philosophy.

Olvera Street restored— stalls, stands, palm trees, and snow.

The Los Angeles Produce Market at Eighth and Wall streets.

The Chicano festival El Día de los Muertos *in Evergreen Cemetery, East Los Angeles.*

Musso and Frank, Hollywood's first celebrity restaurant.

L'Ermitage in Beverly Hills.

Your hosts for the evening at Perino's.

Le Dôme on Sunset Boulevard.

Colorful, elegant—Hiro Sushi in Santa Monica.

Lobster platter at Scandia on Sunset Boulevard.

A white place setting at Perino's.

A setting at Bernard's in the Biltmore Hotel.

A group at the big table at Chung King in West Los Angeles.

Perino's in the Mid-Wilshire district.

Double Decker at Dolores, La Cienega and Wilshire boulevards.

Scandanavian libation, aquavit at Scandia.

The bar at Scandia.

Main peristyle garden of the J. Paul Getty Museum, Malibu.

Mosaic fountain, J. Paul Getty Museum.

Rembrandt's Lady with Plume *at the Huntington Art Gallery, Pasadena.*

The Sculpture Garden at UCLA, adjoining the Frederick S. Wight Art Gallery.

Mulholland Drive near Laurel Pass in February looking across the San Fernando Valley northeast to the snow-covered San Gabriel Mountains.

Malibu Canyon in August looking south across Gold Creek. Old Claretville Seminary on the left.

Laurel Canyon in January at the top of Lookout Mountain Avenue, looking northeast towards the San Gabriel Mountains.

*Forty-five minutes north of Hollywood on Interstate Five looking west
to the snowy mountains of Los Padres National Forest.*

Malibu sunset.

Woodrow Wilson Drive near Mulholland Drive looking west into a stormy autumn sunset.

But the contrasts and colors here do not jar the soul or the eye because they reflect the natural variety which abounds. Blue ocean waves wash white sand beaches, snow capped mountains overlook parched brown deserts, dusty foothills rise from verdant valleys. Tropical palm trees and cascading bougainvillea, scrub brush, chaparral, cacti, wild flowers, and ferns of all kinds find a place to thrive here.

And the vital, indigenous color of the place is in the people. It's part of the way they dress, it's in the things they make, and, more importantly, it's part of their lives.

Unlike other major urban centers, the vast landscape of Los Angeles exudes a dramatic spectrum of color—as part of the environment, as part of the buildings and structures, as part of the people-made decorations, as part of the dishes they prepare, and it's always part of the way they make over the city to fit their everyday needs.

Nature and people arrange and rearrange the palette of reds, blues, and yellows.

Los Angeles, the city of primary colors, in infinite variety.

Port of Los Angeles.

East Coast. Los Angeles, with its new harbor, would become a trading center. Perhaps *the* trading center, greater even than its rival San Francisco. With this bright optimism Los Angeles turned to the twentieth century.

The boom and its collapse had taught the city fathers a lesson in the value of advertising. Los Angeles did not discover this nor was it the first American city to advertise widely. Since the Civil War almost every settlement on the western frontier had its boosters and its publicity. Los Angeles just did it bigger and better and more consistently. California fruit was exhibited widely and the railroads cooperated in rushing the best products to the major fairs and expositions around the country. Copies of Los Angeles' newspapers were sent to publishers everywhere. The chamber of commerce was a cornucopia of publications disseminating the good word. A special "California on Wheels" train toured the Midwest luring unwary farmers aboard and dangling the delights of the *Land of Sunshine* (the title of a periodical published at the time) before their eyes.

Civic boosters might be found in other cities; in Los Angeles they were a separate and distinct species. As one newspaper pointed out: "There is no room for knockers here. We are too busy going ahead." The growth of the city wasn't simply to be desired, it was fully in keeping with the basic plan of the universe. "The prosperity of Los Angeles is founded upon the immutable force of nature," wrote one booster, "combined with the inevitable needs of mankind; and it will remain as the sea and the clouds and the mountains remain, and will increase as the needs of the nation and the race increase."

In 1900 there were 102,000 people living in Los Angeles. By 1910

A 1930s territorial annexation map of the city of Los Angeles.

there were over 300,000. The city was fast outgrowing its frontier image.

In 1910 the world's first international air meet was held in Los Angeles. William Randolph Hearst began his *Examiner* and the city had no less than five daily newspapers. The back of the Southern Pacific's political machine which had long dictated to city hall was broken and the government reorganized. Referendum, initiative, and recall, the latter devised in Los Angeles, entered into the city charter.

There was but one major hindrance: water, or rather the lack of it. Water was one thing nature had not provided Los Angeles. The flow of the Los Angeles River was increasingly depleted, and artesian wells began to show signs of strain. The situation at the turn of the century was hardly critical, but would obviously become so if the city continued its rapid growth.

November 5, 1913: The opening of the Los Angeles aqueduct headgate. President The-odore Roosevelt decided it was more impor-tant to the country as a whole to develop the city of Los Angeles than it was to develop the Owens Valley. William Mulholland, head of the city-owned water department, said at the inaugural ceremonies, "There it is. Take it."

A fabulous scheme was devised by former mayor Fred Eaton: tapping a river which rose in the Owens Valley several hundred miles north of the city and building an aqueduct to conduct it to Los Angeles. Eaton told his plan to William Mulholland, head of the city-owned water department and about to become the city's long-standing water czar.

The story of the building of the aqueduct is one of the more sensational in the city's history because so much is laced with intrigue and evil-doing, or at least the suspicion of evil-doing. When later writers recounted the aqueduct's history they wove a tale of conspiracy, making it the original Watergate. The story, briefly, was that the city's water supplies were in fact more than sufficient to meet its needs. But certain powerful men in the city, chiefly the cantankerous and potent General Harrison Otis, owner of the *Times*, controlled large tracts of land in the San Fernando Valley which were only marginally valuable. Should water be available these lands would skyrocket in price. The Owens Valley plan was nothing less than the effort of these men to get the city of Los Angeles to pay for watering their lands in the valley which at that time was not even part of the city. They did so in part by fabricating a scarcity. This is the story that later was so successfully fictionalized in the movie *Chinatown*.

The problem is the story was basically fiction to begin with. It was true that the city was dominated by General Otis and his friends as few other cities have been dominated. But the fact of his ownership of land was not then a secret. It was well-known at the time Angelenos voted to build the system. Even critics who hammered away at the men who owned the land in the San Fernando Valley had to admit that the city would eventually need the Owens River water.

At the time the Owens Valley aqueduct was begun no one had to scare Angelenos with thoughts of a shortage. Everyone in the city believed devoutly the area could and would grow. If it didn't need the water at once, it would one day. Today, Los Angeles takes every drop it can get from the Owens Valley and needs more from the Colorado River as well.

There was a good deal of skullduggery involved with the Owens Valley project. The U.S. Reclamation Service planned, at one point, to develop the Owens River and to this end secured water rights from trusting valley farmers. These rights later ended up in the hands of Los Angeles and it was charged certain men, posing as reclamation agents, had falsely secured the rights for the city.

But, ultimately, the fate of the Owens Valley was not decided in or by Los Angeles, acting fairly or unfairly. For, at a critical juncture, the U.S. government, in the person of President Theodore Roosevelt, made a key decision which gave the water to Los Angeles. Simply, the American government decided it was far more important to the country as a whole to develop the city of Los Angeles than it was to develop the Owens Valley, as fateful and fearful as the consequences of that decision were to the poor farmers of the valley.

In any case, under chief engineer Mulholland, the massive aqueduct system was completed in 1913. At the inaugural ceremonies as the

DECEMBER 1, 1902: *Initiative, referendum, and recall are adopted into the city charter. No politician's life will ever be quite the same.*

SEPTEMBER 16, 1904: *City Councilman J.P. Davenport is recalled in the first recall of an elected official ever in the U.S. (See above.)*

SEPTEMBER 7, 1905: *Voters approve bonds with which to build the Owens Valley aqueduct.*

JUNE 16, 1908: *The first taxicab appears.*

first gush of Owens River water was unleashed into Los Angeles, Mulholland was heard to utter words later justly famous: "There it is. Take it."

From the turn of the century through the 1920s the sheer physical size of the city mushroomed. In 1896 it occupied about thirty square miles, not much more than it had in Spanish days. By 1920 it was over 300 square miles. Annexation had followed annexation, the most famous being the "shoestring" or strip of land at some points less than two blocks wide which connected downtown with the port at San Pedro. Water was the major weapon in this relentless city-building. The basin's inhabitants were invited to share in the largess the city had acquired from the Owens Valley but only by becoming part of the city itself. Hollywood, San Fernando, Westgate, Owensmouth, Sawtelle, Venice—once independent cities became neighborhoods of the megalopolis.

With area and population growth came new problems. The 1890s and 1900s were, in the rest of the nation, a period of growth for labor unions. Not so in Los Angeles. Here the brotherhood of labor was fiercely resisted—resisted by men such as the crusty General Otis and his equally over-leavened Los Angeles *Times*. He personally felt nothing but disdain for labor and saw no reason why the city shouldn't feel the same. And, more practically, because the absence of unions kept wages low, lower than San Francisco which was thoroughly dominated by labor, Los Angeles was attractive to new industries.

OCTOBER 1, 1910: *The printing plant of the Los Angeles* Times *is dynamited.*

NOVEMBER 4, 1913: *The Owens Valley aqueduct is completed and dedicated.*

AUGUST 28, 1914: *At San Pedro, the* Missourian *docks, the first ship to complete a passage from the East Coast via the Panama Canal.*

MAY 4, 1915: *Voters approve the annexation of 168 square miles of the San Fernando Valley into the city of Los Angeles.*

JULY 30, 1917: *General Harrison Gray Otis, feisty publisher of the Los Angeles* Times, *dies.*

In 1910 a bitter and prolonged strike broke out among the printers of the *Times*. Labor leaders decided now was the moment to stage the final battle for recognition of their movement in the city, and their archantagonist, General Otis, resisted just as doggedly. In October, at the height of the strike, the *Times'* printing plant was rent by a terrific explosion and twenty men died in the ensuing inferno.

Otis blamed the blast upon labor. Labor pointed out the printing plant was a notorious fire trap and fumes from the volatile products used in production of the newspaper wafted freely in and about, waiting for an explosive spark. Detective William Burns, a fabled sleuth, was brought to investigate.

Burns traced the footsteps of a man named Ortie McManigal, who turned out to be little less than a professional bomber (his favorite detonators were Tattoo Jr. alarm clocks). Burns connected McManigal to two brothers, James and Joseph McNamara, officials of a national labor union. The McNamaras were seized in Indiana, and the offices of their union raided. Burns acted throughout without regard to legal niceties.

The McNamaras were hustled back to Los Angeles to stand trial as the perpetrators of the *Times* bombing. Labor at once rose to their

The blown-up offices of the Los Angeles Times. *The result of an October 1910 labor dispute.*

defense and hired the noted civil libertarian Clarence Darrow. Popular sympathy fell to the McNamaras who insisted they were innocent. A year later, as their trial approached, another of their lawyers, socialist Job Harriman, placed first in the city primary for mayor.

In December of 1911 the McNamaras went on trial. The case had not proceeded far when one morning a defense lawyer arose in court and announced that the defendants wished to change their pleas from not guilty to guilty. It would be safe to say there were few more dramatic days in the history of the city than this. The McNamaras admitted they had planned and executed the bombing of the *Times*. It later came out that they had participated in a nationwide series of bombings against recalcitrant employers. In Los Angeles, the banners of labor were torn down overnight. Four days later socialist Harriman was defeated at the polls. History, which in truth contains few real turning points, had one this day.

Clarence Darrow was himself arrested and charged with jury tampering. He was never convicted: one jury could not reach a verdict and a second trial was called off. In return, Darrow agreed never again to practice law in the state of California. He never again defended a radical cause either.

The growth pattern in Los Angeles has been not ups and downs but rather ups and ups. The city spurted ahead in the 1870s, then dozed until the coming of the railroads in the 1880s launched a magnificent boom. The 1890s were less spectacular but steady. With the end of World War I and the onset of the 1920s, a new boom began, one which topped all those that preceded it. The 1920s in the city didn't just roar, they bellowed and surged like a tidal wave.

JUNE 10, 1920: *Census figures show Los Angeles has surpassed San Francisco in population.*

DECEMBER 1, 1921: *Ground is broken for the Los Angeles Coliseum.*

JANUARY 1, 1923: *Sister Aimee Semple McPherson's ornate Angelus Temple is dedicated.*

OCTOBER 6, 1923: *Twenty-five thousand spectators watch USC beat Pomona 23–7 in the first football game played at the Coliseum.*

FEBRUARY 18, 1926: *The cast of Eugene O'Neill's* Desire Under the Elms *is arrested in our Fair City and charged with staging an obscene play.*

The numbers are staggering. Between 1920 and 1930 the assessed valuation of the county grew from under one billion dollars to more than two billion. Twenty-five thousand building permits were issued in 1920; between 1920 and 1930, 400,000 were issued. In 1920 there were 146,000 telephones; in 1930 over 400,000. In 1920 half a million lived in the city; in 1930 almost a million and a half called Los Angeles home and local boosters were disappointed. They had prophesized two million.

Entire new industries opened up, chief of them motion pictures which, while disdained by many in the city's power structure, added substantially to the city's coffers and colored its image forevermore.

Massive new oil strikes at Huntington Beach, Santa Fe Springs, and Signal Hill in Long Beach began the decade of the 1920s. Between 1910 and 1919 a respectable 50,000,000 barrels had been produced in Los Angeles. Between 1920 and 1930 that figure shot up to 180,000,000 barrels.

Oil and its mystique are indelibly part of the hothouse which was Los Angeles in the 1920s. Oil derricks sprouted like sunflowers, aggressively elbowing aside whole residential districts. Overnight boom towns within the city appeared. The promotion of oil stocks and oil schemes of every description, many of dubious good sense and legality, blossomed forth. The master was a colorful character named C.C. Julian who pioneered folksy newspaper advertisements inviting the hordes invading the city to make their fortune through investment in his Julian Petroleum. When Julian's first well indeed came in a gusher, the myth was made. Julian and his successors pyramided their company, always with advertising. Eventually it was revealed the company had floated millions of phony shares and then crashed, bilking Angelenos out of nearly one billion in today's dollars.

Land, too, boomed once again. "Subdivision" was the magic word in the 1920s. Again, as in the 1880s, there were more than enough new customers. At times it appeared the entire Midwest of the United States had moved to Los Angeles. State societies sprang up among the new arrivals; their annual picnics were monstrous affairs attended by thousands.

Writ large across the image of the city was the automobile. In 1910 the city's problem with the car had been speed: autos were forbidden to drive through downtown at faster than twelve miles per hour. Also in that year it was big news when a Cadillac completed a round-trip to San Francisco in just under thirty-three hours. A flat tire in Hollywood had held it up.

By 1920 the automobile had turned downtown into a disaster area. Officially a "congested district," one observer called it an involuntary parking lot." A 1910 law had made it a crime to drive past the intersection of Temple, Spring, and Main streets at faster than a walk. By 1920 if a driver could pass that intersection at such a rate he was very lucky indeed.

Los Angeles realized the growing importance of the car but hadn't yet admitted that the city was in fact inseparable from it. The city's excellent street and intersuburb railway system had been losing money. The Pacific Electric applied to the state for permission to raise its rates. The state agency responsible refused the request, insisting instead steps be taken to increase the regularity of trains in the city and thereby boost patronage. The city decided to ban parking in the downtown area.

What followed was nothing short of miraculous. Overnight, traffic jams disappeared and cars moved rapidly through the city's center. The trains, which had been running an average of one hour behind schedule on every run, were suddenly running on time. Even traffic accidents declined significantly.

There was but one sour note. Downtown businessmen were convinced the limitations on parking were ruining business, and what was bad for business was not allowed in the city of Los Angeles. The city's politicians, notable then for their lack of both leadership and starch, caved in at once. Before long the streets were jammed, the trains were late, and rail patronage was falling again.

December 1924: Via Mulholland Highway, fifty-five miles of direct access to the fields of Elysium.

1904: Picking poppies in Altadena. In the background one of the "Big Red Cars," part of the city's excellent street and intersuburb railway, the Pacific Electric Railway system.

The lesson was that the car and the city were as one. Gilbert Woodill, chairman of the Motor Car Dealer's Association, insisted: "The automobile is an essential part of business and the sooner the city, county, and state authorities realize that hampering the use of the automobile is hampering the progress of civilization the better off we will all be."

OCTOBER 25, 1926: *In Westwood the campus of the University of California at Los Angeles is dedicated.*

JUNE 22, 1927: *The city hall is dedicated.*

MARCH 12, 1928: *Shortly before midnight, the St. Francis Dam, part of the Owens Valley aqueduct system, collapses and 385 die.*

JUNE 7, 1930: *Mines Field, later Los Angeles International Airport, is dedicated.*

It was a decade of contrasts in which amidst well-deserved references to miracles the rigid Protestantism of the newcomers was infused with a tropical libertinage. Puritans felt their inhibitions slipping away in the sun and fought against it. Religious cults of every size and persuasion, a tradition which actually existed here in the last century, were increasing noticeably. Sister Aimee McPherson's dramatized sermons, her Four Square Gospel, and finally her mysterious "disappearance," colored the life of the city. Another minister, antagonist of Aimee, Robert "Fighting Bob" Shuler, pioneered the use of radio. With it he bludgeoned city hall, dictated the city's morals, and eventually elected his own personal mayor who was as lackluster and morally deficient as any who preceded or followed him.

The 1930s were ushered in by the Olympic Games. Olympic Boulevard, a memento of those days, was once Tenth Street, and the 1932 Games were the Tenth Modern Olympiad.

Only slowly did the effects of the Depression begin to be felt. When they were, the city fathers acted in typical fashion. Mexicans, including a number of Americans of Mexican heritage, were unceremoniously herded into railroad boxcars and shipped south. Officials figured the railroad rates were cheaper than paying welfare. Los Angeles police were posted far out of their jurisdictions at the California border where they refused entry to the state to anyone without funds.

Los Angeles was awash with schemes to remedy the Depression. Chief was social commentator Upton Sinclair's EPIC campaign (End Poverty In California) which very nearly succeeded. When it looked as if Sinclair, the Democratic candidate for governor, might win, the city's power structure, from Harry Chandler's *Times* to Louis B. Mayer's MGM Studios, organized against him and ruthlessly destroyed his movement. Next came Dr. Edward Townsend's pensions plan and later Ham and Eggs, a movement to give every retiree a sum of money each month, provided he or she spend it at once.

The 1930s were not all disaster. The city's manufacturing industries—airplanes, tires, clothing—began to recover. By decade's end another 300,000 had been added to the population which now stood at over a million and a half.

Pressure to change the graft-ridden and all but moribund city government came to a head in the late 1930s in a most spectacular fashion. Mayor Frank Shaw was but one of a long line of stand-patters, officially blessed by the city's power elite. To get anything done, it was said, required the ability to speak "corner pocket language." Downstairs in city hall, in the "corner pocket," Mayor Shaw's brother Joe, who officially had no post with the city, held forth.

Civic reformers railed at the status quo and they might have continued baying at the moon had not a detective investigating the administration been greeted one morning by a bomb planted in his car. The culprits turned out to be the police. A recall of Shaw was begun and this time it succeeded. A new and considerably more honest administration under former judge Fletcher Bowron was installed. Soon the turmoil of the 1930s faded against the rising spectre of war.

Los Angeles in the 1940s was one of the great depots supplying men and machines to war. In this decade another half million residents were added. But the prosperity war brought also revealed some sad facts of life in the City of the Angels. Its long-standing racism, for example. In the 1930s city swimming pools bore the odious notice:

DECEMBER 23, 1931: *Experimental television station W6XAO begins operation for one hour a day, six days a week.*

JULY 30, 1932: *The Games of the Tenth Modern Olympiad open in Los Angeles.*

SEPTEMBER 16, 1938: *After a fierce campaign, Mayor Frank Shaw is recalled from office.*

MAY 3, 1939: *Union Station in downtown Los Angeles is opened. It is built on what was once L.A.'s Chinese district.*

NOVEMBER 19, 1939: *Water begins flowing from the Colorado River to Los Angeles.*

DECEMBER 30, 1940: *The Arroyo Seco Parkway, later called the Pasadena Freeway, is opened.*

JULY 21, 1941: *Bertolt Brecht, most famous of the refugees from Hitler's Germany, arrives at San Pedro. He takes up residence at 1063 26th Street, Santa Monica.*

FEBRUARY 19, 1942: *President Roosevelt signs an executive order requiring the internment of the city's Japanese population.*

JANUARY 12, 1943: *The Mexican-American defendants in the "Sleepy Lagoon" murder case are found guilty. Later their conviction will be thrown out by the courts.*

JUNE 3, 1943: *The "Zoot Suit" riots against Mexican-Americans break out in downtown Los Angeles.*

JANUARY 22, 1947: *W6XYZ becomes the first commercial television station on the West Coast. It changes its call letters to KTLA.*

SEPTEMBER 4, 1951: *Proclaimed "Golden Aerial Day" by Mayor Fletcher Bowron, the city celebrates its 170th birthday and the completion of a transcontinental microwave system that will enable ninety-five percent of the nation's TV sets to be turned to the same program at once. Of such is history made.*

OCTOBER 1, 1957: *Citizens are required not to burn rubbish but instead to use trash cans. This will, it is hoped, help fight smog. The penalties are a $500 fine and/or six months in jail.*

APRIL 8, 1961: *The once great Pacific Electric streetcar system, by the side of whose tracks Los Angeles was built, makes its last run.*

DECEMBER 6, 1964: *Dorothy Chandler Pavilion of the Music Center is formally opened.*

JULY 17, 1965: *Simon Rodia, builder of Watts Towers, dies.*

AUGUST 11, 1965: *The Watts riots begin.*

1965: *Groundbreaking of Union Square, first Bunker Hill Project. Beginning of downtown redevelopment.*

NOVEMBER 18, 1967: *USC 21, UCLA 20 in one of the greatest college football games every played.*

"Tuesdays reserved for Negros and Mexicans." The influx of soldiers and sailors into the city heightened tensions which erupted in 1943. Having been first spurred by bigoted newspaper articles concerning the large Mexican-American community, uniformed GIs attacked Mexicans, Filipinos, and blacks. Police stood by, then arrested the victims. The "Zoot Suit" riots were swept as much as possible under the carpet by officials and civic leaders who preferred to see, hear, and speak no evil of Los Angeles.

At war's end the city underwent yet another boom as servicemen, having seen the promised land, returned to take up residence. Fueled by federal subsidies, construction sky-rocketed. In one subdivision as many as a hundred houses a day were being started and 10,000 were finished in two years. Prior to the war, money from the gas tax was used to remove grass growing in the streets of the San Fernando Valley. But by the early 1950s, the population of the valley had multiplied by five hundred percent, massively straining city services. The postwar boom also marked the beginning of freeway construction, which forever changed the topography of Los Angeles.

In a very real sense the Los Angeles of today is but a refinement on the pattern set down in the postwar period, the hurly-burly 1940s and 1950s. Freeways, planned as early as the 1930s, and initially opened in 1940, proliferated. But it quickly became evident that even as designers set the first pencil to a new set of plans, the finished product would be overcrowded. At the same time, the city's failing streetcar system was abandoned in favor of buses. The valuable rights-of-way for the system which we sorely need today passed from the city's control. The once proud "Big Red Cars," which so easily conveyed Southern Californians throughout the area, disappeared.

Instead "smog" appeared. Actually smog had always been here. The earliest Spanish explorers commented upon the inability of the Los Angeles basin to dissipate smoke, and the Indians called it the Land of Many Smokes. Car combustion just made it worse. Yet the city continued to grow and added yet another half million in the 1950s, and by 1960 showed a population of two and a half million in the city and over six million in the county. Estimates for 1980 are almost three million in the city, over seven million in the county, and over nine and a half million in the metropolitan area.

Los Angeles has ceased to be many things. The sleepy pueblo long ago gave way to the brave new turn-of-the-century city which in time birthed today's metropolis without end. A metropolis which for some was as devoid of beauty and of feeling as it was bereft of logic. And it is true the beauty of another age is largely gone. Filled-in are the stately vistas once the rule and which so impressed newcomers: the open fields of waving poppies which framed, in one direction, snowy mountains, and in the other the brilliant blue sea. Yet new vistas have arisen equally impressive, and Los Angeles re-

North Beach Bath House, Santa Monica.

mains a city of unique visual appeal and at its best of absolute splendor.

And what about the feeling? It is here, as it was always here, constantly re-created and nourished by the city's diverse population. Los Angeles has never been a city lacking a heart. It has only been more guarded in giving that heart than its sunny disposition and easy ways might have suggested.

Now Los Angeles confronts its bicentennial. A stately lady of undeniable charm and appeal lifts up her mirror and views an image which contains not a few past indiscretions. Yet no lady would be a woman without her indiscretions, or at least would be a lady of considerably less dynamism! Los Angeles has mellowed with age and has obtained a measure of wisdom. The city is complex and sprawling, yet infinitely fascinating. A place unlike any other place, the city continues to exude fascination and charm, continues to invite and to dare. It is still a city looking forward. Still a city confident of a colorful future.

MAY 1, 1972: *Johnny Carson show comes to Los Angeles from New York. Move symbolized shift of creative center of television industry to L.A.*

1981: *Los Angeles' Bicentennial Year.*

JULY 28 THROUGH AUGUST 12, 1984: *The Games of the Twenty-third Modern Olympiad will be held in Los Angeles. The second summer games to be held in L.A., only the third to be held in the U.S.*

Hale residence on original Figueroa site.

ARCHITECTURE AND HISTORIC PLACES:

Including the Early Adobes, Frank Lloyd Wright, the Bradbury Building, Richard Neutra, and the New Downtown.

By Julius Shulman,
ARCHITECTURAL PHOTOGRAPHER AND HISTORIAN
With Paul Gleye,
LOS ANGELES CONSERVANCY

The vast area of Los Angeles contains a rich legacy of architectural styles from the nineteenth and twentieth centuries that is often overwhelmed by the scale of the city itself. During the first century of Anglo settlement, Southern California was seen as a new and ever-growing land where there was freedom to experiment with new styles and forms. It is endowed with a balmy climate and expanses of land—dry valleys, chaparral-covered hills, and long, sandy beachfronts—that offer unsurpassed architectural challenges.

For the inquisitive visitor exploring this heritage, we suggest in this chapter ten tours arranged by geographical area. We also trace the architectural process in Los Angeles, showing the transition from the works of the earliest masters to the new world of modern design.

Los Angeles has been a testing and experimental ground for architects concerned with quality. In addition to the favorable physical climate is an equally favorable architectural climate; clients show a willingness to allow their architects to develop unorthodox creations. As a result, Los Angeles offers to observers of design, and to those desirous of learning about our heritage, a wealth of diversity. Hardly a style has been neglected.

Master architects have left their imprints on the region. Many of their structures are standing and can easily be observed; scores of them have been designated as Cultural Heritage Monuments. Also, many private individuals have acquired and restored buildings that would otherwise have been demolished or left to decay in disgrace.

We shall illustrate and describe some of these architectural milestones, beginning with the central city. Our chapter is often congruent with Maurice Zolotow's Tours and Favorite Flings, so you can combine your viewing.

TOUR ONE:
DOWNTOWN LOS ANGELES

For those who have lived in urban environments, downtown has often provided a richness of visual experience. The fabric of architectural details is interwoven with faces and sounds. A special vibration enlivens downtown.

There are two ideal ways of exploring the central part of the city. One is to select almost any segment of a downtown street, such as Spring Street with its older Beaux-Arts financial district dating from the turn of the century; or perhaps Broadway, the retail shopping district of central Los Angeles. To the east, Main Street offers vestiges of a more prosperous past, and to the west, along Hill and Olive streets, stand many structures still elegant from a half century ago.

A second technique is recommended for exploring the imposing new development in western downtown that has emerged amidst the historic monuments. Pack a bag for a long weekend and check into the refurbished Biltmore Hotel, at the corner of Fifth and Olive streets. Or stay at the old but still elegant Alexandria, at Fifth and Spring; or the new and more ostentatious Bonaventure, at Fifth and Figueroa streets. (See Hotels, p. 158.) From there one can explore the Broadway Plaza complex with its Galleria. A long weekend of intimate delving into the essence of the city may revive an understanding of and a respect for our civic environment.

However you wish to organize your schedule, here is a walk through downtown Los Angeles that will examine both the old and the new. We will take you to the new Bunker Hill—to a part of downtown which is throbbing with an almost joyous activity, especially if you attend the noon concerts held on the south garden patio of the Bonaventure Hotel. And we will tour the older downtown to the east, with its design statements that, should they disappear, could never be reproduced.

Bonaventure Hotel.

Los Angeles Bonaventure Hotel
Fifth and Figueroa streets
1974–76
Architects: John Portman and
Associates

Let's start by parking near Fifth and Flower streets—or preferably save several dollars by taking the RTD bus. Ascend the Fifth and Flower escalator into the Bonaventure's huge atrium lobby, or to the upper atrium floor that opens on its east side to the pedestrian bridge over Flower Street. It leads to a landscaped park on the Arco Plaza garage, from which there are panoramic new views of downtown. In the past we have not had many high viewpoints from which to observe downtown, and this rooftop is ideal for photography or for just browsing. From here we retrace our steps into the Bonaventure to a second bridge on the same level, leading to the World Trade Center, and thence into Security Pacific Bank's dynamic edifice with its remarkable gardens by Sasaki, Walker.

Exploratory walks dare not be too fast-paced. The waterworks at Security Pacific Plaza are among the best in the Southland. The masses of richly planted containers and ample lawns and seating areas attract many for a lunch escape from air-conditioned and light-absorbing glass interiors.

Finally, to experience yet another species of open space downtown, wander into Union Bank Building's north gardens. Situated along Figueroa between Fourth and Fifth, the building by Harris and Abromowitz, and Albert C. Martin and Associates, built in 1968, is one of the earliest highrises in downtown to be constructed after the removal of the 150-foot height limit in 1957. The gardens, although less decorative than those surrounding some of the newer buildings, nevertheless offer a sense of serenity.

Union Bank Square.

Nearby are several very different architectural statements:

California Club
538 South Flower Street
1929
Architect: Robert D. Farquhar
Private club; not open to public

This sedate, eight-story building is in the classical style long thought proper for organizations of such stature as the California Club. Taught for many decades at the Ecole de Beaux-Arts in Paris, this late nineteenth- and early twentieth-century style became known as Beaux-Arts. The architect was a member of the California Club.

Los Angeles Central Library
Fifth and Hope streets
1922–26
Architects: Bertram B. Goodhue
and Carleton M. Winslow

A special study team of the American Association of Architects in 1978 called the library the perfect symbol for Los Angeles and probably its finest public building, "with an air of serious urban presence and ineffable fantasy." The architects fused traditional and modern elements into a single image. Much of the sculpture and decoration is from Mediterranean, Roman, Hellenic, Byzantine, Islamic, and Egyptian sources—a unity of art and architecture to express the theme of the building, "Light and Learning."

Sculptures are by Lee Lawrie, who later created figures for New York's Rockefeller Center. Inside are 9,000 square feet of murals by Dean Cornwall, representative of the last great period of pre-WPA American mural painting. Every exterior facade and every interior room of this magnificent building hold delightful aesthetic surprises for the visitor.

Los Angeles Central Library.

"Massive," "impressive," "impersonal," are the words most often used to describe the Arco Towers. The windswept plaza between them contains a striking fountain sculpture, "Double Ascension," by Herbert Bayer, and underground is a two-level shopping mall (Pujdak, Bielski and Associates, design consultants) with complex spaces in mirror and tile that are precursors of high-tech.

From the Arco Towers we head east, to a very different downtown. We travel first to Sixth and Olive streets to see the Oviatt Building. Oviatt's was an elegant men's clothier; the entrance was, and still is, decorated with glass from the studio of French designer René Lalique. Upstairs were tailor shops, and under the clock is an Art Deco penthouse. At this writing the Oviatt is being restored, and when completed it will be a downtown jewel.

Atlantic Richfield Plaza
Flower Street between Fifth and Sixth streets
1972
Architect: Albert C. Martin and Associates

Oviatt Building
617 Olive Street
1928
Architects: Walker and Eisen

California Club.

Atlantic Richfield Plaza.

Oviatt Building.

Angel's Flight.

Bradbury Building.

We are now entering old downtown, and let us next visit, as a prelude to the quiet beauty of what still exists there, the site of something that is not there for the time being. At Third and Hill streets, beside the entrance to the Third Street Tunnel that goes under what is left of Bunker Hill, there used to be a small railway that would take residents of the fine old homes on the hill back and forth from the shopping and business center that we are going to visit in a moment. This railway, called Angel's Flight, was long a Los Angeles tradition. It is to be rebuilt and replaced as part of the Bunker Hill redevelopment; but since we are not sure when that may happen, and since we wish not to forget this small piece of old Los Angeles, we include here several photographs of life on the old Angel's Flight. May it rise again.

Our next stop is Broadway and Third Street, where stands a monument of architectural integrity, structural soundness, and visual quality.

Bradbury Building
Broadway and Third Street
1893
Architect: George H. Wyman

Conjuring up an image of entering a cathedral, the Bradbury's skylighted atrium frequently creates a feeling of awe in the visitor. The grand and powerful scale of the space, the delicacy of the wrought-iron staircases, the open-caged elevators—there are so many visual delights that one can stand at any level and marvel at the elegance of the structure.

The Bradbury Building serves as a cornerstone of the old downtown. Among the many fine examples of early commercial architecture in the area, we will point out a few that bring into sharp focus the taste of a period now gone and also demonstrate how much we can learn from the masters of the past. Try to see: Alexandria Hotel, Fifth and Spring streets; Title Insurance Building, 443 South Spring Street; Pacific Stock Exchange, 618 South Spring; I.N. Van Nuys Building, Seventh and Spring; Charnock Block (now Pershing Hotel), Fifth and Main streets; Los Angeles Theater, 615 South Broadway; Eastern-Columbia Building, 849 South Broadway.

This small list is only a smattering of the total wealth of possible downtown visitations. For a more detailed guide to many of these buildings, the Los Angeles Conservancy has published a walking tour of Broadway and Spring Street. The Conservancy's guide is available by calling 623-2489.

TOUR TWO:
THE MUSIC AND CIVIC CENTERS

We suggest the Music Center and its great spaces as a testing ground for a personal contact with architecture. The Jacques Lipchitz sculpture in the mall pool dominating the view of the Dorothy Chandler Pavilion's north facade is one of the artist's most imposing works. The Mark Taper Forum and the Ahmanson Theatre are united by a lofty colonnade which embraces them on their four elevations. And with the reflection and motion of the attendant pools, the complex is a rewarding series of visual impacts.

Los Angeles Music Center
135 North Grand Avenue
1964–69
Architect: Welton Becket and Associates

Los Angeles Music Center.

Department of Water and Power Building
First and Hope streets
1963–64
Architect: Albert C. Martin and Associates

Los Angeles City Hall
Temple and Main streets
1926–28
Architects: John C. Austin, John Parkinson, and Albert C. Martin

This structure's mass, fountains, and lighting complete the enclosure of the Music Center's promenade space. Visit here at twilight in the spring or early summer, when the days are longer, and enjoy with hundreds of other promenaders the delights of a balmy evening, glowing sky, and surging fountains.

At the head of the broad flight of stairs on the east side of the Music Center, one has a fine vista of the Civic Center Mall, with a heroic fountain anchoring its west end, and the City Hall, a twenty-eight-story structure, dominating the east end. If we now proceed to City Hall, we can enjoy another visual and informative treat from its tower. Accessible by elevator, the tower observation deck affords a breathtaking view—on a smogless day, of course. The view of the Civic Center Mall, which we now perceive with a new dimension, and the view of the Bunker Hill redevelopment area, make one realize how Los Angeles has grown during the last decade.

Hall of Records
320 West Temple Street
1961–62
Architects: Neutra and Alexander, Honnold and Rex, Herman Charles Light, and James Friend

The Los Angeles County Hall of Records, to the north of the mall at Temple and Broadway, is notable primarily because it is a highrise structure designed by a team of architects led by Richard J. Neutra. Although he designed several, this was one of the few of his highrises actually constructed.

The preceding walk through the Music and Civic centers is indeed a beginning to the following exploration, which offers an in-depth cross-section of our city's history.

Water and Power Building.

We could begin at the Olvera Street Plaza, leaving the Music Center for the last, but by saving Olvera Street for the finale, a rewarding (and margarita-stimulated) lunch can be realized! So after visiting the Music and Civic centers, turn north through the Los Angeles Mall with its excellent landscaping and abundance of resting places and restaurants. It has six levels, plus four underground parking levels, and is adorned with the Triforium, a sixty-foot high tower of water, light, and music by Joseph Young.

A short continuation to the north along Main Street thrusts one into a small area that evokes early Los Angeles. The Pico House was the first three-story masonry building in Los Angeles, and was built by the last Mexican governor of California, Don Pío Pico. It has recently been restored very precisely, almost as if Ezra Kysor had just built it.

Next door to the Pico House is the three-story Theater Mercedes, the first theater building in the city. Both structures were built in an Italian Renaissance style that must have contrasted sharply with the dusty cow town of the 1880s. Also worthy of inspection is the 1858 Masonic Temple next to the theater at 418 North Main, with its cast-iron balcony.

Los Angeles Mall
Main, between First and Temple streets
1973–75
Architects: Stanton and Stockwell
Landscape architects: Cornell, Bridgers, Troller and Hazlett

Pico House
430 North Main Street
1868
Architect: Ezra F. Kysor

Theater Mercedes
420 North Main Street
1869
Architect: probably Ezra F. Kysor

Los Angeles Mall with a view of the Water and Power Building from City Hall.

Old Plaza Firehouse, 1884.

Olvera Street

Directly north of the Pico House is the Plaza which, although very near the site of the original Pueblo de los Angeles, actually dates in its present form only from 1869. It has been remodeled several times in the last century, most recently in 1962. Facing the Plaza is the Church of Our Lady Queen of the Angels. It is now the oldest place of religious worship in the city, constructed between 1818–1822, although the original pueblo predates it by about forty years. Its present facade dates from 1861. Also on the Plaza is the Old Plaza Firehouse (1884). It has been restored and is now a museum of old firefighting equipment.

Continuing north from the Plaza we enter Olvera Street itself, a block-long Mexican *mercado* featuring hand-crafted goods and souvenirs, plus several restaurants (for that margarita lunch). Although by now it is historic in its own right, its present form actually dates from 1930.

Avila Adobe
10 Olvera Street
628-1274
c. 1818

The Avila is the oldest existing residence in Los Angeles, built around 1818 by the sometime *alcalde* (mayor) of the pueblo, Francisco Avila. It has been completely restored after partial damage in the 1971 earthquake and now serves as a museum of California life in the 1840s.

Olvera Street, Avila Adobe.

Olvera Street is not quite the climax of our tour. Directly to the east is Los Angeles Union Station, the last of the great railroad passenger terminals built in the United States. It is still very much in use, and is now more active than during much of its history.

If you wish to return from here to downtown, catch the RTD minibus across the street by the Plaza.

The following photographs give an overview of what we have seen and what lies ahead on our tours. They were taken under ideal circumstances and portray the breathtaking beauty of our city on *clear* days. Avail yourself of opportunities to get to the upper floors of the taller buildings on clear days or evenings.

The first view is almost unreal—a sunset from Bunker Hill Towers at a moment which, though not too frequent, does occur even in Los Angeles. And yes, the view of San Gabriel Peak, over 6,000 feet high and more than twenty miles away, also rarely experienced, is but another demonstration of the need to eliminate smog. The photograph of the model of Ultimate Downtown Los Angeles depicts the potential of the area's growth.

Union Station
800 North Alameda Street
1939
Architects: John and Donald B. Parkinson

Union Station.

TOUR THREE:
PASADENA

Northeast of downtown Los Angeles, up the Pasadena Freeway, lies the verdant city of Pasadena. The freeway was Los Angeles' first, a milestone of sorts, and was dedicated in 1940. The Arroyo Seco Parkway, as it was originally called, was built as a WPA project, and remains today much as when it was first built. Many of the sycamores that defined the "parkway" are still growing alongside.

Pasadena itself dates from 1874, when the San Gabriel Orange Grove Association acquired much of the old rancho land and sold it to prospective orange growers. During the boom of the 1880s, when the railroads entered the town, it became a fashionable winter resort, and many of the well-to-do visitors never went back home. Today the city contains an elegant and well-preserved heritage of both residential and civic architecture from the early days; we will point out some of the highlights here and guide the reader to sources of further information for exploration of this fine city.

We begin with what is perhaps the epitome of the Pasadena ethic. Appearing on the Southern California architectural scene in the late nineteenth century were two brother-architects, Charles S. and Henry M. Greene. Gifted with a rare sensitivity of design, they

Gamble House.

created homes possessing innovations in space and detailing to such a degree that to this day they represent quality seldom found even among the most sophisticated avant-garde homes of current decades.

Their masterpiece, the David R. Gamble residence, was deeded to the City of Pasadena and the University of Southern California in 1966. It is curated by Randy Makinson, whose book *Greene and Greene: Architecture as a Fine Art* is a must for anyone who wants to be introduced to what *Good Housekeeping* in 1906 described as "a new wave of design coming from out of the far west and contributing many radically new concepts."

As with George Wyman's Bradbury Building, upon entering the Gamble House one is enveloped by an aura of richness in materials and space, and by a sensitivity to materials that transcends a specific time and style. Telephone for current hours.

Within a short walking distance, there are several other Greene and Greene houses—a rich architectural dividend awaits you! For the locations and descriptions of these houses, as well as a guide to much more in Pasadena and all of Southern California, we recommend David Gebhard and Robert Winter's 728-page *Guide to Architecture in Los Angeles and Southern California.*

Gamble House
4 Westmoreland Place
793-3334
1908
Architects: Charles and Henry Greene

Craven House.

We now turn to another of the great architects who influenced succeeding generations of designers in this land: Irving Gill, who followed the Greene brothers by only a few years.

Gill was an architect who gained prominence as a pioneer in creating a disciplined yet romanticized structural form; one of the distinguishing characteristics of his designs was the avoidance of the international style's almost deliberate disregard of nature. True, the latter's philosophy did express a feeling for indoor-outdoor interplay, but it was achieved with rigidity. Gill, on the other hand, infused considerable rapport with nature in his more romantic use of pergolas and arches.

Miltimore House
1301 Chelten Way
South Pasadena
1911
Architect: Irving Gill
Private home; not open to public

Gill's work is appropriately mentioned at this time, for one of his finest houses is not far from the area that embraces so many Greene and Greene structures in Pasadena. This house was built for Mrs. Paul Miltimore in 1911, and has since been retained in nearly original condition; it is best seen on an early morning.

Arroyo Seco

A short drive west on Monterey Road to Orange Grove Boulevard, then north across the Pasadena Freeway will deliver us to lower Arroyo Boulevard. It is difficult to begin outlining a tour of this area of Pasadena; there is such a wealth of landscape and grand homes that it would be almost impossible to view more than a small fraction of the offerings. There are several options for beginning an idyllic and nostalgic adventure. For a starter, turn west on Madeline Drive, off Orange Grove Boulevard. Although it is possible to experience this street in your car, you will miss breathing the quiet air of a Pasadena Sunday morning—the best time for a walk into lost decades of time!

The first few hundred yards of this walk will set the scene for the "name" houses farther along the street. But let us begin with one of the great mansions, completed just before the Great Depression called a halt to such extravagance, except on the part of a few movie stars.

Craven House
430 Madeline Drive
Pasadena   799-0841
1929
Architect: Lewis P. Hobart

This French chateau is one of the finest remaining examples of homes built by the old Orange Grove society. The estate is now the home of the Pasadena Chapter of the American National Red Cross, which is helping to preserve it as a cultural landmark, and welcomes visitors.

Traveling west on Madeline, we notice on the southeast corner of Madeline and Grand Avenue a Spanish-style urban house designed in 1938 by Donald McMurray, copied after a seventeenth-century house in Antigua, Guatemala. Go north on South Arroyo Boulevard to number 850, where we find a house constructed by the same architect in 1927. During much of the late nineteenth and early twentieth centuries there was a serious attempt to find a "true" architecture for Southern California, based primarily on Spanish models. This "Monterey Style" house, so called because it borrows from the combination of California Spanish architecture of the colonial period and importations of styles from the eastern United States during the early Anglo settlement of Monterey, is one of the finest remaining examples in the Pasadena area.

Continuing north on Arroyo Boulevard, one passes under one of the most magnificent bridges in Southern California.

Our brief tour of the Los Angeles area must now leave Pasadena, but there is much more to see. A careful study of the Gebhard and Winter guide to architecture offers a palette of exciting homes not only by Greene and Greene, but also by other productive architects of the same era. We have a precious heritage in this part of Pasadena, South Pasadena, San Marino, Altadena, and other nearby architectural "gold mines." And notice the spectacular tree-lined streets in these areas; the camphor trees are among the most beautiful in the world.

Colorado Street Bridge
Colorado Boulevard over
Arroyo Seco
1912–13
Designer and engineer: John Drake Mercereau

Colorado Street Bridge.

TOUR FOUR:
SPANISH SAN GABRIEL

Remnants of Los Angeles from the Spanish and Mexican periods remain throughout the area. Although they often escape our notice, they have survived a century of explosive urban growth and, in most cases, at least a half century of neglect. But today these relics —including two missions and a number of old rancho homes—have been restored and many now serve as museums and public buildings. On this tour we will point out some of these structures in the San Gabriel area, beginning with the earliest center of Spanish Los Angeles: Mission San Gabriel.

Mission San Gabriel
537 West Mission Drive
San Gabriel   285-5191
1812 (present building)

The Franciscan Fathers established twenty-one missions in what is now California to serve as centers for proselytizing the native residents. San Gabriel was the fourth of these missions, founded on a different site in 1771 and moved here five years later. An earlier mission church was destroyed by a flood in 1810, and the present building was constructed in 1812 using fired brick.

In 1833 the missions were secularized—the buildings were closed, the priests left, and the agricultural lands that had been tilled by the neophytes were divided up among them or given in large parcels to wealthy landowners. For a half century the mission buildings deteriorated through neglect, and what you see today is a very thorough restoration. Natural forces have made changes as well; a tower and much of the ceiling collapsed in a 1912 earthquake. The tower was not rebuilt, but the ceiling was restructured at that time.

On the grounds of the mission is the Lopez de Lowther Adobe, probably constructed around 1806. The house contains memorabilia of the Lopez family, who occupied the house from 1849 until 1964; at present it is open on Sunday afternoons.

Rancho las Tunas Adobe
315 Orange Street
San Gabriel
Private home; not open to public

Near the mission is the oldest continuously occupied home in Southern California; its date of construction is uncertain, but is traced back to several years prior to the erection of the mission church. It was the residence of the padres who supervised the mission's construction. The shingle roof was not an original part of the building but was added in the mid-nineteenth century.

Ortega-Vigare Adobe
616 South Ramona Street
San Gabriel
1795
Not open to public at present

Another eighteenth-century adobe remains in the area; it was originally built in the shape of an "L" in the Mediterranean tradition, although not all of the original building remains. The roof is also modern. Today the home is well preserved and is owned by the Blessed Hope Church of San Gabriel.

Spanish California at the turn of the nineteenth century was still an outpost on the farthest reaches of the Spanish empire. The missions were therefore required to be self-sufficient not only for the padres, but for the neophytes who came to live there. One of the important functions of the missions was to teach the natives Western ways, to transform them "from dangerous enemies and menaces into loyal and industrious subjects of the Crown."

The fields were planted with wheat, barley, and maize, and the *mano and matate* method of grinding the grain was inadequate to feed the growing population; thus a mill was needed. El Molino Viejo was the first mill built for the mission; a more efficient Molino Nuevo was constructed in 1823. After the secularization of the missions, the mill passed into private hands and served many uses, finally falling into disrepair. In the late 1920s it was restored by Frederick H. Ruppel, the restorer of the San Juan Capistrano Mission, using construction methods and materials contemporary with the mission period whenever possible. It is now the southern headquarters of the California Historical Society.

One other home from the Mexican period is not far away. The Adobe Flores (1804 Foothill Street in South Pasadena) is a beautifully restored private residence dating from pre-1840.

Numerous other examples of Spanish and Mexican architecture— such as the De la Osa Adobe at Los Encinos State Historic Park and the San Fernando Mission, which was demolished in the 1971 earthquake and subsequently reconstructed—grace the Los Angeles area. The best source for information is an excellent volume entitled *A Guide to Historic Places in Los Angeles County* edited by Judson Grenier.

El Molino Viejo
1120 Old Mill Road
San Marino   449-5450
1816

TOUR FIVE:
SILVERLAKE AND ECHO PARK

In Pasadena we toured part of its treasure chest of fine old homes, but other areas of Los Angeles also retain their vestiges of an elegant past. In the hills north of downtown, newcomers from two or three generations ago built whole neighborhoods of fine homes overlooking the city or gazing up at the mountains to the north. Some of these homes were precious and pretentious from our vantage point, while others showed great daring in their anticipation of the future. For our brief tour we begin in the east and will slowly circle around downtown to the north and west.

Heritage Square
3800 North Homer Street
Highland Park   222-3150

Heritage Square, just off the Pasadena Freeway at Avenue Forty-three, is a collection of Victorian homes and one railroad depot which the Cultural Heritage Foundation relocated here in an effort to recreate a small part of old Los Angeles' historical architecture. The crown jewel of the exhibits is perhaps the Hale House, moved to this site from its original location on Figueroa Street in 1970.

Charles Lummis House.

Lummis House
200 East Avenue Forty-three
Highland Park   222-0546
1898–1910
Architect: Charles Fletcher Lummis

Nearby is an entirely different experience. Cross over to the west side of the freeway to find Lummis' wonderful house, built of boulders found in the arroyo.

Our next stop is an area still teeming—almost, anyway—with examples of late nineteenth-century "carpenter gothic" houses. Their fanciful use of wood, shingles, and brick illustrates the free thinking on the part of the designer-builders of the day. We will also see an 1888 house by the renowned architect of that era, Joseph Cather Newsom.

This district, known as Angelino Heights, is bounded on the west by Echo Park and on the east by the Pasadena Freeway. In particular, cruise slowly along Carroll Avenue, where the Carroll Avenue Foundation—made up of the street's residents—is restoring several

Angelino Heights

Carroll Avenue.

Victorian homes with dazzling views of downtown Los Angeles. At dusk, Carroll Avenue becomes a jewel. More fine homes are located around the corner on Kensington Road.

This area was one of the finest residential spaces of the city around the turn of the century, and its location tells you why. A little four-wheeled trolley served as early public transportation from downtown; when the Shulman family arrived here from Connecticut in 1920 we resided nearby, and I clearly recall riding to visit friends in that swaying, rocking vehicle!

Silverlake:
Richard Neutra and R.M. Schindler

While the international style was coming to maturity in Europe through the teachings of the Bauhaus, it was also making one significant appearance in the United States, primarily in Los Angeles. The two great architects whose designs contributed significantly to this movement were Richard J. Neutra and Rudolph Schindler.

Both originally from Vienna, the two architects worked together in Los Angeles in the early 1920s. Their buildings have left indelible imprints on the pages of architectural history.

Schindler, during his early days in Los Angeles, worked closely with Frank Lloyd Wright. He designed and supervised much of Wright's Olive Hill (Aline Barnsdall) projects while Wright was in Tokyo supervising construction of the Imperial Hotel. Actually, most of Schindler's effort from 1917 to 1921 was spent on Wright's projects, during which time there was a liaison between Wright, his son Lloyd, Irving Gill, Schindler, and Neutra. The cross currents of their lives in this architectural outpost allowed them to exert profound influences on each others' work; these were the formative years of what was to become a rich contribution to architectural history.

Much of the work of Neutra and Schindler was carried out in the area called Silverlake, which offers panoramic winter vistas of the snow-capped mountains to the north. Smog had not yet been discovered, and property was most reasonable—for $5,000 the lots with the finest views were available, and even moderate property could be had for $2,500. Neutra built his original Research House along the lake in 1933; it burned in 1963 and was replaced by a new design by Richard and Dion Neutra in 1964. It may be seen at 2300 East Silverlake Boulevard.

Treweek and Sokol Houses
2250 and 2242 East Silverlake
Boulevard
1948
Architect: Richard Neutra
Private homes; not open to public

Neutra visualized the prospect of creating a colony—a true community that would demonstrate a broader role for the architect than designing a single dwelling on an isolated lot. The key to his community was a profound concern for the privacy of each resident; by carefully positioning each house on its site, he could achieve privacy and at the same time provide all residents an excellent view of Silverlake Reservoir. Architectural elements were interwoven so skillfully that from most viewpoints the harmony and the fabric of the dwellings are like a Bach toccata and fugue reincarnated in physical forms.

Lovell House
4619 Dundee Drive
1929
Architect: Richard Neutra
Private home; not open to public

The Silverlake houses came late in Neutra's career; he had assured himself a place in architectural history nearly two decades prior to beginning his colony, with his revolutionary Lovell House to the west in the Hollywood Hills. In 1929, when the Craven family had commissioned a French chateau, the Lovells were receiving this

David Treweek House. (Note: Sokol House at right rear.)

Buck House.

Lovell House.

crisp, white, steel-fabricated "factory for living" that created an international sensation. Stories on the house were published in almost every country in the world. And today, a half century after being built, the house looks as crisp and modern as when it was new; its design seems almost timeless, and that is perhaps the highest compliment in architecture.

Lipetz House
1843 Dillon Street
1936
Architect: Raphael S. Soriano
Private home; not open to public

This was Raphael Soriano's first house. The living room curves at one end in the sweeping lines of the streamline Moderne.

Walker House
2100 Kenilworth Avenue
1936
Architect: R. M. Schindler
Private home; not open to public

It was also here, on the hills to the west of Silverlake, that R. M. Schindler built a number of distinctive houses. His designs were a dramatic counterpoint to Neutra's purer international-style dwellings across the reservoir. The 1936 Walker residence, photographed here in 1938, is dramatically situated in a location that was originally bare of other houses. Schindler prepared his designs to express the interior as part of the architectural totality, and he constructed his buildings so that the clients could enjoy the spaces im-

Droste House.

mediately and furnish the interiors at their convenience, as the photograph of the Walker House interior shows.

With the increasing concern for the preservation of our architectural heritage, many early works of Schindler and other architects have been faithfully restored, including Schindler's 1940 Droste House, very near the Walker House. It is clearly a structure of utmost simplicity, yet it blends into the difficult, steep site.

Schindler's Buck House has also been restored recently, and it was accomplished in such an admirable fashion that we feel Schindler would have been delighted. He favored the Buck House, as his talents were tested there because of the tight corner site. The photograph was taken in 1937, before landscaping enclosed the garden.

Two other of Schindler's houses are worthy of brief note here. His McAlmon House, at 2721 Waverly Terrace in the Hollywood Hills, is a dignified and restrained piece of architectural sculpture. Nearby, his Sachs Apartments at 1811–13 Edgecliff Drive is one of Schindler's finest works.

Droste House
2025 Kenilworth Avenue
1940
Architect: R. M. Schindler
Private home; not open to public

Buck House
805 South Genesee Avenue
1934
Architect: R. M. Schindler
Private home; not open to public

Schindler Sachs Apartments.

TOUR SIX:
FRANK LLOYD WRIGHT

Of all the architects working in Southern California, Frank Lloyd Wright stands out as one who has achieved the highest international standing. Wright's earliest work was not in Los Angeles but in Chicago; his Prairie School designs were contemporary with the craftsman-styled homes of Greene and Greene on the West Coast. In the unique community of time and design that was Chicago at the turn of the century, Wright's monumental qualities surfaced and became evident through his great ability to infuse into his designs an elegant craftsmanship and detailing, even to the smallest, seemingly inconsequential elements of a space.

Although Wright's work in Southern California was carried out in another medium, that of pre-cast concrete blocks, his structures here are of almost monumental proportions compared to his suburban-home Chicago work. His Los Angeles work was considerably influenced by pre-Columbian Mayan designs from Yucatan and Central America, as well as by the integrity and formality of Japanese architecture.

Wright's designs were distinctly individual, but many similarities do exist between his buildings and those of others working in similar media at the same time. One similarity is the new and pronounced emphasis on the *horizontality* of form, marking an almost violent departure from the verticality of the Victorian influence, as illustrated in our "carpenter gothic" houses.

Vestiges of the Wright tradition in particular can be observed in the 1958 work of architect Edward Durrell Stone in his Stuart Pharmaceutical Building at 3300 East Foothill Boulevard in Pasadena. Stone in the 1950s had embarked on a design course utilizing concrete masonry in a decorative manner beyond anything that Wright had achieved. Yet Wright's influence is immediately evident! Stone's designs were so impressive that they considerably influenced American architects for several years.

Perhaps the most "visual" of all Wright's work is his Ennis House, a monumental "Mayan temple." Perched on a hillside in the Los Feliz section of the Hollywood Hills, it is visible from many nearby vantage points.

Many of Wright's creations are well-hidden, and the observer can view them only after considerable maneuvering. But there are a few other accessible locations. Our next stop, to the south of the Ennis House, is now a public monument.

Ennis House
2607 Glendower Avenue
Hollywood
1924
Architect: Frank Lloyd Wright
Private home; not open to public

Barnsdall ("Hollyhock") House
Hollywood Boulevard at Vermont
Avenue
Hollywood   662–7272
1917–20
Architect: Frank Lloyd Wright

Aline Barnsdall was an oil heiress who commissioned Wright to build a residence for her and a theater and cultural complex for the residents of Los Angeles. Her favorite flower was the hollyhock, and Wright decorated the main house with stylized designs of this flower. The accompanying Studio A was designed largely by R. M. Schindler under Wright's supervision. The property was deeded to the city of Los Angeles in 1927, and was promptly neglected for a couple of decades. Some of the estate was even sold. But in a belated awakening, the city has restored the house and has developed what is left of Barnsdall Park into a cultural center.

Hollyhock House.

Storer House
8161 Hollywood Boulevard
West Hollywood
1923
Architect: Frank Lloyd Wright
Private home; not open to public

This house, on Hollywood Boulevard west of Laurel Canyon Boulevard, is not as monumental in scale as the Ennis House, but it retains the sensitive detailing and imaginative use of the concrete block that Wright had designed. He believed that masonry was the appropriate building material for the Southern California climate.

Freeman House
1962 Glencoe Way
Hollywood
1924
Architect: Frank Lloyd Wright
Private home; not open to public

Selected by many architectural critics and authorities as a "perfectly scaled structure," this house peers out over Hollywood from the hills directly above Franklin and Highland avenues, from which vantage point it is best viewed. Schindler's association with Wright during the early 1920s involved the creation of the interior space of this house.

Millard House
645 Prospect Crescent
Pasadena
1923
Architect: Frank Lloyd Wright
Private home; not open to public

Traveling east to Pasadena, we can view the Millard House, part of the magical upper Arroyo Seco neighborhood, and a short walk from Greene and Greene's Gamble House. Years of landscape growth have obscured much of the Millard House, but a glimpse is worthwhile nevertheless.

As a final note, we suggest that the Frank Lloyd Wright enthusiast drive to Montecito, just south of Santa Barbara, where at 196 Hot Springs Street is Wright's *first* Southern California house, built in 1909–10 for the Stewart family. It is a Prairie School design set in verdant hills, with hardly a hint of his future direction in Los Angeles.

Ennis House.

Hollyhock House.

Freeman House.

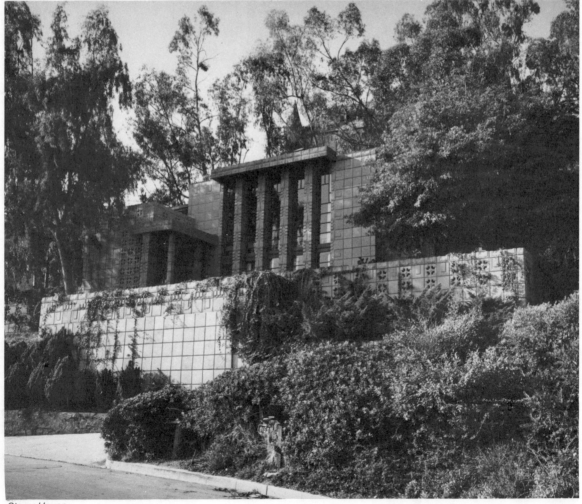

Storer House.

Millard House.

TOUR SEVEN:
A DIFFERENT LOOK AT HOLLYWOOD

KCET
4400 Sunset Drive
Hollywood   666–6500

The architecture of a motion picture studio from the early years is a unique offering of Los Angeles. And to see one that has not been commercially exploited, go to public television station KCET.

As Stephen Manes wrote in his *Sixty Years of Studio*, old studios were fair game for the wrecker's ball; the ethic of the movie industry was to create and then disregard sets for a film, and much studio architecture was treated the same way. What are now the KCET studios have housed production companies since 1912; yet they remain today much as originally constructed. It is one of the oldest remaining studio structures in filmmaking. KCET conducts tours of its television production facilities, including the original buildings.

KCET.

Another architectural form, not at all related to the entertainment industry, also typifies Los Angeles, especially the areas developed during the early decades of this century—such as Hollywood. This period saw the construction of many small, attached housing units that remain as beautiful and as functional as are many newer and more fanciful structures. These "courtyard homes" or "bungalow courts" were small apartment houses that surrounded an open courtyard, often beautifully landscaped.

This housing type has been researched by three University of Southern California School of Architecture professors who have uncovered scores of these remarkably contemporary achievements. The illustrations we include are from their forthcoming book on the subject; they demonstrate the elegance with which these projects were developed. All those illustrated are fully occupied, with waiting lists!

Pan Pacific.

Although courtyard housing may be found throughout older sections of Los Angeles, we illustrate several examples from Hollywood that are easily accessible. Please respect the privacy of the residents.

Our third look at Hollywood takes us to the Pan Pacific Auditorium. This cavernous hall is faced with a green-and-white facade that epitomizes mid-thirties Los Angeles. Architecture in the depression years was influenced by a curious blend of forces. First, it was necessary to minimize costs; no longer could we afford marble-clad exteriors and lavishly decorated lobbies. So here only the facade was consciously decorated, while the actual building is straightforward and uninspired. Second was the influence of speed; in particular the influence of the swift ocean liner, for during the thirties it was *the* prestigious form of travel. Thus on the Pan Pacific facade we see balconies with railings where all corners are curved and flagpole standards shaped like ocean liner wind funnels. "Streamlining" was more than evoking ships, however; note that the curves of the building are like the curves of the automobiles in our photograph taken shortly after the structure opened. A building, of

Pan Pacific Auditorium
7600 Beverly Boulevard
1935
Architects: Wurdeman and Becket

course, is not an aerodynamic object; the windswept lines are but an exercise in imagery. What it all amounts to is a "fantasy of efficiency" that we can read into 1930s society. Here it is expressed in architecture, while elsewhere in the world it was being acted out by totalitarian governments.

At this writing the Pan Pacific is subject to extreme controversy, for the land on which it sits is destined to be a flood control basin. The principal alternatives appear to be either to preserve the entire building, and perhaps relocate it, or to preserve only the facade, perhaps as a gateway to the proposed Pan Pacific Park. As a piece of sculpture, only the facade is of note; but as a monument to the social vision of nearly a half century ago, the entire structure stands as an integral unit.

Our special tour of Hollywood may have left the reader wondering about the "real" Hollywood. If so, Maurice Zolotow's "Tours and Favorite Flings" chapter should slake your thirst. Also, the Los Angeles Conservancy has prepared a walking tour of Hollywood Boulevard; call 623-2489 for details.

TOUR EIGHT:
THE NEAR WEST SIDE

In the 1890s and 1900s, Los Angeles expanded to the north and east. But in the 1920s and 1930s it expanded west to the ocean, along what is called the Wilshire corridor. Wilshire Boulevard became the great artery feeding this westward growth and serving as its "downtown"—it is perhaps the world's first linear downtown—as it carried residents and vacationers from Los Angeles to the beach at Santa Monica. In its wake, Wilshire Boulevard has left a fifteen-mile stretch of architectural history, of which we shall study a small portion in this tour. Our origin is the corner of Wilshire and Western Avenue.

Pellissier Building
(now Franklin Life)
Southeast corner, Wilshire
and Western
1930–1931
Architects: Morgan, Walls,
and Clements

This twelve-story building sheathed in turquoise terra cotta is a fine example of Art Deco architecture, or what is locally called Zigzag Moderne. The pre-Depression days (even lasting into the early 1930s in architecture, for buildings were designed some time before their construction) were booming and lucrative, especially in Los Angeles. Commercial architecture expressed this mood. No longer were buildings brown or gray stone, but rather they could be green, blue, white—or shining black with gold trim, as was the Richfield Building downtown, where the Arco Towers now loom. Buildings glittered in the sun, and their decoration expressed that glitter in complex patterns suggesting pulsing movement. The whole world was mechanism, where science and free enterprise were building an ever-greater future. Although zigzag buildings don't move, their form and decoration evokes an image amusingly similar to that which greets the visitor to the It's a Small World pavilion at Disneyland. Thousands of dolls move in different ways, but all in unison to the same song.

In the corner of the building is the Wiltern, one of the masterpieces of Art Deco theaters; it's worth attending whatever is playing in order to experience the interior.

Wiltern Theater

As you leave the Wiltern Theater, travel east on Wilshire toward downtown and you will pass three religious institutions worthy of note. The Byzantine-influenced Wilshire Boulevard Temple, with its mosaic-inlaid dome and murals of Jewish history by Hugo Ballin, stands at 3663 Wilshire. In contrast is the very modern St. Basil's Catholic Church, found at Wilshire and Kingsley Drive and designed in 1974 by Albert C. Martin and Associates. And a few blocks farther east, at Wilshire and Normandie Avenue, is the Italian Romanesque Wilshire Boulevard Christian Church (1922–23), by Robert H. Orr.

Three sanctuaries

During the era represented by this stretch of Wilshire, Los Angeles was a great repository for what has come to be called "programmatic architecture." Form followed function in a literal sense different from that envisioned by "serious" architects. If a shop sold doughnuts, it should be shaped like a doughnut; if it sold tamales it

Brown Derby Cafe
3377 Wilshire Boulevard
1926

Bullock's Wilshire.

looked like a tamale. Most of these little items are gone, but a few remain. A camera shop with a facade shaped like a huge camera still exists at 5370 Wilshire, and the Tail o' the Pup hot dog stand, shaped like a you-know-what, still stands at La Cienega and Beverly boulevards. And here we have the Brown Derby in the shape of its namesake; there used to be a large sign on top that said, "Eat in the Hat." The derby, which was architecturally more prominent when the building was new, suggests an image of poshness; therefore the restaurant must be posh. And it is, too, somewhat.

Bullock's Wilshire
3050 Wilshire Boulevard
1929
Architects: John and Donald
Parkinson

Next we come upon one of the great architectural monuments of Los Angeles, the Art Deco flagship of the Bullock's department store chain. When it was built on this site in 1929, the area was a suburb of Los Angeles; Bullock's location here exerted a great influence on the westward expansion of the city. The main entrance is not on Wilshire; behind the store is a parking lot with a large *porte-cochère* that shelters the entrance. Even in 1929 the automobile was the mode of transport for Bullock's customers.

Bonnie Brae Street.

If you have already seen the exterior, go back again to see the incomparable interior. Here is a store where the experience of shopping is rewarding in a timelessly elegant fashion.

Bonnie Brae Street

Continue east on Wilshire to Bonnie Brae Street, and turn right to enter another enclave of fine homes reflecting the imaginative and often provocative design spirit of builders nearly a century ago. Along Bonnie Brae about two blocks south of Wilshire we find several Queen Anne homes; the two at 818 and 824 South Bonnie Brae, both c. 1897, display particular whimsy and playfulness.

Alvarado Terrace

If you are pursuing our tour by bicycle, pedal down Bonnie Brae to Pico Boulevard and consider for a moment the crescent design of Alvarado Terrace. The crescent terminates at Hoover Street, and is occupied by seven rather palatial structures from the early 1900s.

We must be continually aware of Los Angeles' growth syndrome; much of this area was created in one of the city's periods of explosive growth, generated largely by real estate promoters and developers. Some of these designers were thoughtful; Alvarado Terrace, with its park facing the opposite side of the street, makes for a spacious and generous openness even today. But the same tendencies toward explosive growth have destroyed similar areas existing from an earlier period. Los Angeles must find ways to continue growing without destroying, for areas such as this cannot ever be replaced.

Alvarado Terrace.

The plan for Alvarado Terrace was created by Pomeroy Powers, a real estate promoter of the turn of the century. His house at 1245 Alvarado Terrace is an opulent Mission Revival mansion, one of the most imposing on the street; it was designed in 1902 by A.L. Haley. We cannot help but wonder at the design flexibility of the early Los Angeles architects and buildings—they were certainly seldom at a loss for a vernacular style! Complementing the homes on the terrace is the 1912 First Church of Christ Scientist at 1366 South Alvarado Street, designed by Elmer Grey in the Italian Romanesque style.

Santa Sophia Greek Orthodox Church
1324 South Normandie Avenue
1948
Architect: Gus Kalionzes

Edifice conscious? Then traverse the short distance west on Pico Boulevard to Normandie Avenue for an example that seldom fails to leave viewers awe-struck. Its embellished exterior and interior are incomparable.

TOUR NINE: WEST ADAMS

To those of us who have resided in Los Angeles for decades, the progression and simultaneous destruction of so much of the city has evolved before our eyes. Boyle Heights, extending eastward from the Los Angeles River, was a very desirable late nineteenth-century residential area; it was close to the central city, and the hilly terrain offered fine vistas and dry building sites.

Concurrent with the maturing of Boyle Heights, the West Adams district, several blocks to the south of Alvarado Terrace, emerged

Doheny Mansion.

as another fine neighborhood. Palatial mansions of superlative design were erected. To this day, even with the deplorable razing of so many, a cruise along West Adams Boulevard reveals a large number of remaining mansions. Although most are no longer private homes, many are well maintained.

Chester Place

This small street remains a showplace. At the turn of the century it was a private enclave of twenty acres, containing thirteen dwellings, and of those that remain, the most notable is the Doheny (originally Posey) House, today called the Doheny Mansion.

Doheny Mansion
8 Chester Place
746-0450
1899–1900
Architects: Theodore A. Eisen and Sumner P. Hunt

This building is truly a classic of opulent residential architecture, and is well known because it frequently appears on television as a set. The interior can be seen in the accompanying illustration—and what an interior! Tours are available. Across the street, at number 7, is the Wilson House, a Mission-Islamic concoction dating from 1897. Chester Place is worth an hour or two at least, merely sauntering around.

St. Vincent de Paul.

The nearby Childs House, at Arlington Avenue and Adams Boulevard, is the center of another small enclave of imposing homes. This structure, now the Children's Home Society, is a Colonial Revival mansion built about 1900.

St. Vincent de Paul Roman Catholic Church
612 West Adams Boulevard
749-8950
1923–25
Architect: Albert C. Martin

Much of the history of architecture in Southern California, prior to the general acceptance of the international style, shows a concern for finding an "appropriate" architecture for this new land. There was no indigenous architecture to speak of; the Gabrielino natives lived in small huts made of twigs—actually, they lived outdoors most of the time. And the missions built by the Spanish colonists were fairly complete architectural importations. Yet the "Spanish" in some form largely dominated this search for a proper Southern California architecture, either as a derivation of the missions or of other styles the Spanish had brought with them to Mexico.

One of these styles was the Churrigueresque—named after the Spanish baroque architect José Churriguera, who adorned plain walls with huge panels of intricate, unrestrained meta-baroque ornament. This style was brought into Mexico and adopted with great relish by colonial church architects.

In 1915, amidst the search for a Southern California architecture, Bertram Goodhue was appointed designer of the Panama-California Exposition in San Diego, which was held to celebrate the opening of the Panama Canal and to advertise San Diego's proximity to it. (The Panama-Pacific Exposition in San Francisco was held at the same time and for the same purpose.) As the architectural theme of the San Diego exposition, Goodhue chose a "Spanish Colonial" model, of which the Churrigueresque was a prominent style.

The exposition was extremely influential architecturally; for the next fifteen years one of the most widely emulated monumental styles in the Southland was the Churrigueresque; and the St. Vincent de Paul Church is one of the finest remaining examples. Although most buildings were derivations of earlier styles, it is possible that a new and unique architectural tradition could have emerged from that search. But the Great Depression called a halt to it; the new and very necessary ethic was efficiency, and the various modern styles seemed to answer that need best of all.

Not all monumental structures expressed this need for an indigenous style, of course. The nearby Second Church of Christ, Scientist, at 948 West Adams, comes directly from Rome, bypassing Spain altogether. The bank of six Corinthian columns make it a true temple in appearance.

In this tour we have been concerned more with older designs than with contemporary architecture, particularly with regard to homes. We believe it is a matter of great urgency to display the qualities of these dwellings, for they should be studied and respected as viable and useful elements of our environment. They are irreplaceable.

Second Church of Christ Scientist.

TOUR TEN:
CENTURY CITY

Modern architecture is also important, however, and Century City is a new town worthy of a visit. It stands on the site of the old Twentieth Century-Fox movie lot between Santa Monica and Olympic boulevards, west of Beverly Hills.

Sunday is perhaps the best time to stroll through Century City, when its pace is slower. There are waterworks, many places to enjoy a brown-bag lunch, and numerous fine restaurants.

Century City.

The list of participating architects of Century City reads like a Who's Who. The varied designs present a startling and revealing cross section of the state-of-the-art of architecture as it has evolved during the past two decades. From the original Welton Becket Gateway Buildings on the Avenue of the Stars at Santa Monica Boulevard, to the twin triangular-shaped Century Plaza Towers by Minoru Yamasaki, there is a provocative visual treat for those desirous of exploring design trends. Architects of other Century City buildings include: A.C. Martin and Associates (1900 Avenue of the Stars); Helmuth, Obata, Kassabaum (1901 Avenue of the Stars); Skidmore, Owings, and Merrill (10100 Santa Monica Boulevard); Minoru Yamasaki (Century Plaza Hotel); Charles Luckman and Associates (Century Park East Condominiums); Maxwell Starkman (First Los Angeles Bank, Avenue of the Stars and Constellation Boulevard); Welton Becket and Associates (San Diego Savings and Loan, Santa Monica Boulevard and Century Park East).

The shopping mall has an inviting variety of stores and merchan-

Century City.

dise. It is reached via pedestrian bridge across Avenue of the Stars. The mall's wide walkways with their trees, benches, vendors, and street musicians create a congenial public space.

This chapter has shown in photographs and text the cream of Los Angeles architecture. It only begins, however, to indicate the richness and depth that await the architectural explorer. Additional reference books (see Appendix, p. 347) and organizations like the Los Angeles Conservancy and the Cultural Heritage Foundation can point the way to a more thorough examination. As these groups are proving, there is a great deal not only to enjoy but to save from destruction.

Just as Los Angeles' immensity and diversity tend to engulf its architecture, they also engulf its history. But the history exists very much in the architecture, and one can fully appreciate Los Angeles' past and present only by discovering and exploring the structures of our human environment. Architecture is more than just buildings; it is a living representation of the spirit and style of its time.

Simon Rodia's Watts Towers.

TOURS AND FAVORITE FLINGS:

A Guide to Special Tours Including Raymond Chandler's Los Angeles, Los Angeles on Foot, Los Angeles by Car, Where Movies Are Made, Venice, and More.

By Maurice Zolotow,
LOS ANGELES MAGAZINE

"**D**own these mean streets a man must go," wrote Raymond Chandler, describing his hero-detective Philip Marlowe, "a man who is not himself mean, who is neither tarnished nor afraid." The streets on which Marlowe went were the streets of Los Angeles. The paradox of these streets is that so few of them are mean.

Los Angeles has the same social problems as other large urban centers. Poverty and prejudice, anger and frustration, the priority of economics over aesthetics—these take their toll on our community, too. But the marvel is that so little of this is reflected in our physical environment. In other cities oppression is built into the walls; the crumbling social structure finds exact metaphor in the rows of dark, decaying tenements, jammed with people or empty and burnt out. Los Angeles is remarkably free of these scars. Of major cities, ours is the most inhabitable.

Much of the credit goes to its dispersed layout; when each of us can find a bit of space, there is less tendency to devolve into the "crowded rat cage" experiment that most cities are in the process of constantly replicating. This, plus the tolerant disposition of our citizenry, produces a human setting for the Los Angeles experiment: constructing a livable future, both for us and for the rest of a civilization too often resigned to the terminal.

Before we begin our tours, I must cite some examples of the compatability with which Angelenos live. The first arises out of an interesting experiment in sight and sound which I devised. It is a trick I play on visitors to whom I am displaying the joys of my city. We find a well-traveled intersection with pedestrians on the sidewalks and many cars. My favorite is the intersection of Hollywood Boulevard and Highland Avenue. I play my trick when we are en route from Musso's to C. C. Brown's (this is part of our Hollywood excursion which I will subsequently chart for you). We have paused, let us say, for the light at Highland. The avenue is thick with automobiles going north to get on the Hollywood Freeway at the Highland on-ramp. And Hollywood Boulevard is, of course, crowded with vehicles. And there are people walking up and down the streets, which were some of Philip Marlowe's favorites. (He once "lived" in a flat on Yucca Avenue, not far from where we are standing.) I will ask, "Do you hear anything unusual? Do you see anything unusual?" My tourists look about intently. They listen intently. Sometimes they guess. They are invariably mistaken. Finally, they give up. And I tell them what it is.

"Do you hear any horn-blowing?" This, I assure you, will especially

Hollywood and Vine.

stun a person from Paris, where the air is cacophonous with the angry screams of horns. We just do not blow horns in Los Angeles. It is really something to hear, believe me, this automotive silence. I don't know of any city in which your average driver is so quiet and understanding. I think I blow my horn maybe once or twice a month —usually to warn a car making a blind swing out of a driveway. I never blow my horn at a pedestrian. We don't hate pedestrians in Los Angeles. We respect them. We protect them. We cherish them. This, I assure you, will astound a New Yorker or a Roman. Sometimes we have taken that little trip from Musso's to C. C. Brown's, which is a ten minute stroll, and we have not heard even one klaxon screeching. And my visitors do not believe their own ears, even when I have pointed out this phenomenon.

And then I tell them about the unusual sight: all the walkers will not cross a street until their light is green, and when the light turns red all the walkers halt. This is absolutely unheard of in Paris and Rome and New York, where walkers and drivers engage in a battle of nerves.

But wait, there is something even more. Where there are no traffic lights, we often have pedestrian crossings, thick white parallel lines, about which drivers are warned by the sign "Ped Xing." And I give you now a miracle, like unto the miracle of the parting of the Red Sea. I love to watch an old lady or gentleman stride out bravely, looking neither right nor left, ignoring the automobiles charging down; and then the cars brake, the automotive waters part, and the walker passes through the traffic, thus demonstrating a faith in morality over machinery which is heartening in these depraved times.

Now these phenomena are so marvelous, and yet so everyday, that we forget that they exist uniquely in Los Angeles. They do not exist to this degree in any other city, these three aspects of our life: the silence of the cars, the respect for traffic lights, and the cherishing of pedestrians. You will not find them listed in any automobile club guide to the city, and the tour guides will not show them to you because they take them for granted.

But you should not take for granted or on faith how well our people and their environment stand up under duress. See for yourself on a drive through Watts; see how far we have come toward making the words "slum" and "ghetto" obsolete. (And see, admittedly, how far we have to go.) Given a decent setting, the human spirit can thrive. Set among these modest homes is a monument to that spirit, the Watts Towers, built by immigrant tile-setter Sabbatino (Simon) Rodia of ceramics, shells, and glass. Clustered lacy spires of beauty rise from what is as close as Los Angeles gets to mean streets. The towers are at 1765 East 107th Street, next to a community art center.

Watts Towers

Another group of inspiring towers—these built by thousands of men rather than one—rise from what was once the backlot of

Century City skyline.

Century City

Twentieth Century-Fox Film Studios. Century City, a soaring complex of office buildings, condominiums, hotel, and entertainment center, dominates the West Los Angeles skyline.

My favorite approach is to drive west on Pico Boulevard. (Strangers to our city can orient themselves by looking for the foothills—the Santa Monica Mountains in this case—which are north.) We will assume you have begun the journey at La Cienega Boulevard and are going west on Pico, through West Hollywood and Beverly Hills. The towers loom ahead. You pass Century Park East and then Avenue of the Stars. On your left, observe the hedges and brick gates of the Hillcrest Country Club. If you know a member, do wangle an invitation to lunch, so you can partake of the noblest buffet west of the Mississippi. Hillcrest is an elegant country club with a magnificent golf course and a card room where Hollywood-style gin rummy is played by scores of brilliant players. There is a splendid gymnasium and sauna and a lovely dining room looking out on acres of greenery. In one corner, by a window, is the famous round table, at which for decades some of the wickedest Hollywood wits bantered words. Once Groucho Marx, Jack Benny, Milton Berle, George Burns, George Jessel, and many others too humorous to mention held forth at the round table.

Twentieth Century-Fox

At Motor Avenue, make a right turn at the Twentieth Century-Fox Studios. You will not be able to proceed very far unless you have a pass. While you are attempting to persuade the guard to let you park for five minutes, you can glimpse the exterior sets constructed for *Hello Dolly!*, starring Barbra Streisand and Walter Matthau. Look up the wide boulevard leading to the soundstages and offices of the studio, and you will see what looks like a very real New York Third Avenue Elevated Railroad and the St. Patrick's Cathedral and the New York Public Library Main Building with its lions. You will see ballrooms and railroad stations and brownstone mansions and marble palaces with wrought iron gates and stained-glass windows. It's just as well you are forbidden to come too close. For if you were to touch the marble, you would know that it is wood, and the wrought iron—wood, and the expensive stained-glass windows aren't glass, and the bricks are wood, the railroad tracks are wood, everything is wood.

Now when you drive about Century City and observe the curvilinear facade of the Century Plaza Hotel, or wander among the shops of the Century Square shopping mall, or take the escalators to all levels of the ABC Entertainment Center, with its theaters, shops, restaurants, and Mondrian-like ambience, I would remind you of the ghosts that once inhabited these hills and plains. These hundreds of acres, from Pico Boulevard all the way to Santa Monica Boulevard, were once the complete domain of Twentieth Century-Fox. It was a walled city, with one of the great backlots of Hollywood, where they could (and did) have jungles and oceans and deserts and snow-covered mountains. Battles on land and sea were fought over these prospects, now dominated by contemporary buildings, curiously curving walkways, and futuristic multilevel areas. This was once the country of Tyrone Power and Betty Grable, of Richard Widmark and Ginger Rogers, of Cary Grant, Mitzi Gaynor, Robert Mitchum, and Marilyn Monroe.

Remember, as the gateman makes you turn around and go back to Pico Boulevard, that this was one of the greatest dream factories of our time. They rarely went on location when they had to film a movie in those days. They had the whole world in the backlot. They had the continents and the oceans and they had—and still have—the greatest gathering of technical experts ever concentrated in the service of a visual art. Twentieth Century-Fox is still one of the great illusion manufacturers, but the backlot is now just a few acres of streets, lagoons, and facades. Directors, stars, and technicians go out into the "real world" when they make a film nowadays. Curiously enough, the world looked just as "real" on film, when the magicians were fabricating illusions on the backlots.

MGM

Heading out from Twentieth Century-Fox, cross Pico going south on Motor Avenue until you see the MGM water tower up ahead, and Motor dead-ends into Washington Boulevard in Culver City. Before you stands the high wall of the most formidable walled city ever put up by the movie industry in its great years—the 1930s, the 1940s, the 1950s. Here walked "more stars than there were in the heavens": Clark Gable, Greta Garbo, Robert Taylor, Lana Turner, Joan Crawford, Spencer Tracy, John Gilbert, the Marx Brothers, and Katherine Hepburn. This is where Louis B. Mayer was King and Irving Thalberg the creative force.

Go left on Washington until you find space to park. Then walk towards the studio. On a little street named Grant, near the Smith and Salsbury mortuary offices, you will find the most celebrated of all studio administration buildings—the four-story late Art Deco Thalberg Building. You can walk in here and look around the reception room but you can't go upstairs, and you can't enter through the gates and see the films and television shows being shot. The Thalberg Building is the nerve center of MGM, and now there is a new emperor, Kirk Kerkorian. This man rescued the studio when it was on the verge of bankruptcy, by converting the mythos and imagery of Hollywood and seizing upon one of MGM's classic films, *Grand Hotel*, and getting the studio into the gambling business, with an MGM Grand Hotel in Las Vegas and Reno. Now the studio is prospering again and is manufacturing cinema dreams once more in Culver City—and also enabling other dreamers to inhabit castles-in-the-air in Nevada.

Cinerama Dome on Sunset Boulevard.

The Milky Way

After departing MGM, go north, returning via Motor Avenue. Make a right turn at Olympic Boulevard and go east. At Beverly Drive, go left and park. Walk to The Milky Way at 326½ South Beverly Drive. Inside you will discover a little-known and marvelous cafe. Posters of recent films—*Jaws, Close Encounters of the Third Kind*—adorn the walls. Tapes of classical music soothe the ear. Say hello for me to the *patronne*, a lithe and lively lady with a sweet smile and close-cropped blond hair. Her name is Mrs. Adler. You would take her to be a French film actress. She is the mother of Steve Spielberg. Spielberg directed her favorite pictures, listed above.

I ask you, on what other Hollywood tour do you get to personally meet the mother of one of our most brilliant young film directors?

Going from the sublime to the academic, fare forth and take Beverly north to Wilshire Boulevard, turn right, and travel east a mile or so until you come to Lapeer Drive, a few blocks past Doheny Drive. By the way, when you are going east or west as you will often be doing while traversing Los Angeles, try to avoid Wilshire, Sunset, Hollywood, and Santa Monica boulevards as they are often busy. The experienced natives use Fountain Avenue, Beverly Boulevard, Olympic Boulevard, and Sixth Street for criss-crossing the city. Avoid freeways between 7 and 9 a.m. and 4:30 and 7 p.m. At other times you will discover to your delight that not only are the freeways mostly unclogged, but the surface streets, even downtown, are not densely choked. It is usually possible to find street parking, with or without a parking meter. Watch for signs that indicate no-parking hours.

At Lapeer and Wilshire visit the headquarters of the Academy of Motion Picture Arts and Sciences, the same academy whose members select the persons and films awarded the gilded statuettes we call "Oscars" every April (open from 9 a.m. to 5 p.m., Monday through Friday). Visit the handsome well-lighted library on the fourth floor. In the stacks repose about 1.6 million stills from movies, as well as candid publicity photographs. The library has fifteen thousand books on film and millions and millions of newspaper and magazine clippings which are filed. Scholars and popular writers on movies and movie stars frequent this library. From time to time there are exhibits of costumes in the glittering grand lobby off the foyer, and these are open to the public.

Academy of Motion Picture Arts and Sciences

On the second floor is one of the two finest movie theaters in Los Angeles: the Sam Goldwyn Theatre. The screen and sound are perfect and the projection is accurate. Two life-size Oscars flank the screen. The theater is only for the use of members and for press and publicity screenings when a studio or exhibitor leases it for the evening. The other—and even better—movie theater is the Cinerama Dome on Sunset Boulevard near Vine Street, whose screen is truly wide and high and whose sound system is superb.

Cinerama Dome

We drive east on Wilshire and hang a left on La Cienega Boulevard. Proceed north, noticing the many dining places on both sides which have caused this stretch to be named Restaurant Row. Continue until you come to Fountain Avenue, which begins here and wends its way east until it becomes Hyperion Avenue and ultimately leads into Brand Boulevard in Glendale. Traveling along Fountain, you will see many of the 1920s apartment buildings in creamy white with plaster garlands and gargoyles. You will pass, near Crescent Heights Boulevard, the walled estate where Loretta Young once resided. In these streets of West Hollywood many of the stars lived before they moved to Beverly Hills and Bel Air. They also lived in what we call the Hollywood Hills, which are the wind-

**Restaurant Row
Fountain Avenue**

ing, twisting, narrow streets above Sunset Boulevard, and many famous personalities still live there. As you move farther east you will be getting into old Hollywood, and you will see many bungalows with open porches, wooden Ionic columns, and overhanging eaves. These are very typical of the low-cost homes on small plots in which lived the people who worked at the Goldwyn Studios, the Chaplin studios, at RKO and Columbia and Paramount —all studios which existed or still exist in this part of town.

Hollywood Memorial Park Cemetery

Turn right on La Brea Avenue and then left on Santa Monica Boulevard and proceed until you come to the Hollywood Memorial Park Cemetery at 6000 Santa Monica Boulevard. There are many fine cemeteries in greater Los Angeles and all of them have famous men and women coffined away. But Forest Lawn (the original over in Glendale) is the only other one worth a visit, though I think you will find it disappointing because, except for Jean Hersholt, most of the deceased celebrities are either in crypts, like beautiful memories filed away in drawers, or, what is even worse, are laid on a hill with only a flat marker to tell you the name. It is the Forest Lawn principle to be against headstones and vaults and great crypts. I guess "Death, Be Not Proud," is the slogan over there.

Tomb of Douglas Fairbanks in the Hollywood Cemetery.

For persons like myself, be they ancestor worshipers or epicureans of necrophilia, the finest of all resting places is Hollywood Memorial Park Cemetery. It is open every day. There is ample free parking. At the administration office, you will be provided, gratis, with a map of the grounds and the locations of the final resting places of such persons as Rudolph Valentino, Gene Stratton Porter, and Marion Davies—William Randolph Hearst's paramour—who is buried under her maiden name of Douras, in a Douras family vault. Tyrone Power has a fine marble above-the-ground tomb with a Shakespeare inscription and elaborate carvings. The most stunning grave is Douglas Fairbanks'. It is the only one truly worthy of a great Hollywood star. There is a sunken garden with a long pool, a vast stone, and Fairbanks in silhouette on a medallion. It is beautiful. You will also see the graves of Cecil B. De Mille and Harry Cohn, "Beloved Husband Father." Cohn, the crude, violent, tyrannical boss of Columbia Pictures, was the most hated man in Hollywood. He died on February 27, 1958, and a crowd of thousands turned out to attend the services. This caused a local wit to say, "You give the public what they want, and they will always come out for it." The joke has been attributed to many wits about many Hollywood tyrants, including Louis B. Mayer and Jesse Lasky.

One grave which is not marked on the official map is that of Virginia Rappe. She lies with just a simple plaque above her remains in section eight, near an artificial lake. In 1921 Virginia Rappe went to San Francisco and attended a wild party at the St. Francis Hotel at which it was alleged that Roscoe "Fatty" Arbuckle attempted carnal penetration with a bottle of Coca-Cola, or so goes the legend. Her bladder was ruptured and she died. He was tried for murder and acquitted, but his career was ended.

Going south on Gower Street to Melrose Avenue, it is but a headstone's throw to Paramount Pictures. Not too far away and also on Melrose, is the Mexican restaurant, Lucy's El Adobe, which is one of Governor Edmund Brown, Jr.'s, favorite hangouts. Jerry Brown and Linda Ronstadt often dine here on carne asada. El Adobe is a modest place. (See Dining Out, p. 149.) I am sure that you, like all of us visiting Los Angeles, will forever be on your own personal star treks, and I will now digress and give you some favorite watering holes of the stars, for which I am sure they will hate me. People over at Paramount may go to Lucy's El Adobe, to Oblath's, a very old and very traditional 1930s type of cocktail lounge with leatherette banquettes, right across from the Bronson Gate at Paramount. Nickodell's is another local haunt. Further west, the Studio Grill— a fine and expensive joint—is frequented by people from the Goldwyn Studios. (See Dining Out, p. 141.) You can see various celebrities on Sunday brunching at Nate 'n Al's delicatessen on Beverly Drive (see Shopping, p. 268), at Butterfield's on Sunset, at Moustache's on Melrose near Crescent Heights (see Dining Out,

Watering Holes of the Stars

p. 138), and at the Beverly Wilshire (see Hotels, p. 156). The Polo Lounge of the Beverly Hills Hotel is where many stars like to conduct interviews and where people meet to haggle over deals. (See Hotels, p. 154.) It is also rumored to be a place where you can pick up some of the highest-priced and most beautiful *hetairae* in Los Angeles, if your tastes and wealth run in this direction. I wouldn't know about such things. The Bistro at lunch—if you can get in, which is damn near impossible—is another hunting ground for stars. (See Dining Out, p. 126.) I would like to beseech you just to look—don't touch. Please do not annoy famous men and women by badgering them for autographs while they are dining. Respect their need for privacy and peace. Every star I've ever interviewed has told me that the most painful aspect of being famous is the loss of privacy.

Paramount Studios

You will not be able to get into Paramount unless you have influence, but you can stand outside those famous wrought-iron gates and remember that scene in *Sunset Boulevard*, in which Gloria Swanson, playing a once-famous star and now-faded flower, returns to her old studio in her Hispano-Suiza, driven by Erich von Stroheim, and is barred by the studio gateman. (Do not be frustrated with all the studios you have not been able to enter. Soon I will tell you about one whose portals will open for you, and at a very reasonable price.)

You will now go west on Melrose Avenue, hang a left at Vine Street, and go south, past Beverly Boulevard, where Vine becomes Rossmore Avenue. At 570 Rossmore is the Ravenswood, a fine white Art Deco apartment building, which is owned by Mae West, who resides in the penthouse suite. Nearby is the even more exotic looking El Royale. These were once among the most expensive and fashionable apartments in town. There is still a waiting list to rent a flat in them because they are finely made with high ceilings, thick walls, enormous spaces. Going south to Wilshire Boulevard, note the Ambassador Hotel, still a fine caravansary, whose Cocoanut Grove during the 1930s and 1940s was a favorite dancing place of celebrities. There were name bands and fine food and cocoanut trees with cellophane leaves. (See Hotels, p. 153.) Near the Ambassador is the Original Brown Derby, whose exterior is shaped like a derby. It was a time of structural fantasy for Los Angeles, the city in which the spirit can express itself in exuberant fol-de-rol. There are other Derbies, one on Wilshire in Beverly Hills and a famous one on Vine Street near Hollywood Boulevard. While you're in the mid-Wilshire neighborhood you might, since we shall not come back to this area on the tour, drop into Perino's, at 4101 Wilshire, the once and present center of haute cuisine in L.A., a place of exquisite remembrances where many stars celebrated important events in their lives, and where many banquets were given, and are still given. (See Dining Out, p. 129.)

Ambassador Hotel, Cocoanut Grove

Original Brown Derby

Perino's

Let us return via Rossmore and Vine to Melrose, then drive a block east and turn onto El Centro Avenue. Here at 815 El Centro is the

Original Brown Derby restaurant on Wilshire Boulevard, April 1941.

Los Angeles Orphans' Home—Marilyn Monroe

Los Angeles Orphans' Home. The most famous orphan who inhabited it was Marilyn Monroe. I remember once being taken on a guided tour by the superintendent of the home and standing in the room little Norma Jean shared with three other orphans. From her window you could see the RKO logo with its lightning-bolt. Marilyn told her girlhood fantasies of being an actress and star at RKO. Not too far from the orphanage is the famous Studio Club, where Marilyn also lived for a time. It used to be an all-girls boarding house, under the supervision of the YWCA, for young women who were trying to make careers in movies. It is at 1215 Lodi Place. Stroll about the patio and gardens. Taste the quiet. Remember that these flatstones were once trodden by Marilyn Monroe and Gale Storm, by JoAnn Worley, Kim Novak, Donna Reed, Janet Blair, Evelyn Keyes. And, ah, by poor Sharon Tate, wife of director Roman Polanski, murdered by the Manson family in Benedict Canyon.

Studio Club—famous boarding house for starlets

Let us now go west on Santa Monica Boulevard, make a right on Cahuenga Boulevard and proceed north, being careful to bear rightwards when Ivar Avenue is born out of Cahuenga. Park between Sunset and Hollywood boulevards. On the west side of the street you will see the USO Building with a plaque of Bob Hope in profile on its stark wall. Across the way, convenient to any sexually frustrated members of the armed services, is Plato's Retreat West, a new establishment dedicated to dining, dancing, and bathing in the

Ivar Avenue

L.A. Public Library, Hollywood Branch

nude, as well as other sports practiced *en deshabille*. Getting our mind onto higher things, we look into the Hollywood branch of the L.A. Public Library at 1627 Ivar Avenue, a very 1920s type of California mission structure, with an interesting tile facade and a small fountain. Inside is a lovely library with a two-story ceiling. Many writers and directors and stars came here during the 1920s and 1930s, when this part of town was the heart of the movie colony. And we definitely know of one famous fictional character who came to this library—Philip Marlowe—in Raymond Chandler's *The Big Sleep*.

Hollywood Knickerbocker Hotel

Nathanael West lived at 1817 Ivar during the writing of *Day of the Locust*, the best novel of 1930s Hollywood. We can retrace West's footsteps in fancy, walking up Ivar and crossing Hollywood Boulevard. There is the Hollywood Knickerbocker Hotel, once a rather grand and important hotel, and now a senior citizens' apartment house owned by the government and closed to the public. Here is where D.W. Griffith lived out his last years, alone and unrecognized.

Vine Street Brown Derby

The NBC studios (it was radio then) were located nearby at Sunset and Vine, and CBS was quartered in a dramatically contemporary art moderne building at 6121 Sunset—still a beautiful example of the spirit of that age and worth a look. The Vine Street Brown Derby, now a fairly sedate retreat, teemed with excitement, especially at lunch, when famous persons were paged on the loudspeaker and columnists like Hedda Hopper, Jimmy Fidler, Louella Parsons, and Sidney Skolsky table-hopped. NBC is now in beautiful downtown Burbank (over the hill and into the valley) and the CBS television studio is an already dated square fortress on Beverly Boulevard and Fairfax Avenue, cheek to cheek with the Farmer's Market. You will, I know, visit Farmer's Market, so take a free tour of the CBS facilities.

Hollywood and Vine

Capitol Records Building

Nathanael West's home

Hollywood and Vine, which some ignorant outlanders still think of as the center of Hollywood, and which used to be affectionately known as the "double crossroads of the world," is a shabby intersection nowadays. Going toward Yucca Avenue, look to the east and observe the rounded contours of the Capitol Records Building, shaped like a stack of gargantuan phonograph discs, with a twenty-foot chimney in the shape of a stylus. This, I believe, was the first circular office building in the world. As soon as you cross Yucca Avenue, there is a steep and beautiful street that breathes the spirit of the 1920s and 1930s, the street between Yucca and a flange of Franklin Avenue. Climb to the top of Ivar. You have passed small houses and large houses, Tudor imitations, Spanish colonials, and California moderne. This is how it looked when Nathanael West lived here. At the top on the eastern slope stands the magnificent white mansion once inhabited by Marie Dressler and now subdivided into much-desired and expensive apartments. About halfway down the block, at 1817 Ivar, is the Parva-Sed-Apta apartments, one of those pseudo-Tudors, with a small tile decoration outside and small plants and a terra-cotta figure of a small laughing child.

Capitol Records Building.

Home of Nathanael West.

Tiles of various designs and colors were a basic design element in homes and office buildings during these years, and they are always lovely accents when you find them. West's old home is still well maintained. It is a two-story walkup, with a Victorian ornamented glass front door.

Las Palmas Avenue

Musso and Frank Grill

Larry Edmunds Book Shop

Going south on Ivar, we turn right on Hollywood Boulevard, as West did so many times, and go to Las Palmas Avenue, where once was located Stanley Rose's bookshop. West liked to hang out in the bookshop's backroom, drinking wine and sharing observations with other writers—William Saroyan, F. Scott Fitzgerald, John Fante, William Faulkner, Budd Schulberg. Now the site has been converted into part of Musso and Frank Grill, which boasts that it is the oldest restaurant in Hollywood—"since 1919." West, as did many of his *copains*, often drank and dined at Musso's. It is still a hangout of writers and actors and directors. With its dark oak paneling, faded murals, starched linen tableclothes and napkins, and marvelous waiters, it is, believe me, a reconnaissance into old-time Hollywood. (See Dining Out, p. 121.) Another reconnaissance is right across the way at the Larry Edmunds Book Shop, 6658 Hollywood Boulevard, which has the largest selection of new and out-of-print books on film and movie personalities anywhere in the world. It also stocks thousands of stills, posters, even cancelled checks of celebrities!

Grauman's Egyptian and Chinese Theatres

Ambling along Hollywood Boulevard westward, walk down the long entranceway of Grauman's Egyptian Theatre, red carpeted, with murals of Egyptian figures and statues in niches. By the ticket taker is an amusing mural of hieroglyphic writing and Egyptian personalities. On the other side of Hollywood Boulevard, and a few blocks further west, is another of Sid Grauman's brainchildren—the world famous Grauman's Chinese, recently extended into three theaters and occupying the entire block. The new owner is Ted Mann, who has tried to rename it Mann's Chinese, but we habitually call it Grauman's. This used to be the theater of the great flood-lighted premières, the kind where they had rows of grandstands built so rubberneckers could gawk at the stars. The first gala pre-mière was De Mille's *King of Kings*. The crazed star-worshippers broke through police lines and rioted. Several persons were seriously injured. West made this event the basis of the climactic episode of *Day of the Locust*. At Grauman's Chinese, you will want to take some time to meander around the forecourt in which are printed the hands and feet of many stars and their scribbled signatures—all put down in wet concrete. The Chinese with its red pagodas and oriental spires is another expression of that exuberant Los Angeles spirit which is the key to our city, and one freely given to those who are receptive.

C.C. Brown's Ice Cream Parlor

Just a few strides west and you will find C.C. Brown's, the ice cream parlor of the stars. Here is created the most depraved hot fudge sundae you will ever eat. On a base of roasted almonds, there rests an enormous scoop of the richest vanilla ice cream I ever have

C.C. Brown's Ice Cream Parlor.

Schwab's Pharmacy in 1947.

Schwab's Pharmacy today.

known, and upon that glistens a mound of whipped cream and, to pour over, a small pitcher of hot fudge—light, delicate, sweet, concocted with a secret recipe by Mr. Brown in 1922. During the silent movie era the C.C. Brown hot-fudge sundae and banana split were famous among actresses tormented by strict starvation meals during filming. When a film was in the can, they took their dieters' revenge with a sundae orgy at Brown's. Joan Crawford, Carole Lombard, Jean Harlow, Jean Arthur, and many others endured the terrible slenderizing diets because they knew there was a hot-fudge sundae at the end of the tunnel.

West Hollywood

Schwab's Pharmacy

Having had one (remember, Brown's doesn't open until 1 p.m.), you now have the strength to walk back to your car, on Ivar Avenue. Drive west and you are back in West Hollywood. Turn left on Fairfax Avenue, right on Sunset Boulevard, left on Laurel Avenue, and then park. Walk up the block and visit the famous Schwab's Pharmacy (there are other branches but this is the famous one). This is the one where, it is said, Lana Turner was sitting on a stool at the counter having an ice-cream soda when she was discovered by an MGM talent scout. Well, she *was* discovered while sitting at a counter—but it was not at Schwab's; it was at the Top Hat Malt Shop, opposite Hollywood High School, which she attended at Hollywood Boulevard and Highland Avenue (one of the few Art Deco high schools of its time). The Malt Shop is no more. But there are still aspiring starlets sitting in Schwab's. And famous stars, usually New York visitors, here to do a movie or teledrama and staying at the nearby Chateau Marmont or Sunset Marquis, come here for breakfast in the backroom. Sunday brunching at Schwab's is another habit of actors, so add it to your list of star-watching places. A little side excursion over to the Chateau Marmont, a relic of the 1920s and still a favorite hostelry for visiting actors, is recommended. (See Hotels, p. 159.)

Chateau Marmont

Chateau Marmont overlooking Sunset Strip.

Going back now, look for 1401 Laurel Avenue. This is a lovely garden courtyard with an elegant gray Normandy-style stone building. It is a beautiful example of our garden apartments. Towards the back, in apartment six, F. Scott Fitzgerald occupied a duplex, during the last years of his life when he was trying to live without alcohol and was writing his final and unfinished novel, *The Last Tycoon*. And a little farther down is the most breathtaking of all 1920s style garden apartments in Hollywood: the Villa d'Este at 1355 Laurel. Even its garage is lovely. People wait as long as five years for an apartment at the Villa d'Este. It has fountains, great tiles on the walkways, and lemon trees, banana trees, and olive trees. Around the corner at 1433 Hayworth Avenue, is another lovely garden courtyard apartment and here lived Sheilah Graham, in a downstairs flat, amidst the flowering azaleas and weeping willows. She was Scott Fitzgerald's last mistress. He died of a heart attack in her apartment in 1940.

Now perhaps you have always dreamed of buying one of those guides to the homes of the stars. Maps purporting to show the streets and house numbers of these homes are hawked on Hollywood Boulevard. I think it is sheer madness to go gallivanting around Beverly Hills and Hollywood with a map and stopping here and going there and wearing yourself out for nothing, really, because in many cases the stars who are supposed to be living there no longer do. If you must indulge in this whimsical form of voyeurism, I recommend that you take the StarLine Tour One, in which you will see about eighty homes. It is a two-hour trip and most of the year tours leave every hour on the hour, 9 a.m. to 6 p.m. The price is $6.50 for adults and $3.25 for children. For those who either possess indomitable strength, or are dedicated masochists, there is also the Grayline Grand Tour of Los Angeles. Here you will get a once-over lightly of the entire city in about ten hours. It is an all-day excursion and the price is $16.00 for adults, $8.00 for children.

There is, speaking of tours, one tour about which I am enthusiastic. It is the Universal Studios Tour. This is the only way in which most people are able to get through the gates and into a studio. But it is much more than that. The basic tour takes two hours and is a delightful experience. It costs $7.25 for adults and less for juniors and children. From Laurel Avenue, go to Sunset, turn right on Laurel Canyon Boulevard and drive over the hills to the San Fernando Valley. Take the Hollywood Freeway going east and leave it at the Universal City off-ramp, then make a right into Lankershim Boulevard and follow the signs to the tour parking area. From the time you buy your ticket and get into the queue, you will be entertained. At the queuing-up place, you will see a "waxworks" statue, sometimes it is Boris Karloff as Frankenstein, sometimes it is Lon Chaney as the Phantom of the Opera. You start walking by and suddenly the horror comes to life and reaches out to shake your hand. After you have recovered from the shock, you can enjoy the spectacle of subsequent tourists getting a scare. You will be herded into long tram cars, each with an individual guide. The guides are all in-

Laurel Avenue—F. Scott Fitzgerald

Villa d'Este.

Commercial Tours to Stars Homes

Universal Studios Tour

telligent young men and women, most of whom plan to be writers, directors, actors, or technicians. They are passionate about movie history and movie techniques, and your tour will not only encompass every aspect of movie production, in terms of actual demonstrations of lighting effects and special effects and camera tricks, but will encapsulate a history of Hollywood, with interesting stories and gossip. (See Family Entertainment, p. 239.)

Beverly Hills

Beverly Hills Hotel

And now to Beverly Hills. Let us return, via the Hollywood Freeway and the Ventura Freeway, exiting from the Coldwater Canyon off-ramp, which will lead you past the Beverly Hills Hotel, a pink stucco extravaganza. You might park here and stroll through the Polo Lounge and the Patio Lounge and then out in back among the flowered paths and the expensive bungalows. Under the rubric of must-see hotels, I also include the Beverly Wilshire and, further out on Sunset, the Hotel Bel-Air, one of the most unusual you will ever see. (See Hotels, p. 154.)

Beverly Hills Presbyterian Church

And now park your car a few blocks south of Sunset, either on Beverly Drive or Rodeo Drive. Walk south until you pass Santa Monica Boulevard. At Santa Monica, on Rodeo, the fine Spanish-style Beverly Hills Presbyterian Church has a quiet inner courtyard (where you may want to sit and calm your nerves after the ordeal at Universal Studios). Continue south and you will pass another Santa Monica Boulevard which is parallel to the first. The second one we call "little Santa Monica Boulevard" and it is the one with shops and restaurants.

Polo Lounge at the Beverly Hills Hotel.

At 9507 little Santa Monica is a fascinating three-story white stucco building with a high fashion boutique downstairs. This is the Writers' and Artists' Building, whose small offices are, according to the directory, inhabited by Michael Blankfort, Joanna Lee, Ray Bradbury, Jack Albertson, Jack Nicholson, Mann Rubin, John Riley, Bernard Wolfe, Rubin Carson, and other eminent writers and actors. Some of them still work in the building. It is another one of those places for which people wait for years until a famous writer dies and his space is free. The owner, an eccentric gentleman, only rents space to creative people. One of the second floor offices has E. Hemingway on the door. This office is actually occupied by Chuck Barris, producer of "The Gong Show." Many people would question whether Chuck Barris is creative. But he is. He wrote a novel once in the E. Hemingway office. It was a rather good novel.

Writers' and Artists' Building

Crossing Rodeo (Ro-dáy-o) Drive, you will observe Carroll and Company, which is cater-corner to the Writers' and Artists' Building. Dick Carroll is one of the most influential men's stylists in the city. He stocks beautiful suits, shoes, shirts, and also many kinds of hats. It is very hard to find a good place which sells hats. He is the brother of Sidney Carroll, a screenwriter, who wrote, among other works, *The Hustler*. Another eminent men's wear virtuoso is also a Dick—Dick Dorso, formerly an agent and now owner of an elegant shop on Camden Drive, just around the corner. The two Dicks probably clothe most of the male celebrities in Los Angeles. *Très chic* and *très chère*. Meandering down Rodeo Drive, which is the Rue de la Paix of L.A., you will behold, behind startling windows and exciting facades, the shops of Courrèges, Gucci, Van Cleef and Arpels, Céline, Ted Lapidus, Jerry Magnin, Ruth Matthews, Battaglia, and Giorgio. The Beverly Rodeo Hotel with its red stucco front is amusing, and the Cafe Rodeo, open in warm weather, is a pleasant place to lunch, as is the patio in the rear of the Swiss Cafe up the block. By the way, like the Polo Lounge, the bar of the Beverly Rodeo Hotel is rumored to be a place to meet the most elegant and skillful *femmes de nuit*. Like I say, I wouldn't know about such things personally, but that is what my wicked friends tell me.

Rodeo Drive

While I would have you shun stars' homes, there is one side excursion I like to make and will share with you. Driving west on Sunset, just past the Beverly Hills Hotel, turn right on Benedict Canyon Drive and then proceed north a few lights until you come to Tower Road. Take your car slowly up Tower Road. You will pass many small and beautiful homes, and as you rise higher and turn onto Tower Grove Drive the houses become fenced estates, and stone walls conceal the homes, and you are suddenly in almost wild country where quail cross the road and coyotes are in the hills. You are going to see the former residences of the two greatest romantic heroes in movie history. At 1345 Tower Grove Drive is Falcon's Lair, where John Barrymore once lived and loved and caroused and laughed and went into melancholy fits. And then as you climb higher and wind around curves you will come to the very top, to 1400 Tower Grove Drive. Here you can park on the edge of the

Tower Grove Drive—Barrymore, Gilbert, and Garbo

mountain while below you stretches a breathtaking vista of Beverly Hills. Turn around and look at the multilevel white Spanish colonial mansion, a most beautiful and exquisite house, with tile roofs. Think of it, in ten minutes you have been able to cross over from the heart of Beverly Hills to this quiet, wild landscape. Here is where John Gilbert loved Greta Garbo. Here, once, Duesenbergs and Packards and Isotta-Fraschinis and Cords wound up the roads, just as you have done. That is all I am going to say on the subject of homes of the stars.

Westwood Memorial Cemetery
Marilyn Monroe's final home

Except for one more. The final home of Marilyn Monroe. It is a little crypt in a little cemetery in Westwood, at Glendon Avenue and Wilshire Boulevard, the Westwood Memorial Cemetery, over in the northeast crypt area. The plaque simply says, Marilyn Monroe, 1926–1962. By it is a vase. There are always roses in it. Twice a week, on Tuesdays and Fridays, Joe DiMaggio sends roses, remembering the woman he loved so intensely and whom he had married and who had divorced him long ago. Visitors to the cemetery often take a rose as a momento. And so, if you go on Thursday, you may only see two roses left in the vase. And sometimes only one. They always leave one.

Having paid tribute to Marilyn Monroe in Westwood, we are now ready to explore the new and the old in downtown Los Angeles. If you, gentle reader, are a traveler from London, Paris, or other European cities, many of which still have Roman ruins, you will think we are absurd to speak of anything "old" in this city. I cannot show you antiquities. I cannot even show you significant 200-year-old historical sites and houses as they can in Philadelphia, Boston, and Charleston. Perhaps it would be more precise to speak of what we have to show you as the brand new, the recently new, and the less new. Well, a journey of a thousand landmarks begins with a single building, to paraphrase the Chinese proverb, and the building I have chosen is El Alisal, which means "the Sycamores" in Spanish. (There are many sycamore trees all over the city that shed leaves in September, thus giving us an autumnal illusion.) From downtown, take the Pasadena Freeway going north, and get off at
Highland Park the Avenue Forty-three ramp, which is in Highland Park. A few blocks left, at 200 East Avenue Forty-three is El Alisal, the Charles F. Lummis home, a strange two-story edifice, sprawling over a half acre. It is made entirely of rocks and was built by Lummis himself over a period of thirteen years with the aid of one Indian assistant. He dragged the rocks from the Arroyo Seco ("dry river bed") and set them in cement. The Lummis house looks like a small fortress. It
Lummis Home was finished in 1910. Lummis was the first city editor of the Los Angeles *Times*. He wrote many books. He loved many women. He was a passionate defender of the Indians of the Southwest. He came from Chillicothe, Ohio, and fell in love with Los Angeles at a youthful age. This house of rocks was, in its time, a cultural center, where the local illuminati gathered for suppers, conversation, concerts, and poetry readings.

Lummis was not only a fighter for Indian rights but an admirer of their arts and artifacts, and not far from his house of rocks you will find, upon a high hill, a blissful example of California mission, a fine museum of Indian relics, crafts, and history which he founded: the Southwest Museum at 234 Museum Drive (See Museums and Galleries, p.213). The roots of La Reina de Los Angeles are Spanish and Mexican and Indian and we often return to these original motifs.

Southwest Museum

Continue right on Avenue Forty-three a few blocks, and then turn right on Homer Street which dead ends into Heritage Square (free guided tours the second Sunday and third Wednesday of the month with docents who are intelligent, passionate, and informed lovers of Victorian architecture). Just as the Southwest Museum stands as a monument to the Indian spirit, Heritage Square, which is still in the process of development, will be an authentic re-creation of Los Angeles during the late Victorian and early twentieth century. There are already four superb examples of Queen Anne, Eastlake, Flat Front Italianate, and Mansard style homes which have been moved from their original locations, saved from the wrecker's ball, placed here, and lovingly restored. Only the Hale House, a gorgeous specimen of redwood Victoriana, is open, but you can see the others being restored. Ultimately it is the dream of the Cultural Heritage Foundation to make this place a genuine reconstruction of a late nineteenth century quarter of our city, using true structures and shops. It should be comparable to Williamsburg, Virginia.

Heritage Square

Hale House

Now return to the Pasadena Freeway and go south. Approaching downtown L.A., you are afforded from this height a breathtaking prospect of one of the wonders of the modern world, the four-level interchange, the beating heart of our circulatory system, in which four freeways—the Pasadena, the Santa Monica, the Harbor, and the Hollywood—meet and separate. Four hundred thousand automobiles a day, every day, change lanes and shift from one freeway to another, often at a fast clip, a heaven of engineering at 11 a.m. and a hell of bumpers at 5:30 p.m.

Freeways—the four-level interchange

Approaching the interchanges, be alert. Bear to the left toward the downtown exits, taking the Sunset Boulevard off-ramp all the way down to Main. Turn left on Main to Vignes Street. We will make a slight detour here to see a real old-fashioned jail that looks like a frontier lock-up in a John Wayne movie. It is a real jail which houses real prisoners. It is the most prison-looking jail in the city. There are bigger and more contemporary holding tanks, like the one in Parker Center (police headquarters over on First and Los Angeles streets), which criminals call the Glass House. But I love this old jail near Vignes Street. If I had to serve time, I hope it would be here. It is my favorite jail.

Old Jail

From here, go a few blocks, hang a left on Alameda Street and cruise along until you see the parking area of the Union Station on the left. This railway terminal is one of the most gorgeous evoca-

Union Station

Freeway east of downtown at the Pasadena and San Bernardino interchange.

tions of Moorish and Spanish feeling in the contemporary mode, pure Southern California. It was used by hundreds of thousands of travelers and is still in operation. Like the Pasadena Freeway, Union Station was a make-work project of the Depression, started in 1933, opened in 1939. Wander through the colonnades of arches and the waiting room with its tile floor and high ceiling.

El Pueblo de Los Angeles Olvera Street

Then, with the nostalgic smell of trains still lingering, cross Alameda street to El Pueblo de Los Angeles State Historic Park. Here is the original plaza, the first of a thousand plazas, where the city started with a few families 200 years ago. *Gracias a Dios*, they have not built skyscrapers on this place. Some vestiges of the past remain and are in good condition. The Pico House was our first hotel, an imposing three-story stone building, next to the Merced Theatre, and the Masonic Hall. Cross Main Street to visit the old Plaza Church and Mission, which dates back to 1812 and which has been considerably restored. It is a simple and clean example of mission style. (There are free guided tours of the entire plaza and its historic buildings, Tuesday through Saturday, every hour on the hour, 10 a.m. to 3 p.m..) In the heart of the plaza is the gazebo-like *kiosko*, a circular bandstand, trimmed with tiles. Concerts are given here on Saturday and Sunday. The Avila Adobe, which dates from 1818, is the oldest house still standing in L.A. Francisco Avila was an *alcalde*, or mayor, of the settlement. The house is furnished with old Spanish furniture and has pots and pans and crockery of the period.

*Los Angeles' Chinatown
—a warm blend of East and West.*

Leaving Olvera Street, cross Macy Avenue to Ord Street and you are now in old Chinatown. Around North Spring Street, Main Street and North Broadway you will see a Bank of America branch shaped like a pagoda, a motel shaped like a left-over piece of Grauman's Chinese Theatre, and old brick buildings that go back to the 1870s and the first Chinese settlers. Chinatown today is a cheerful, sunny, and optimistic area. You can see a small seated statue of Dr. Sun Yat Sen, founder of the former Chinese Republic, at the entrance of Ginling Way, which is a Chinese version of the plaza motif. This is a real quarter, peopled by Chinese families, and not some Potemkin type of village put up to catch tourist dollars. There are plenty of authentic Chinese herb pharmacies and live poultry shops and

Chinatown

exotic groceries. You can, if you know your way around, buy good Chinese tonics and aphrodisiacs.

At 913 North Broadway, you will please examine the facade of the Golden Palace restaurant, a striking instance of that commingling of cultures so typical of L.A. For here are thirty-foot high murals with Chinese themes, those blue delft colors of sing-song girls at bridges and dragons and warriors, and they are fashioned out of tiles, yes, Mexican tiles. The murals are not great masterpieces but amusing as a spontaneous expression of our exuberant spirit.

City Hall

From here, it is a ten-minute walk to City Hall, but I suggest you drive, from Union Station over to Second and Spring streets. Opened in 1928, the City Hall is done in conservative Art Deco. Walking up the stairs you will see arched corridors in another variation of the colonnade theme with tiled murals and terrazzo floors. Walk to the center and see the impressive rotunda. Take an express elevator to the 22nd floor and then the tower elevator to the 27th. Here, in an open area, with a wrought-iron railing which is uncomfortably low, you can view the city.

Los Angeles Mall, The Triforium

An underground passage leads from City Hall over to the new Los Angeles Mall, which is just another version of a Spanish-Mexican plaza. Here you can see the notorious Triforium, which, according to a brochure put out by the Los Angeles Convention and Visitors Bureau, is the "Mall's theme tower . . . three banks of illuminated, colored glass prisms operated by computer to display live, electronic or recorded musical performances in light and color." The Triforium has been ridiculed by the art critics of the city as being an ugly, malproportioned, and atrociously conceived public sculpture. For one thing, it has never functioned properly. I guess I have wandered around the mall a dozen times and never once have I seen and heard that vaunted *son et lumière* concert which the Triforium is supposed to produce "electronically." Nor has anybody else of my acquaintance. And yet I have a confession to make. I am fond of the Triforium. I just love great ugly defiant structures, which are so ugly that when stared at long enough they become fascinating, and consequently possess a beauty of their own. The Triforium is three enormous wishbone-shaped concrete figures interconnected and set in water. At the lower level is a stylized totem pole in a fountain, and many shops. This entire mall with its underground shopping area and Triforium is probably the single most despised achievement of modern city planning in L.A. Still, it must be seen. It must be seen to be depreciated.

Music Center: Dorothy Chandler Pavilion, Ahmanson Theatre, and Mark Taper Forum

Walk west on Temple Street until you come to the Music Center, which should be seen by night. In sunlight it looks too stark. In the evening, with its illuminated fountains, with audiences streaming to one of its three houses (the Dorothy Chandler Pavilion, the Ahmanson Theatre, and the Mark Taper Forum), with the lobbies glistening with light, and the sculpture looking powerful in the lights and shadows, it is a thrilling sight. (See Going Out, p. 172 and 176.)

Los Angeles City Hall.

World Trade Center

Bonaventure Hotel

Let us now return to our cars and drive up Temple Street and turn left on Figueroa Street, then left on Fourth Street, and left again on Flower Street, parking in the World Trade Center garage. From here it is but a hop, skip, and jump to the Bonaventure Hotel and the Security Pacific building. Wherever you will go in this quarter you will see the five mirrored-glass cylinders of the Bonaventure Hotel gleaming in the sunlight or shining at night. They look different at different times of day and from other locations. Sometimes as you walk in the underground mazes of these twentieth-century fantasies, or stand close to their bizarre giant shapes, you may feel disoriented and alienated, a frightened victim in a science-fiction movie. (See Hotels, p. 158.)

Security Pacific Building.

Across from the World Trade Center garage, on Flower, is a flight of stairs which you climb. You now find yourself on a lengthy and deserted walkway over Flower transiting a twilight zone of depersonalized concrete. Below you the cars and pedestrians are tiny. Just keep striding bravely along this high overpass. You will see a passage into the fifty-two story Security Pacific National Bank Building. Through the corridors you discover a central area, open to the light. Heavenly waterfalls are splashing into a fountain, lovely willow trees dip down to the pool. Now return to the lobby. Take the escalator to the next level, and you are on Hope Street. Go outside. There you will see an entrancing sight—a gigantic tentacled *stabile* sculpture by Alexander Calder, about 100 feet tall, painted Chinese red. Not far from the Calder is a lovely secret garden, with flowers and shrubs and waterfalls. I suggest you sit on one of the benches in this garden and contemplate the vista of the Bonaventure's cylindrical towers, with the contrasting squat structure of the World Trade Center—an interesting juxtaposition of abstract masses. From this distance, the buildings themselves become sculptures as well as habitations.

Security Pacific Building

Now we will walk down Hope Street. See that cone-shaped top of the tower over the Public Library? It is one of the architectural curiosities of L.A. You descend a downhill flight to Fifth Street, and below, looking up, you will see that the staircase has been disguised by a facade resembling a California mission-style fortress. This is a false front, worthy of the backlot at Universal Studios. The grounds of the Public Library are well landscaped. They provide pleasant sleeping quarters for derelicts from our local port of missing men, which is not far away.

Los Angeles Public Library

Let us proceed down Fifth—it will be downhill all the way, my friends. Now you are at Pershing Square. Inclined as I am to admire anything which is interesting, I can't see anything to like about Pershing Square. It is banal. It is a favorite place for winos and drifters. And yet, on one side of the square is the beautiful Biltmore Hotel, a handsome brick structure of classical dimensions, which looks like it was designed for London or Boston. The dignified exterior, however, does not even hint at the treasures inside—the lobby and those stairs with wrought-iron balustrades. The tiles, Spanish wood ceilings, and baroque murals would take you hours to absorb. (See Hotels, p. 158.)

Pershing Square

Biltmore Hotel

Outside, past Hill Street, you come to Broadway, one of the few avenues in Los Angeles which is truly a crowded city street. Broadway is the shopping center for the Mexican-Americans among us—and there are over one million Chicanos out of a total L.A. population of about seven million. They add color, warmth, and a relaxed and life-embracing quality to our city. You will want to walk through the aisles of the Grand Central Market, an incredible bazaar of bakeries, fruit and vegetable stalls, butcher shops, and groceries selling a dozen kinds of chili. The interplay of shoppers and salespeople is intriguing.

Broadway

Grand Central Market

Grand Central Market.

Down the street is the first of Sid Grauman's fantasy theaters, the Million Dollar, opened in 1916, and still a gorgeous showplace. This was a time when Broadway was the theatrical heart of the city and when the Alexandria Hotel on Spring Street was the gathering place of the movie stars. Across from the Million Dollar Theatre is the celebrated Bradbury Building. The exterior is chaste. The interior, however, is an incredible open design of iron staircases, a skylight, marble floors and walls, and a sense of quiet and aristocratic elegance. It has been the scene of a thousand moments in films and television dramas. The Bradbury Building is occupied mostly by lawyers. One office, on the second floor, has an eye on the frosted glass and the identification, "Samuel Spade, Investigations." The door is always closed. You can let your imagination loose and

Bradbury Building

New Otani Hotel.

Gardens at the New Otani.

imagine Humphrey Bogart in there with Mary Astor. (See Architecture, p. 42 .)

The New Otani Hotel, a lovely Japanese inn, is at 120 South Los Angeles Street, but it is a million cultural miles away. Here, if you take the elevator to A Thousand Cranes Restaurant, is another secret garden, on an upper level, a planting of rocks and pools and splashing waters in little fountains, hundreds of white azalea bushes, all exuding that quality of Nipponese delicacy and restrained manners which has also been added to our melting pot. (See Hotels, p. 156.) The streets around the hotel are worth a ramble for their Japanese shops and restaurants.

New Otani Hotel

Clifton's Brookdale Cafeteria

Now we peregrinate up Broadway, until we are past Fourth Street. At 648 South Broadway is Clifton's Brookdale Cafeteria. Before you enter, look at the sidewalk, at the terrazzo images there—aspects of life in Southern California as it was in 1935 when this most unusual of cafeterias opened, and as it is today. Clifford E. Clinton, who died in 1969, was one of those cranks and individualists, one of those inspired reformers, one of those Upton Sinclair types, who flourish in Los Angeles—Howard Jarvis being the latest. They are wonderful specimens of untrammeled humanity. Clifford Clinton believed that a diner who didn't like his food didn't have to pay. Your word was good enough for him. And if you did not have the dollar or two to pay for your meal, even though you liked it, you could pay him whatever you could afford to pay. He also gave you free pamphlets. He was a philosopher. He wrote his own pamphlets. He believed in giving you food for your stomach and food for your mind. Well, the food is still good and the atmosphere is relaxing, but there is no more economic philosophy. There is the sidewalk terrazzo, though, as Clifford Clinton's monument.

Movie Palaces

You will find, as you stroll Broadway, other terrazzos, though more abstract. There are several spectacular theaters, survivors of that exuberant period of movie palace construction during the 1920s and early 1930s, and all of them should be savored and studied—the marquees, the exteriors, and the lobbies. The Los Angeles Theatre, 615 South Broadway, has enormous Corinthian columns above the marquee, and, within, a gorgeous lobby of crystal chandeliers and mirrors, a pastiche of the Hall of Mirrors in Versailles. The smaller Palace Theatre at 630 South Broadway has interesting terra-cotta decorative touches. The Tower, at the corner of Eighth Street, has an incredible facade and small lobby, said to be a pastiche of the Paris Opera. The Orpheum Theatre, at 842 South Broadway, is another example of the period.

Doremus Building, Art Deco masterpiece

At Broadway and Ninth Street is what I consider the single greatest masterpiece of the Art Deco and L.A. moderne mode of the late 1920s and early 1930s—the Doremus Building, formerly known as the Eastern Columbia Building. Enjoy the fantastic clock tower and numerals in abstract modern with clean straight lines and a bluish green color. (See Architecture, p. 44.)

Herald-Examiner Mansion

Broadway has one more *sui generis* edifice to give us, and that is the *Herald-Examiner*'s stately mansion at 1111 South Broadway, a mingling of many styles which exude wealth and power. (See Architecture, p. 44.) It is meant to stun you and it does. It was designed for William Randolph Hearst, who founded the *Examiner* in 1903. It was his favorite paper. The lady who designed this gorgeous palace was Julia Morgan, who also designed the stately pleasure dome for Citizen Hearst at San Simeon, but that, my footsore friends, is another tour.

Now let us retrace our steps and go over to 617 Olive Street and the Oviatt Building, the second great example of period fashion (the third is the Bullock's Department Store on Wilshire Boulevard in the mid-Wilshire district). James Oviatt, a leading haberdasher of the time, commissioned the designer René Lalique to create etched glass panels and ceilings and fanciful doors and mailboxes. Above the building is a stunning campanile and clock.

Oviatt Building, Lalique glass panels and ceilings

Entrance of the Oviatt Building.

Theatre Jewelry Exchange

At Seventh and Hill streets is the Theatre Jewelry Exchange, housing dozens of small dealers in baubles, bangles, and baguette diamonds. Note the terrazzo designs in the lobby and quotations from the New Testament. Look above you at the decorative terra cotta and the baroque tower. Along Hill, between Seventh and Sixth, is the heart of the wholesale and retail jewelry establishment of Los Angeles. Diamonds worth fortunes are passed around like jellybeans from one dealer to another.

St. Vincent's Court

Wandering up Seventh now, you may miss the little alley called St. Vincent's Court. Don't. It is a charming space, somewhat reminiscent of London.

Broadway Plaza, Hyatt Regency Hotel

The Global Marine House, at 811 Seventh Street, is an incredible building both inside and out, and was made in 1925 in the Romanesque spirit. Two gigantic naked male statues sprawl over the entrance. The lobby has a little pool and amoretti and incredibly beautiful tiles from the Pasadena factory of Ernest Batchelder and, as one of its most unusual features, small booths, like confessionals, with paintings displayed inside them. The art is changed monthly. The spirit which imbued the designers and builders of this Global Marine House is still present, as you can see when you cross the street and go to the Broadway Plaza, perhaps the most exuberant and florally abundant of interior plazas. Two levels contain shops and dining places and many plants and trees. The Hyatt Regency Hotel is located here. You should go up the tower to the Angel's Flight Restaurant, one of those revolving affairs which make a complete 360-degree turn every fifty minutes.

St. Paul's Cathedral, secluded retreat

I know you are getting weary, but I still have another plaza for you and some more sights to see as long as we are downtown. Walk up Sixth Street, all the way to Figueroa, to St. Paul's Cathedral, an Episcopal church in fine mission style. Though it is off the Harbor Freeway, and though it is in a seething maelstrom of traffic, this little church and its gardens make a quiet, secluded retreat. Let us sit down at one of the stone benches in the garden and contemplate that elegant brick building across the way which looks like a very expensive hotel, and then, in the other direction, that strange building with the rounded marble facing at its corner and then, opposite that, as we can see by the labels, is the Arco Plaza. Well, the elegant brick building is the Jonathan Club. The Jonathan Club and the California Club, an equally imposing structure located at 538 South Flower Street, are both private clubs, both citadels of the Los Angeles power structure. Here many of the men who own and control the banks of our city, the oil companies, the insurance companies, the real estate, and some of the politicians come to dine and plan.

Jonathan Club and California Club

Linder Plaza

The building with the curved marble edging is the new Linder Plaza building, 888 West Sixth, but when you touch the "marble" it turns out to be tin, cleverly disguised.

Twin Towers of Atlantic Richfield

The twin towers of Atlantic Richfield are worth a visit. Three levels of shops and restaurants are inside. Outside is a circular splashing fountain with a superb and lofty abstract sculpture that seems to go in and around itself like a Möbius curve. The best vantage point to see it is facing the Bank of America windows. It is beautiful in the noon sunshine and even more haunting in the evening when the light makes the fountain spray iridescent and softens the sculpture into a mysterious and powerful thing that seems to move in and out of the waters.

Having ransomed your car, you will exit on Figueroa, make a left and then head to Olympic Boulevard. Go west on Olympic until you come to Alvarado Street. You are about to visit one of the loveliest and least-known quarters of the city—the Echo Park district. But before we get there I have a little surprise in store for you. At the corner of Olympic and Alvarado is the Papa Choux Restaurant. Walk into it. You will observe a series of *fin de siècle* semiprivate dining rooms, with red curtains and red swags, all terribly *louche* and out of the 1890s. Yes, these are *salles privées*, just like they have in certain Parisian restaurants which date from the same period. You would swear this restaurant is eighty or ninety years old. But it was built during the 1960s by Seymour Jacoby, spiritual sibling to Charles Lummis and Simon Rodia.

Alvarado Street

Papa Choux Restaurant

But wait, we have not done with the Jacoby inventions. Next door to Papa Choux is the Olympian Hotel, a fine establishment whose slogan is "Have your next affair at the Olympian." Though the management no doubt means your "catered affair," one assumes that it is willing to accept all affairs, including those of the heart. In the Olympian Hotel is the most fascinating coffee shop in L.A. It is a fine place for dinner and there are long lines at lunchtime. One reason is the glass wall that displays little tropical birds flying about little tropical trees. Years ago monkeys also lived in this Eden which Seymour Jacoby created to entertain his customers. Yes, a flock of little rhesus monkeys and spider monkeys. And every now and then a lady monkey would get in estrus and intimacies would occur while persons were drinking and dining. Well, word got around town, and you had to reserve tables weeks in advance to get into the Olympian Coffee Shop. It was the only X-rated restaurant in town. Then somebody reported these monkey orgies to the police department, and the proprietor was charged with . . . well, I don't know exactly *what* they charged him with. He fought the case, he even served one day in jail. He said he loved monkeys, that's all. But he finally gave the monkeys away to the Griffith Park Zoo. Now there are only birds to watch. They are not quite as interesting from an erotic viewpoint.

Olympian Hotel Coffee Shop

Turn right on Alvarado and proceed northward past MacArthur Park until you come to Montrose Street. Turn right on Montrose and go east until you see Echo Park Lake before you. From here you have a splendid view of the Angelus Temple, a semicircular build-ing with Moorish arches and a Byzantine dome. This was the church of Aimee Semple McPherson, the great evangelist of the

Angelus Temple

1920s. Thousands came here every day of the week, and especially on Sunday, to hear her sermons, to be saved, to be baptized. There was (and still is) a huge baptismal tank into which persons were plunged every Sunday. She broadcast on the radio. She was the first of a long line of hell-fire and damnation Los Angeles radio and television evangelists. The temple itself is not open to the public except during services but if you go to the offices and say you would like to see it, they may open it for you. It is a handsome church. They still baptize in the tanks after the 6 p.m. Sunday services. Overhead is a massive spherical ceiling, painted blue, with a round lamp in the center. It is one of the world's largest unsupported domes.

Echo Park Lake

St. Athanasius Church

Of all our bodies of water and all our parks, the one of which I am fondest is Echo Park with its lake, like an oval mirror ringed with palms. The best time to see it is at dusk, when the sun is setting. Go and stand on the verandah of St. Athanasius Church and look across the park, facing west, and you will be transported out of yourself. It is one of the most emotionally gratifying views in the city. Echo Park is also a nice place to walk, and it is never crowded. Around you on the hills you will see many Victorian houses. This neighborhood has recently become interesting to young couples and artists. After having fallen into shabby desuetude for a long time, it is now undergoing a revival.

Carroll Avenue, Victorian houses

Return to your car and turn left on Bellevue Avenue, make another left on Edgeware Road, and climb a few blocks to Carroll Avenue. Drive to the 1300 block. You have now escaped from the present and, by means of a time machine, you find yourself in a completely untouched block of superb Victorian houses. Many amusing and picturesque details ornament these homes, all of which are privately owned and cannot be entered except during an annual fundraising tour. You could walk up and down this street and stare at these houses for hours and still not finish relishing all their details.

Santa Monica Pier

Saving the grandest lady of our city till last, let us visit the Pacific Ocean. Drive west on the Santa Monica Freeway and exit on Lincoln Boulevard going north. Make a left on Colorado Avenue and park when you see the water. You are on a bluff and the beach is below. To the north is Palisades Park, a lovely strip overlooking the ocean. Ahead is the Santa Monica Pier, featuring one of the oldest carousels in the U.S. The owners claim it to be ninety years old. It was almost torn down, but was saved by public protests. The merry-go-round building is a strange circular structure painted in garish tones of red and yellow. Read the message signed by the forty-three horses of the merry-go-round, thanking the L.A. citizens for saving the pier in 1973. Once there were small apartments above the carousel, but now there are only the horses and the music and the price is still twenty-five cents. There is a scooter ride on the pier and a skeeball game and a pinball arcade and a lady named Sandra who looks into her crystal ball for you for two dollars and a shooting gallery and two restaurants, Moby's Dock and the Boathouse. The Boathouse is almost on the water. It is nice to walk

Angelus Temple.

to the end of the pier and see the fisherfolk. At the other end of the pier, you can go down to the Santa Monica Promenade and walk south, your life being endangered by roller-skaters and bicyclists. The promenade is free of automobiles and it is a wonderful walk. On Saturday and Sunday it is one of the happiest places in the city. You are close to the beach, which never seems to be crowded, and you are close to the sky and the palm trees. (See Beaches, p. 229.) If you walk to the end of the promenade, you will see, at Pico Boulevard, an imposing red-brick building. It used to be the Del Mar Club, an upperclass beach club, with a fine dining room and floorshows. Later it was taken over by the U.S. Navy as a rest and rehabilitation retreat for men who had seen action in the Pacific. Eventually the Synanon Foundation took over the property to work with drug addicts and alcoholics. Then Synanon fell upon hard times, and in 1977 Nathan Pritikin's Longevity Center took over this building and now operates it as an expensive spa to which persons go for three weeks to diet and exercise and restore their health.

Santa Monica Promenade

Every beach city, and there are so many up and down the Pacific Coast, is interesting in its own way. From Santa Monica, we will proceed farther south, either by car or on foot, until we come to Venice. Venice, like so many *arrondissements* in L.A., is going through a transition from being a ramshackle slum and a hang-loose place to an expensive and even elegant beach colony. But the Venice street-people still abound, and the painters' and sculptors' studios are still active. It is still a Latin Quarter. One hopes this is never lost, for then Venice would no longer be Venice, but would become a condominium-choked, high-rise community.

Venice

Ocean Front Walk

To start the Venice walk, park your car in the municipal lot on Rose Avenue, right at the beach. When you stroll this Ocean Front Walk, especially on weekends, you will encounter many gaudily dressed street-people, some of whom are amusing flim-flam artists, and others of whom are honestly uninhibited hedonists. There are strolling players and mimes and musicians. They put on free entertainment and solicit donations. On one walk, I heard an extraordinary steel-band playing reggae and calypso music. There are sometimes tap dancers and jazz flutists and rhythm trios. And there are many people with whom to converse. It is about a two-mile walk, with the beach on one side with benches for resting and now and then playgrounds for children. On the land side are the usual kind of beach houses and a few stores. There are streets behind streets of more beach houses and that informal bathing-suit-atmosphere of every beach colony. This is still a neighborhood of writers, painters, musicians, sculptors, and bohemians of every kind, and they give it that ambience of freedom which is so pleasant.

Land's End Cafe and Sidewalk Cafe

Two of my favorite sidewalk cafes are Land's End and another one, simply called the Sidewalk Cafe. (See Dining Out, pp. 135 and 131.) There are few experiences more satisfying than a brunch or dinner on Ocean Front Walk, looking out at the sand and ocean waves, watching the skaters glide so smoothly in and out of the pedestrians. At Market Street, which has several art galleries, there is one of the many wall murals in which the city abounds—this one is a spaceman-cowboy fantasy desert scene. A little farther along is

Windward Avenue

Windward Avenue, where you will see the colonnades of what used to be the St. Charles Hotel and are now shops and a night club named F. Scott's, after the writer. (See Going Out, p. 188.) Here is

Terry Schoonhoven's mural

the finest wall painting in the city—Terry Schoonhoven's mirror-image mural of the scene we see opposite. It is one of the most delicious *trompes l'oeil* ever.

Continue south on Ocean Front Walk and turn left on South Venice Boulevard. Go about two blocks to a tiny bridge. The cross street is almost a dirt lane, and there is a sense of disorder as if it is going to wrack and ruin. And, in one sense, it is. In another sense, though, it is at a height of grandeur; it is a dream.

The dreamer was Abbott Kinney. Kinney was a millionaire cigarette manufacturer. He retired to Santa Monica at the turn of the century. He loved Venice, I mean, the original Venice in Italy. The one with the Grand Canal and the Doge's Palace and St. Mark's Piazza. Kinney put together many parcels of property south of Santa Monica. He believed that the temperature and spirit of this area was like Italy's, so he decided to make a little copy of Venice on the Pacific Ocean. He made it come to life in 1904. From Rose Avenue on south, these streets, now paved, were once canals. Kinney put up little houses like those he had seen in Italy. He built bridges over his canals. He even imported gondolas and gondoliers. He dreamed of it becoming an artistic center. He dreamed of it as a

Old Santa Monica Pier.

place where painters could work in an atmosphere of sensual beauty, where they could paint as Titian and Tintoretto had once painted in old Venice. Well, what happened to Mr. Kinney, shouldn't happen to a doge. He sold his houses and he made even more money, but instead of the great Renaissance city-state he had envisioned, he had just another petit-bourgeois beach town. And it got more and more honky-tonk, and soon it fell apart. Finally L.A. annexed Venice. Most of the canals were drained in 1925, and Main Street, once the center of the canal freeway system was paved over. But wait—a few survived.

When you look toward your right from South Venice Boulevard, you will see, instead of a street, a long gently flowing canal, with small beach bungalows on either side. This, my friends, is the Grand Canal, our own Grand Canal. Walk it slowly and carefully, along broken sidewalks and dirt paths and through overgrown shrubbery meandering up Carroll, Linnie, Sherman, and Howland canals. You can make an unusual one hour walk just going up and down these canals. Sometimes the bridges are wooden, sometimes they are the original concrete.

The Grand Canal

Abbott Kinney, you succeeded after all. Your monument is these lovely canals and the lovely atmosphere of the houses of the canal people. There are no longer gondolas, it is true, and there are no ducal palaces. But the most important aspect of your vision finally came true when Venice changed from a honky-tonk Coney Island bazaar into a bohemian neighborhood. It drew the painters, musicians, and writers, who are the dominant inhabitants of your strange little city with its canals, its bistros, its galleries, and its ocean walk. They express the free spirit that is the heart of Venice and Los Angeles.

Lush decor of Bernard's at the Biltmore Hotel.

DINING OUT:

A Discriminating Guide, from Sushi to Châteaubriand.

By Carole Lalli,
LOS ANGELES HERALD-EXAMINER

"It was a wasteland," is how Jean Bertranou of L'Ermitage describes the restaurant scene he found when he arrived in Los Angeles in 1965. Bertranou had just spent four years in a French restaurant in Las Vegas, so he knew a wasteland when he saw one. The owner of Au Petit Cafe, who opened his place in 1963 and established the style for smart and rather expensive little cafes that would prevail for another decade, found he needed a liquor license to survive. People in Los Angeles didn't drink much wine with dinner in those days. The before-dinner scotch and water could move on with the escargot, the pâté maison, the coq au vin, and the raw mushroom salad which was considered daring back then.

Los Angeles' restaurants caught up in a hurry, and after they caught up, they kept going, until finally, for French food at least, Los Angeles has overtaken San Francisco as the premier dining city on the West Coast. No more describing a restaurant as "good . . . for Los Angeles," no more three-day trips up north to sensitize the taste buds and mainline French fare. If you want a textbook meal of pike quenelles with sauce nantua followed by rack of lamb, with a nice chocolate mousse for dessert, you can certainly get that in San Francisco, but the new excitement in restaurants is in Los Angeles.

One chef told me that the reason for the new enlightenment is that "people can be just so dumb for just so long," but a steady stream of young, very ambitious and talented chefs, waiters, and restaurateurs helped. According to Belgian-born Eddy Kerkhofs, one of the partners at the new Le Dôme, the young French chefs who want to come to the United States choose New York, Chicago, or Los Angeles; few want to go to San Francisco, which he says is thought to be "passé" and a tourist town. Many are attracted to L.A. simply by the image that attracts everyone else: "fast fun, sunshine, and pretty girls." And the increasingly knowledgeable and demanding local clientele provides a beneficial challenge to the talents of young chefs.

Another recent French émigré, a thirty-year-old chef who has already had his own successful place in London and is now the executive chef of one of the best new restaurants (and is already scouting for a place of his own) has a more practical assessment: "The greatest opportunity is here; more restaurants are needed, and there is more money to open them and more money around to spend in them."

Outside of good French food, however, Los Angeles is not overly endowed with excellent restaurants serving from other European cuisines. Visitors from the East Coast complain that we haven't enough good Italian restaurants, although why that surprises them surprises me. Our coast faces a different direction, and the millions of immigrants who entered the United States through West Coast ports came from China, Japan, and Southeast Asia, and *that* is the basis of our particular ethnic richness. Whereas I can choose a single best Italian restaurant in L.A. with ease, it is difficult to limit my choices of Thai or Japanese places to a half dozen each.

The other part of our ethnic richness comes from Mexico, but if you think you're about to find out about some wonderful Mexican restaurant here, you're in for a disappointment. I too thought the streets of Los Angeles would be lined with swell Mexican restaurants before I got here, but I was wrong, but then I also thought that artichokes, avocados, and raspberries were going to be cheaper than they are three thousand miles from where they're grown, and I was wrong there also. Los Angeles has many good Mexican restaurants, but no great ones.

Left to my own devices—in other words, free of the burden of a weekly restaurant review—I would dine out most frequently in good but inexpensive ethnic places, where my first demand, for good food, would be met, even though service and ambience might be missing. I would save my dollars for occasional *haute cuisine* splurges, and then my demands would escalate dramatically. At forty dollars per person for dinner, I cannot think of too many excuses for less than excellent food, service, and surroundings, and I am ceaselessly amazed that so many others will. And, unless one of those "small, modest little French places" excels at some dish I am yearning for, I usually find their charms elusive indeed, and their relatively low price not low enough to represent real value.

This is a list of personal favorites, and I am quite open to the notion that someone else's favorite Thai or Japanese or even Chinese (though I doubt it) restaurant is as good as mine. And I know that there are folks out there who do not share my appreciation for Perino's; I suppose you could call that a matter of taste, although some people's taste is clearly better than other's. I do not, however, think it is arguable that L'Ermitage and Peppone are best in their class. (This introduction appeared in a slightly different form in *Esquire* magazine, March 13, 1979. Reprinted with permission.)

AMERICAN

A real effort is made to secure the widest variety and freshest fish available each day, but this is not a chef's restaurant, and simplest preparations are most successful. Steamed clams, sea bass, salmon, swordfish, or shark grilled over mesquite charcoal are the best bets. Steak-cut potatoes are recommended over corn on the cob or rice pilaf. The clam chowder is to be avoided, and if you're lusting for sashimi, go to a Japanese restaurant. The service by aggressively healthy-looking California kids is more friendly than competent, but somehow forgiveable so close to the beach. Moderate.

Gladstone's 4 Fish
146 Entrada Drive
Santa Monica Canyon   454-3474

Lawry's was the first single-entrée restaurant, and after twenty years it is still the standard for others. Excellent roast beef, Yorkshire pudding, creamed spinach, and a suitable late-Victorian dining hall ambience. Surprisingly good wines, well priced, and truly professional service. There are no reservations taken here and the wait can be long at peak times. Moderate.

Lawry's the Prime Rib
55 North La Cienega Boulevard
Beverly Hills   652-2827

Musso and Frank Grill
6667 Hollywood Boulevard
Hollywood   467-7788

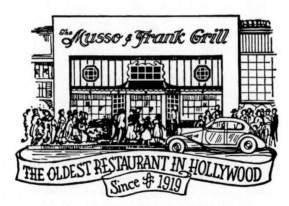

Musso's is sixty years old; from the comfortable faded look about the place, it appears that little has changed. Hopefully, it will not. Musso's has a menu considered large by today's efficiency-conscious standards, but typical of its time. Oysters and clams on the half shell, excellent salads, and a very good tomato soup are comforting appetizers. Simple grills and sautés—lamb chops, sand dabs, chicken—as well as chicken pot pie, corned beef and cabbage, and other daily specialties are best bets. Whatever else you have, have creamed spinach too. Moderate.

Original Pantry
877 South Figueroa Street
Downtown   972-9279

The good news is, it's open twenty-four hours a day; the bad news is, no booze. The Pantry is a bare, barny, no-nonsense sort of place, but friendly, in its gruff way. Big baskets of excellent sourdough bread and fresh celery, radishes, and carrots arrive with your waiter. The menu runs to good, pan-grilled steaks (T-bone or porterhouse recommended), lamb or pork chops, and one or two old-fashioned dishes—ham hocks, short ribs—that will stick to your ribs. Breakfasts are magnificent. Inexpensive to moderate.

Pacific Dining Car
1310 West Sixth Street
Los Angeles   483-6000

Huge sides of prime beef and lamb hang in the cool aging rooms underneath the original structure of the Pacific Dining Car, a Red Line commuter car. The place has been an L.A. landmark almost since it opened in 1921, and is Palm's only serious contender for number one steak house. However, be *very* specific about how you want your meat cooked, especially if you like rare lamb. French-fried onion rings, and spinach in cream are the best side dishes; the unlikely but tasty custard topped with crushed Grape Nuts the best dessert. In some quarters, the Dining Car's reputation rests more solidly with its large, impressive, and well-priced wine inventory than with its meat lockers. Moderate to expensive.

Palm
9001 Santa Monica Boulevard
West Hollywood   550-8811

As in any other town lucky enough to have one, L.A.'s Palm is the best steak house in town—not to mention most expensive, although it is hardly surprising that the best, prime, corn-fed beef and the biggest live Maine lobsters would be expensive. Following the tradition started by the newspaper reporters and cartoonists who hung around the New York Palm about fifty years ago (it was a speakeasy then), the Los Angeles Palm has graffiti, too. Ours is cleaner, however, and more reminiscent of *Welcome to L.A.* than *Front Page*. There are some good Italian dishes—clams oreganate, linguine with fresh clams—to vary the straight-forward American menu. Excellent steaks, roast beef, or lobster (although we've encountered mushy claws on our last two giant crustaceans). Best side dishes are cottage fried potatoes and buttery fresh spinach. For dessert, cheesecake, of course. Expensive.

The Saloon
9390 Santa Monica Boulevard
Beverly Hills   273-7155

And a very elegant saloon it is, with stained glass panels in the swinging doors, a handsome circular bar dominating the front room, and faintly British hunting scenes touching off the clubby atmosphere of the main dining room. Best appetizers include briny fresh clams and oysters, clams Corsino (with shallots, butter, and bacon) and oysters Rockefeller. The ingredients at the Saloon are of top quality, and the place excels at rather simple preparations of red meat; calf's liver, New York steak, or veal steak are always perfect. The ribeye steak is possibly even better, with a slightly chewy texture and a hearty taste nicely underscored by a stock-and-wine-rich sauce Bordelaise. Whatever fish or seafood is available—giant red scampi, fresh scallops—is well turned out. The Saloon has a large and classy wine list, with well-chosen French and California labels, and plenty of good bottles in the nine to fifteen dollar range. (See Where to Drink, p. 168.) Expensive.

The crowd here, a horsy set of the Damon Runyan type, is a match for the room's well-detailed speakeasy decor, and the entire ambience is underscored by stylish piano playing. The food at Sneeky's is, as you might guess, simple and sturdy, solidly based on the American appetite for large cuts of red meat. New York steaks (plain or topped with the excellent pizzaola sauce), a thick slice of prime rib that practically covers the plate, and barbecued prime baby back ribs. The veal piccata is surprisingly good; the whole broiled little chickens are superb. Moderate to expensive.

Sneeky Pete's
8907 West Sunset Boulevard
West Hollywood   657-5070

Hamburgers

It looks like a hangout for some characters in a James Cain novel: a little white cottage, ancient discolored wallpaper, and ceiling fans. The hamburgers are good, of the overwhelming California style—"with everything." There is also fine baked ham, sliced thin and piled high onto sandwiches. Unfortunately, the French fries are frozen. Excellent cinnamon-spiked apple pie and berry pies served with the best slightly sweetened whipped cream make for luscious desserts. Inexpensive.

The Apple Pan
10901 West Pico Boulevard
West Los Angeles   474-9344

A group of food stalls offering health food, barbecued chicken, fried fish, and other foods, served cafeteria-style, to eat indoors or in the large open patio. Inexpensive.

Brentwood Country Mart
225 Twenty-sixth Street
Santa Monica   395-6714

One of the best hamburgers in L.A., made from carefully trimmed, prime beef ground on the premises daily. The burgers are wide, not very thick, served on Cassell's own flavorful, made-to-spec bun. There are also wonderful ham, tuna, or cheese sandwiches served on outsize slices of splendid, thin-sliced rye or egg bread. The simple accouterments of nifty hamburger dining (potato salad, lemonade) are all homemade and of stunning quality. Inexpensive.

Cassell's Patio Hamburgers
3300 West Sixth Street
Los Angeles   480-8668

A classic 1940s drive-in, Dolores offers pert car hops and fine burgers. You can grab a Double Decker to go while you cruise Wilshire, or eat inside in an oasis of time. If you didn't think nostalgia could be unselfconscious, dine at Dolores. Inexpensive.†

Dolores
8531 Wilshire Boulevard
Beverly Hills   655-8638

Over thirty varieties of hamburger in combinations ranging from the sublime to the curious (a burger topped with soft ice cream?) are served on justly renowned buns. It happens twenty-four hours a day. Inexpensive.†

Hamburger Henry
3001 Wilshire Boulevard
Santa Monica   828-3000
4700 East Second Street
Long Beach   433-7070

The other best hamburger in L.A., thick and juicy with a variety of toppings from bleu cheese to peanut butter. A good salad bar, French wine by the glass, and beer on tap. Comfortable, vaguely rustic rooms, and a pleasant secluded patio. Inexpensive.

Hampton's Kitchen
1342 North Highland Avenue
Hollywood   469-1090

CHINESE

Chang Sha
1017 North Broadway
Downtown   223-9183

If you're careful, this extremely modest-looking restaurant can be one of the best in Chinatown. Crab with bean sauce, eggplant with shredded pork, and chicken with walnuts are all super, but there are many dishes here that are not. Ask for help. There is an order-ahead menu of special dishes. Inexpensive.

Chinese Friends
984 North Broadway
Downtown   626-1837

Ten customers at once is just about capacity here, and English is not the favorite language. The staff are lovely and helpful anyway, and expert at the spicy dishes of Szechuan and Hunan. Hot, peppery shrimp are wonderful; bean curds and sea slugs, cooked various ways, are specialties. Inexpensive.

Chung King
11538 West Pico Boulevard
West Los Angeles   477-4917

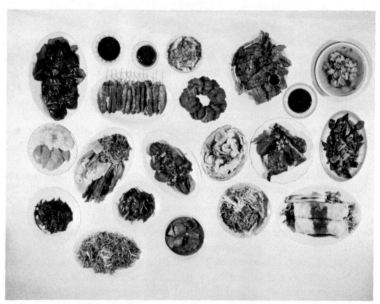

A big, plain storefront with the best Szechuan food in town. Excellent entrées: chicken or beef with tangerine flavor, chicken with peanuts and chilies, shredded pork with Szechuan pickles, camphor tea duck, Chung King hot sauce whole duck, eggplant with garlic, green bean thread noodles. Inexpensive to moderate.

Green Jade
747 North Broadway
Downtown   680-1528

Hidden off a sidestreet in Chinatown, the Green Jade is a little-known but extraordinary restaurant. They serve Hunan cuisine, exclusively for those who like it hot and spicy. Service is slow, but it's worth waiting for the snappy shrimp dishes, beef combinations, and truly sublime sweet and sour pork. To enjoy more exotic specialty meals not available to the walk-in trade, you can call in your order a week in advance. Inexpensive to moderate.†

Gung Hay
14800 Crenshaw Boulevard
Gardena   770-3777

The drive to Gung Hay is worth twice the distance for what may be the best Cantonese food in town. The huge restaurant has nine chefs who handily turn out the hundred or so dishes on the regular menu and the dozen or so extraordinary ones listed as "Traditional Dishes from Old China." Excellent dumplings (siu mai) with a rich pork filling and the special eggrolls (in paper-crisp caul fat instead of a dough wrapper) are the best appetizers from the regular menu. The best soup is made with winter melon, abalone, pork, and authentic (and therefore, expensive) shark fins. Picking only a few entrées is impossible, but duck roasted with honey and spices rubbed into its skin, and deep fried squab are remarkable. And, since quality is so high, even standards from the Chinese-American repertoire such as lobster Cantonese or simple steamed whole fish gain new dimensions. If possible, the best bet is to plan at least forty-eight hours ahead, gather up a party of at least six friends and order stuffed, deep fried squabs, extraordinary Peking duck served with steamed buns (kwa lu opp), or a whole duck boned and stuffed with lotus seeds, Chinese ham, barley, and exotic seasonings, or a simple sauté of large shrimp and fresh lobster. Moderate.

Mandarin, Szechuan, and Hunan dishes are featured in one of the best restaurants in Chinatown. Hot sautéed sugared walnuts and various cold appetizers (spicy duck and dried bean curd are best) are the signature appetizers. Best entrées include spicy sliced squid, fried cuttle fish with shredded pork and shredded tripe. For aficionados, however, the spicing may be too mild. Steamed rock cod with broad bean paste, shredded pork with Szechuan pickle, and the very spicy and delicious Szechuan sliced pork (twice-cooked) all are outstanding. Service here can be casual, or it can be indifferent; it's a matter of luck. Inexpensive to moderate.

Hunan
980 North Broadway
Downtown   626-5050

Awfully good Szechuan and mandarin dishes. Cold jellyfish, beef or chicken with chilies and raw peanuts, moo-shu pork, braised eggplant are recommended. Inexpensive to moderate.

Lucky Restaurant
1643 North Cahuenga Boulevard
Hollywood   463-0464

Restaurateur Cecilia Chiang opened her Beverly Hills restaurant in 1976; her Mandarin in San Francisco's Ghirardelli Square was by then eight years old. Now, the pretty Beverly Hills establishment is as firmly established. Best dishes: steamed dumplings, hot and sour soup, Peking duck (order ahead), lamb stir-fried with scallions, Kung Pao chicken, Szechuan whole fish, eggplant, string beans, stir-fried spinach with cellophane noodles. Moderate.

Mandarin
430 North Camden Drive
Beverly Hills   272-0267

Chef P.C. Lee is a renowned teacher and consultant to Chinese restaurants. His restaurant is devoted to the five major Chinese regional cuisines—Szechuan, Hunan, Canton, Peking, and Shanghai. The location, in what was once the coffee shop of the old Roosevelt Hotel in Hollywood, seems unlikely, but there it is. A sampling of some of the dishes available indicates the scope of Mr. Lee's effort: shredded hog maw in hot peppercorn sauce, extraordinary camphor tea duck, fish in hot garlic or black bean sauce, Kung Pao squid, sautéed spinach or romaine lettuce with garlic, dry-cooked string beans, several excellent bean curd preparations, and cold jellyfish appetizer. Inexpensive to moderate.

Mandarin Chefs
1714 Ivar Avenue
Hollywood   467-6981

Man Fook Low
962 South San Pedro Street
Downtown　623-3375

This unassuming place offers home-cooked food just like mother used to send out for. Best way to enjoy it is for lunch with Chinese chicken salad and yummy tea cakes. Inexpensive to moderate.†

Mr. Chow
344 North Camden Drive
Beverly Hills　278-9911

This is a smart room—high style in black and glass, Art Deco details, and Oriental precision. It attracts an equally chic crowd, with no small measure of celebrity. Unfortunately, the food is far less consequential than the art direction, but careful ordering can produce a respectable (if not quite authentic) Chinese meal. The signature appetizer is gambei, a salted, deep-fried green; but the steamed mei chi dumplings and shrimp toast are equally good. Best entrées are imitation crab, fresh scallops (or shrimps) in spicy sauce, or deep-fried beef with a lavish garnish of tender, thinly julienned orange peel. Avoid drunken chicken. Expensive.

Shanghai Winter Gardens
5651 Wilshire Boulevard
Beverly Hills　934-0505

Along with the beautifully poetic name, Shanghai Winter Gardens offers mandarin cuisine. Specialties include Peking duck and barbecued chicken salad. The restaurant is decorated with traditional Chinese holiday trappings and provides both intimate dining and prompt service. Moderate.†

Yang Chow
816 North Broadway
Downtown　625-0811

Keep your eyes on the slippery shrimp (spicy and crisp), the beef scallops with broccoli, and the shredded chicken with garlic sauce. Yang Chow is a small Chinese restaurant catering to those who like their food hot. Good service, reasonable prices.†

CONTINENTAL

Adagio
5259 Melrose Avenue
Hollywood　465-8250

Adagio is one of those peculiarly Californian restaurants that attempt to combine a French bistro style with pure organic cooking; here at least, the result is not a total lack of distinction. There is a uniformity of quality and able cooking, and a diverse menu that offers abundant salads, quiches, soups, and omelets, as well as full entrées. Veal scallops with sherry and cream, and the daily seafood preparations are best bets. Adagio is not the dining experience of a lifetime, but the service is considerate, the room is charming and comfortable, and the price is right.

The Bistro
246 North Cañon Drive
Beverly Hills　273-5633

In a city where even "traditions" have half-lives, it is remarkable that the Bistro has remained on top of the fashion heap. In spite of the splendid places that have opened since the Bistro in 1963, this still is one of the prettiest rooms, with as much cachet as the rest put together. It is authentic enough in its art nouveau interior to be photographed extensively in *Irma la Douce*; it is also significant enough in Beverly Hills' society for the naughtiest scene in *Shampoo*.

Food, as one might expect, is a less important element at the Bistro than the decor or the splendid service; but careful ordering from the blackboard menu can produce a fine meal. The best dishes are simple ones. Fresh seafood, mustardy shrimps Bistro, and gazpacho are favorite appetizers. Fresh white fish is almost always available in a variety of simple styles; veal chop forestière, Bistro hamburger, chickenburger, chicken Grandmère, chicken Casanova, and calf's brains beurre noir are signature entrées. At lunch, cold poached salmon, eggs Benedict or Moscovite, or creamed chipped beef with poached eggs are best. The chicken pot pie may not be authentic (the pale golden oval of exquisite puff pastry served with the large pieces of tender chicken and vegetables is not baked on top) but it deserves its reputation. The classic dessert is Bistro chocolate soufflé. Expensive.

As one canny society-watcher put it, "A lot of women go to lunch to be seen, and the Bistro was just too dark to be seen *in;* now, they can go to the Bistro Garden." Indeed. The interior is a slightly slimmed-down version of the Bistro, with all the charm intact, although when the room is at full pitch, the acoustics can be a bit frightful. The garden is superb, the perfect spot for those who want to be seen (but not by just anyone passing; it is walled from the street) and for those who simply like to take lunch outdoors. The menu is tinier than the Bistro's, but it features some of those sturdier dishes as well as some new ones with a decided brasserie cast: choucroute garnie, cold beef vinaigrette, a trio of little grilled medallions (veal, lamb, beef) with a faultless béarnaise, an assortment of cold plates, and even a fresh tostada. Expensive.

The Bistro Garden
176 North Cañon Drive
Beverly Hills   550-3900

Chasen's is not among my favorites because I have rarely had good service there. Of course, there are those (mostly of recognizable name or face) who are known and treated royally. It makes it worse, somehow, to know that the place is capable of good behavior for some and not others. If you insist on visiting this vestige of the golden age of Hollywood, avoid any attempts at fancy, Continental dishes (remember, Chasen's was built on a foundation of chili). Stick to the homier American specialties like chicken pot pie, fresh fish, grilled steaks and lamb chops, and the justifiably renowned Hobo steak. The chili is rich, creamy, and moderately spicy. Expensive.

Chasen's
9039 Beverly Boulevard
Beverly Hills   271-2168

Fabulously pretty rooms and the chance to observe the wildly successful "at table" are the highest recommendations here. Jimmy Murphy was a famed maître d' at The Bistro, and is concentrating on the same luxuries of service and style that forgave *that* average kitchen. However, the latest chef is Otto Cloetta, who was a fine head chef at Scandia; presumably he will bring the kitchen up to a point that at least matches the wallpaper. One or two dishes have been impressive—a lemony salad of fresh abalone and French green beans, a perfect kiwi tart—while others—roasted baby lamb, broiled salmon—have at least not been embarrassing. Order cautiously. Wines are expensive. When the room is at capacity, service tends to be inadequate. Expensive.

Jimmy's
201 South Moreno Drive
Beverly Hills   879-2394

La Difference
10948 West Pico Boulevard
West Los Angeles   475-7535

A cozy room, with natural pine paneling and comfortable booths, and a personal eclectic collection of art and artifacts. The daily selection of fresh fish, seafood, and meat is on display in front of an open kitchen, where all orders are grilled over wood fires. Dinners include salad and a selection of Middle Eastern appetizers—roasted peppers, puréed eggplant, mushroom and dill salad, chopped chicken livers—all to eat with flat bread. Potatoes are served with the entrée; there are also à la carte vegetables. Fish and seafood are recommended, although the meat is also good. Best dessert is Lindy's New York cheesecake. Moderate.

L'Escoffier
Beverly Hilton Hotel
9876 Wilshire Boulevard
Beverly Hills   274-7777

Textbook Continental menu, formal service, luxurious decor, plenty of tableside preparations. There are, besides the numerous offerings of the menu, two multicourse *prix fixe* dinners that are worth the prices. Otherwise, the menu is strictly à la carte, with particularly good soups and a tendency to fine, complicatedly sauced dishes. Dancing to a live combo. Expensive.

Manny's Bistro
1748½ Westwood Boulevard
West Los Angeles   474-6277

This is the ultimate restaurant indulgence. Manny is, shall we say, a little eccentric. His twenty seat restaurant is an extension of his home. If he wants to play the guitar, he will; if you want to smoke a cigarette, you won't. Which is just part of the reason for going there. The rest is Manny's careful cooking, his eclectic taste, and his insistence on quality. The *prix fixe* multicourse dinners change and cover a wide territory according to the whim of the chef. The carne asada is superb. Reservations are essential; if Manny feels like going away for a week or two, he will. Moderately expensive.

Perino's
4101 Wilshire Boulevard
Los Angeles   383-1221

After forty-seven years, this is one of the last great Continental dining rooms. Perino's still maintains its soft rose upholstery, its crystal chandeliers, its old-world service, and its enormous à la carte menu. The meticulous preparations needed to produce textbook sauces, dozens of fresh salads and vegetables, superb soups, and a dazzling selection of poached, roasted, and sautéed seafood and meat are carried out in the old-fashioned way, by an enormous staff—100 serve a daily clientele of no more than 135. Maître d' John Hammerton personally acquires excellent and sometimes rare bottles for Perino's cellar; not all his selections are on the wine list. Expensive.

An informal, clubby atmosphere and late hours make the Rangoon a comfortable hangout. The menu is Continental—esoteric, with a vaguely British tilt. The grand days of the Empire are celebrated with decent curries and fine chutneys, but there are dead-on American treats such as C. V. Wood's World Championship Chili and good steaks, as well as harder to define treats such as deep-fried potato jackets lined with peanut butter. Expensive.

Rangoon Racquet Club
9474 Santa Monica Boulevard
Beverly Hills   274-8926

Scandia
9040 Sunset Boulevard
West Hollywood   278-3555

Scandia has been a landmark at its current location for more than twenty years, but Ken Hansen, who founded it, has been a legendary restaurateur for longer than that. The original tiny Scandia, which was wildly popular long before the '50s, was famous for its Smorgas Brika, its wonderful herrings, its divine Danish apple cake, and the flaming Viking sword. Then of course, there was veal Oscar, a dish Hansen revived through his exhaustive studies of recipes (the dish was originally created to honor King Oscar) and which eventually became something of a restaurant cliché. The original Scandia was successful, but it hardly began to tap the talent and energy of its owner-chef. It was the current Scandia that achieved and maintained a position among the very top-ranked Los Angeles restaurants, and it was the one that constantly challenged Hansen's resources.

The cozy Danish hunting lodge atmosphere of the old Scandia dictated the style only of the new Skal Room; the restaurant has, in addition, a large, elegant main dining room, a plant- and sun-filled garden room, and an intimate, carefully appointed wine room for small private parties. The Scandinavian delicacies that previously dominated the menu became the nucleus of a large, ambitious, and endlessly varied Continental bill of fare. The occasional visitor may concentrate on dishes that made Scandia famous—bif med log, the faultless gravlaks, shrimps in dill sauce, Danish plaice or poached turbot, skewered baby lobster tails sauced with caviar and dill. The constant diner, on the other hand, will be tantalized still by new dishes. If nothing else, Scandia is a great fish restaurant.

Hansen sold Scandia recently. He's still there, of course, but now one looks for subtle changes, signs of crumbling in the corners. The favored dishes are still as tasty, the extraordinary wine list apparently well-maintained, and the prices still modest considering the quality of the place. Perhaps the fine edge is off the service. But then, the fine edge was always off the service when Hansen was off the premises. Hansen is an original, after all, with intelligence, taste, drive, and *nerve*. The restaurateurs who have the taste and talent are rarely the ones with the nerve to push it on such a scale as Scandia's. Moderate to expensive.

Stratton's
10886 Le Conte Avenue
Westwood   477-4907

When it opened in 1976, Stratton's, which is housed in Westwood's oldest building, had been appropriately decorated to approximate the style of an English country dining hall. The centerpiece of the expensive facelift is a Stratton family heirloom, a genuine Gainsborough. The menu, too, is British at its center—Cornish fish pie, shepherd's pie, and rare roast beef with Yorkshire pudding—but with Continental, particularly French provincial, accents. The front patio at Stratton's adds to the charm of lunch or dinner here. The wine list, while small, is chosen with much discrimination and is well-priced. Moderate to expensive.

ECONOMY GASTRONOMY

Alice's Restaurant
1043 Westwood Boulevard
Westwood   478-0941

Made and named after the movie *Alice's Restaurant*, this charming cafe in Westwood is an excellent choice for a low-cost light lunch or dinner. Although Alice's serves full dinners, we recommend going there for one of their fine salads, a sandwich, or soup. The whole-wheat bread covered with crushed oats is a treat in itself.†

Anna Maria's Ristorante Italiano
1356 South La Brea Avenue
Los Angeles   935-2089

Just a few steps off La Brea Avenue, you can sit under the stars on a warm evening and feast on all sorts of luscious Italian fare. Featured dishes include manicotti and chicken cacciatore.†

Bicycle Shop Cafe
12217 Wilshire Boulevard
Brentwood   826-7831

Dine in a unique atmosphere at the Bicycle Shop Cafe. Nestled between the plants and the checkered tablecloths, clinging to the walls, and hanging precariously over-head are dozens of bicycles, tricycles, unicycles, and many other forms of pedal-powered vehicles. Good dining bets are the salads, crêpes, and omelets.†

Bratskeller Restaurant
1154 Westwood Boulevard
Westwood   477-9535

A landmark in Westwood, the Bratskeller serves hearty Renaissance sandwiches for lunch. For dinner try their chicken Haiti or shrimp and beef kabobs. The interior decorations are exquisite; you will feel you have wandered into an old world German cathedral.†

Cafe Pierre
317 Manhattan Beach Boulevard
Manhattan Beach   545-5252

Cafe Pierre is a small restaurant with the flavor of a French country inn. Their nightly specials, usually one beef and one fish dish, come highly recommended. However, if you're not in the mood for a large meal, Cafe Pierre has a wide selection of light repasts. Their salads, all accented by tarragon dressing, are often enough for a meal in combination with the sourdough French bread that is brought warm to your table. Also good are the quiche Lorraine, a wide variety of omelets, and crêpes.†

In 1937, Ralph and Mona Damon opened Damon's with the idea of serving a limited but quality menu of steaks and salad. The good, basic food plus tropical decor—circa 1937—with palm trees, cocoanut heads, and a large sea turtle make Damon's quite an adventure. The dining room is small, so expect a wait in their standing-room-only bar.†

Damon's
118 South Central Avenue
Glendale   956-9056

Long established as a place to take a man-sized appetite, Edward's Steak House has been dishing up New York steaks, roast beef, and seafood since 1946. Expect a wait almost every noon and evening.†

Edward's Steak House
733 South Alvarado Boulevard
Los Angeles   385-0051

You could drive down Third Street every day of your life and not know that Joe Allen's Restaurant is there. But the place has been discovered and has become a favorite hang-out for struggling young actors. The food, whether it be salad or steak or chops, is always tasty.†

Joe Allen
8706 West Third Street
Los Angeles   274-7144

For a light dinner, La Poubelle offers twenty-two varieties of crêpes. If this isn't enough, you can choose from a selection of omelets, quiche Lorraine, or French onion soup.†

La Poubelle
5909 Franklin Avenue
Hollywood   462-9264

Centrally located at the intersection of Melrose Avenue and La Cienega Boulevard, the Melting Pot is quite a treat. The soups are fresh, the salads have countless ingredients, and their full dinner selections (including fish and beef) are freshly prepared and very good. Although an outdoor patio is available, eat inside. The roar of traffic at peak hours is unbearable.†

The Melting Pot
8490 Melrose Avenue
West Hollywood   652-8030

An excellent place to take a break from a Sunday afternoon of rollerskating, the Sidewalk Cafe offers a variety of light meals such as omelets and salads. They also have a dinner menu with more substantial main dishes.†

Sidewalk Cafe
1401 Ocean Front Walk
Venice   399-5547

Even if it weren't open twenty-four hours a day, and even if breakfast wasn't available at all times, Southtown would still be notable for its gumbo, fried catfish, Louisiana hot links, grits, Mammie Jammies, and peach cobbler!

Southtown Soul Food
1515 North Wilcox Avenue
Hollywood   461-3245

Her slogan is "Eat Here Better Than at Home and Cheaper Too," and Maurice Prince means it. This is dead-on American home cooking with some southern influences. The fried chicken is first-rate; pork chops, and order-ahead macaroni and cheese better than Mom's. Bring your own booze.

Maurice's Snack n' Chat
5553 Pico Boulevard
Los Angeles   931-3877

ENGLISH

As soon as you see the plaid carpeting you know you've entered onto the British Isles. The lunchtime buffet is excellent. Prime rib and steaks are very good; kidney pie and Yorkshire pudding are special. The Sunday brunch offers everything from muffins to bagels. Moderate.†

Cock 'n Bull
9170 Sunset Boulevard
West Hollywood   272-1397

The Great Scot
2980 Los Feliz Boulevard
Hollywood   664-0228

The beer is ordered by the yard and special tables have been installed to accommodate the huge steins. Decorated in an intimate old English style, the Great Scot offers a complete sandwich bar for luncheon. Prime rib, roast beef, and ham all clamor for attention, and a piano bar is open Tuesday through Saturday. Moderate.†

Oscar's Wine Bar
8210 Sunset Boulevard
West Hollywood   650-9124

Oscar's is not so much a wine bar as a very good British-Continental restaurant translated to a funky little bungalow on Sunset Boulevard. Excellent appetizer courses and luncheon dishes: pâtés, terrines, rich custardy quiches, avocados, asparagus, steamed artichokes or broccoli, always fresh and properly at room temperature. Best of all, angels on horseback (bacon-wrapped oysters on toast). Steak tartare, home-baked ham, roast Cornish hens with a rich forcemeat, steak and kidney pie, and oatmeal-coated sautéed mackerel are favorite entrées. All the desserts, from the bread and butter pudding to the elegant fruit tarts and sinful cheesecake, are top-drawer. The wine list is small but select and mostly French, with the bulk of the bottles well-priced in the fifteen to twenty-five dollar range. Moderate.

T.J. Peppercorn
Hyatt House Hotel
6225 West Century Boulevard
L.A. International Airport
670-9000

In the middle of this airport hotel you can find a spacious dance floor with live entertainment Tuesday through Saturday. Entrées include delicious prime rib, lamb, and roast duck. Construct your own salads and desserts with a huge array of ingredients at T.J.'s salad and dessert bars. Moderately expensive.†

FRENCH

Albion's Bistro
13422 Ventura Boulevard
Sherman Oaks   981-6650

What a wonderful room! An eclectic blend of late ninteteenth-century styles—a flower-patterned rug, a statue of an art-nouveau beauty—exquisite table appointments and soft background music. Albion's is one of the most romantic restaurants in town. The food, however, is very much of our time, quite stylish, awfully good, and elegantly presented. Appetizers—all courses—are substantial, quite generous enough to be shared. Snails in a fragrant sauce of butter and fresh basil are piled into Albion's faultless feuilleté; a pretty duet of fish mousseline is served with two rich sauces; there are various "salads" that are in fact elaborate cold plates involving lobsters, fresh bright green French beans, artichoke hearts, asparagus, prawns, foie gras. Fresh seafood—scallops in a silky beurre blanc, sea bass with cucumbers—changes with the season. Favorite mainstays of the entrée menu are the chicken in mustard sauce, the densely herb-flavored pink rack of lamb. For dessert, fresh fruit tarts in crumbly, buttery shells of pâté sucree. The wine list is not large, but it is carefully selected, and, all things considered, reasonably priced. Expensive.

Ambrosia
501 Thirtieth Street
Newport Beach   (714) 673-0200

Newport Beach's most significant claim to *haute cuisine* has a large choice of classic dishes, of good quality and deft preparation, but there are few surprises on this menu. Luxury is the specialty here. The formal decor runs to velvet, brocade, and lace; there are plenty of tableside preparation and dining room pyrotechnics. Ambrosia's style is best understood by its Victorian treatment of women: there are little footstools to rest the dainty feet and the dubious nicety of a ladies' menu without prices. The wine list here is huge and impressive, with several collectors' items at appropriately high prices. Expensive.

Some of the dishes that seemed daring when Au Petit Cafe opened fifteen years ago are familiar today to even the least sophisticated diners, but Au Petit still delivers quality and competence. The famous raw mushroom salad, the admirable pâtés, the warm *al dente* asparagus bathed in sweet butter are all recommended classics. But then, there is the mussel salad with a fresh lacy garnish of finely julienned carrots, celery, and leeks, one of the dishes on Au Petit's new *cuisine minceur* menu. Entrées tend toward simple sautées and braises, finished with uncomplicated but carefully made sauces, and interesting fresh vegetable garnishes. The wine list, built up over fifteen years, is almost exclusively French; as a result, it shows some lovely labels but few bargains. Moderate to expensive.

Au Petit Cafe
1230 North Vine Street
Hollywood   469-7176
♦♦

By now, Aux Delices has become a landmark on Ventura Boulevard, and the San Fernando Valley's first stronghold of first-rate French cooking. The room is solidly bourgeois (the outstanding art is a street map of Paris) and just slightly frumpy. The service, however, is for the most part outstanding, except on those rare occasions when some parties are lingering over *cafe filtre* and others are waiting in the tiny foyer. The food is equal to places far hautier.

Aux Delices
15466 Ventura Boulevard
Sherman Oaks   783-3007
♦♦

Beautiful, complicated cold dishes have always been favorite hors d'oeuvres here; the prettily arranged duck terrine and the first-rate quennelles are as good as you're likely to find anywhere. Chicken in a smooth red wine sauce, veal Normande (or a seemingly endless variety of other veal preparations), and a wide assortment of fresh fish dishes are best entrées. A faultless tarte tatin, Paris-brest, and feuilleté with fresh berries are the best choices from the excellent homemade pastries. The wine list is small but knowledgeably selected, with prices moderate to high. Price of entrée includes an excellent green salad vinaigrette and soup, usually creamed vegetable. Moderate.

This is the best hotel dining room in town and one of the only two serious downtown restaurants (the Tower is the other). Part of Bernard's reputation rests on its impeccably formal (but not supercilious) service, and on the room, the painstakingly restored vintage 1920 dining room of the legendary Biltmore Hotel updated with classic contemporary furnishings. The rest is based on the elegant cuisine, mostly fish dishes prepared according to the *nouvelle cuisine*, notable for freshness, eye appeal, and excellent sauces. Best appetizers: the trio of tiny fish terrines with watercress sauce, poached oysters in braised lettuce leaves, mussel soup. Entrées: poached salmon with kiwi, bass over salmon mousseline

Bernard's
515 South Olive Street
Downtown   624-0183
♦♦♦

with lobster sauce. Bernard's uncommon civility is carried out with a gentle harp, an admirable collection of Don Flou brandies and eaux de vie, and fine cigars. Expensive.

The Cellar
305 North Harbor Boulevard
Fullerton   (714) 525-5682

The Cellar is a restaurant of enormous quality with an individual style that emerges, masterfully, from a firm foundation of classical and *nouvelle cuisine* styles. It is located in a landmark building in Fullerton, a nice enough town that does not happen to be one of our dining centers. Best appetizers include a sensational duck liver mousse served in a pretty pastry duck, a tender sea bass terrine with a chive-spiked sauce mousseline, and, most impressive of all, a seafood soup, very much like a bisque, enriched with puréed frogs' legs and plump mussels under a golden crust of brioche.

Seafood entrées include enormous prawns in a simple cognac-spiked cream sauce garnished with lumpfish roe, and poached trout filled with silky pike mousseline. There is real ambition and invention at the Cellar. Roasted duck arrives in a smooth brown sauce lightened with lime juice and garnished with fresh kiwi fruit; tarragon, sherry vinegar, and cream sauce accompany chubby fresh squabs; succulent breast of pheasant is served with white raisins, green olives, and a whole fresh fig. Even more familiar dishes, such as the interpretation of veal Normande, are exceptional. Desserts at the Cellar are perhaps less inspired than the rest, but there is a good chocolate mousse and a fine Grand Marnier soufflé. The wine list is impressive, and fairly top-heavy, but with intelligent California labels in the middle range. Service is formal, with only occasional lapses towards pretentiousness on the one hand, and familiarity on the other. Expensive.

Chambord
8689 Wilshire Boulevard
Beverly Hills   652-6590

Chambord has service to match any of the higher-ranked and higher-priced restaurants. The room is comfortable but correct, and gracefully appointed. The menu, which used to seem too timid for the talent of its kitchen staff and for the sophistication of Chambord's clientele, is now more adventurous, more reflective of the best new food fashions. However, mainstays of the old menu—asparagus vinaigrette, first-class smoked trout, fish mousselines—

are still deeply satisfying. Fish, lamb, and veal dishes are first-rate. The wine list is modest in selection and price. Moderate to expensive.

Gregoire and his gregarious family run this place—an odd assortment of little rooms—seemingly as an extension of their home. In fact, it looks like a house that was only recently, and abruptly, turned into a cafe. Dinners begin with a slim slice of warm quiche, with a flaky crust and rich filling; soup or salad is also included with price of entrées here. Best entrées are lamb mignonettes, cooked perfectly medium rare, served with tarragon-spiked sauce; crisp-skinned duck with green peppercorns; steak au poivre; and a freely interpreted, hearty bouillabaisse which is thick with tomatoes and heavy with saffron, fennel, and Pernod. Crème brûlée and individual soufflé are best desserts. Moderate.

Chef Gregoire
15464 Ventura Boulevard
Sherman Oaks   789-2711

Simple yet subtle French seafood is served in a gracefully appointed room on the beach at Venice. Sole with bananas and almonds and sea bass with a mushroom-caper sauce tasting delicately of Pernod are standouts. The wine list is small but well chosen. Moderate.†

Land's End
323 Ocean Front Walk
Venice   392-3997

When it opened, they said it was too expensive for the San Fernando Valley, whatever that meant. In time, others' prices caught up, and anyway, going to the valley (really, a rather pleasant drive over Coldwater Canyon) for such a pretty room and such good food seemed reasonable. La Serre is a greenhouse, attractively decorated with lattice, tile floors, pretty table appointments, and a *lot* of plants hanging or standing about. It is a perfect setting to show off the kitchen, which, under a highly talented young chef, Jean-Pierre Peiny, quietly and consistently produces elegant French food. The preparations are characterized by well-constructed sauces and fresh ingredients. Seafood—scallops, salmon—is always special. Pear tart and Grand Marnier soufflé are just a couple of the fine desserts. Expensive.

La Serre
12969 Ventura Boulevard
Studio City   990-0500

In La Toque Los Angeles has yet another important, highly original French restaurant. It is run as a partnership between Ken Frank, a young American chef, and Henri Fizer, previously the maître d' at L'Ermitage. La Toque is smallish, comfortable, and pretty, in an understated way, with a convenient location at the east end of the Sunset Strip. Service is competent, if less than formal, but food dominates here. Sauce making and precise cooking characterize this kitchen; the style is based on a deep understanding of the *nouvelle cuisine*. Some of the trademark dishes are scallops in a complicated marinade that includes raspberry vinegar; escargots in an intensely flavorful sauce of port and green peppercorns; sliced rare breast of duck in red wine with poached pears. But the menu is rewritten every day and often includes striking cold dishes, often of fanciful arrangements of pristinely fresh seafood as well as elegantly sauced fish entrées. Desserts (there is usually a home-

La Toque
8171 Sunset Boulevard
West Hollywood   656-7515

made ice cream of the day) are creatively conceived and masterfully executed. Expensive.

Le Cellier
2628 Wilshire Boulevard
Santa Monica   828-1585

One of the best of a small clutch of modest but reliable French restaurants on the West Side, Le Cellier offers competent service, an extremely pleasant, well-run room and a wide choice of well-priced French wines. Le Cellier's regular menu is a list of reassuringly familiar favorites, and there are daily specials. Wednesday's coulibiac of salmon and Sunday's calf's sweetbreads are worth planning for. The bouillabaisse, available each day, is one of the best in Los Angeles. Soup and salad are included with entrées. Moderate.

Le Dôme
8720 Sunset Boulevard
West Hollywood   659-6919

It's hard to imagine where all those chic people went before Le Dôme. Le Dôme is like a cabaret, even though there's no music and no dancing. Somehow, a sophisticated decor, carried out in dark green, plum, and chrome, a round bar and rare Chinese pottery is housed in an eccentric, pseudo-Grecian temple on the Sunset Strip. And somehow, it is just the right backdrop for elegant brasserie dining.

Best Le Dôme hors d'oeuvres are fat, marinated herrings, chicory salad with lardons, Danish salmon. Among the entrées are grilled shark with anchovy butter, grilled lobster, boudin noir with sautéed apples and mashed potatoes, and, when it is available, the thick veal chop with potatoes, onions, and lardons. Desserts are great, especially the fruit tarts. The wine inventory is constantly changing, in a desperate effort to provide enough good bottles at the best possible prices. A good selection of champagnes. Moderate to expensive.

Le Restaurant
8475 Melrose Place
West Hollywood   651-5553

When it opened more than seven years ago, Le Restaurant was part of the movement from the small, high-quality bistros which had defined Los Angeles' best French restaurants, to a more serious attempt at *haute cuisine*. It remains firmly established as one of our finest—not quite on the highest level occupied by L'Ermitage and Ma Maison, but right behind—and it can compete with any for attractive surroundings and fine service. Smoked salmon, impeccable salads, and excellent soups (especially the extraordinary lobster bisque) are among the best first courses. The consistently classy signature dishes include lobster in a basil-infused sauce; duck breasts in a fine *bordelaise*; and grilled pigeon, although its garlic-cream sauce is often too understated. Careful attention is paid to the preparation and presentation of vegetables, and pastries are superb. Wines are mostly French and mostly high priced. Expensive.

L'Ermitage
730 North La Cienega Boulevard
West Hollywood   652-5840

When Jean Bertranou opened his L'Ermitage restaurant in 1973, he raised the standard for French dining in Los Angeles and the expectations of the dining-out public. Until then, our best French restaurants were producing very good, and in some cases, excellent bistro food. It wasn't so much that Bertranou had to show anyone else

how to cook better, but in time L'Ermitage showed those who were apprehensive before, that the public would not be terrified by a cuisine that combined classic techniques and innovative ideas.

L'Ermitage is by now famous for Bertranou's obsession to find more and better ingredients for his kitchen. Seafood and game are flown in from all over the country and from abroad; poultry is raised according to the chef's directions; and the best fruit and vegetables the season can offer are served (sometimes it is the season in South America or Australia that is being celebrated). Occasionally the demands of L'Ermitage helped create a market for certain items. What could be flown in for L'Ermitage could be flown in for other restaurateurs who could afford the price. The steady stream of pastry chefs who apprenticed at L'Ermitage and moved on to other L.A. restaurants has had its own effect on the dining consciousness of Angelenos.

L'Ermitage is formal, graceful, comfortable, and beautifully appointed. The service is usually correct, but not pretentious. The requirement that Americans speak French fluently when dining in their own country has thankfully passed out of existence. Well-priced wines are frequently featured, but the wine list is, generally speaking, classy and expensive, with emphasis on French labels. Expensive.

Elegant beyond belief, L'Orangerie was one of the extravaganzas that opened at the end of 1978 and elevated Los Angeles to the town with at least the best *looking* restaurants. L'Orangerie is one of

L'Orangerie
903 North La Cienega Boulevard
West Hollywood   652-9770

those rare rooms that manage to be formal and beautiful as well as thoroughly comfortable. The menu is limited, although the restaurant is already famous for some of its dishes (seafood salad dressed with raspberry vinegar, poached eggs with chicory, lardons, scrambled eggs with caviar, the individual thin warm apple tart). Best entrées include grilled sea bass with fennel, fresh poached scallops, double rib of beef (for two) charred on the outside, pink to red and running with juices inside. Service is nearly perfect. Expensive.

Ma Maison
8368 Melrose Avenue
West Hollywood   655-1991

At first it seemed as if it would be just another average bistro that would pass quietly in and out of fashion. Then it acquired a chef barely old enough to work in a place that had a liquor license. Wolfgang Puck turned out to have fierce ambition and talent to match. With a serious kitchen and a brilliantly run "front" (owner Patrick Terrail is about the best maître d' in town), Ma Maison moved safely past considerations of mere fashion. Nevertheless, it is more intensely fashionable now than ever. The kitchen was grandly renovated recently, but the unaffected funkiness of the dining rooms has thankfully not been tampered with.

Puck has created more than one dish that helped make his reputation—fish en croûte filled with mousseline, à la Bocuse; a sinful marjolaine—but recommendations are almost futile. The menu at Ma Maison is a mere departure point; there are numerous daily specials, with always significant fresh fish included. Putting yourself in the chef's hands is a clever way out of the dilemma. Expensive.

Michael's
1147 Third Street
Santa Monica   451-0843

Michael McCarty, the owner and executive chef of Michael's, brought the latest in intensely chic decor and new wave French cooking to Santa Monica. Inside, Michael's offers soft neutral colors and tasteful original art; the outside patio is even better and in fine weather just may be the best outdoor eating spot in town. The food is also fashionable, handily executed by a thoroughly professional staff of talented young Americans and distinguished by sleek arrangements on oversized white plates. Intriguing daily specials are often constructed around fresh fish flown in from France; the regular menu usually features salads of watercress and endive topped with a poached egg or chicory dressed with walnut oil and topped with a piece of warm *chevre*; charcoal-grilled squab perched on duck *foie gras* and sauced with raspberry vinegar; steak *frites*; grilled chicken with tarragon. Michael's has a fine wine list, which features an intelligent selection of California labels. Expensive.

Moustache Cafe
8155 Melrose Avenue
West Hollywood   651-2111

Casual cafe atmosphere, a sunny dining patio. A full selection of omelets, salads, sandwiches, crêpes, and more substantial entrées. Spinach salads, chopped steaks, seafood salad, eggs Florentine are recommended, although this kitchen ought not to be taken too seriously. Continuous service from before noon to after midnight. Inexpensive to moderate.

Since it opened in 1964, everything about the Tower—its silverplate, its distinctive logo, its flawless caviar—has been the work of Raymond Andrieux, an elegant Frenchman who has been involved in American *haute cuisine* for more than forty years. Thanks to Andrieux's diligence, the Tower is distinguished by high quality, especially in its appetizer menu (smoked trout, smoked salmon, real turtle soup), and surprisingly, for a cool room perched on the thirty-second floor of a steel and glass skyscraper, the Tower is also strong on provincial cooking (petite marmite, chicken Mascotte, lamb braised with beans, duck with olives). The sweet,

Tower
1150 South Olive Street
Occidental Center
Downtown   746-1554

pink, lamb noissettes generously perfumed with fresh tarragon are consistently excellent. On Fridays there is an abundant, headily fragrant bouillabaisse. The Tower's wine list is enormous, mostly top-heavy French, and, consequently, expensive (but not over-priced). The restaurant has lagged at dessert time, but now some interesting pastries are being made. A stunning mille feuille, layered with crème St. Honore and strawberries, and an unusual tart of poached pears over chocolate custard was added to the cart recently. Otherwise, there is a rather uninspiring array of custards and mousses and some commercially baked cakes. A fancy, flaming concoction of soufflé crêpes (order ahead) seems dated today. Sometimes the Tower's service is not up to the standard set by the prices or the pretensions, but it still is one of our important restaurants. Expensive.

INTERNATIONAL

Dar Maghreb
7651 Sunset Boulevard
Hollywood 876-7651

Other Moroccan and North African restaurants have opened (Moun of Tunis is also recommended) but this was the first of significance. It is still the standard against which others are measured, and it is certainly a showplace of painted tiles, rugs, and cushions. Multi-course dinners consist of Moroccan salad, b'stilla, couscous, chicken with lemon, with only the principal course varied according to the choice of your entire party. Incomprehensibly, the couscous is the least successful dish. The wonderful b'stilla may be even further improved (for an additional charge) if prepared with squab instead of chicken. Moderate to expensive.

Gitanjali of India
414 North La Cienega Boulevard
West Hollywood 657-2117

Samosas and the assorted Indian breads alone could make a meal. The menu is sophisticated, cooking precise, and the use of spices sure. Lamb kathmandu and spicy vegetarian thali are highly recommended dishes. Moderate.

Kavkaz
8795 Sunset Boulevard
West Hollywood 652-6582

This is the reigning spot, perched high above the Sunset Strip, for Russian-Armenian eating and carrying on. The signature dish is sedlo, a leg of lamb tenderized and flavored for days in a marinade of pomegranate juice; Russian cabbage borscht and chicken Kiev are other favorites. A great sampling of vodkas goes with the high-spirited music and Russian dancing on weekends. Moderate.

La Tranquera
4760 Melrose Avenue
Hollywood 666-9133

An enormously friendly, family-run restaurant specializing in well-prepared Chilean food. This is a cuisine of deep flavors, but not overtly spicy, with many delicious dishes based on pork and potatoes. Dinners are served with soup and salad. Inexpensive.

Paul Bhalla's Cuisine of India
10853 Lindbrook Drive
Westwood 478-8535

One of the top-ranking Indian restaurants in town. Paul Bhalla is said to possess the only traditional tandoor oven in the city; it yields a superb, rosy-red, attractively garnished tandoori chicken. The curried chicken vindaloo is the spiciest dish on the menu. If there is a criticism of Paul Bhalla's, it is probably that the subtly flavored Punjab-style thrust to the menu could gain dimension from more hot preparations. General quality is uniformly excellent, however, with lamb curry, eggplant curry, and the intensely flavored lamb and spinach sauté leading the list. Dal (curried lentils) and excellent chutneys are served with dinner. Moderate.

Rosalind's is the only restaurant in Los Angeles serving the sturdy, highly seasoned cuisine of West Africa. A variety of finger-food appetizers includes akara, bread-like little fried balls of ground black-eyed peas, O Jo Jo meat balls, plantains, and other delicacies served with hot pepper sauce (pilli-pilli). Best entrées are ground nut stew, Nigerian-style spinach (with fish and meat), and chicken yassa from Senegal. Accompany with beer and round off the meal with cocoanut pie for dessert. Inexpensive.

Rosalind's West African Cuisine
1941 South La Cienega Boulevard
Los Angeles   559-8816

A large, spare, immaculate storefront restaurant run by a refugee family from Saigon. At twice its prices, Saigon Flavor would still be one of the best restaurants in Los Angeles. The underpinning of such praise is the owners' deep pride in the Vietnamese cuisine and a relentless pursuit of quality. The best of the appetizers is a sampling from the enormous variety of Vietnamese finger foods: fried imperial eggrolls with pork, bean sprouts and egg wrapped in rice paper, a fresh spring roll which holds shrimp, pork, raw spinach, cellophane noodles, and mint. Shrimp wrapped around raw sugar cane and grilled over charcoal is then folded into a rice pancake with mint, cucumbers, slivers of carrots, and crisp slices of green apples. The signature dish at Saigon Flavor is the very fresh Dungeness crab (purchased live whenever possible) roasted with clarified butter, spices, and a *lot* of darkly browned garlic; the most interesting meat entrée is moderately spicy, charbroiled pork. Inexpensive to moderate.

Saigon Flavor
1044 South Fairfax Avenue
Los Angeles   935-1564

One wall of Ardison Phillips' restaurant is dominated by one of his huge paintings, while others are decorated with his spare colored pencil and crayon drawings. Otherwise, the unpretentious space is left as an uncluttered backdrop for the eclectic culinary art of chef Tom Rolla. A brief review of just a few of the favorites from the Studio Grill menu shows a wide range: zarzuela (a Spanish seafood stew), clams or mussels in a garlic-intense green sauce, couscous, marrow bones, cassoulet, lamb curry, Thai-inspired grilled shrimp with ginger and lime juice, and scallops in a chili-spiked cucumber sauce. There are simpler, but no less outstanding roasts of lamb, pork, and duck. The new expansion of the Studio Grill will be accompanied by a larger selection of Italian dishes on the menu. The wine list here is superb, with all bottles, even those that are necessarily expensive, very well priced. The signature dessert here is the incredible walnut torte. Moderate.

The Studio Grill
7321 Santa Monica Boulevard
Hollywood   874-9202

ITALIAN

Adriano's opened early in 1979 and quickly became the most promising new Italian restaurant in the city. The place is tucked into a tiny shopping center near the top of Beverly Glen. Clever decorating

Adriano's Ristorante
2930 Beverly Glen Circle
Los Angeles   475-9807

evokes some of the style of an Italian piazza. The menu is large and imaginative, although the all-important antipasti course is somewhat limited. Antipasti della casa and insalata di mare sound better than they are; scampi with straw potatoes and calamari fritti are better choices. Adriano's reputation, however, could rest with its pastas. Tortellini with a delicate chicken stuffing, silky fettucine "Tre P" (peas, prosciutto and Parmesan) and the satiny ravioli with a deeply rosemary-scented meat filling are all homemade, apparently by a pasta genius. Best entrées include a generous mixed seafood grill, bass poached with red wine sauce, veal slices with capers and anchovies, fresh California squab or quail, sweet little lamb medallions with butter and garlic. The dessert specialty is a kind of crème brûlée baked with liquor-marinated strawberries. Moderate to expensive.

Dan Tana's
9071 Santa Monica Boulevard
West Hollywood   275-9444

It seems to be *de rigueur* at Dan Tana's that you should wait at the bar for your table, even with a reservation, and even at ten o'clock at night. Apart from that little nuisance, the comfortable, laid-back style the place acquired when the nearby Troubadour was the hot rock ticket lingers; Tana's is a casual hang-out with good food, late hours, and amiable, if sometimes harried, service. The fettucine Alfredo is better than average here, the cannelloni tender, hot and running with top-quality cheese. Although the kitchen is capable of some of its *alta cucina* ambitions, the best dishes are simple ones: excellent grilled New York steak or the thick veal chop; fine, fresh spinach sautéed in rich olive oil, and, if you ask, a *lot* of garlic. Moderate.

Emilio's Ristorante
6602 Melrose Avenue
Hollywood   935-4922

It has pretty tiles and a real fountain in the middle of the front room, fake grapes, real flowers, a wine room to dine in, and just about everything else a good Italian trattoria can offer. Emilio's is enormously popular and successful, and, though the menu holds few surprises, the food is consistently above average. Hearty soups—stracciatelle Fiorentina, with egg and spinach, or rich chicken broth with toast and poached egg—are always satisfying. In season, mussels steamed in a thin, peppery sauce with mushrooms, or calamari stewed in tomatoes and fresh herbs can be had in appetizer or entrée portions.

Emilio's is justifiably well known for its spaghetti puntanesca, spicy and mushroom-studded; *al dente* linguine with olive oil and garlic (and anchovies, if you ask for them) or the homemade potato gnocchi are as good. The kitchen here is slightly heavy-handed, and consequently more successful with hearty dishes than delicate ones. The simple, charcoal grilled thin veal steak, steak pizzaiola, and the various chicken dishes are the best entrées. The wine list is extensive and fairly priced. Moderate.

Italia
1909 Wilshire Boulevard
Santa Monica   394-9788

Italia is recommended for its kitchen, which, under owner-chef Mario Palagi can usually produce at a level that almost overcomes some horrendous lapses in the service. The most serious chronic lapse is the discrepancy between the time a table is booked and the time it is available, but then, further delays, lost or mistaken orders, are not unheard of.

The menu is mostly derivative of one or two northern Italian styles, with a couple of Continental flourishes, and little is unfamiliar to anyone who frequents Los Angeles' Italian restaurants. Best appetizers include mozzarella marinara, tender calamari stewed in a spicy tomato sauce, and, when it is freshly prepared, spiedini alla Romana. Tortellini "panna and proscuitto" in a thick cheese and cream sauce; cannelloni Mario, a paper thin crêpe folded around parsley-flecked ricotta; and linguine with garlicky clams in a white sauce are unarguably fine pastas. Best entrées are simple fish and seafood dishes such as sautéed whitefish, scampi with garlic and lemon sauce; and a generous seafood frito misto. Veal scampi Fiorentina and veal cutlet Andrea are the most successful meat entrées. It's not very original, but the quality is high. Moderate to expensive.

Wonderful homemade pasta—ravioli verde, fettucine—excellent veal and seafood, chicken with spinach or spicy Italian sausages. This is a very high-spirited place, with friendly, caring service. Moderate to expensive.

La Dolce Vita
9785 Santa Monica Boulevard
Beverly Hills   278-1845

A charming trattoria decorated with patchwork patterns and nostalgic tintypes and photos of someone's family. The fresh pasta is superb; homemade fettucine or tortellini needs only a toss with sweet butter and chives to satisfy. Spicy tomato sauce arrabiatta can be had with tuna or calamari over *al dente* linguine or silky tagliarini, or it can be the zuppa for zuppa di mussels, when they're in season. Wonderful grilled chicken, herbed or spiced as you like it, steak with peppers, fried zucchini, sautéed spinach, fish of the day—simple, but perfectly turned-out dishes. Knowledgeable service and a fine wine list. Moderate.

La Famiglia
453 North Cañon Drive
Beverly Hills   276-6208

For those of us who are not part of gilt-edged Beverly Hills society, the famous La Scala may mean indifferent service and lukewarm meals. If you find yourself dining here, and you like your pasta *al dente*, make sure you tell your waiter. Best dishes: Leon's salad, carpaccio (lunch only), striped bass Portofino, veal scallopini piccata, and grilled sweetbreads. Expensive.

La Scala
9455 Santa Monica Boulevard
Beverly Hills   275-0579

The little trattoria that is La Scala's cousin has less pretension, is far less expensive, and is altogether more charming. The perfect spot for a simple, satisfying lunch—mozzarella marinara, terrific cold grilled chicken, chopped salad Leon, shrimps marinara. Lunch only, no reservations. Moderate.

La Scala Boutique
475 North Beverly Drive
Beverly Hills   550-8288

It is, simply, the best Italian restaurant in town, a small, unpretentious shopping-center trattoria of extraordinary scope and ambition. A list of "best" dishes would unfairly limit the possibilities.

Peppone
11628 Barrington Court
Brentwood   476-7379

Peppone's menu is large, but the verbal recitation of daily specialties, particularly of seafood, nearly doubles the options. The best bet is to construct an Italian-style meal, of small, shared courses—antipasti, primi (pasta), and secondi (entrée)—in order to taste more. In summer, of course, it would be folly to miss the pesto, or, when they are available, fresh imported porcini mushrooms tossed into fettucine. The relentless Gianni Paoletti, Peppone's owner-chef, has spent endless hours collecting fine Italian and California wines for the restaurant's constantly changing cellar. Moderate to expensive.

Ristorante Chianti
7383 Melrose Avenue
West Hollywood   653-8333

This place has slipped drastically from its position of a few years ago as one of the top-rated Italian restaurants in town. It is still a wonderful, small but sophisticated room, however, and the fettucine, the salads, the osso buco, and the saltimbocca are well above average. The wine list has always been good but expensive; the zabaglione is outstanding. Moderate to expensive.

Valentino
3115 Pico Boulevard
Santa Monica   829-4313

This room is frequently overbooked, the bar is often rambunctious, the acoustics can be frightful, and the overextended waiters and captains (who are otherwise able professionals) may neglect their stations. Nevertheless, the kitchen is competent, if not brilliant, and pastas (gnocchi, silky fettucine) are well made with interesting sauces. This is a good seafood restaurant, although sometimes they overcook. The restaurant is justifiably known for its fine calamaretti fritti, even though the babies are often grown up by the time we eat them. Valentino has one of the deepest and most extensive cellars of Italian and California wines. Moderate to expensive.

Villa Capri
6735 Yucca Street
Hollywood   465-4148

The definitive Italian-American neighborhood restaurant. The menu is mostly derived from Neapolitan and Sicilian styles, which have unfortunately become passé in the wake of the current fashion for northern dishes. Villa Capri produces dishes like eggplant par-migiana, pork chops with bell peppers and pan gravy spiked with vinegar. Extraordinary calamari fritti compete with the best Italian home cooking. Fresh pasta (to fashion into chubby cheese-filled ravioli, or tender spinach noodles) is prepared daily, as is the dough for the superb thin-crusted pizza and the wonderful, wheaty bread. The service at Villa Capri ranges from pleasant and com-petent to pleasant and willy-nilly. The decor is a throwback to a past Los Angeles taste for dim rooms and blood-red tufted booths. Moderate.

JAPANESE

An especially esoteric assortment of sushi ingredients, with sea ur-chin and various roe included. Also, pretty sashimi and chirashi, in which sushi ingredients are arranged over sushi rice in a bowl, to be eaten with chopsticks. Moderate.

Hamayoshi
3350 West First Street
Los Angeles   384-2914

One of the few sushi bars in Santa Monica, Hiro Sushi offers a good general menu as well as lower than average prices. The chefs are more than happy to slice your food "by the numbers" as you watch,

Hiro Sushi
1621 Wilshire Boulevard
Santa Monica   395-3570

a ritual particularly fascinating for the sushi novice. Respectful murmurs of appreciation are obligatory.†

Ichiban Cafe
108 South San Pedro Street
Downtown   622-4453

When you slice up radishes and wrap them in rice and seaweed it's called oshinko maki. At the sushi bar in the Ichiban Cafe, the dish is unbelievably good. The decor here is a little unusual—bits of Japanese-style, American-style, even Chinese-style architecture. Prices are reasonable, quality of food is high.†

Imperial Gardens
8225 West Sunset Boulevard
West Hollywood   656-1750

The sushi bar here is not the most comfortable, but the chefs occasionally rise to artistic heights to delight the Sunset Strip clientele. Excellent sunomono of tiny clams and cucumber. Moderate to expensive.

Inagiku Oriental Plaza
Bonaventure Hotel
404 South Figueroa Street
Downtown   614-0820

The regular restaurant here is only adequate with shabu-shabu clearly the best of some very familiar choices, but the sushi bar is remarkable, even in a city where great sushi is easier to come by than great hamburgers. Salt-cured salmon, smoked imported Japanese scallops, many types of roe (salmon, herring, crab), and fresh sea urchins are deftly fashioned into pretty sushi and norimake. The sunomono—cold vegetables dressed with rice vinegar—are also inventive here. Moderate.

Masukawa
1328 West Rosecrans Boulevard
Gardena   323-1922

A good, middle class, and moderately priced sushi bar. The style is less refined than at fancier places, and the sushi is unceremoniously plunked down on the shiny black lip of the counter, but the atmosphere is as friendly as a neighborhood tavern, and quality is tops. Best sunomono around.

Considered by some to be the best sushi bar in Los Angeles. The food is consistently delicious and the prices within reason. It's usually crowded but worth the wait. The one sushi chef for every three customers assures personal service with much flourish. The menu comes complete with English translations. Moderate.†

Teru Sushi
11940 Ventura Boulevard
Studio City   763-6201

This is one of the prettiest Japanese restaurants in Los Angeles, a good-looking, contemporary room (traditional tatami rooms are also available) overlooking the rooftop garden and waterfall of the New Otani Hotel. The menu is far more esoteric than most, having been designed with the Japanese guests in mind. Complete dinners include clear soup and sunomono. In addition, there is a large a la carte selection of appetizers, the best of which are salt roasted clams, very fresh seaweed, and cold green tea noodles, beautifully garnished and arranged. Shabu-shabu and yosenabe (fish and vegetable stew, cooked at the table) and chicken yakitori are of high quality. The sushi bar is above average. The condition of all sushi ingredients is impeccable, and the sushi chefs are pleasant and artistic. Moderate.

A Thousand Cranes
New Otani Hotel
120 South Los Angeles Street
Downtown   629-1200

Offers tempura, shabu-shabu, and teppan as well as sushi. The chefs operate within easy reach and they're glad to demonstrate their slicing technique to interested diners. Moderate.†

Tokyo Kaikan
337 East First Street
Downtown   625-2538

Yagura Ichiban
Japanese Village
101 First Street
Downtown   623-4141

The first Los Angeles restaurant to specialize in robata-yaki, or country-style Japanese cooking. Robata-yaki is available only at its own counter, however, and the food served in the sit-down area of Yagura Ichiban is not recommended. The counter operates along the same principles as a sushi bar, with an enormous selection of fresh fish, meat, and vegetables that are cooked to your order, while you watch, and then passed to you on a wooden paddle. Besides robata yaki, in which the ingredients are skillfully grilled over charcoal, Yagura Ichiban offers kushi-age, a light, crisp, greaseless frying style (it is not in a tempura-like batter, however). The selection here is staggering and the quality impeccable: seafood includes fresh smelts and imported Japanese scallops with their coral still attached; best meat choices are top-quality slices of beef wrapped around string beans or asparagus, and garlicky little pork meatballs. Moderate.

MEXICAN

For reasons not easily explained, Los Angeles never has developed the first-class Mexican cuisine our geography seems to indicate. We have some very good places, and a seemingly endless number of interchangeable, adequate places, where, if you keep your expectations in check, you will not be disappointed. But for the most part, the Mexican fare here only touches the surface of what that large, complicated country with its strong and stylish regions can offer. In our city, the Mexican places at the top of their class do not compare to the best restaurants in other classes.

Ana Maria's
3541 East First Street
Los Angeles   269-1713

A neat, but plain storefront only slightly relieved by a nice hanging collection of clay pots. The menu is more than slightly familiar, but it is executed with enormous care and skill. Highlights are chicken en mole, pork in chili verde, and an extraordinary shredded beef, combined with eggs and succulent seasonings. Equal attention is paid to smaller details, like the finely chopped, cilantro-spiked guacamole, and the warm, pastry-fine tortilla chips. Inexpensive.

Antonio's Restaurant
7472 Melrose Avenue
West Hollywood   937-8763

Besides the all too familiar tacos, taquitos, and enchiladas, Antonio has something he calls Mexico City Specialties, three or four dishes prepared each day that begin to widen our perceptions of the great Mexican cuisine. Favorites are Friday's red snapper Veracruzano; Saturday's sirloin in a complex mole sauce, and a veal shank braised in wine, red chili, and herbs; Sunday's pollo en pipian. Inexpensive to moderate.

El Cholo
1121 South Western Avenue
Los Angeles   734-2773

Fifty-one years of old hacienda atmosphere complete with a Spanish garden and a fountain make El Cholo a beautiful place to dine. Sonora-style enchiladas and margaritas made with Cuervo 1800 Gold are standouts. The sangria brunch on Sunday will put a glint in your eye. Inexpensive.†

The specialty here is the pregnant burrito, plus wine margaritas and a year 'round supply of infamous Noche Buena Christmas Beer. The burritos are not only delicious, they're huge. Inexpensive to moderate.†

El Nopal
112 National
West Los Ang

A cheerfully decorated family restaurant dedicated to high-level homemade dishes. A specialty is carne adobado, thin slices of juicy pork, marinated in chili, onions, and other seasonings for twenty-four hours before char-grilling. Tender roasted pork with scallions and cilantro is also recommended. The rest of the menu is more or less familiar, but it is carried out with the same care as the specials. A good selection of Mexican beers and Penafiel fruit-flavored soda waters. Inexpensive.

Guadalajara Inn
4466 East Gage Ave
Bell   773-9882

Homemade tortilla to bite, part-time magician to delight. A "top of the list" restaurant where you can smell the tortillas being rolled and kneaded as you wait. The atmosphere is festive and will remain that way long after you leave if you drink more than two of the formidable margaritas.

La Cabaña
783 Rose Avenue
Venice   399-9841

Fresh, handmade tortillas as you watch. Excellent tostadas and chile rellenos. Try the house specialty at $3.75, and you will not be disappointed.

La Choza
11785 Olympic Boulevard
West Los Angeles   473-9293

Of the many spots in the Olvera Street area at which to stop and snack, this one is probably the best, in its extremely modest way. Set up like a typical colonial-style kitchen, La Luz del Dia offers handmade fresh tortillas and cafeteria-style food. The chicharron en salsa verde is serious stuff, not for sissies. Inexpensive.

La Luz del Dia
624 North Main Street
Downtown   972-9578

There are thirteen Los Arcos and Acapulco restaurants in the southland area. The San Francisco special *is* special. Crab meat enchiladas, margaritas, and rellenos are all tasty. Despite the large number of restaurants involved with this chain, the quality of food is consistently high. Clean and well lit—definitely the best chain.

Los Arcos
8431 Sunland Boulevard
Los Angeles   767-4240, 240-5970

Good arroz con pollo, enchiladas rancheras, and taquitos, and you can have them for less than you'd expect to pay. The food, however, doesn't match the margaritas, which are excellent.†

Lucy's El Adobe
5536 Melrose Avenue
Hollywood   462-9421

The king crab enchilada stands up and demands your attention. The red snapper is an unexpected pleasure. The chile rellenos will warm your corazon. Mijares offers service with a smile and get-what-you-pay-for prices.

Mijares
1145 Palmeda Drive
Pasadena   356-9348

Calabazas rellenas are first-rate. They're made of zucchini stuffed with spiced ground beef smothered in melted cheese with sour cream folded in. But the real specialty here is the atmosphere: a two-story garden dining room with foliage to rival anything south of the border. Moderate.†

Pancho's
3615 Highland Avenue
Manhattan Beach   545-6670

THAI

For the average Angeleno, Thai food is appreciated although by now familiar. To most visitors from almost anywhere else in the United States, this part of our ethnic richness is high adventure. The Thai cuisine is complicated and sophisticated, derived from, but no longer quite like, Indian, Philippine, and Chinese cuisines. Thai dishes are characterized by the constant play of contrasting tastes—sweet and sour, spicy and astringent, sweet and hot. Fresh green, red, and yellow chilies; dried red chilies, whole or crushed; and sliced green chilies in vinegar are integrated into dishes or used as condiments. Healing herbs, mint, cilantro, and basil, are added for relief or contrast or pounded into a paste to flavor curries; dried wild lime leaves, lemon grass, ginger, and laos (like ginger) are cool and fragrant. Fermented fish sauce or shrimp paste may add yet another complex taste.

Thai dishes fall into three basic types: liquid curries or soups, called kaengs; dry or thick-sauced dishes, krueng kiengs; cold, salad-like dishes, yams or yums. Within each category, of course, are subdivisions. Curries may be yellow (mild), red chili (moderately hot), or green (extremely hot, if made correctly).

There is an entire category called nam prik—endless combinations of fermented fish sauce or shrimp paste with garlic, chili, dried shrimp, sugar, lemon or lime juice, cocoanut cream, cilantro, or tamarind. Sate sauce, constructed from pulverized peanuts, is typical nam prik and is most commonly served with slim slices of barbecued pork or beef on bamboo skewers.

Other staple dishes include taut mun or todd mann—ground fish cakes (usually cod) studded with slices of fresh green chilies. And there are numerous noodle dishes; mee krob or mee grob, combining crisp-fried rice noodles, shrimp, and pork in a caramelized sauce; phat Thai or pud Thai (practically the Thai national dish), Chinese egg noodles garnished with dry shrimp, crushed peanuts, red chili pepper, bean sprouts, and scallions. In addition, bean threads (cellophane or glass noodles) may be combined with vegetables or cooked in a soup. Stir-fried dishes combining fresh herbs and chilies with chicken, beef, or shrimp are most common, as are barbecued beef, chicken, and duck which may be served hot from the grill or as the principal component of a yam.

Thai meals may be served in the authentic style, which means all dishes, including soups, are brought to the table at once, and a kind of free-form noshing commences. When the curries get too intense, it may be time to sample a yam; the searing effect of squid with chilies may be tempered by a plunge into the sweet mee krob. In the U.S., however, many Thai restaurants follow Western custom and serve in courses. Also, the availability of Chinese dishes on a Thai menu does not indicate lack of authenticity; the practice is just as common in large Thai cities like Bangkok which have enormous Chinese populations. With Thai food you drink beer or Thai iced coffee or tea.

The following list of Thai restaurants in Los Angeles covers several good places, but there are many, many others. Because menus tend to be somewhat predictable, only a few unusual or exceptional dishes are noted. Most Thai restaurants are in the inexpensive to moderate price range.

Musman—a mild beef-peanut-potato cocoanut milk curry; prik king —string beans with pork in red chili oil.

Bangkok 1
1253 North La Brea Avenue
Hollywood   876-0633

Barbecued chicken; beef curry with mint; stuffed squid and pork soup.

Chao Praya
6307 Yucca Street
Hollywood   464-9652

Extraordinary mee krob; chicken and spinach with sate; chicken soup with cocoanut milk and lemon grass; homemade cocoanut ice cream.

Chuladul's Restaurant
9552 Washington Boulevard
Culver City   559-3666

Braised ham hocks; hot and sour shrimp soup; squid and cellophane noodle soup.

Siam
5158 Hollywood Boulevard
Hollywood   666-9138

Wonderful yams (or yums): roast duck, squid, bean threads with pork; squid with hot green chilies and mint; fish cakes.

Thai House
1080 North Western Avenue
Los Angeles   464-9931

Beef sate; crisp fried eggplant; vegetable soup with shrimp and lime; pud kaprow (pork, chicken, or beef with Thai basil and green chilies); cellophane noodles with shrimp and pork; mee krob.

Thai Spoon
8553 Santa Monica Boulevard
West Hollywood   855-9311

The mission-style Beverly Hills Hotel set in its twelve-acre garden estate.

HOTELS

By Nancy Hathaway

California has a history of hospitality that dates back to the early missions. Stretching from San Diego to Sonoma, they dotted the coast the way Holiday Inns do today. In those days, many of the missions were spaced at one-day intervals from each other, so the efficient traveler could leave one mission in the morning and arrive at the next by sundown, in time for a hearty meal and a welcome bed.

Today's visitors have a considerably broader choice of lodging than did the early Californios, but the habit of hospitality persists. The list that follows does not pretend to be complete; instead, it is selective. Every hotel listed here is very special in one way or another. If you cannot afford to stay at any of them (and they are all relatively expensive), you still might consider visiting them for a drink, a meal, a stroll through the gardens, or a look at the architecture. In addition to the restaurants listed in the marginal notes, most of the hotels have coffee shops and lounges. And they are all great places to sit and watch the passing parade.

When the Ambassador Hotel first opened in 1921, Wilshire Boulevard was a dirt road. Since then, the hotel has become part of the texture of the city. Between 1930 and 1943, Academy Awards were held here six times. At least five presidents have visited, many famous movie stars had bungalows here (as did J. Edgar Hoover), and almost every band played at the Cocoanut Grove. Today, the grounds are an unexpected delight in a very urban part of town.

Ambassador Hotel
3400 Wilshire Boulevard
Downtown   387-7011
Royal Ambassador (French)
Celebrity Room (buffet luncheon and Sunday brunch)

And if a wedding, convention, or bar mitzvah seems not quite so romantic as, for instance, seeing Ginger Rodgers win an Oscar (in 1940, for *Kitty Foyle*), or hearing the Andrews Sisters in the Cocoanut Grove, at least the memory lingers on. The old world charm, the racquet club, and brunch in the Celebrity Room are all fine points in a hotel whose history is part of the city it serves.

Hotel Bel-Air
701 Stone Canyon Road
Beverly Hills   472-1211
Bel-Air Dining Room (Continental)

In a humbler incarnation, the Hotel Bel-Air was once a stable—but even then, it was the stable of an oilman. Today, the comfortable adobe building serves a more exalted function. Offering superb, individual service, the hotel is surrounded by beautiful gardens. All manner of flowers bloom here, and a pond is home to a pair of white swans. Even the interior attempts to bring the outside world inside. Designer Manuel Alvarez has furnished the sixty-eight rooms and suites (plus one cottage) in a variety of yellows and greens—and the results are impressive enough to have been written up in *Architectural Digest*. If there is a complaint to make about the Bel-Air, it would be that the dining room is not up to snuff (although the wine list is a good one). It doesn't matter; the grounds, the quiet intimacy, the hotel itself, and the gin fizzes in the lounge more than make up for that small lapse.

Pool-side comfort at the Beverly Hills Hotel.

Beverly Hills Hotel
9641 Sunset Boulevard
Beverly Hills   276-2251
The Coterie (Continental)
Polo Lounge
Loggia (breakfast and Sunday brunch)

Anyone who has ever stumbled accidentally into, say, the middle of a Shriner's Convention, will appreciate the Beverly Hills Hotel, which boasts "Never a Convention." Even nametags are banned at this fine old hotel, although business meetings can be arranged. Many of the 325 individually decorated rooms and bungalows are equipped with wood-burning fireplaces, bars, patios, kitchens, and antique furnishings. Rambling across a twelve-acre garden estate, this mission-style hotel (the main building was built in 1912) offers swimming, tennis, a cinema room for private screenings, fine shops, a profusion of palm trees, and several restaurants, including the chic and—if you're lucky—celebrity-filled Polo Lounge.

The Huntington-Sheraton in Pasadena is the only hotel that enters a float in the annual Rose Bowl parade, and that fact may give a clue to the unique character of this hotel. Visiting Rose Bowl teams stay here, where they can enjoy a model ship collection in one of the restaurants, an exhibit of early railway pictures and posters, and the "Picture Bridge," decorated with forty-two paintings of California historical sights by artist Frank Moore. Surrounded by lovely gardens, the building was completed in 1914 and designed so each of the rooms would receive direct sunlight at some point during the day. If you plan to be in Pasadena, especially at Rose Bowl time, this is the place to stay (even though the visiting team may sulk a bit after losing to USC).

Huntington-Sheraton Hotel
1401 South Oak Knoll Avenue
Pasadena   792-0266
Ship Room (Continental)
Crystal Terrace (American)

The Huntington-Sheraton Hotel built in 1914.

Built overlooking the ocean, the Miramar-Sheraton offers sweeping views and easy beach access. Since 1976 the hotel has been in the process of change. A new entrance way is being built, and lobbies and guest rooms have been refurbished to the point that nothing in them is more than two or three years old. Although it has been around for almost sixty years, the Miramar-Sheraton today is becoming a brand new hotel. Still, its main attraction is its location; approximately two-thirds of the rooms overlook the ocean (not to mention the lovely Santa Monica Palisades Park), and the beach is close. For those who prefer smaller bodies of water, there is a heated swimming pool.

Miramar-Sheraton Hotel
Wilshire Boulevard at Ocean Avenue
Santa Monica   395-3731
International Room (Continental)
Garden Room (American)

New Otani's rooftop garden and restaurant.

New Otani Hotel
120 South Los Angeles Street
Downtown   629-1200
A Thousand Cranes (Japanese)
The Black Ship (Continental)

The New Otani has been designed with care. From the doorknobs (wooden, to prevent static electricity) to the elevator buttons (set low, for those in wheelchairs) to the health spa (which offers shiatsu massage), meticulous attention to detail is apparent. Atop the fourth floor is a Japanese garden; and if the surrounding view of downtown L.A. doesn't exactly add to the serenity, who's to quibble? Most of the rooms are Western, but three Japanese-style suites are available. The restaurants similarly offer a fusion of cultures. Downstairs, seventeen shops display beautiful, very expensive Japanese goods. A new shopping complex next door, planned for completion in the spring of 1980, will house sixty-six additional stores.

Beverly Wilshire Hotel
9500 Wilshire Boulevard
Beverly Hills   275-4282
La Bella Fontana (Continental)
El Padrino (bar-rotisserie)
Don Hernando's (Mexican)

More than any other hotel in town, the Beverly Wilshire is the work of one man—Hernando Courtright, first president of Century City, who bought the ailing hotel in 1961 and turned it around. He rejuvenated the original building, added a new wing, and moved the main entrance from Wilshire Boulevard to El Camino Real, a private side street now lined with mission arches and gaslight lanterns from Edinburgh castle. Each floor in the new wing is done in a different style, from Spanish decor on the first floor to "Avant Garde Modern" on the sixth. Throughout, the hotel reflects Courtright's belief in fine materials, comfort, and superb, highly personalized service. In 1971, the Beverly Wilshire became the first hotel in America to receive the Grand Luxe hallmark, previously given only to European hostelries. It is still winning awards today. Located at the foot of Rodeo Drive, it has 500 rooms and suites, various shops, several restaurants and bars, a pool just like Sophia Loren's, and easy access to the most prestigious shopping in the country. "The greatness of a city," Hernando Courtright says, "is measured by the standards of its hotels." He sets a worthy example.

The old Wilshire Boulevard entrance to the Beverly Wilshire Hotel.

Historic lobby of the Biltmore Hotel, with its hand-painted ceiling and ornate artwork.

Biltmore Hotel
515 South Olive Street
Downtown   624-1011
Bernard's (French)

In a city where the new is often more striking, and easier to find, than the old, where automatic gas fireplaces seem more common than real ones, the Biltmore is a delightful surprise. Ceilings in the Biltmore are not only high, they were handpainted in the 1920s by Giovanni Smeraldi. Due to its richly detailed architecture, the hotel was named a historical landmark in 1969. Since then, it has been renovated at a cost of $30 million. Each room is decorated in shades of a single color of the rainbow; there are live plants in every room; and the work of artist Jim Dine is featured throughout the building. Even if you don't stay at the Biltmore, it's worth a trip downtown to see this fine old building and, while you're at it, to dine at Bernard's. (See Dining Out, p. 133.)

Bonaventure Hotel
404 South Figueroa Street
Downtown   624-1000
Inagiku Oriental Plaza (Japanese)
Beaudry's (Continental)
Top of the Five (American)
Carl's Jr.

From the outside, the mirrored towers of the Bonaventure add a dramatic, even gaudy note to the downtown landscape. From the inside, this convention-oriented hotel looks like the set for a grade-B science fiction movie. Riding the space age glass elevators can be stomach-turning; and once you've ridden them, the idea of sitting down to a leisurely meal in a restaurant that revolves may seem revolting. But—if your stomach can stand it—the view is terrific, especially at sunset on a clear day. Take along the Dramamine and treat yourself to a drink and a fine view of Los Angeles.

It depends on your tastes; the Century Plaza is a large, commercial hotel with neither the charm of the Biltmore nor the beauty of the Bel-Air, but the fact is that year after year, eleven times since it opened in 1966, it has been awarded the Mobil Travel Guide's Five Star rating. All the amenities are there, and it is popular for conventions. The building, a long curve of cement and glass, houses 800 rooms and suites, each with a balcony overlooking the city. There are several restaurants (most notably the award-winning Yamato, which offers both tatami rooms and Western-style dining), a variety of shops, swimming and wading pools, and an elegant lobby. Special attention has been paid to the blind; relief maps in rooms show the location of all furniture, and the restaurants have braille menus. The hotel is near the ABC Entertainment Center and across the street from a large and pleasant shopping center.

Century Plaza Hotel
2025 Avenue of the Stars
Century City   277-2000
Yamato (Japanese)
Granada Room (Continental)
Garden Restaurant (American)

Long, curving face of the Century Plaza Hotel.

If any single hotel symbolizes old Hollywood, it would be the Chateau Marmont, which housed luminaries like Clark Gable, Carole Lombard, Jean Harlow, and even Howard Hughes. Built in 1927 in the style of a Norman castle and set down inconsiderately on Sunset Boulevard, where it is surrounded by billboards, the Chateau Marmont is like a fading movie star who, fifty years later, suddenly achieves a new popularity. In 1975 the hotel was losing $2,000 a month. New owners Ray Sarlot and Karl Kantarjian have rejuvenated the place, and once again quiet elegance more reminiscent of Europe than of Hollywood prevails. Today, famous actors, artists, writers, and musicians frequent the Marmont, which was named a Cultural Heritage Monument in 1976. Although it has no restaurants, the hotel does serve a continental breakfast.

Chateau Marmont
8221 Sunset Boulevard
Hollywood   656-1010

Tom Bergin's lively bar.

WHERE TO DRINK:

Bars, Saloons, and Watering Holes.

By Denis Hamill

Visiting all the fine saloons in our thirsty metropolis would be a life's work doomed to failure. This noble task would remain ever unfinished. In a yeasty flux, new places open, old ones fold, and others, sadder still, lose their special social magic. A good bar is a fragile organism; a change of bartenders, a self-conscious awareness of its own excellence, the wrong remodeling job—all can be fatal. But just as often a place gradually gets better. It acquires the ability to transform a mere crowded room into a charmed circle of conviviality. It becomes, quite simply, a fine saloon.

So the quest goes on. An everchanging universe of funky dives, sleek lounges, and stalwart neighborhood taverns awaits exploration. We will list a few of our favorites, but there can be no substitute for finding your own. Sampling the diverse watering holes of Los Angeles is a marvelous endeavor. But first a caution.

Drinking in L.A. is different from other cities. The dangerous side of that difference involves the automobile. Not only is drinking and driving on our freeways dangerous to life and limb, but even the casual imbiber who can handle his liquor well is prey to the quotas of the California Highway Patrol.

Side-of-the-road drunk tests are as common in Los Angeles as side-of-the-road palm trees. Highway cops can put a driver through a routine not unlike basic training on the shoulder of the Santa Monica Freeway even if the driver has touched nothing stronger

Harry's Bar and Grill.

than Welchade all evening. From here you can be dragged into a police station and asked to submit to either a breath, blood, or urine test to determine the alcohol content in your body. If that content is over 1.5 percent you will be held in lieu of $375 bail. Court appearances and lawyer fees will almost certainly follow. If you pass the test you will be released but not before your evening has been ruined.

So the obvious advice to any visitor to L.A. who cares for a night on the tiles is to take a taxi to and from the saloons. Or see to it that someone else drives. And try to frequent establishments closer to your hotel or home. If you go out in a group for a bar-hopping spree be sure to hit the joints farthest from home first and drink your way back. There is nothing worse than finding yourself half-jarred at the 2 a.m. closing time fifty miles from bed with a steering wheel in your hands.

Choosing which saloons you will visit before you go out is advisable. If you're looking for, say, a disco, pick one and call first to get all the necessary information including directions, dress code, cover charges, parking facilities, and hours before you embark on your journey.

There is nothing more infuriating than to traverse thirty-five miles of freeway to find out you will not be admitted to a bar because you are wearing jeans. Or because you need a membership card or a twenty dollar cover charge.

In Los Angeles the saloons cover many styles: young singles' joints, also referred to as "body shops," that are invariably jammed on weekends and should usually be avoided (unless you enjoy waiting an hour between drinks and gargling in an atmosphere equivalent to a rush hour bus); quiet saloons with no music but with conversation as the main attraction; what I call "pinball emporiums" where the emphasis is on electronic toys for adults who miss hanging out in pizza parlors; restaurant bars (these are the most abundant) which offer pre-prandial libations while you await a table; and the good old fashioned corner taverns—places of solace and retreat to drown the blues or celebrate small triumphs.

Unless you are an uncontrollable star gazer, the celebrity hang-outs should be shunned. To begin with, if you are not a "name" in most of these places you can stand like a wooden Indian for ages waiting to get a table or a drink at the bar. The celebrities usually go to these places to avoid rabid fans and will have nothing to do with autograph seekers and tourists with Instamatics. But the bouncers will have something to do with you, and that often means a bum's rush through the door. These places are usually unbelievably pretentious and overpriced anyway and do little but dash the illusions of loyal fans.

Los Angeles saloons offer some pleasant surprises to visitors. The finest margaritas north of the border are made here and should be tested by tequila lovers. Mexican beers such as Dos Equis, Bohemia, and Carta Blanca are among the best in the world and a pleasant change from the monotony of American beer—which brings us to Coors beer, enshrined here in L.A. as the best American brew. While opinions vary on this subject, Coors is abundant and cheap in Los Angeles and the thirteen-year union boycott on this grog has finally been lifted so feel free to slug.

California house wines in Los Angeles are also very good and very cheap. The average price is a dollar for an eight-ounce glass and this is well worth the price. Buying it by the liter is even cheaper.

Certain areas of the city boast specialized bars. Santa Monica, for example, is jammed with British-style pubs where darts, shepherd's pie, British ales, and fish and chips bring in the ladies and gents.

Hollywood boasts an ever-swelling throng of show-biz bars where deals are made and the trade papers are often left out for light reading. Beverly Hills caters to those people who like to hand the valet parking attendant the keys to their Rolls. The San Fernando Valley offers less pretense and more value, with good working man's saloons where Irish music or a sports motif appeals to the serious drinker who has never heard of Perrier water or a Singapore Sling.

All of these places—whether it is an Italian restaurant with the best cappuccino in town out in San Pedro or a black bar in Crenshaw with a $4.50 all-you-can-eat soul-food spread or a famous Irish bar in Pasadena—have good things going for them. But to get to them you need wheels.

And in Los Angeles today the only thing worse than a half-tanked car is a driver in the same condition.

Must-Hit List: The following eighteen saloons are among the best drinking joints in L.A. Any one of them is well worth a night on the tiles.

This saloon is one of the oldest drink tanks in town. It was originally owned by a couple of guys known as Bing Crosby and Pat O'Brien in partnership with Tom Bergin. It sells one of the best Irish coffees in L.A. The handsome rustic wood atmosphere and reasonable prices attract a big Joe College crowd, but order is maintained by beefy bartenders who also make beefy drinks. There is no music or entertainment here, so the emphasis is on the fine art of conversation.

Tom Bergin's
840 South Fairfax Avenue
Los Angeles   936–7151

Located on the marina at Redondo Beach, the Blue Moon offers a Saturday and Sunday afternoon novelty—New Orleans jazz dancing. The musicians perform on an outdoor deck where you can either sit and listen or get up and shimmy. This is all played against

The Blue Moon
207 North Harbor Drive
Redondo Beach   374–3339

the nautical backdrop of the marina, which makes for a beautiful weekend afternoon of fun.

Casey's Bar
613 South Grand Avenue
Downtown   629–2353

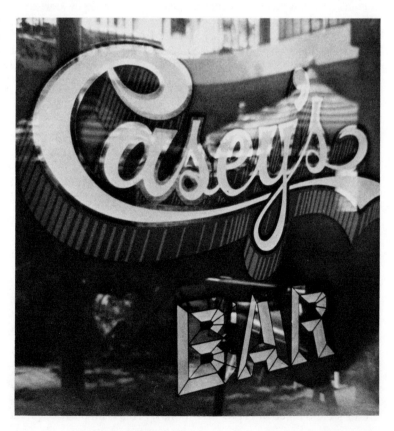

Although burrowed near the tallest skyscrapers in Los Angeles, this Irish pub might convince you that you've returned to the "old country." Especially if you've downed one or two of the house specialties: Tica Irish Spring or one of the other Irish coffees available (made with liberal splashes of Irish whiskey). Tuesday through Wednesday there's a piano player and on Friday, a band. To quote one of the waitresses, "You come into this place after five on Friday and there's no way you're not going to be either picked-up, picked out, or stone drunk." That translates as a busy cocktail hour. Lunch and dinner. Closed Saturday and Sunday.

This is a small but charming watering hole near the ocean. Excellent, cold tap beer sells very cheap. There are no pretenses, no hassles, and no rip-offs here. Just a fine drinking establishment to relax in and rinse the salt air from your mouth.

Chez Jay
1657 Ocean Avenue
Santa Monica   395–1741

An excellent place to drink. The atmosphere is boisterous, and the chic meet here. The bartenders are superb and lightning fast. The prices are fair by Beverly Hills standards, which means fairly high. However the drinks are freely poured and generous. Piano music mixes well with conversation. The drawback to this saloon is that it often becomes unbearably crowded, something management cannot help. When you offer so much you suffer from overpopularity.

The Gingerman
396 North Bedford Drive
Beverly Hills   273–7585

Great American Food and Beverage Company
826 Wilshire Boulevard
Santa Monica   451-1411

This is a nut house. And that is meant in the most complimentary of ways. Not the kind of place to go for a quiet drink and reveries of lost loves. It is a place to go and celebrate. Every night is a small riot here. Food is served at fair prices in huge portions, and beer is sloshed around by the pitcher at equally fair prices. Wine is also available. No hard liquor is sold here. Entertainment is provided by the waiters and waitresses who double up on the piano or on guitars. Often the whole saloon will join in the song. This place also has one of the most extensive ice cream menus in town so you can bring your granny if she has a strong heart.

Harry's Bar and American Grill
2020 Avenue of the Stars
Century City   277-2333

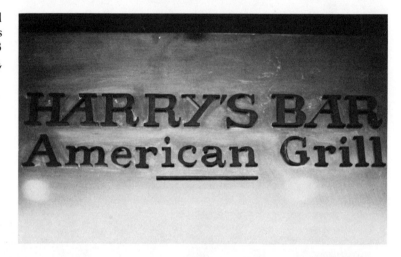

Harry's is an exact replica of its namesake (of Papa Hemingway fame) in Venice, Italy. This one doesn't overlook the Grand Canal, however; it's located in the middle of the Century City ABC Entertainment Center. Lots of fine linen and walnut woodwork accentuate the continental decor. The crowd is made up of businessmen, young up-and-comings, and, every now and then, a genuine certified Star. Bar specialties include a "Bellini": fresh peach puree and champagne. Lunch and dinner are served.

Heckles
424 Fair Oaks Avenue
South Pasadena   799-0857

At Heckles you'll find a bar and restaurant with a lively attractive crowd, good prices, a sports motif, and very professional bartenders. There is dancing and live entertainment regularly here and management puts an emphasis on all-out fun. Prices are reasonable.

Ireland's 32
1321 Burbank Boulevard
Van Nuys   785-4031

Here is the best Irish bar in L.A. It offers good Irish music both live and on the juke box, a fair glass of Guinness, good cheap pub grub, and an excellent atmosphere for both drinking and song. This place attracts sports enthusiasts and those nostalgic for the Emerald Isle.

John Bull English Pub
103 South Fair Oaks Avenue
Pasadena   795-0240

This is an old theater converted into a very handsome saloon. It has a long bar, imported ales, very reasonable prices, live entertainment, ample seating, cordial management, fast bartenders, and good food. What else is there to say? Go.

A find neighborhood tavern, O'Mahony's draws people in search of good Irish coffee and cold, clean tap beer. There is music every night and O'Mahony's can take you for a climb up the Blue Ridge Mountains, whisper soft jazz into your ears, or shake you with pure folk rock. A good weeknight hit. Grace, the bartender, is one of the most efficient women in this trade.

O'Mahony's Irish Whip
2029 Main Street
Santa Monica   392–6621

Monahan's
110 Lake Street
Pasadena   449–4151

A beautiful-looking bar with beautiful waitresses who serve beautiful drinks at good prices, Monahan's is probably the most popular saloon in Los Angeles. It has been immortalized by cop/author Joseph Wambaugh who likes to bend his elbow here between shifts and chapters.

This is the gathering place for L.A.'s urban cowboys. Known especially for oater music, the club charges a cover, is usually crowded, does not have the world's greatest table service, but the Thursday night amateur contest is unrivaled in town for laughs and an occasional obscure bit of talent. (See Going Out, p. 189.)

Palomino
6907 Lankershim Boulevard
North Hollywood   765–9256

Des Reagan's
10618 Burbank Boulevard
Burbank   762–0707

Fortified with a long serviceable bar and ample seating, Des Reagan's is one of the best fun joints in the San Fernando Valley. Saturday night in Reagan's is bust out time with live Irish music and the dance floor clogged with members of four and five generations. The prices are very reasonable and service is excellent. Darts are available most nights and *fun* every night.

The Saloon
9390 Santa Monica Boulevard
Beverly Hills   273–7155

On Friday evenings there's standing room only in this New York style pub. Drinks average two dollars, but people drive from all over to frequent this Beverly Hills bar. Clientele includes all types, from three-piece suiters to the Levi's set. There's lots of "social interaction," to give it a name you could use with your mother. A fine restaurant serves lunch and dinner. (See Dining Out, p.122.)

Trani's is an Italian restaurant that has prospered in San Pedro for half a century. Bartender and owner Lou Trani is one of the most personable men in this noble trade. He can give the entire history of the infamous Beacon Street, once called the toughest street in the world, over one of his fantastic cappuccinos. Drinks here are plentiful and moderately priced. Sports talk is encouraged at the bar, with great debates over the superiority of either USC or UCLA athletes. A rare blend of longshoremen, professional athletes, businessmen, entertainment types, and sports nuts frequent the bar.

Trani's Majestic Cafe
145 West Sixth Street
San Pedro   831–0788

Good drink at good prices in a great bar that puts up the best soul food spread in L.A. Enjoy ham hocks, chitterlings, fried chicken, collard greens, and black-eyed peas at $4.50 for all you can "greeze." Tommy Tucker, the gentleman who runs this saloon, insists on well-behaved patrons and plenty of good fun. The Playroom is located across the street from a fine nightclub called the Parisian Room, and dinner and drinks at the Playroom and a live soul or jazz act across the street make for a spectacular evening out on the town.

Tommy Tucker's Playroom
4907 Washington Boulevard
Los Angeles   936–3720

This is easily the most beautiful saloon in Los Angeles. It has three—count 'em—bars located on a split tier design. Yesterday's attracts a mostly young UCLA college crowd, and live entertainment is provided nightly. Unlike most singles bars, Yesterday's charges no cover at the door. There is also no dress code requiring eighty-six dollar French jeans only. Prices are exceptionally fair by Westwood standards, and the margaritas and other fancy drinks are tops here. It's the best college haunt in town.

Yesterday's
1056A Westwood Boulevard
Westwood   479–4131

Lobby of the Pantages Theatre.

GOING OUT:

Concerts, Theaters, Discos, and Clubs.

By Kathleen Dautremont Olson,
NEW WEST

Night life in L.A. is sensuous and warm. Music is its pulse, film its fantasy. The quality is superlative; for movies and popular music, Los Angeles is the undisputed capital of the world. Other performing arts also flourish in our accepting environment. From the innovative to the traditional, from high art to playful diversion, entertainment fills our nights like the blue sky fills our days.

Live theater is one of L.A.'s fastest growing cultural resources. Some productions start here and go on to Broadway, and many touring Broadway shows play in the large theaters around town. With the Mark Taper Forum leading the way, there is a healthy dose of experimental drama. Theater people are especially proud that in recent years several former movie houses have changed to legitimate theater. Further proof of the vitality of theater in L.A.!

Being in the movie capital of the world has its advantages. Aside from unexpectedly lunching next to one of the stars or seeing someone famous on the street, you can see new films here appreciably before they are screened in other parts of the U.S. Revival houses show old and rare films, and several theaters specialize in foreign films.

L.A.'s rock clubs are legendary for showcasing the hottest new talent as well as established stars. This is the industry's—and many of the musicians'—home, so this is where performers come for the stimulus of competition and the reward of record contracts. Jazz offers some of the most exciting music in L.A. today. From bop to fusion, it is enjoyed at a growing number of clubs. And disco offers an exhilarating alternative to those who want to do more than just *listen* to music.

Symphony and dance concerts round out the entertainment scene, including local companies such as the Los Angeles Philharmonic and internationally famous artists on tour. Los Angeles has excellent facilities for these events, from the elegant Dorothy Chandler Pavilion and the Ambassador Auditorium to relaxed and casual outdoor amphitheatres.

THEATER

The Big Houses

Ahmanson Theatre
Music Center
135 North Grand Avenue
Downtown   972–7211

Located in the Music Center and seating 2,100, the Ahmanson produces four subscription plays beginning in October and ending in June each year. The season provides a mixture of traveling plays from Broadway, revivals of classic plays, and some world premières. Well-known actors from movies and TV often star in these productions. During the summer, touring musicals from Broadway take the stage. Hearing can be a problem from the upper balconies.

Mark Taper Forum
Music Center
135 North Grand Avenue
Downtown   972–7211

An intimate theater with excellent seating, the Mark Taper Forum holds about 750 and has a three-quarter round stage. Noted for producing new plays, the Mark Taper Forum/Laboratory is a place where writers, directors, and actors can work on original material and offer the public interesting developmental theater. In addition to new plays from the U.S. and abroad, the Taper produces classic revivals and some traveling shows. A festival of new plays is held every spring. Parking costs $2.50 in the underground Music Center garage. Lower-priced parking is available at the corner of Temple Street and Grand Avenue.

Huntington Hartford Theatre
1615 Vine Street
Hollywood   462-6666

A venerable old place built in 1927, the Huntington Hartford was purchased by the A. and P. market scion in 1954 when it was one of the few large theaters in town. Over the years it has hosted some of the best productions, both West Coast premières and Broadway shows, and it continues to present fine comedies, musicals, and dramas. Although the Hartford is no longer the most elegant theater around, it is the only one where you can still order a drink before the show and have it waiting for you at a reserved table at intermission. The tables are few so reserve one before the curtain. The Intermission Bar is on the mezzanine. Theater parking is available in nearby commercial lots.

In the Music Center of the County of Los Angeles, Mark Taper Forum (foreground) and the Ahmanson Theatre.

A gala opening at the Huntington Hartford Theatre.

Shubert Theatre
2020 Avenue of the Stars
Century City   553-9000

With red plush seats and ample leg room, the Shubert is one of the newest and most comfortable theaters in town, and it's a nice place to get dressed up for. Full-scale Broadway productions that run for months are the bill of fare here, and ticket prices are high. Park in the underground garage.

Pantages Theatre
6233 Hollywood Boulevard
Hollywood   469-7161

The Pantages is a wonderful old theater originally built as a movie house in 1930 by Alexander Pantages. In 1977 it changed to live drama. Done in opulent Art Deco style, the building itself is a work of art. Seating 2,288, it is the largest house in L.A., and touring Broadway productions are staged here. Four commercial parking lots are close by.

Variety Arts Center
940 South Figueroa Street
Downtown   623-9100

A sense of history enriches the Variety Arts Center. Built in 1924 to house the first women's club in L.A. (the Friday Morning Club), the structure is poured concrete and steel and was the first earthquake-safe building in the city. With beautiful old beamed ceilings, and stained-glass windows, it has been restored to its former elegance by Milt Larsen, who bought the building from the club in 1977. Now the home of the Society for the Preservation of the Variety Arts, it is a membership club that is also open to the public. The building holds an extensive collection of books, posters, playbills, and personal memorabilia of the vaudeville greats, including Ed Wynn, Eddie Cantor, W.C. Fields, and others. Carl Fleming runs the library where many of these treasures are kept, and he is a great source of knowledge on the vaudeville era.

The Variety Arts Theater on the main floor seats 1,158 and is the site for many productions. Old radio dramas, complete with a sound-effects man and commercial interruptions, are presented on Wednesdays at 8 p.m. in the Little Theatre on the third floor. Call ahead to make reservations for these popular productions. On the top floor is a lounge, with a lovely old bar and comfortable couches and chairs, and the Roof Garden for dining and dancing on Friday and Saturday nights. Dinner is served beginning at 6:30 p.m., and the band starts playing at 8:30. Valet parking is available.

Westwood Playhouse
10886 Le Conte Avenue
Westwood   477-2424

Across the street from UCLA, the Westwood has 498 seats, all good. The quality of the productions is quite dependable. The theater does both new and old plays, some of them moving here after successful runs elsewhere. During intermission drinks are served in the courtyard adjacent to Stratton's restaurant, which is a lovely place to dine before or after the show (see Dining Out p.130). Park in the Security Pacific Bank lot a few doors west or on the street.

Solari Theatre Ensemble
201 North Cañon Drive
Beverly Hills   550-7077

The Solari Theatre Ensemble is another medium-sized theater, like the Westwood Playhouse. It is named for actor-director-teacher Rudy Solari, who converted it from a movie house in 1975. The plays are of high quality and often star famous performers. Street parking is available.

Three other theaters, smaller than the Westwood and the Solari, don't have regular seasons, but do have good plays. They are the Coronet Theatre, 366 North La Cienega Boulevard, West Hollywood, 652-3191; the Las Palmas Theatre, 1642 North LasPalmas Avenue, Hollywood, 469-1981; and The Theatre, 817 North Hilldale Avenue, West Hollywood, 275-9872.

Coronet Theatre
Las Palmas Theatre
The Theatre

The Equity-Waiver Houses

In 1972 Actors Equity, the union for actors, agreed to permit its members to perform without pay in theaters with ninety-nine seats or fewer. Professional small theaters that operate under these conditions are known as equity-waiver houses. The plan has many benefits. New actors and directors striving for a break in TV or the movies get a chance to practice their craft and possibly be "discovered." Successful actors who have already appeared in TV or films can maintain their ties with the stage. For the theater industry the costs of mounting a production are greatly reduced, so there is more leeway to experiment with new plays. And the public gets to see live theater for about the price of a movie.

Carlo Maria Giulini, Music Director of the Los Angeles Philharmonic Orchestra.

These smaller theaters have adopted the "no frills" plan, for the most part. They are unpretentious, often just bare seats and a stage, with coffee served at intermission. Performances are usually Thursday through Sunday. Curtains are most often at 8 p.m., but may be at 7:30 or 8:30. Tickets are in the six dollar range. Since these theaters are small, it is best to make reservations. Some theaters require payment twenty-four to forty-eight hours in advance, since selling all the seats is crucial to their survival.

Not all professional theater companies are equally good. Following is a list of those that have maintained high quality over the past few years. That doesn't mean that every play these companies produce is a hit, or that one of the other ninety companies won't do something great. You can check small theater listings in the Sunday Calendar section of the Los Angeles *Times* before going to a play. The productions that are deemed especially good are listed in the Best Bets section at the beginning of the current theater listings, and there is a quote from the review.

Actors' Alley is a seventy-five-seat theater with a three-quarter round stage. Located in the San Fernando Valley, it does both new plays and classic revivals. Parking is available next to the theater.

Actors' Alley
4334 Van Nuys Boulevard
Sherman Oaks   986-7440

American Theatre Arts occupies a renovated old building, and is a charming theater that produces both revivals and new plays, with the emphasis on new material. One of the plays developed here was *The Gin Game*, by D.L. Coburn, which subsequently ran on Broadway and won the Pulitzer Prize. Parking is available behind the theater.

American Theatre Arts
6420 Hollywcod Boulevard
Hollywood   466-2462

The Company of Angels
5846 Waring Avenue
Hollywood   464-9634

The Company of Angels, one of the oldest, was founded by Richard Chamberlain, Leonard Nimoy, Vic Morrow, and others. The theater has fifty seats and does mostly established plays. Parking is available by the theater.

Globe Playhouse
1107 North Kings Road
West Hollywood   OK-GLOBE

The Globe is a one-half scale replica of the original Globe in Shakespeare's time. This company specializes in Shakespeare and is recognized by the Folger Shakespeare Library in Washington, D.C., as one of the top three professional Shakespeare companies in the country. There is limited parking next to the theater.

Los Angeles Actors' Theatre
1089 North Oxford Avenue
Hollywood   464-5500

The LAAT was founded by Ralph Waite, of "The Waltons." There are two stages, and the company is devoted to doing new plays, often with a political slant, some of which come out of their workshop. Parking is on the street.

Melrose Theatre
733 North Seward Avenue
Hollywood   465-1885

The Melrose is one of the oldest companies around; they put on revivals and some new plays. The theater seats sixty in a restored Art Deco building. Parking is on the street.

MET Theatre
649 North Poinsettia Place
Hollywood   937-8614

An intimate fifty-seat theater, the MET has received acclaim almost since its opening in 1973. The theater is committed to producing new plays, but also does some established ones. Parking is on the street or in lots on the corner of Fuller and Melrose.

Odyssey Theatre Ensemble
12111 Ohio Avenue
West Los Angeles   826-1626

Under the artistic direction of Ron Sossi, the Odyssey stages four or five plays each season in its two small theaters. The repertoire includes dramas, political plays and even light opera. This adventurous company is willing to try everything.

Theatre 40
241 South Moreno Drive
Beverly Hills   277-4221

Located on the Beverly Hills High School campus, Theatre 40 is a well-respected company that performs in an air-conditioned ninety-nine-seat theater. They specialize in classic plays, but occasionally do a new work. Park in the school lot.

MUSIC AND DANCE

The Concert Halls

Dorothy Chandler Pavilion
Music Center
135 North Grand Avenue
Downtown   972-7211

Dorothy Buffum Chandler is credited with almost singlehandedly creating the Music Center. The wife of former Los Angeles *Times* publisher Norman Chandler (the *Times* is now published by their son Otis), she was able to unite disparate elements in the city's social structure and get them to contribute the money necessary to build the cultural complex. The largest building bears her name.

The Dorothy Chandler Pavilion is probably the most elegant public place in Los Angeles proper. It faces the Mark Taper Forum across a reflecting pool. With marble walls and gleaming gold-and-white mosaic columns in the mirrored lobby, and with exquisite crystal chandeliers throughout, the building is magnificent. The pavilion is

the winter home of the Los Angeles Philharmonic, whose season runs from November to April. The Los Angeles Civic Light Opera sponsors productions here during the remaining six months. Other concerts, usually of the finest quality, are also booked. The New York City Opera comes here in November for about six weeks, and the American Ballet Theatre visits in February. Seating 3,197, the Chandler is so large that a single performer on stage looks minute from the last rows of the balcony. Seats in the orchestra or the Founders Circle are best. Parking is available in the underground Music Center garage. (See Tours, p. 104 .)

The Ambassador Auditorium is part of Ambassador College, which is owned and operated by the Worldwide Church of God. The Ambassador rivals the Dorothy Chandler in elegance and in the quality of its performers. Like the Chandler, the Ambassador is bordered by reflecting pools. It was built with materials from all over the world. Baccarat candelabra from France and a crystal chandelier from West Germany grace the grand lobby, and a beautiful purple and gold carpet from Hong Kong covers the foyer, in an abstract design. The regal purple and gold motif is carried over into the carpet and seats of the auditorium itself.

Renowned artists in music and dance from all over the world perform here. The season runs from September to May. Sparkling apple juice and coffee are available during intermission out on the

Ambassador Auditorium
300 West Green Street
Pasadena   577-5511

veranda (weather permitting). There is parking on the streets around the auditorium and free parking in the underground parking structure (enter on St. John Avenue).

Terrace Theater
300 East Ocean Boulevard
Long Beach   436-3661

Part of the Long Beach Convention and Entertainment Center, along with the Center Theatre and the Long Beach Arena, the Terrace is the home of the Long Beach Symphony, whose season runs from September through June. Guest artists performing classical and popular music are also booked at the Terrace. Plenty of parking is available around the Convention Center and in the adjacent parking structure.

Shrine Auditorium
665 West Jefferson Boulevard
Downtown   749-5123

The Shrine has the largest stage west of the Mississippi and seats 6,500. Built in 1926, it is like an aging dowager. Moorish arches at the entrance, a beautiful ceiling, and now-musty red plush seats bear witness to her former splendor. Used primarily for touring companies of international note, the Shrine has hosted the Bolshoi Ballet, the Grand Kabuki Theater of Japan, the Performing Arts Company of the People's Republic of China, and the Royal Ballet of London, to name a few. Several parking lots are in the vicinity.

Wilshire Ebell Theatre
4401 West Eighth Street
Mid-Wilshire   939-1128

The Wilshire Ebell Theatre is a lovely older facility without a bad seat in the house. Its Spanish-influenced architecture and magnificent wood paneling are a delight after the stainless steel and chrome that we're subjected to in modern buildings. In addition to musical concerts, the Ebell also hosts the Los Angeles Ballet. This young but promising company was formed six years ago by John Clifford, then a principal dancer with Balanchine's New York City Ballet. The company is presently having its first subscription series.

Royce Hall
Beckman Auditorium

In addition to the theaters listed above, professional performances in classical and popular music and dance are presented at UCLA's Royce Hall in Westwood, 825-2953, and at California Institute of Technology, otherwise known as Caltech, Beckman Auditorium, in Pasadena, 793-7043.

The Outdoor Amphitheatres

One thing to remember about Southern California nights is that the temperature drops sharply. You may arrive at these outdoor events in shirtsleeves, but you'll go home shivering so bring a heavy sweater, coat, or blanket.

Hollywood Bowl
2301 Highland Avenue
Hollywood   87-MUSIC

Nestled in the Hollywood Hills on a site that forms a natural amphitheatre, the Hollywood Bowl is the summer home of the Los Angeles Philharmonic Orchestra, along with visiting conductors and guest artists. Some concerts include audio-visual performances such as Tchaikovsky's *1812* Overture, with fireworks and cannon salute. There are also pops nights on the schedule. A pre-season Fourth of July celebration, including fireworks, is always held. The

Hollywood Bowl.

season runs from July through September. Concerts begin around 8:30 p.m., and it's fun to take a picnic supper and dine on a blanket in the beautiful gardens surrounding the bowl. Since this is a popular way to begin the evening, come between 6 and 6:30 p.m. to get a spot. If you happen to have box seats, you can reserve your own little table and dine in the box. It is not uncommon to see box-holders using china, crystal, and silver utensils for their picnics, and even silver candelabra! The restaurant on the grounds serves a buffet, but make reservations beforehand through the box office. Incidentally, you may need the picnic blanket to pad the wooden benches in the amphitheatre, or you can rent cushions for that purpose on the premises. The higher seats at the bowl afford a view of the surrounding hills, but the sound is better close up.

There are three ways to approach parking. You can park in one of the free park-and-ride lots, located in different areas of the city, and take a bus to and from the bowl for fifty cents each way. Or you can park in one of the lots in North Hollywood with shuttle service to the bowl. For further information about these alternatives, call the box office. You can also park in one of the lots at the site. It takes about twenty or thirty minutes to get out of the parking lot after the concert, which is surprisingly quick, considering the number of people accommodated.

The Greek Theatre is in Griffith Park, which is also a nice place to picnic before a concert. The Greek hosts a potpourri of dance, opera, classical, and popular music. The Joffrey Ballet, the D'Oyly Carte Opera, and singers from Shaun Cassidy to Perry Como have performed here in the past few years. The sound is best in the

Greek Theatre
2700 North Vermont Avenue
Hollywood   660-8400

reserved seating section. If you end up in the general admission section, it may be possible to move down to the reserved section provided there are empty seats after the concert begins. Concerts start around 8 p.m. Parking is no problem, and the exit is relatively speedy.

Universal Amphitheatre
Universal Studios Lot
Universal City   980-9421

The Universal Amphitheatre is a great place to see rock and popular singers and comedians. The amphitheater is laid out in a fan shape and all seats are within 150 feet of the stage. Frank Sinatra, Linda Ronstadt, Donna Summer, Boz Scaggs, and Steve Martin represent the kind of talent booked here. The problem for non-residents is that tickets are sold by mail weeks in advance, and it can be difficult to get tickets the week of the performance. Concerts usually begin at 8:15 p.m. Parking is on the premises.

NIGHTCLUBS

Most clubs operate on the cover and minimum system. Cover charges range from $2.50 to upwards of $9.00, depending on the talent. Weekends are often higher, but the best talent is booked then. Right now, the average cover charge is $5.00, and there is usually a two-drink minimum.

Comedy

Mitzi Shore opened the Comedy Store as a workshop for aspiring comedians, a place where they could practice their routines before live audiences and really learn the craft. Entertainers at all levels of expertise perform here, and visiting the Comedy Store can be a painful experience—your sides ache from laughing so hard. The club has three rooms: The Main Room is the largest and has the best talent, sometimes big-name acts; the Original Comedy Store seats 230; the Belly Room is small and intimate and exclusively for female entertainers. With this set-up, there is an audience size to fit any comedian's needs!

Shows are nightly, beginning around 8:30 p.m. Monday is Potluck Night when anyone can go onstage by signing up before 7 p.m. (on Mondays only, the show begins at 8 p.m.) Improvisational comedy groups and stand-up comedians entertain during the week. The best entertainment is on weekends, when there is less of a workshop atmosphere and comedians who are going to be appearing in Vegas or on national TV take the stage to warm up their acts. There is a two-drink minimum, and you must be twenty-one to be admitted. For valet parking, pull into the hotel driveway on the east side of the club.

Comedy Store
8433 West Sunset Boulevard
West Hollywood   656-6225

Comedy Store West
1621 Westwood Boulevard
Westwood   477-4751

Another branch, the Comedy Store West, has been opened in Westwood. All ages are welcome here, and beer and wine are the only alcoholic beverages served.

New Ice House
24 North Mentor Avenue
Pasadena   449-4053

During the twenties, the Ice House was actually a cold-storage place that sold ice. However, in the fifties it was turned into a first-rate comedy and music establishment that hosted the likes of Steve Martin and Lily Tomlin. Inside, rough pine walls and the exposed brick of the original buiding create a cozy setting for the entertainment. The largest room, with lots of small tables for four crowded around the stage, is devoted to comedy and magic. Usually two comedians and one magician entertain and the acts change every week. The Music Cabaret is like a little theater, with cushioned fold-down seats and attached tables for refreshments. There are different acts each night, everything from jazz to folk to country to rock. Shows in both rooms run Wednesday through Sunday, beginning at 8:30 p.m. In the dining area, a performing magician circulates among the tables. The menu is straightforward all-American, including hamburgers, spaghetti, snacks, and desserts. Beer and wine are the only alcohol served. Parking is near the entrance of the Ice House, via the alley, as well as in the J.C. Penney parking lot across Mentor.

Improvisation
8162 Melrose Avenue
West Hollywood   449-4053

The Improvisation is another fine comedy showcase. Budd Friedman is the owner and master of ceremonies, and he does a great job of making the audience feel at home, as well as entertaining them with his own jokes. The Improv was opened to give theater people a place to perform, and big names, such as Bette Midler, Lily Tomlin, Richard Pryor, and Christopher Plummer, show up from time to time. Interestingly, when this happens, the cover charge is not raised. And since these performers just pop in, usually on a Friday or Saturday, you may be lucky enough to see one of them on a night when you're there.

A week at the Improv goes something like this: Sunday is audition night; Monday is Improv at the Improv—improvisational comedy groups; Tuesday and Wednesday are for aspiring comics and new singers and songwriters; stand-up comedians take the stage on Thursday. The best talent is booked on Friday and Saturday. A word to the wise: If you sit in the front seats, you're part of the show! Call for reservations, especially on weekends. Parking is on the street.

Off the Wall
1204 North Fairfax Avenue
West Hollywood   655-0226

Off the Wall is the brilliant improvisational comedy troupe that spawned Robin Williams, of ''Mork and Mindy'' fame. The eight members, some of whom are as gifted as Williams, use audience suggestions to create zany sketches. Being made up on the spot, this brand of comedy is both unexpected and exciting. Background piano music is immensely successful in setting the tone for each scene, and Off the Wall can turn even the most mundane suggestions into hilarious skits. The humor gets wilder as the evening goes on; the troupe is really hopping in the second half of the show.

There's nothing fancy about the location. The show takes place in a rented ballet studio that holds about ninety-nine folding chairs. Nonalcoholic drinks and snacks are served during the short intermission, and actors mingle with the audience. Shows are on Friday and Saturday at 8:30 p.m.; doors open at 8 p.m. Because of limited seating, it is advisable to make reservations early in the week. Parking is in the adjoining lot.

Jazz

Acts change frequently at the jazz clubs. To find out who's appearing, consult the What's New section of *New West* magazine. Two fairly new publications, the *L.A. Weekly* and the *Reader*, also carry current listings. Many clubs advertise their line-ups in the music section of the Los Angeles *Times* Sunday Calendar.

The Baked Potato is a popular and well-thought-of place for jazz. Its charm lies in its intimacy—almost a living-room atmosphere—with crowded-together tables facing the stage. About a third of the audience is wearing Baked Potato shirts or jackets, which are for sale on the premises. It's definitely an insiders' club. The name comes from the menu, which features huge baked potatoes served with a choice of eighteen different stuffings, ranging in price from $2.50 to $4.95. Beware of rude waitresses here. The house band, Don Randi and Quest, plays Wednesday through Saturday, and there are guest bands the other nights of the week. The music is quite loud, considering the size of the room. Shows begin at 10 p.m. There is a small parking lot at the back of the club, and street parking.

Baked Potato
3787 Cahuenga Boulevard West
North Hollywood   980-1615

Concerts by the Sea
100 Fisherman's Wharf
Redondo Beach   379-4998

Concerts by the Sea is part of a two-level cluster of shops and restaurants along the beach. Laid out like a little theater five rows deep, this club is the best-suited of all for listening. With black leather seats, red carpeting, and fancy chandeliers, it is also one of the most elegant. However, since this is a popular place, you may find standing room only. Top jazz musicians, such as Ahmad Jamal, Woody Shaw, Cal Tjader, and Milt Jackson, are the rule here. There are shows Thursday through Sunday, with three sets per night, beginning at 9 p.m. (doors open at 8:15 p.m.). Thursday is half-price admission night. No one under twenty-one is admitted. There is plenty of parking in the underground garage at the pier.

Donte's
4269 Lankershim Boulevard
North Hollywood   769-1566

If you like good jazz and good Italian food, you'll love Donte's. Red and black decor, with murals of jazz greats such as Dizzy Gillespie and Louis Armstrong, and the charisma of owner Carey La Brett create a mellow setting for listening and dining. With the yummy, garlicky smells emanating from the kitchen, you'll be hard-pressed to resist the food. However on weekends the kitchen gets very busy around 9 p.m., so it's advisable to come for dinner before 8 p.m. The room is relatively small, but not as crowded as some nightclubs, with tables for dining and some just for listening, as well as seats at the bar. Donte's hosts all kinds of jazz, with bop and crossover played frequently. You'll find seasoned talent as well as new young musicians (both Joe Pass and Chuck Mangione got started here). Well-known musicians and singers often turn up in the audience. Shows begin around 9:30 p.m., Monday through Saturday. Parking is on the street.

Lighthouse
30 Pier Avenue
Hermosa Beach   372-6911

The Lighthouse bills itself as a "jazz club and waterfront dive," and that, ladies and gentlemen, is exactly what it is. The decor is early fifties tacky, but the Lighthouse is firmly entrenched on the L.A. jazz scene because it books some of the best talent around—Kenny Burrell, John Lee Hooker, Horace Silver, and others. There are three sets each night at 9:15, 11, and 12:30. The Lighthouse is usually closed on Monday. Park on the street or in a twenty-four-hour metered parking lot behind the buildings across the street.

Parisian Room
4960 West Washington Boulevard
Los Angeles   936-8704

In 1978 Dizzy Gillespie called owner Ernest France to ask to be released from his contract to perform at the Parisian Room—it seems he was invited to appear at the White House on the same night. The Parisian Room has been around since 1937 when it was one of the first drive-in restaurants in L.A. Now it is a hang-out for jazz musicians, and some of the greats play here—Joe Williams, Ahmad Jamal, Yusef Lateef, and Hugh Masakela, in addition to Gillespie. Nightly shows get started around 9:30 p.m., with a showcase for up-and-coming musicians on Mondays. Patrons must be twenty-one. Plenty of parking is available adjacent to the club.

Rock

Rock clubs have some things in common: They are dark, smoky, and have a wanton atmosphere, possibly because, as researchers have recently discovered, rock music, with its incessant bass beat, stimulates the sex organs. People who hang out in these places are quite young, often teenagers. They usually wear jeans or other casual garb, the funkier the better.

Cover charges vary with the quality of the talent at most clubs, and seating is on a first-come basis. It is not unusual to stand in line for as long as an hour or even longer on weekends. During the week, when space permits, there is sometimes dancing at these clubs, but they are primarily showcases for original rock. To see who's appearing in the rock clubs, consult listings in *New West* magazine, the *L.A. Weekly*, or the *Reader*. Most of these clubs advertise upcoming performances in the music section of the Los Angeles *Times* Sunday Calendar.

The Roxy is the hottest club in L.A. for rock stars. It has a great sound system, and record companies use the club to showcase their talent. So musicians who are bringing out a new album often appear here to publicize the event. But the Roxy is not exclusively for rock—pop music and comedy are sometimes on the bill. With olive walls and Art Deco touches, the Roxy seats 500. It attracts a slightly older, more sophisticated crowd than the other rock clubs. The waitresses are surprisingly nice, and there's even valet parking. Shows are at 9 and 11:30 p.m., and tickets are sold in advance at the box office. For big-name acts, lines form hours ahead of time to get into the show.

Roxy
9009 West Sunset Boulevard
West Hollywood   878-2222

The Starwood is a mainstream rock club that is a haven for the teenage crowd. (If you are over twenty-five and come in here wearing a business suit, you will look like a dirty old man!) On weekends there are scores of teenagers hanging out outside the club. Inside the Starwood are two large rooms—one for disco dancing and one for listening to live rock bands. Lots of kids stand in front of the stage to hear the bands, but there are also tables with a two-drink minimum. Most of the tables are occupied by the "older" folks—aged twenty-one to thirty. The VIP Lounge on the second floor overlooking the stage is by invitation only—primarily for record industry people.

Starwood
8151 Santa Monica Boulevard
West Hollywood   656-2200

The Starwood books local talent and sometimes well-known bands. There is no age limit here and shows take place nightly at 8:45 and 11:30 p.m. The cover charge admits you to both the disco and the showcase area. If you just want to dance, come on a night when a lesser-known band is playing, to avoid paying a high cover charge. Street parking is a problem.

If you're looking for something other than the black walls and low lights founds in most rock clubs, try the Sweetwater. The walls are natural wood paneled and adorned with Indian weavings. Because of a twenty-one minimum age, the crowd is slightly older, although most patrons are in their early twenties. The Sweetwater hosts up-and-coming rock bands, country-western performers, and occa-

Sweetwater
264 North Harbor Drive
Redondo Beach   372-0445

sionally big-name talent. On Thursdays there's dancing to music by the Twisters, who play songs by the Beatles and the Stones, as well as their own compositions. Shows begin at 9 p.m. The only alcohol available is beer and wine. There is parking in the lot by the club.

Troubadour
9081 Santa Monica Boulevard
West Hollywood 276-6168

Doug Weston hosted the likes of Linda Ronstadt, Gordon Lightfoot, the Eagles, and Jackson Browne in the early seventies when they were on their way up. His club, the Troubadour, has a reputation for launching new talent. The showroom is a big music barn—high ceilings and exposed rafters, with long plank tables around the stage, and a loft with church-pew seats. The first row in the loft is an excellent place to sit, but come early to get the best seats. Monday is Hoot Night, a showcase for the aspiring. There are two or three acts the other nights of the week, with the best talent booked on weekends. Shows begin at 9 p.m., and tickets go on sale beforehand. Street parking is a problem.

Whisky a Go Go
8091 West Sunset Boulevard
West Hollywood 652-4202

If you go to the Whisky a Go Go, especially on a Friday or Saturday night, expect to stand on line for up to an hour. It's not as bad as it sounds, provided the weather is fine, because just watching the people on Sunset Strip is a show of its own. The Whisky hosts mostly original rock groups, and the local bands have groupies who dress like their rock heroes to come to the concerts. The people in line with you will tell you something about the entertainment! Inside, the Whisky has the *de rigueur* black walls found in most clubs. "Groundlings" can stand in front of the stage, and there are tables seating four or more. Upstairs there's a bar and tables for two on a balcony overlooking the stage. This is the best place to sit. Shows are at 9 and 11:30 p.m. nightly. Tickets are available through Ticketron or at the Whisky office. Parking is a nightmare, especially on weekends. Park on the street and come early to stand in line for the best seats.

Because of altercations between police and rock fans at a concert in 1975, rock stars have shied away from doing big concerts inside L.A. city limits. So the two best places to see rock bands, other than in the clubs, are the Santa Monica Civic Auditorium and the Forum in Inglewood, both outside of L.A. proper.

Santa Monica Civic Auditorium
Pico Boulevard and Main Street
Santa Monica 393-9961

The Santa Monica Civic has good sound, but sometimes they take out the seats and sell standing room at general admission prices. This gets both crowded and tiresome after standing for a while. Otherwise, there are rows of old-fashioned fold-down wooden seats at graduated prices.

Forum
Manchester Boulevard and
Prairie Avenue
Inglewood 673-1300

The Forum is also a site for sports events—the Lakers and the Kings play here. The quality of sound depends on the bands themselves and how well their equipment is suited to conditions in the Forum. But some of the "biggies" play here, including Linda Ronstadt and Rod Stewart.

Other Music

The Backlot at Studio One seems classier than most nightclubs. Maybe it's because of the white tablecloths, or the competent waiters, or the congenial crowd. You can see well from all the seats, which are laid out on two levels facing the stage. The Backlot usually has nationally known entertainers. Phyllis Diller, Carmen McRae, and Melba Moore have all recently appeared here. Shows are at 9:30 and 11 p.m., but tend to get started a little late. The cover charge varies with the talent, and acts are usually booked for a week. Dinner is served from 7:30 to 9 p.m., with piano music to dine by. There are six entrées on the menu, including fish, chicken, steak, and pork, priced from $7.50 to $10.50. The Backlot has valet parking.

Backlot
657 North Robertson Boulevard
West Hollywood   659-0472

Bla Bla Cafe
12446 Ventura Boulevard
Studio City   769-7874

The Bla Bla Cafe is a friendly little place that serves good American food and offers all kinds of entertainment, from comedy to music to improvisational theater to magic. Owner Albie Hora opened the Bla Bla to give performers a chance to work at something other than a one-week gig, and acts change nightly here. Most of the talent is booked from auditions, which are held on Sundays from noon to 6 p.m., so the Bla Bla is a good place to see new performers (Al Jarreau is one who started out here). Shows are at 9 and 11 p.m.

The menu is surprisingly large, with breakfast served until 4 a.m. on weekends. There are the usual sandwiches and burgers, and some fun foods, like potato skins and sour cream (delicious) and a spinach fritata. The service is good, and Albie is a congenial host. Beer and wine are the only alcoholic drinks. Since the Bla Bla is relatively small, reservations are advised, especially on weekends. Call on the day of the show to confirm. There's no problem with street parking.

F. Scott's
25 Windward Avenue
Venice   396-7444

F. Scott's is in the heart of Venice, the area built at the turn of the century to be a facsimile of the Italian city. (See Tours, p.115 , and Beaches, p.297 .) What used to be the Saint Charles Hotel, with arched, Venetian-style portals, now houses this delightful little nightclub. Owner Barry Levich has installed a mirrored Art Deco bar, and an original Venice gondola hangs on the wall. Ceiling fans and exposed brick walls complete the setting Levich calls "classic Berlin cabaret." The entertainment is quite good—songs from the thirties and forties and Broadway show tunes, with Levich sitting in now and then to play cafe-society piano. The entertainers tend to be gifted and versatile young people on their way to the top. Shows begin at 9 p.m. and F. Scott's is open Wednesday through Sunday. The audience sits at small, crowded tables, and the drink specialties are creamy concoctions with names like "Tender Is the Night" and "The Great Gatsby." The clientele is casually sophisticated (translation: don't wear jeans, but you don't need a tie). Park across the street.

Mayfair Music Hall
214 Santa Monica Boulevard
Santa Monica   451-0621

Furnished in baroque Victorian style, with red plush seats, ornate gilt light fixtures, and dark wood paneling, the Mayfair Music Hall re-creates the atmosphere of its turn-of-the-century English counterparts. The entertainment is a mixture of slapstick, comic songs, and stand-up comedy, enhanced by evocative period costumes. The goings-on are laced with audience participation, cat-calls, and sing-alongs, and it gets to be a rowdy evening. Mousie Garner, who was one of the Three Stooges and a member of the late Spike Jones's band, is a cast regular. The actors mingle with the guests after the show around the incredible Circle Bar in the lobby. Shows are at 8:30 p.m. on Wednesday, Thursday, and Sunday, and at 8 and 10 p.m. on Friday and Saturday.

For openers there is the Underground Restaurant, which, oddly enough, is upstairs on the second floor. The menu wisely sticks to six entrées: three beef dishes, including roast beef and Yorkshire pudding, Cornish hen, catch of the day, and a daily special. Dinner is served from 6 p.m. Sandwiches, chili, and English chips are available in the Grub Pub on the main floor. There is ample parking in nearby public lots.

McCabe's
3101 Pico Boulevard
Santa Monica   828-4497

Going to McCabe's is like taking a trip back to the sixties. You will find men with long hair in jeans and plaid shirts, and women wearing jeans and embroidered peasant blouses or long dresses. And McCabe's offers sixties entertainment—some of the best folk music in L.A. McCabe's is also a guitar shop and hundreds of beautiful and expensive instruments hang on the walls. The light reflecting off them gives a golden glow to the surroundings and makes it seem even more warm and homey. The auditorium holds about 200 folding chairs. There are usually two acts on the bill, with homemade cakes and tea or coffee at intermission. Shows are at 8 and 10:30 p.m. on Friday and Saturday, and sometimes at 7:30 p.m. on Sunday. Tickets go on sale two weeks before each concert, or they can be purchased at the door, if they're not sold out. It's safer to pick them up beforehand at the guitar shop. Parking on the surrounding streets is a problem. Best bet is to come early.

If you're looking for those good old country comforts, by all means visit the Palomino. This is hands down the best place for country music in greater L.A. Some of the performers who appear here are on the Grand Ol' Opry circuit, and many, like Emmylou Harris and Jerry Lee Lewis, are successful recording artists. The club is filled, and on weekends *packed*, with folks in jeans and cowboy shirts who sing along and applaud whatever they like during the show. There is a patio to accommodate the overflow, but there are no speakers outside. Come early to get a seat indoors, so you can really hear the music.

Palomino
6907 Lankershim Boulevard
North Hollywood   765-9256

Dinner is served from 6 p.m. Steak and lobster are the house specialties. However, the kitchen gets swamped on full-house nights, and under those conditions, the food is mediocre. The waitresses are especially nice and helpful. Shows are nightly at 8 and 11 p.m., with amateur night on Thursday and a $100 prize for the winner. There is parking on the premises. (See Where to Drink, p. 167.)

Sur la Mer is elegant, sophisticated, and very big-city in atmosphere. The decor is contemporary chic—stainless-steel framed chairs with upholstered seats in bright red and blue, plush carpeting, white tablecloths, and a panoramic view of the marina. The staff is enthusiastic in presenting a French dining-cabaret atmosphere. Cabaret as a genre works very well as dinner entertainment, and Sur la Mer specializes in show tunes, the kind that we all want to hum along with. A hydraulic stage raises the three or four singers in the revue so that they can be seen by people on both levels of the two-tiered restaurant. There are two acts to each show, presented at one-hour intervals from 7:30 p.m. Revues change every month, and some are better than others.

Sur la Mer
4351 Admiralty Way
Marina del Rey   822-7000

The menu offers French-Continental entrées and there is a fine but limited wine list. Dinner for two costs about fifty dollars. Dinner is served from 6 p.m. with seating until 10:30 p.m. Not all tables have a view of the stage. Since the bar stays open until 1 a.m., this is a good place to stop at the end of the evening. The last act is at midnight, and you can see the show for the price of a drink. Valet parking is available.

Discos

There are lots of bars with dance floors in L.A., but, strictly speaking, they are not discos. A disco is an establishment whose *raison d'être* is dancing. In addition to records, "discs," they also have light shows using strobes and revolving and flashing colors to add atmosphere. And often the dancers have a higher-than-average level of expertise. Surprisingly, discos are quite dressy. Women wear bare disco dresses or pants that fit like a second skin, in lamé, satin, or leather. Men sport three-piece disco suits with open-collared shirts, although slacks, an open shirt, and a jacket are acceptable. At some discos even jeans are okay. The dance floor gets very hot, so be sure to dress lightly. Discos are most crowded on weekends, and cover charges are usually higher, averaging four to five dollars. On these nights, many discos stay open until four or five in the morning, and it's a fun way to end a night on the town.

Bootleggers
11637 West Pico Boulevard
West Los Angeles   478-7555

Bootleggers is a semiprivate club open to nonmembers as space permits. The circular dance floor is on the small side and is flanked by tables for two. There is a semicircular lounge separated from the dance area by a glass wall that offers respite from the loud music without obstructing the view. Bootleggers is open until 5 a.m. on weekends, and you must be twenty-one to be admitted. Dance lessons are given on Monday and Tuesday. There is parking in the adjacent lot or on the street.

Chippendales
3739 Overland Avenue
West Los Angeles   838-0173

Chippendales has a living-room atmosphere, with upholstered couches and chairs, a fireplace, and even a few backgammon tables. The dance floor is not terribly large, but the dancers are adept. The crowd is dressier than at some other places; no jeans or T-shirts are allowed. On the list of out-of-the-ordinary events here are a dance contest every Monday night, dance lessons Monday through Wednesday, and male dancers who entertain for women only on Wednesday, Friday, Saturday, and Sunday evenings until 10 p.m.—in other words, a skin show for the ladies. Chippendales is open until 4 a.m. on weekends and is for patrons twenty-one and older. Valet parking is available.

Circus Disco
6648 Lexington Avenue
Hollywood   462-1291

Circus Disco is decorated with circus posters and is like a three-ring circus in its own right. Anyone over twenty-one is welcome and the crowd ranges from campy to gay. Jeans, disco outfits, and some outrageous clothing are seen here. The dance floor is huge, hot, and crowded; the music is ear-splitting and the dancers some of the best. There are two long bars at either end of the dance floor and standing room only along the sides. Circus mirrors, the kind that distort the image, flank the entrance. The club is open until 4 a.m. on weekends, and there is parking in the adjacent lot or on the street.

Dillon's is near the UCLA campus, and college students make up the greater part of the clientele. You enter at the back by the parking lot and ride up to one of the three dance floors in a brass elevator. The decor throughout is très chic—a blend of contemporary furniture, mirrors, and lights. However, the dance floors are small, hot, and crowded. One of the floors is reserved for those twenty-one and older, the others are open to anyone over eighteen. There is live music on one floor and disco music on the others. Dillon's is open until 2 a.m. and has the most expensive cover charge, six dollars on Saturdays.

Dillon's Westwood Village
1081 Gayley Avenue
Westwood   478-5088

Moody's is a classy dance hall done in purples and blues. The disco is downstairs. A large dance floor and a nice light show complement the serious dancers. The crowd, in their twenties, shows up in disco dresses, satin jeans, or disco suits. There is a restaurant serving burgers, omelets, and salads on the ground floor, and a comfortable lounge on the third level completely removed from the noise downstairs. Moody's is open to those twenty-one and older, until 4 a.m. on weekends. Saturday is the biggest night, and it gets crowded around 11 p.m. Park in the adjacent lot, on the street, or in several public lots nearby.

Moody's
321 Santa Monica Boulevard
Santa Monica   451-5003

Studio One is the oldest disco in the city. Like the Circus, it has a huge dance floor. It also features nonstop earsplitting music and a light show. The crowd is almost exclusively gay men, and the dance floor is always hot and crowded. No one under twenty-one and no one wearing open-toed shoes are admitted. Dancing is nightly from 9 p.m. until 2 a.m. Parking is available in the adjacent lot or on the street.

Studio One
652 North Lapeer Drive
West Hollywood   659-0471

Los Angeles County Museum of Art. "Monument to Balzac" by Rodin at the entrance.

MUSEUMS AND GALLERIES:

Including the Norton Simon, the Museum of Natural History, the Los Angeles County Museum of Art, the Huntington Gallery, the Getty Museum, and Galleries.

By Michael Kurcfeld, NEW WEST
And Anne Gilbar, LOS ANGELES MAGAZINE

André Malraux said that art museums were the cathedrals of America. It is certainly true that large cities invest a great amount of effort and pride in their museums, often hiring the finest architects to design grand edifices for their collections and exhibitions. Los Angeles is no exception. Blessed with a number of art-loving philanthropists who went so far as to put real estate where their hearts were, Los Angeles can boast a fair selection of privately and publicly operated cathedrals.

The architecture runs the gamut from baroque to quasi-Chinese to Graeco-Roman to contemporary, with hybrid variations in between that reflect Angelenos' taste for crossbred styles. The collections of art, artifacts, and scientific curios may not always be the most extensive in the world, but they are usually commendably representative. It is important to view them as part of a rapidly growing legacy to future generations. As this is written, new wings are being planned for the Huntington Galleries, the Museum of Science and Industry, and the Los Angeles County Museum of Art. A local group of art patrons have organized to create an altogether independent contemporary art museum, perhaps along the lines of the Whitney in New York.

Whether or not a museum offers lavish auxiliary programs, such as LACMA's film revival series and packaged overseas tours, is beside the point. If you spend an afternoon at any of the following places, alone as easily as with companions, you should come away edified and eye-delighted.

Barnsdall Municipal Art Gallery
4804 Hollywood Boulevard
Hollywood   660-2200

Located in hilltop Barnsdall Park next to Frank Lloyd Wright's Hollyhock House, Barnsdall Municipal Art Gallery is a handsome exhibition space for the work of Los Angeles artists of every persuasion. Director Josine Ianco-Starrels has found the perfect solution to the problem of exhibiting contemporary non-celebrity art to a general audience: theme shows. She gives uncluttered rationale to a diverse series of artists by finding common threads in their work that anyone can respond to. Recent shows have focused on xerography, craft patterns reflected in non-craft artworks, portraits, social criticism, and environmental issues. There are also frequent retrospectives highlighting the work of distinguished local artists like Helen Lundeberg and Matsumi Kanemitsu.

The Gallery Theatre in Barnsdall Park.

The annual Magical Mystery Tour, held at Christmas, is a collage of fun and unusual artworks by any number of artists. A separate North Gallery features one- and two-person shows of generally very deserving young talents.

Docents at the Barnsdall Art Gallery do a fine job of getting visitors involved in the art that confronts them, asking questions and coaxing reactions.

California State Museum of Science and Industry
700 State Drive
Los Angeles   749-0101

The Museum of Science and Industry is a sprawling, ever-changing educational toy, a combination of Aristotle and P. T. Barnum. Next to the Smithsonian Institution, it's the largest museum of its kind in the country. Built in 1912 and vastly remodeled in 1951, it operates rigorously on the participation principle. Visitors are exhorted to push buttons, pull levers, pick up telephone receivers and, above all, have fun. It is dedicated to the proposition that education needn't be painful, and it is a measure of its success that more than three million people come through annually, most of the younger visitors squealing with delight.

Exhibits are of inconsistent quality, if only because newer ones can't help but be more sophisticated. Those sponsored by private industry are mostly excellent, since they are created by top designers and educators. IBM, for instance, commissioned Charles Eames to mastermind its superb Mathematica exhibit, our favorite. You don't have to be a kid to marvel at the smart graphics and ingenious apparatuses that illustrate complex theories of celestial mechanics, multiplication, probability, topology, minimal surfaces, and everything else that might otherwise be dull and inaccessible. A sea of quotations by history's great mathematical minds plus vivid timelines of scientific discovery complete this magical classroom.

Another of the museum's fourteen permanent exhibition halls features General Motors' The Turning Wheel display. In clear, colorful models, charts, exposed engines, and visitor-operated devices the evolution and complex workings of the automobile are revealed. Particularly timely are the visual dissections of different energy systems: steam, electric, internal combustion, and so on. Kids become spellbound by the fully animated cutaway Chevrolet chassis showing how power flows through the car.

Other highlights include a 240-foot dioramic model railroad complex, a Pacific Telephone exhibit on telecommunications, a tic-tac-toe-playing computer, a mockup of an air traffic control tower which simulates the cockpit view of a landing plane, a Metropolitan Water District exhibit on (you guessed it) water, and a fantastic push-button wonderland on Electricity that cost Southern California Edison over $1 million. In the Animal Husbandry Hall, a giant see-through incubator hatches 150 chicks daily.

Adjacent to the main building is the sleek new Hall of Health, a museum unto its own. It is a first-class showcase of the mysteries of the human body, conceived with state-of-the-art visual aids that are lucid and riveting. Circulatory Man is an abstract electronic figure with pulsing florescent veins and arteries, surrounded by models of the body's organs and a circular console of telephone hookups. Visitors use these to learn about all aspects of the circulatory system, at one point listening to their own heartbeat. Other attractions include Neuroman, an eight-foot push-button bundle of nerves; Transparent Woman, a translucent mechanical gal who lights up her vital organs and explains their functions; a multimedia presentation inveighing against Drugs and Narcotics in sober, documented terms; The Five Senses; and, for those faced with telling their offspring about the facts of life, a no-nonsense exhibit on Human Reproduction. The eqully imaginative Dental exhibition hall is right next door.

"Neuroman"—a highlight of the Hall of Health exhibition at the California State Museum of Science and Industry.

Artistic designs form part of the captivating "Mathematica" exhibit at the Museum of Science and Industry.

Aside from the regular fare at the museum, there are some sixty rotating temporary exhibitions a year, many of which are quite daring. In the past, curators have addressed themselves to immortality, parapsychology, human values, and more orthodox subjects like bonsai, photography, and Aztec artifacts. This is definitely not a sleepy little dustcatcher of a museum.

Across the way from the museum's new Kinsey Auditorium, in the old Armory Building, is the inchoate Space Museum. A graceful Thor-Agena missile stands out front in proclamation of the hangarful of space hardware on long-term loan that rests within. As yet, the collection is scatter-shot and incohesive, more in a state of storage than exhibition. But a master design plan has been approved and the completed hall promises to be equal to its subject. Big plans are also in the works to erect a Museum of Finance, a sort of paean to our free enterprise system.

The museum is located in Exposition Park, just south of the USC campus. The park is an oasis of landscape, learning, and leisure which also includes the Los Angeles County Museum of Natural History, a seven-acre rose garden, the Memorial Coliseum, and the Sports Arena. The rose garden, once the site of a racetrack, is redolent with the fragrance of 146 well-groomed beds of roses in as many varieties. A central fountain, benches, arbors, and winding paths contribute to a setting of year-round sublimity.

Craft and Folk Art Museum
5814 Wilshire Boulevard
Los Angeles   937-5544

In Japan, the artisans who do the finest job of preserving traditional crafts are deemed national treasures. That kind of respect for handcrafts both contemporary and endangered permeates the Craft and Folk Art Museum. This spirited little sanctuary of ethnic and folk artistry regularly offers exhibits like Textiles of Afghanistan, Traditional Toys of Japan, Artesanos Mexicanos, and Early American Quilts. The museum is set up on the first and third floors of a quasi-Colonial building across the street from Hancock Park and the Los Angeles County Museum of Art. The mezzanine, overlooking the main gallery, is occupied by The Egg and The Eye, a tasteful little restaurant that features fifty-five varieties of omelet as well as soups and salads.

The museum boasts a very inviting craft shop filled with all manner of jewelry, ceramics, toys, tapestries, and miscellany by local craftspeople as well as a nookful of African arts. The shop has rotating "mini-shows" highlighting the work of particularly distinguished California artisans. The bookshop has a fairly wide selection of titles relating to the museum's themes. Everyone who works in this nest of eyecatching curios is friendly and helpful, and there's something euphoric about being in the midst of all these lovingly wrought objects.

The most captivating artwork at the Getty Museum is easily the building itself. When billionaire J. Paul Getty's art collection outgrew his eight-gallery house in Malibu, he commissioned a lovingly exact copy of an ancient Roman country house, the Villa dei Papyri. This villa, which stood outside the city of Herculaneum overlooking the Bay of Naples, was totally buried by volcanic mud when Mt. Vesuvius erupted in A.D. 79. With the aid of precise notes taken during the villa's partial excavation in the eighteenth century, Getty has given us not only an enchanting look at suburban Imperial Rome but a perfect setting in which to view his collection of Greek and Roman antiquities.

The approach to the museum, up a densely landscaped Appian driveway, hints at the breathtaking pastoral beauty of the site. Ascending from the ground-level parking structure to the loggia above it, one beholds the long sweep of the Main Peristyle Garden and the impeccable museum facade beyond. The floors of the deep surrounding porticoes are inlaid with marble and mosaic, the walls are embellished with *trompe-l'oeil* murals, and the long cerulean pool in the center of the courtyard is skirted with a fret of immaculate little hedges. The scene is completed with grape arbors, Doric columns, Pompeian lanterns, and ornamental roof tile ends. The same attention to detail is reflected throughout the Getty. At various points farther on, the visitor will discover an equally geometrical Roman herb garden, Inner Peristyle Garden, West Garden, and East Garden, the last dominated by a marvel of a mosaic fountain.

The main level of the museum contains what some consider to be one of the three most important collections of Greek and Roman antiquities in the United States. It includes marble and bronze sculpture, mosaics, vases, and various minor arts. Works of major significance include the fourth century B.C. Getty Bronze, the Lansdowne Herakles, and the Elgin throne. In general, the strongest areas of the sculpture collection are Greek and Roman portraits and fourth century Attic grave reliefs. Our favorites are the statues of Orpheus and the Sirens. There is also a commendable if small selection of Etruscan objects in the Etruscan Vestibule, en route to the Basilica of Cybele, the Temple of Herakles, the Hall of Aphrodite, and other classical chambers to be encountered on the main level. The Villa Display Room, off the main entry vestibule, provides vivid descriptions of the original Villa dei Papyri and how it was recreated for a mere $17 million.

The upper floor houses a hit-or-miss collection of paintings that fitfully represents all major schools of Western art from the late thirteenth to the early twentieth centuries, with emphasis on Renaissance and baroque. With the museum's extraordinary endowment of $700 million, however, there's no telling how formidable it may become. Highlights include a couple of fine Rembrandts in the Dutch Painting room, Gentile da Fabriano's *Coronation of the Virgin*, Van Dyck's *Portrait of Agostino*

J. Paul Getty Museum
17985 Pacific Coast Highway
Malibu   454-6541

The center courtyard at the J. Paul Getty Museum.

Another view of the Getty's center courtyard from one of the surrounding porticos.

Pallavicini, Boucher's *The Fountain of Love*, George de la Tour's *The Beggar's Brawl*, a *Madonna* by Paolo Uccello, and *The Holy Family* by Raphael. Hopeless romantics will love Bougereau's *Young Girl Defending Herself Against Eros* and Alma-Tadema's *Spring*. From one damask-walled gallery to the next, one may find works by Rubens, Gainsborough, Tintoretto, Van der Weyden, Monet, Canaletto, Titian, and Poussin.

Elsewhere on the same floor is a collection of mostly French decorative arts, ranging in date from the early years of the reign of Louis XIV to the French Revolution. One can see from a golden array of furniture, carpets, tapestries, ceramics, clocks, chandeliers, and various small decorative items made of gilt bronze that the French nobility really knew how to live. Wonderful panelled rooms that duplicate old aristocratic Parisian hotel rooms in all their rococo glory are the stage for this part of the Getty holdings. It is amusing to remember that all of this Regency finement is being snugly housed in a first-century Roman villa.

The bookstore, also off the main entry vestibule, has a fairly good inventory of books germane to the museum's collections, not to mention postcards, posters, slides, a wide range of museum publications, and a few reproductions of classical statuary.

Advance parking reservations are recommended for guaranteed admission because visitors who have not made them can enter only if parking is available.

Huntington Library
1151 Oxford Road
San Marino 681-6601

Henry E. Huntington liked to do things on a grand scale. Not only did he develop a highly efficient transportation system for turn-of-the-century Los Angeles (the Pacific Electric Railway virtually defined the city's present anatomy), he turned his immense San Marino estate into what has become a research and cultural center of international eminence. The present 207-acre property is a utopian milieu: In the midst of some twelve distinct gardens that are lovingly and expertly tended, there is a stately English manor that houses a respectable period art collection, and a monumentally classical library building containing more than a half million books and five million manuscripts. The Huntington is a western mecca for scholars of British and American history and literature, and it is an exquisite afternoon's excursion for everyone else.

The Huntington Art Collection has recently metamorphosed from an undistinguished cache of eighteenth-century British and French fine and decorative art to a promising West Coast version of New York's Frick Collection. Its calibre has been thus increased by the bequest of a substantial number of French, English, Dutch, Flemish, and Italian masterpieces of the seventeenth through nineteenth centuries. Local collector Mildred Browning Green and her husband, Judge Lucius Peyton Green, left the Huntington a $7

Entrance to the Huntington Library and Art Gallery.

million-plus estate that includes a superb Rembrandt portrait and notable works by Anthony Van Dyck, Watteau, David, Fragonard, Claude Lorrain, Canaletto, and Boucher—forty-two paintings in all. In addition, there are eight portrait miniatures and about thirty decorative objects.

The bonus is just how splendidly these new works complement the Huntington's existing bounty and setting. Each room of the Huntington mansion has been modeled after interiors of the *ancien régime* and lavished with paintings, sculpture, furniture, tapestries, and decorative objects that present a vivid picture of Georgian opulence. The Green collection has added considerably to what was already the pride of the Huntington holdings: a large, skylit hall of full-length British portraits. These grand renderings of pomp and personality, including the renowned *Blue Boy* by Gainsborough,

Detail from "Blue Boy" by Gainsborough in the Huntington Art Gallery.

Pinkie by Sir Thomas Lawrence, and Sir Joshua Reynolds's *Mrs. Gibbons as the Tragic Muse,* have been augmented by another of each of these artists' works plus paintings by George Romney, John Russell, and the Scot, Henry Raeburn. In contrast to these elaborately devised paintings, there are rotating exhibits of an extensive store of British drawings and watercolors. Works by Blake, Turner, Constable, and Rowlandson have an air of freshness and spontaneity, particularly the landscape watercolors. Located variously throughout the art gallery and parts of the library, one can find collections of Renaissance bronzes of mostly mythological subjects, Sèvres porcelain figures, British miniatures (portraits), Renaissance paintings by minor masters like Roger van der Weyden and Sebastiano Mainardi, snuff and comfit boxes, and one of the richest assemblages of French eighteenth century sculpture in the U.S. There is also British sculpture, mostly busts, and several hundred examples of British silver. The finest craftsmanship seems to have gone into the French furniture of the late eighteenth century, in which it is possible to follow the transformation from rococo to neo-classical style. The entire setting lacks only a mincing marquis in white powdered wig.

While Huntington's original art acquisitions were of limited scope and inconsistent quality, he was superbly advised in the area of books and manuscripts. The library houses a truly remarkable collection of literary and musicological treasures, many of them on view to the public in the Exhibition Hall. In this beautifully wood-panelled, two-story room, it is possible to see the Ellesmere Chaucer, a circa 1410 illuminated manuscript of *The Canterbury Tales.* From this celebrated gem, the viewer is invited to inspect a virtual history of the English language under glass. There is an open copy of The Gutenberg Bible (printed in 1455 on the inner skin of a calf), an unexcelled assortment of Shakespeare first editions, Benjamin Franklin's *Autobiography* in his own handwriting, along with letters and papers of Washington and Jefferson, and Audubon's masterpiece of natural history, *The Birds of America.* While these last items are displayed in handsome, hexagonal upright cases, there are also some twenty-eight supine glass cases arranged somewhat chronologically around the hall. One does not have to be a bibliophile to be moved by Huntington's eleventh-century Bible of Bishop Gandulf and other hand-scribed medieval manuscripts. The development of printing is traced through an early Boccaccio to fifteenth-century editions of Plato, Dante, and other classics. Highlights of the subsequent historical fare include the King James Bible, a 1481 map of the New World, Milton's *Paradise Lost,* Blake's *Songs of Innocence and Experience,* the *Declaration of Independence,* Thoreau's *Walden,* a handwritten Jack London manuscript, and first editions of Swift, Pope, Wordsworth, Coleridge, Dickens, Poe, Whitman, and Joyce. The manifold public display only hints at what lies in the upper gallery of the hall and in the chambers beyond. Only advanced scholars are invited to find out.

What began as just another Southern California citrus ranch and California's first avocado grove is now an Eden of 9,000 kinds of plants. The Huntington Botanical Gardens provide ideal laboratory settings for ongoing horticultural experiments, a sublime sanctuary for the cityworn, and a visual feast for even the most jaded plant lover. A walking tour of the sprawling grounds requires a good hour and a long mile. Among the more unusual displays is the twelve-acre desert garden, an extraterrestrial-looking landscape of agaves, ice plants, puya, tree aloes, Living Stones, a dragon tree, yucca, aeoniums, and a bristling assortment of cacti. There is a lush Japanese garden with four kinds of pine, a traditional Japanese house, small pagoda, stylized bridges, and an adjacent Zen rock garden. A smaller courtyard contains a collection of bonsai trees. There are fragrant rose gardens, a subtropical garden, an Australian garden, a camellia garden, a palm garden, a Shakespearean garden arranged with flora mentioned in the bard's works, a lovely lily pond surrounded with stands of bamboo, an herb garden, and a jungle garden. The Elysian ambience is completed with fountains, temples, statues, urns, jardinieres, wellheads, and benches that grace the grounds. The North Vista is a long quad of lawn flanked by thirty-one stone mythological figures and crowned with a baroque fountain, the perfect spot for a tryst.

One of the best things about the Long Beach Museum of Art is its setting. The galleries are contained in a charismatic 1912 cedarshake mansion overlooking the Pacific, on grounds that are lushly landscaped and happen to include a well-kept carriage house converted to a bookstore and gallery. The ambience is homey and inviting, the contemporary art shown there is high calibre. The permanent collection of paintings, prints, and sculpture, specializing in twentieth-century American art, has about a thousand pieces, sixty percent of which are by Californians. Much of the sculpture can be viewed in the garden. The museum hosts a regular schedule of changing exhibitions which might consist of anything from seventeenth-century French drawings to the most arcane video installation.

Long Beach Museum of Art
2300 East Ocean Boulevard
Long Beach   439-2119

The museum's most important present role is as "video central" for Southern California. It operates a video post-production studio and extensive archives in another building. Screenings can be arranged for visitors wishing to discover what's current in underground video art.

Once visitors to the Los Angeles County Museum of Art are resigned to the fact that this fledgling institution is no Louvre, they may enjoy it for the intimate string of departmental galleries that it is. Los Angeles' bid for a world-class art museum falls in the same area of abeyance as its ambition of becoming a major center of contemporary art. It's a question of patronage. A museum is as much a reflection of the city's enthusiasm toward art, expressed in part by the largess of its wealthy citizens, as it is of its own goals. It's only

Los Angeles County Museum of Art
5905 Wilshire Boulevard
Los Angeles   937-4250

European Art Galleries in the Ahmanson Gallery.

fair to add that LACMA, founded in 1910 as part of Exposition Park's Museum of History, Science, and Art, has always eschewed specialization in favor of representing the entire range of art history. That's a staggering task. The museum has had neither the time nor the endowment, especially in an increasingly fierce art market, to catch up with the art strongholds doted upon by generations of sovereigns, tycoons, and benign bureaucrats.

Since the museum's move into its present three-pavilion complex at Hancock Park in 1965, acquisitions have accelerated encouragingly, to the point where only about ten percent of the museum's holdings can be displayed at a given time. And as of this writing, the locally based Atlantic Richfield Company has pledged $3.5 million toward the construction of a new contemporary art building on the museum property.

At present, visitors will not find gleaming multitudes of recognizable masterpieces at LACMA. Its collections of the more celebrated periods of art history are modest by most standards. But there are definitely treasures to be found and a good number of surprises. The museum has actually assumed international distinction

Reliefs from the palace of Ashurnasirpal II, Assyria (Kalah) 9th Century B.C.

in certain areas. Its prized Heeramaneck collection of Indian, Tibetan, and Nepalese art objects (345 superb paintings, sculptures, textiles, jades, and crystals) is one of the three greatest in the Western world. The recently acquired Heeramaneck ancient Near Eastern collection of 2,500 objects plus 650 Islamic paintings, ceramics, metalwork, and textiles has made Los Angeles a major center for the study of Near Eastern civilizations.

Many of these works are provocatively displayed on the atrium, plaza, and fourth levels of the Ahmanson Gallery, which houses the museum's permanent collection. Although the skylit atrium rising up the four stories of the Ahmanson Gallery affords some dramatic perspectives, like a boxed Guggenheim, precious exhibition space had to be sacrificed, and the remaining quarters are increasingly cramped.

Other highlights of the permanent collection are the Hammer collection of 5,000 Daumier prints, the Gilbert collection of rococo and regency silver (plus the exquisite eighteenth-century silver-and-gold *Gates of Kiev*), an assembly of post-Renaissance mosaics unrivalled outside the Hermitage, and one of the most extensive arrays of costumes and textiles in the world (including a coveted cache of pre-Columbian Peruvian textiles and a rich assortment of Indonesian pieces).

The gracefully curated Far Eastern Gallery features art from all over Asia, from Paleolithic to modern times, with a strong sampling of Japanese paintings and screens of the Edo period and Chinese funerary sculpture of the T'ang Dynasty. There's a fine assortment of Rodin bronzes to be seen, the more monumental ones located in the museum's surrounding sculpture garden. The Prints and Drawings Department does an excellent job, within its limitations, with Picasso aquatints, Rembrandt etchings, de Kooning lithographs, a Robert Henri monotype, and other gems.

"Heads of Jeanette" by Henri Matisse.

Works by Pissarro, Degas, Toulouse-Lautrec, Cézanne, van Gogh, and Picasso form the nucleus of the museum's impressionist and post-impressionist collection. The New York school is represented with a few paintings by Gottlieb, Kline, Rothko, and Pollock. The overall selection has the look of filling holes in a very thin weave covering a very broad area. European painting and sculpture from 1860 to the present and American art since the Armory Show of 1913 occupy galleries on the third floor of the Ahmanson, while a fun, if undernourished, line up of contemporary art can be found on the upper level of the Frances and Armand Hammer Wing. This center pavilion is also where temporary loan exhibitions and traveling extravaganzas like Tut are offered to the public, at the rate of about four a year.

The museum's collection of old masters has a long way to go, but in the last few years it has acquired works by Rembrandt, Hals, Jacob van Ruysdael, Fra Bartolommeo, and Veronese. One particularly beautiful painting is George de la Tour's *Magdalen with the Smoking Flame.*

Other individual artworks to watch out for are the Assyrian palace reliefs, the Nepalese *Mandala of Vishnu*, the Japanese *Jizo Bosatsu*, an amazingly modernistic *Cycladic Figure*, Hals' *Portrait of Pieter Tjarck*, Houdon's *Bust of George Washington*, Degas' *Bellelli Sisters*, Cézanne's *Still Life With Cherries and Peaches*, Picasso's *Portrait of Sebastian Juñer Vidal*, Matisse's *Heads of Jeanette*, Thomas Cole's *L'Allegro*, Winslow Homer's *The Cotton Pickers*, George Bellows' *Cliff Dwellers*, Diego Rivera's *Flower Day*, Frank Stella's *Getty Tomb*, and Richard Diebenkorn's *Ocean Park Series #49*. And be assured there is quite a lot more worth seeing.

Siva, 10th Century South India.

The museum handbook is an informative, well-written, and indispensable guide to the museum's considerable number of esoteric items that only a curator could love at first sight.

The third pavilion, the Leo S. Bing Center, houses the Bing Theater, which offers excellent film series (such as the International Tournée of Animation, the International Festival of Children's Films, and endless classic film revivals), and the inconsistent Art Rental Gallery on the lower level which displays work by young local artists mostly. Also located in the Bing Center is the execrable Plaza Cafe. Its sole virtue is that its patio tables overlook the sculpture garden. A better bet for lunch is The Egg and the Eye Restaurant in the nearby Craft and Folk Art Museum.

The newly relocated Museum Shop, now dominating a plaza once nicely laden with sculpture, is a chocolate glass box brimful of art books, posters, postcards, slides, catalogs, reproductions, jewelry, textiles, and trinkets.

A well-endowed natural history museum is a good place to revive a flagging sense of wonder and to measure oneself against other cultures, other species, and other elements. Los Angeles is blessed with one of the country's finest, one that easily fulfills all the essential requirements of a natural history museum.

Los Angeles County Museum of Natural History
900 Exposition Boulevard
Los Angeles   746-3775

It is imposing. The original central building, erected in 1913, is a fine Romanesque edifice that is beautifully detailed and massively scaled. Floors in the main rotunda are of fitted marble; walls, columns, and semi-domes are of travertine; ceilings are ornate and airily high. The whole is just the sort of monumental municipal architecture that is perfect for the display of timeless artifacts. Exhibition halls seem to go on forever. Getting lost and pathfinding willy-nilly from birds to African masks to early American automobiles heightens the feeling of discovery. The awesome scale of the museum dwarfs one back into childhood, a precondition perhaps vital to enjoying this place.

It is informative. Explications are clear, legible, well-illuminated, and logically organized. There is more subject matter than you'll need to keep yourself fascinated of a quiet afternoon. Permanent

Entrance to the oldest wing of the LACMA.

exhibits include pre-Columbian ceremonial objects, invertebrate fossils, insect life (with wonderful bits of insect lore), a replete Hall of American History (everything from Thomas Jefferson's clothes to an 1889 streetcar), the popular Hall of Western American Indians, spiffily restored antique autos, political memorabilia, and brimming presentations of marine and bird life.

California fossils in the main foyer.

There's more than meets the eye. Public displays are really just the tip of the iceberg: not fully shown is the second largest fossil vertebrate collection in the country, the museum's three million insect specimens (rivaling the Smithsonian), one of the most important collections of fish specimens, and vast storerooms of anthropological material such as the Hearst collection of 200 Navajo textiles and 4,000 baskets from all cultures. In fact, for every curiosity on view to visitors there are probably dozens more waiting to be placed on rotating temporary exhibition. The museum's fabulous collection of African tribal art is never seen otherwise.

It is picturesque. Let's face it, museums are for looking. The four darkened, cavernous animal-habitat galleries alone are good for hours of inspection. This is taxidermy at its most scenic, with consecutive tableaux of North American, African, and exotic mammals set in dramatically lit native environments, accurate down to the season, foliage, and insect life of each habitat. It's the kind of stop-action realism that allows one to ponder improbable confrontations with wildlife and, with the aid of intermittent recorded narrations, enter an assortment of *terra incognita*. Displays like Cultures of the South Pacific and the many-splendored Hall of Gems and Minerals are visually rich and absorbing. Here's a dazzle that ain't Hollywood.

Mural in pre-Columbian Hall.

It's exhausting. Wear comfortable walking shoes and be prepared, unless you're giving the most superficial look-see, not to attempt all 400,000 square feet in one visit.

The Ethnic Arts Shop offers distinctive, high-quality arts and crafts from around the world. Available in the shop are such diverse items as ceremonial sculpture from West Africa, amber jewelry from Scandinavia, and handwoven tapestries from Mexico, Ecuador, and Peru. Also for sale are authenticated antiquities and a variety of colorful ethnic clothing, including Chinese hand-embroidered silk robes.

The Book Shop (at the south entrance) carries up-to-date titles in all areas of natural history, with a particularly fine pre-Columbian section. Also offered are wildlife notes and cards, museum postcards, and a large assortment of children's educational books, puzzles, kits, and toys.

If you've a taste for the avant garde, and wish to see what younger Los Angeles artists are up to, the best place to begin is LAICA (pronounced lie-ka). Since its inception in 1974, this member-sponsored, grant-supported complex has provided local artists with an alternative to traditional museums and commercial galleries. Some of the most imaginatively curated exhibitions in town have been seen here, from displays of artist-designed clothing and books to collections of "autobiographical fantasies" to a show of artworks based

**Los Angeles Institute
of Contemporary Art**
2020 South Robertson Boulevard
Los Angeles   559-5033

entirely on sound. Well-knowns like Peter Voulkos, William Brice, George Herms, and Bruce Nauman often unveil their latest work at LAICA. In addition, there are full programs of video and performance art and regular series of underground films.

LAICA is more than a gallery to the Los Angeles art community; it's a vital nerve center. It runs the largest artists' registry (bios and slides) in the country, initiates government-funded educational and artist employment programs, hosts conferences, and publishes *JOURNAL*, the most promising contemporary art publication on the West Coast. And LAICA usually has a handle on everything else of interest in local art affairs.

There are as many as six exhibitions running at any given time in LAICA's combined galleries, including a downtown window display space. Though somewhat cramped, the galleries are quiet and well-illumined and rarely without surprises.

Newport Harbor Art Museum
850 San Clemente Drive
Newport Beach   (714) 759-1122

One might expect Southern California's most ambitious showcasing of contemporary art to be at the Los Angeles County Museum of Art, or at least somewhere in Los Angeles proper, but it isn't. That distinction goes to the gutsy, community-supported Newport Harbor Art Museum. It was founded in 1961 by a resourceful, tough-minded group of local women who wanted to bring "the art of our time" to Orange County. Since its humble beginnings on the second floor of a seaside turn-of-the-century dancehall, the museum has offered outstanding exhibitions: Morris Graves, Karel Appel, Ed Ruscha, Robert Rauschenberg, Edward Hopper, Frank Stella, Jasper Johns, and the excellent "American Painting of the 1970s."

Since 1977 NHAM has enjoyed full-blown museum status on a two-acre site donated by the omnipresent Irvine Company, in an understated, functionally designed single-story building that reflects the area's clean-lined conservatism. The clue to its even being a museum, seen from the outside, is the long laminated-wood sculpture by Tony DeLap that rests out front.

NHAM is busily building a permanent collection of American art of this century, with a desperately needed emphasis on West Coast art of the last forty years: other museums just aren't doing the job. Grateful to the hand that feeds it, the museum energetically serves the community a feast of panel discussions on modern art, films, classical and jazz concerts, creative workshops for children, and an art rental program.

Aside from its two enormously adaptable gallery spaces, the museum boasts an everchanging rental gallery and a small sculpture garden. A glass-enclosed cafe in the garden serves good light food in a pleasant greenhouse atmosphere. The bookshop, though limited, does have rotating displays of fine craft items and a good selection of art periodicals and catalogues.

A brief but worthwhile stop while in Pasadena is the Pacific Asia Museum. It's a compact Oriental jewel of a place dedicated to nurturing the cultural ties between East and West. Through a continuous program of exhibitions, dance and music concerts, lectures and classes, the museum keeps a broad window open on the Pacific and Far East. Past displays have included Japanese Screen Painting, Chinese Painting—The Last 100 Years, Korean Folk Painting, Indonesia: Fabled Islands of Spice, and The Contemporary Paintings of India.

The museum, built in 1924 to house local art enthusiast Grace Nicholson's collection of Orientalia, was designed in traditional Imperial Palace Courtyard style, complete with decorative roof tiles, finials, and stone carvings imported from China. An authentic Chinese courtyard garden, a highly symbolic kind of landscaping, has been added recently, providing a contemplative focus to the art in the surrounding galleries.

Upstairs in the two-story edifice, tiny shops offer crafts and *objets d'art* from all over Asia. A quaint little tea room serves spice teas and almond or sesame cookies. Upon leaving, one finds a small bookshop with a narrow range of titles on Eastern arts, as well as postcards and some posters. In all, one comes away grateful for this anomalous pavilion of cultural goodwill in the middle of downtown Pasadena.

Pacific Asia Museum
46 North Los Roble
Pasadena   449-2742

Hands-on display in the children's gallery.

Most people think of Los Angeles as having spontaneously materialized in an orange grove, perhaps next to some Spanish mission plunked down by Father Junipero Serra. Any prior history of the area is more vague still, so much so that the George C. Page Museum in Hancock Park provides a real revelation. It is a smartly designed "total concept" museum devoted to La Brea's 40,000-year-old tar pits and the choicest discoveries of the 100 tons of fossil bones excavated there. The richest source of Ice Age fossils in the world, La Brea has been the site of paleontological digs since 1905. Until recently, the fossils were housed and displayed seven miles away at the Museum of Natural History. But in 1972, local philanthropist George Page proposed building the current on-site museum. The rest is prehistory.

The museum's shell is one of its greatest attractions. It's a low pyramid of grassy slopes that seems to have erupted naturally out of the park grounds. The temptation to climb up onto it is irresistible. Across the top is a sweeping aluminum lattice-work that leaves the beautifully landscaped atrium below simultaneously enclosed and open-air. This overhead span is bordered on all four sides with a continuous simulated-sandstone frieze depicting extinct beasts in an Ice Age landscape. The total effect is of some pre-Columbian burial mound, a sight that is particularly dramatic in the evening.

George C. Page Museum
5801 Wilshire Boulevard
Los Angeles   936-2230

This is unquestionably one of the most clearly laid out exhibition spaces around. Visitors simply make one clean circuit from the information center at the entrance to the gift shop at the exit. En route, you will encounter the fastidiously catalogued and displayed skeletal remains and fully reconstructed skeletons of everything that ever passed through L.A.: sabre-tooth tigers, dire wolves (with an eerie grid of 404 skulls), a twelve-foot-high Imperial mammoth, ground sloths, antique bison, extinct varieties of camel, mastodons, birds not seen for thousands of years, dwarf antelopes, and innumerable small and more familiar creatures. There's even the 9,000-year-old "La Brea Woman"; she doesn't look a day over 7500.

Twin mini-theaters feature an identical fifteen-minute triple-projection presentation on the way animals became entrapped in the gooey asphalt and how the museum developed. Just as enlightening is the Asphalt is Sticky exhibit, where visitors are invited to pull up on large dipsticks immersed in tar, an eloquent demonstration of how ensnared an animal's leg would become. There are WPA-style murals illustrating the migration of early humans across the Bering Strait and down to L.A., and a charming country scene in Late Pleistocene Los Angeles. Unique to this museum is an open-view paleontological laboratory where visitors can observe research in progress.

The Dinosaur Theater runs a film that breaks the hard news to many misinformed visitors that dinosaurs disappeared 65 million years before the La Brea pits were even formed. There are two excellent graphic displays at the end of the course: a wall painting that gives a capsule view of the Earth's five billion year history; and the La Brea Time Wall, a sequence of twenty colorful, backlit transparencies in 2,000-year segments depicting the evolution of life around the tar pits in correlation with major historical events like the birth of Christ and the building of the pyramids. The entire exhibition is thoughtfully planned, uncluttered and as involving as a museum full of bones can possibly be.

Norton Simon Museum at Pasadena
Colorado and
Orange Grove Boulevards
Pasadena   681-2484

Thanks to a canny businessman named Norton Simon and his abiding passion for masterpieces, Southern California has a collection of art treasures of international rank. In 1974, Simon took over the ailing, fifty-year-old Pasadena Art Museum in order to house and display his evergrowing store of premium paintings, prints, tapestries, and sculpture. Amid a storm of controversy over his imminent autocracy, Simon modified and expanded the exhibition space of the museum. The exterior remained a curvy, symmetrical fortress of glass and tawny red ceramic tile, squat and contemporary against a vintage neighborhood.

Although Simon entered late into the competition for old master and impressionist works, he has been uncompromising in the quality of his acquisitions, paying enormous sums for items he felt he had to have. The museum is technically coordinated through two foundations Simon created to ease the travails of possession, but he

Degas Gallery.

wields a heavy hand in virtually all curatorial matters. It cannot be denied that the collection absolutely reflects the taste and temperament of one man. Fortunately, not only is Simon a wily customer in the art market, but he does his homework and knows what to look for. The $100 million he has spent since 1954 translates into an all but flawless inventory of art objects.

The collection represents early Italian, Dutch and Flemish, Spanish, seventeenth through twentieth century French, German expressionist, and Asian art. Although everything can be seen on a single long visit, those who prefer to stroll casually and savor slowly should take note of these particularly important works: Rembrandt's *Titus, Bearded Man in a Wide-Brimmed Hat*, and *Self-*

Entrance to the Norton Simon Museum of Art.

Portrait as well as an extensive array of his etchings; Raphael's *Madonna and Child with Book;* Tiepolo's *Triumph of Virtue and Nobility over Ignorance;* the fourteenth century Guariento altarpiece; Giovanni di Paolo's *Branchini Madonna;* Renoir's *Pont des Arts;* Zurbaran's *Still Life with Lemons, Oranges and a Rose;* the Galka Scheyer collection of the Blue Four painters (Feininger, Klee, Kandinsky and Jawlensky); the Filippino Lippi altarpiece; Ingres's *Odalisque and Slave;* Rubens's *Holy Women at the Sepulchre;* Memling's *Christ Blessing;* Manet's *Ragpicker;* Bacciccio's *St. Joseph and the Infant Christ;* Guido Reni's *St. Cecilia;* a Canaletto painting of the Venice Piazza; Monet's *Rouen Cathedral;* Rodin's *Burghers of Calais;* Cranach's *Adam* and *Eve;* Cézanne's *Tulips in a Vase;* and Il Bassano's *Flight Into Egypt.*

Moreover, the intimate subterranean galleries boast one of the largest collections of Goya etchings in the world, a roomful of Degas paintings and his enchanting ballerina modèles, a delightful little trove of Dutch oils just beyond the *Book of Tulips,* and a number of rotating exhibitions from the museum's print vault. These might include any of the excellent sets in house—Rouault, Moore, Fragonard, Lorrain, Picasso.

An upstairs chamber contains Simon's vast, haunting collection of Indian and Southwest Asian sculpture. This congregation of deities is highlighted by the exquisite Shivapuram Nataraja. The controversial bronze dancing god, believed stolen and smuggled out of India, is now officially on loan from the Indian government until 1986.

For those who love impressionist painting, the Norton Simon Museum provides. There are choice works by van Gogh, Matisse, Pissarro, Cézanne, Monet, Manet, Renoir, Seurat, Utrillo, Bonnard, and others. There is a full wall of cubist paintings by Picasso, Braque, and Gris. One gallery features sculpture by Moore, Hepworth, Brancusi, and Noguchi. And major French art of the seventeenth and eighteenth centuries includes sumptuous works by Poussin, Chardin, Watteau, Boucher, and Rubens.

Visitors should be sure not to miss the sculpture garden, with its elegant fountain and reflecting pool, as well as monumental pieces by Maillol, and Matisse's *The Backs.* The garden affords a welcome respite half-way through an afternoon of picture-gazing..

But enough itemizing. If the preceding honorable-mentions aren't enticement enough, the remaining surprises won't be either. Flush as the museum is with quality art, the display is tasteful, uncrowded, often intimate. Works are dramatically illuminated and imaginatively arranged. It is clear that the curator has taken pains to suggest stylistic relationships between artists that might not always be immediately obvious, as in the placing of Manet's *Ragpicker* next to Goya's *Saint Gerome,* or a bronze Kashmiri Buddha amidst sixteenth-century French tapestries.

The museum seems to be completely scrupulous about its attributions, clearly pointing out where experts disagree on, say, whether *Portrait of a Courtesan* is the work of Titian or Giorgione. It is a low-profile institution, eschewing splashy media events like Tut in favor of quiet self-esteem. There is a glow of pride about the place, from the blithe ticket lady on up to Simon himself. And the museum guards are not only personable and eager to help, but they're usually quite knowledgeable about the art in their charge.

The museum bookstore is the best around, amply stocked with hard and softcover art books of all periods. The shop also offers fine original prints, reproductions, slides, and postcards. There is an excellent selection of books on contemporary photography (see Shopping, p. 213). Unfortunately, the museum lacks a dining facility, so visitors ought to have lunch before venturing in.

Southwest Museum
234 Museum Drive
Highland Park   221-2163

The Southwest Museum goes a long way toward correcting the Hollywood image of the American Indian. Built in 1912, it's a small but well-provisioned institution devoted to researching and displaying the fascinating details of Indian life, stretching back some 10,000 years and covering terrain between Mexico and the Bering Strait. The museum's collection of Western Indian artifacts, particularly its vast holdings of basketry by most tribes west of the Mississippi, is among the finest in the country.

The best way to enter the museum is via a tunnel that begins down on street level. It's lined with the first of many dioramas that portray tribal scenes and are the central focus of each hall. An elevator takes you up to the main galleries. Exhibit cases are laden with ceramics, hunting weapons, cooking utensils, ceremonial paraphernalia, costumes, and all else that completes the picture of life among the Pueblo Indians, Plains Indians, Eskimos, and other territorial groups. The simplicity and respect for natural forces that characterizes Indian ceremonies and crafts are well worth viewing, as much to dramatize our own prodigality as to learn more about California's ancestry.

Frederick S. Wight Gallery
UCLA
Westwood   825-9345

This two-story campus gallery offers more than the conventional student shows. Sophisticated exhibitions such as Art About Art, Olivetti Designs, and a spectrum of ethnic and craft art shows make the Wight Gallery worth a visit. Stroll through the UCLA Sculpture Garden just outside.

ART GALLERIES
by Anne Gilbar

Choosing art is one of the most individual of activities. Each person's taste varies; it is difficult to predict or advise what the best galleries are. But, depending on what artists or kind of art you like, there is a gallery in Los Angeles that will satisfy your tastes. We have listed a few of the most prestigious and respected galleries (and some art supply shops) in and around the city, along with a random sampling of the artists they represent. For timely information on shows, check the listings in the Sunday Calendar section of the Los Angeles *Times,* in *Los Angeles Magazine* (a monthly), and in *New West* magazine (a biweekly).

Ace Gallery
185 Windward Avenue
Venice   392-4931

One of the most renowned galleries in Southern California, Ace handles important modern and contemporary paintings, drawings and sculpture. Its distinguished list of artists includes Helen Frankenthaler, Donald Judd, Ellsworth Kelly, Roy Lichtenstein Robert Motherwell, Robert Rauschenberg, Roland Reiss, Ed Ruscha, Frank Stella, Andy Warhol.

Donati Exhibition in the Ankrum Gallery.

Ankrum Gallery
657 North La Cienega Boulevard
West Hollywood   655-7562

A lovely gallery, designed to show small sculptures as well as monumental pieces, Ankrum specializes in original works by the latest American artists. Shows are always rotating, so be sure to call for the latest or upcoming exhibits.

Ashé
608 Venice Boulevard
Venice   822-0906

Owner Steve Saitzyk has collected one of the largest selections of Oriental calligraphy and sumi supplies on the West Coast. There is an astounding variety of rice papers, some inlaid with images, including leaves and ancient Japanese symbols. You'll also find more ordinary art supplies, including brushes, papers, and inks. The atmosphere is delightful, and Steve is happy to answer questions and offer advice and even minor instruction.

They offer contemporary paintings, sculpture, assemblage, collage, and occasional primitive art exhibitions, such as Masks of the World, including India, Tibet, Ceylon, and Africa. Some of their artists: Tim App, Slater Barron, Natalie Bieser, Tim Boyer, Carole Caroompas, Daniel Douké, Dennis Farber, Joanne Julian, Peter Liashkov, Betye Saar.

Jan Baum—Iris Silverman Gallery
8255 Santa Monica Boulevard
West Hollywood   656-8225

A large portion of this space houses an extensive lithography workshop. Jean Milant, the gallery director, is also a master printer and has published editions of such artists as Michael Balog, Chris Burden, Via Clemens, Tony DeLap, Joe Goode, Craig Kauffman, Bruce Nauman, Ed Ruscha, William T. Wiley.

Cirrus Gallery
542 South Alameda Street
Downtown   680-3473

Here you'll find a good selection of important contemporary paintings, sculpture, and drawings. The gallery exclusively represents Billy Al Bengston, Laddie John Dill, Ed Moses, and Ken Price.

James Corcoran Gallery
8223 Santa Monica Boulevard
West Hollywood   656-0622

This gallery handles primarily contemporary painting, sculpture, drawings, and photography. Artists represented include Karen Carson, Ron Cooper, Guy Dill, Steve Kahn, Peter Lodato, Maria Nordman, Leland Rice, Alexis Smith, Keith Sonnier, Ann Thornycroft.

Rosamund Felsen Gallery
669 North La Cienega Boulevard
West Hollywood   652-9172

Perhaps the most well-known gallery and lithography studio on the West Coast, this lovely gallery (housed in a building by famed L.A. architect Frank Gehry) has consistently prestigious shows. You'll

Gemini G.E.L.
8365 Melrose Avenue
West Hollywood   651-0513

David Hockney Installation at Gemini G.E.L.

215

find the newest works of Robert Rauschenberg, David Hockney, Jasper Johns, and many more. In the back is a collection of originals that is probably the most comprehensive around. Be sure to ask to see Gemini's catalogue, as it is a truly complete selection of American modern art.

G. Ray Hawkins
7224 Melrose Avenue
West Hollywood   550-1504

Considered one of the finest photographic galleries on the West Coast, Hawkins represents Ansel Adams in Southern California, **as well as Richard Avedon, Yousuf Karsh, Max Yavno, and Paul** Outerbridge. The gallery carries a large (and enviable) selection of vintage and contemporary photographs.

Joyce Hunsaker and Associates
812 North La Cienega Boulevard
West Hollywood   657-2557

Consultants to private and corporate collectors, this gallery shows contemporary paintings, prints, drawings, sculpture, and fiber **works by established as well as young American artists including Lita Albuquerque, Jerry Burchman, Ron Davis, Kay Whitney. Open** by appointment.

Icart Vendor
8111 Melrose Avenue
West Hollywood   653-3190

For deco prints, art nouveau pieces, graphics, and antique framing services you can't go wrong with this lovely shop. They carry primarily original graphics and posters, but you'll find a good selection of copies of turn-of-the-century posters.

Janus Gallery
21 Market Street
Venice   399-9122

Jan Turner has amassed an impressive collection of contemporary paintings, drawings, and sculpture by, among others, Lita Albuquerque, Joel Bass, Larry Bell, Mary Corse, Matsumi Kanemitsu, Gloria Kisch, Margit Omar, Larry Poons, Michael Steiner, and Michelle Stuart.

L.A. Louver Gallery
55 North Venice Boulevard
Venice   396-6633

Contemporary paintings, drawings, and sculpture. Artists represented include Max Cole, John Gordon, Loren Madsen, Sally **Shapiro, Paula Sweet. Prints by Richard Diebenkorn, Jim Dine,** David Hockney, Jasper Johns, Frank Stella. Exclusive representative for Petersburg Press on the West Coast.

Margo Leavin Gallery
812 North Robertson Boulevard
West Hollywood   273-0603

Respected nationwide as a gallery with a wide selection of paintings, sculpture, and drawings, Margo Leavin's space always has museum quality pieces on display. Even though her shows are popular attractions, Leavin's gallery walls are continuously covered with an array of some of the most famous artists in the U.S., including Arakawa, Lynda Benglis, Jud Fine, Sam Francis, **Jasper Johns, Ellsworth Kelly, Agnes Martin, Ann McCoy,** Louise Nevelson, Claes Oldenburg. Note: The Leavin Gallery is hard to find. If you continue on Robertson Boulevard north of Santa Monica Boulevard, it is located in an old mansion on the right hand side of the street.

Tortue Gallery
2917 Santa Monica Boulevard
Santa Monica   828-8878

Important major works, modern and contemporary paintings, sculpture and drawings by, among others, Claire Falkenstein, Sam Francis, Patrick Hogan, Ed Kienholz, Shirley Pettibone, Gregg

Work of Claire Falkenstein in the Tortue Gallery.

Renfrow, David Schirm, Stephen Seemayer, Mark Tobey, Joyce Treiman.

This gallery offers a respected collection of internationally-known works from the 1840s to today by some of the world's finest photographers, including Edward Weston, Phillipe Halsman, Dorothea Lange, Irving Penn. It is both a pleasant showcase and a popular hangout for lovers of fine photography.

Steven White Gallery
835 North La Cienega Boulevard
West Hollywood   657-6995

Handles contemporary paintings, drawings, and sculpture, specializing in California artists, including Charles Arnoldi, William Brice, Ron Davis, Joe Goode, Robert Graham, Tom Holland, David Hockney, John McLaughlin, Gwynn Murrill, Bruce Nauman.

Nicholas Wilder Gallery
8223½ Santa Monica Boulevard
West Hollywood   656-0770

This charming shop carries antique prints. You'll find a selection of fabrics and trims with which to frame your prints or theirs (they offer framing services). The choices are remarkable—you'll see their unique process of framing antique prints with trim and matting made from unusual and old fabrics.

Yesteryear, Ltd.
8684 Melrose Avenue
West Hollywood   659-5080

A whimsical greeting at Disneyland.

FAMILY ENTERTAINMENT AND CHILDREN'S PLACES:

From Disneyland to Magic Mountain, including Marineland, Knott's Berry Farm, And Children's Attractions.

By Michael Kurcfeld,
NEW WEST

A selective listing of amusement parks and outdoor entertainments—places to get away from it all for a day—might not seem like the best set of clues to the unique character of Los Angeles, but it could be. For L.A. is a city of escape artists. People come here in a flurry of flight patterns from Anytown, looking for bigger windmills to tilt and a better tan to flaunt. By sheer cosmopolitan momentum, L.A. is becoming more and more the Oz that New York was to generations of dreamers. L.A.'s industries teem with escapist by-products: music, television, film, fashion, and, in its way, aircraft. As a city predicated on private transportation, it's a place where people routinely escape encounter with one another. The weekend communal pleasure outing, for most Angelenos, is therefore a very serious matter.

Los Angeles is often thought of as Fast Food Heaven, a sprawling plastic tray of greasy cuisine to go, packaged in the primary colors of diluted ethnic themes and million-dollar ad campaigns. Amusement parks are the fast food of fun, aimed more at our viscera than our minds. The themes that are boiled down and served at Magic Mountain, Disneyland, and Knott's Berry Farm are quick and easy onion rings of real life.

At the heart of the fantasy and entertainment offered by L.A.'s theme parks is a discernible relationship with Hollywood. It was a film animator who created Disneyland and filled it with the most sophisticated illusionistic devices ever seen in a park setting. The purchase of Marineland by Hanna-Barbera, the well-known TV animation firm, continues this connection. All the parks use stage sets, animal characters, and actors. They put on theatrical productions and transport the visitor to imaginary places. The magic of cinema is most openly extolled in the Universal Studios Tour and at Movieland Wax Museum. Even the Griffith Observatory offers astronomy shows that appeal to the most jaded film-goer.

And let's talk about the weather. The Los Angeles climate, a special combination of semi-arid, semi-tropic, and Mediterranean, is hospitable to virtually all plantlife. That's probably why theme parks here are so lushly landscaped, and why places like Descanso Gardens and Huntington Gardens are among the nicest spots to spend an afternoon.

There are more clues that link Los Angeles' character to its public places. As interested explorers, you are challenged herewith to find them.

Children's Museum
310 North Main Street
Downtown   687-8800

The Los Angeles Children's Museum is the youngest in a thriving family of such museums dedicated to the nurturing of wonder and perception in young minds. Judging by the ingenuity and vitality of the place, it will no doubt thrive like, well, a child. It's a place where children may lay their hands on and sink their teeth into the things that make up the urban environment, past and present.

In a colorful, multi-level plywood maze of more or less sequential "please touch" exhibits, children can play the game of Discovery at their own pace. They can discover the mysteries of City Streets, including a cutaway fire hydrant, transparent parking meter, photomurals, and police motorcycle. Beneath the raised street is the Sewer Room, a crawl-through display of sewer conduits and pipes.

They can discover the architectural possibilities of Sticky City, a nook-filled space lined with adhering fabric, and stocked with large foam-rubber shapes. The shapes are also covered with adhering fabric and can stick to each other and to the walls. A child's talent for demolition plays as vital a role here as anything constructive.

The past is the theme of Before You and Me, where children discover the nostalgic appointments of Grandma's Attic and Grandpa's Workshop. Here, in the most atmospheric of the exhibits, children dress up in period clothing, hook rugs, churn butter, try out old tools, and generally immerse themselves in days gone by.

The Shadow Box is a room covered in phosphorescent vinyl that freezes shadows thrown by a time-released strobe light. The resulting silhouettes of jumping bodies appear as magic to children. The Workshop Place supplies the little visitors with a smorgasbord of recycled materials donated by private industry; they can create an ongoing model city or anything at all. Children may also weave on a real loom and paint pictures on a communal plexiglass wall.

One of our favorite attractions at the museum is called Everyone Is You and Me. Two people sit facing each other at a small table, separated by an upright glass divider whose surfaces reflect and pass light in a way that melds the sitters' faces together. A simple optical trick says volumes about the family of man.

The museum staff has big plans for the future. By the time you read this, they may already have added a TV newsroom with real video equipment and kiddy anchormen, children-powered Instant Theater, a water exhibit, a greenhouse, and more.

Built of cunningly scavenged materials (everything from manhole covers to tire retreads), the museum will probably survive any punishment your young ones can mete out. The arrangement of ramps and landings is designed with the handicapped and the toddler in mind. Entering the building from the central mall courtyard, visitors will find an information center displaying posters, children's books, T-shirts, and an assortment of small toys. Groups larger than ten require reservations. Visitors are allowed in by first-come-first-served limited groupings, so there might be a wait.

Any amusement park that refers to itself as "The Happiest Place on Earth"—and lives up to the boast—belongs in a category of its own. Disneyland has transcended mere amusement to become an internationally cherished legend. It is an irresistible marvel of technology, set design, myth, and master planning. Much of its success lies in its consummate ability to charm adults as much as children.

Disneyland
Harbor Boulevard exit,
Santa Ana Freeway
Anaheim   (714) 533-4456

Walt Disney had a genius for entertaining people, and when he decided to create his Magic Kingdom he understood the psychological appeal of both fantasy and orderliness. He mythologized America into her most benign aspects, added a spritely cast of beloved storybook characters to stir the cheerfulness of childhood, and set it all in a jeweled clockwork of cinematic transport. The park's fifty-eight attractions, costing some $200 million to date, effect a harmony that challenges rather than ignores the real world.

Disneyland is a seventy-six-acre stage, entered via Main Street USA. This miniaturized composite of small-town America circa 1900 is a perfect opener. The ambient optimism of the period propels you right on through the rest of the park. As in every other corner of Disneyland, the motifs are completed to perfection, down to the ornamentation of the calliope in the Penny Arcade. This fastidious artistry makes it easier to surrender to the dreamlike quality of everything. Main Street features horseless and horse-drawn carriages, oldtime fire engines, a silent movie house, ice cream parlor, and shops galore. The Opera House offers a juicy display of Disney memorabilia and a first encounter with Disney's remarkable audio-animatronics: Great Moments with Mr. Lincoln. (Computer-animated performers such as he, more often furry and funny, are of the most exact entertainment science, down to the barely perceptible movements of the eyes. It is one of the keenest examples of Disney's technological sophistication and goes back to his roots in animated film.) The splendid Disneyland railroad train commences its circuit of the park at the Main Street Station.

Beyond Main Street is the Plaza around which revolve the other six theme lands and a number of cafeterias. The Plaza is "Disney-landscaped" with some of the 800 plant species that are lushly arranged around the park. There are few times when the crowds here are abated, but there is never any litter. In another departure from real life, legions of custodial personnel keep Disneyland immaculate. It always looks new, and therefore happy.

From the Plaza the choices unfold in an easy clockwise sweep. Adventureland is built around a single excursion, a scenic jungle cruise down a reel of rivers that pretends to wind through a misty Amazon rain forest, a hippo-filled Congo, and a stretch of Nile rapids. Crocodiles guard an ancient shrine, Indian elephants bathe contentedly, and off on an African veldt lions, zebras, and giraffes eye passengers suspiciously. Neither these nor the headhunters are real, but the waterfalls and plantlife are. It's a safari without mosquitoes, just real enough for the kids. Overlooking the river is Swiss Family Treehouse, a cozily appointed rustic hideaway that inspires daydreams of tropical idylls. And there's the Enchanted Tiki Room, a South Seas musical fantasy decked in exotic birds and flowers.

Frontierland right next door portrays the Old West in a characteristically sanitized fashion. It shares the circular Rivers of America waterway with adjacent New Orleans Square and Bear Country. Visitors have a choice of vessels: the Columbia, a magnificent fully-rigged sailing ship; the Mark Twain, an elegant Mississippi stern-wheeler; keelboats, canoes, or log rafts to Tom Sawyer's Island to explore Fort Wilderness and climb Castle Rock. The Indians look stuffed and eerily picturesque, rather like a museum diorama. Some of the best entertainment in the park can be found at the Golden Horseshoe, a "saloon" (the only thing depressing about Disneyland is that it's dry) which offers vintage dancehall atmosphere and can-can stage productions. Scheduled for opening is a major attraction called Big Thunder Mountain Railroad, billed as a "rumblin' runaway mine train adventure." Judging from the elaborate set being erected, it'll be great fun.

Anyone who's wistful for a Southern gay-nineties atmosphere will love New Orleans Square. This maze of narrow winding streets, intimate courtyards, quaint shoppes and flower marts is detailed down to the iron filigree on the balconies. Diners in French and Creole cafes are entertained in Dixieland fashion. Intermittently, jazz combos and Mardi Gras parades re-create the sounds of old New Orleans. The Pirates of the Caribbean is a cruise on flat-bottom bateaux that course through haunted undersea grottoes and into a Caribbean seaport. The village is attacked by pirates, pillaged, plundered (Disneyland frowns on rape, however), and burnt. Our favorite attraction is the Haunted Mansion, a masterpiece of illusion. Single-file "doombuggies" convey visitors through a gauntlet of 999 animated ghosts and goblins, often etherealized by the magic of holography. This is the other side of Disney's technical wizardry, setting the park apart from all others. This ingeniously macabre fantasy climaxes in a graveyard scene that will just kill you.

Bear Country is set in the Great Northwest of the late 1800s and is graced with stands of tall pine. The central feature is the Country Bear Jamboree, a vaudeville of mechanically animated bears starring Teddi Barra.

Sleeping Beauty's Castle dominates the approach to Fantasyland and is the most photogenic landmark at Disneyland. Once through its entrance and cluster of shops, visitors discover a round of rides based on popular Disney storybook fare. The Casey Jr. Circus Train pushes through Storybook Land to Cinderella's Castle, Pinocchio's Village, and the homes of the three little pigs. For those with a sweet tooth, It's a Small World takes you on a boatride through cutesy but beautifully designed tableaux of mechanical doll-children representing over 100 countries, each group singing in its native language a tune that sticks long after you've exited. The high point of this terrain is the fourteen-story Matterhorn, a scale replica of the real thing. The coaster ride has been updated, adding crystal ice caverns, an abominable snowman that's easy to miss, and tandem bobsleds. The tamer of the two thrill rides in the park, its lines are nonetheless among the longest.

Take the Skyway Tram over to Tomorrowland, Disney's sanguine vision of the future. It features progressive modes of transportation such as the quietly efficient, if limited, monorail and a PeopleMover system of shuttle cabs. "Atomobiles" are used in the Adventure Thru Inner Space ride that takes visitors through a microscope into ever-diminishing scales of atomic phenomena. Amidst the various dramatizations of science and technology, there is inexplicably found another animated animal show called America Sings. Emceed by a cartoonified bald eagle and owl, this spirited narrative takes the revolving audience in the Carousel Theater through America's musical history. The Bell System's America The Beautiful exhibit is a dizzying 360-degree sequence of film footage, some aerial, of emblematic American places like the Grand Canyon and the White House.

The best ride in the park for thrillseekers is Space Mountain. This latest addition is a twenty-million-dollar simulated flight into deep space. The entry line passes through a fun NASA set to waiting "rockets," which are hoisted up a roller coaster ascent in a wonderful optical-effect chamber and proceed to whiz passengers along a harrowing slalom of hairpin turns accented with space travel lighting effects like meteor showers—great if you can keep your eyes open. It's breathtakingly scary, unless you're a coaster pro.

Disneyland takes on a different enchantment after dark. Everything flickers and glows, the Plaza trees are lit up as if by fireflies and the trim lights of the Mark Twain, which now resounds with its own Dixieland band, twinkle across the water. Very romantic. The Main Street Electrical Parade is a charming spectacle of fantasy floats festooned with myriad lights and cadenced to another catchy theme tune. The parade is followed by the most exhilarating, elaborate fireworks in California. This pyrotechnical *pièce de résistance* is offered every evening at 9 p.m. from mid-June to early September. Don't miss it.

Music can be heard throughout the park in the evening, from dancing Tahitians in Adventureland to contemporary sounds over in Tomorrowland and a summertime list of big name entertainers that has included the likes of Count Basie, Pearl Bailey, Stevie Wonder, and Chuck Berry.

The eating is plentiful if not necessarily gourmet. The best dining spot is the Blue Bayou Restaurant, built over the Pirates of the Caribbean river. Visitors should make reservations early for this popular if overrated place. Artificially moonlit, it does have a certain intimacy found nowhere else in the park.

Park services are the most complete we've seen anywhere, ranging from pet kennel to on-call nurses to lockers for checking packages. The gift shops at Disneyland are far too numerous to cite, as are the arcades, snack spots, and lesser rides. Suffice to say there is more than anyone could ever need. Guided tours are available for first timers. Call for rates. Disneyland Hotel connects by monorail and offers good lodging and dining.

For sheer sylvan serenity, there are few places in and around Los Angeles that match the 165-acre former private estate that is now Descanso Gardens. With its native California oak forest, nature trails, and idyllic atmosphere, Descanso (meaning "rest" in Spanish) is an apt name for the gardens.

Descanso Gardens
1418 Descanso Drive
La Cañada   790-5571

Beneath the oak forest is one of the world's largest displays of camellias with over 100,000 plants representing over 600 varieties of camellias. This vast collection is in bloom from late December through March. Nearby is the Teahouse, a refreshment pavilion designed in the Oriental tradition. Surrounding it is a beautiful Japanese garden featuring pools, waterfalls, and carefully selected stones. The Teahouse offers only tea and cookies, and there are no other dining facilities in the gardens. But visitors may pack a lunch and eat in the picnic area adjacent to the Gate House.

Teahouse in Descanso Gardens.

The gardens also contain a four-acre All-American Rose Selection Garden and a History of Roses Garden with plants arranged in chronological order dating back as far as the first century A.D. The peak of the blooming season is May and early June.

Visitors should call the gardens for schedules of flower shows, art festivals, and summer concerts and plays that are held there.

Griffith Observatory
2800 East Observatory Road
Griffith Park   664-1191
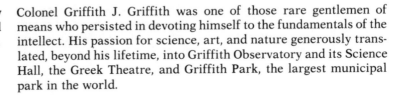

Colonel Griffith J. Griffith was one of those rare gentlemen of means who persisted in devoting himself to the fundamentals of the intellect. His passion for science, art, and nature generously translated, beyond his lifetime, into Griffith Observatory and its Science Hall, the Greek Theatre, and Griffith Park, the largest municipal park in the world.

Situated high on the southern face of his great 4,000-acre chaparraled reserve, Griffith Observatory is an august scientific temple, unique in being the only planetarium open to the public. It was built in 1935 to enable Angelenos to watch the heavens and, it turns out, their city below. It appears on the hillside as a gleaming Art Deco mosque, tri-domed and impregnable. A six-faced obelisk of astronomer-saints (Galileo, Copernicus, and company carved in radiant Delphic heroism) guards the approach to the monumental facade.

Entering through heavy wroughtwork portals emblazoned with iconic medallions, visitors find themselves in the central rotunda. Suspended from the 40-foot dome is the Foucault Pendulum, a 240-pound hollow bronze sphere whose 42-hour revolutions were once used to prove the Earth's rotation on its axis. The dome is graced with a sweeping thirties mural of Greek deities on the subject of Progress. The building is a treasure of detail and a shrine to the grand perspective.

The view of the city would be enough to commend the observatory, especially to the lovers that flock here on warm nights. But inside there's a fifty-foot-high domed theater that offers a provocative bill of shows featuring some very heavenly bodies. It's astronomy with stage presence. The shows can be anything from simulated trips to the moon and Mars, to thought-challenging tributes to Albert Einstein, to Christmas specials about the Star of Bethlehem. They are presented in ways that outmaneuver any visual aid I've seen before. The shows are made possible by a snazzy piece of technology called the Zeiss planetarium projector, equipped with twelve projectors that can produce over 100 effects. The narrator, ever droll, describes it as "a giant ant with thyroid problems." With this device the dome becomes a canopy of sky and the audience-in-the-round is treated to exhilarating displays of rapid nightfall, megawatt constellations, and time travel. Stonehenge and King Tut's Egypt are a couple of items on the itinerary.

No one is indifferent to the mind-boggling statistic. Once you learn, for example, that the light shining from some stars we see today began traveling before the Atlantic Ocean existed, you're hooked. Four to five shows a year are created for cosmos addicts.

The Laserium, an independent feature shown after evening planetarium events for a separate admission fee, is really just a glorified light-effects demonstration. Complex stunts of limited-palette laser beams are created to mesmerize the audience. The configurations go from pure geometry to neon carnival to a frenetically doodled expressionism. The accompanying soundtrack is an eclectic medley heavy on the electronic and disco. The music for the planetarium show runs more to Mozart and Brahms.

Outside there is a winding balcony skirting the observatory. The view does as good a job of shrinking you as do the shows inside. Precision pay-telescopes are available all along the parapet. They're great for peering down into the city at ten-power: flattened perspective creates *camera obscura* wafers of urban life in motion.

The big picture, however, is up on the roof. Here the public is invited to gaze through a powerful twelve-inch telescope at whatever is visible in the night sky: Saturn, Jupiter, Mars, the moon, and sundry celestial phenomena. Also on the roof are three solar telescopes, which offer views of the prominences at the edge of the sun, the solar spectrum and the sun itself. The telescopes are generally open from after dark until 10 p.m.

Arrive early enough before shows to allow time for the Hall of Science. It has seismological instruments, a six-foot moon globe, meteorites, a giant Tesla-coil, a cosmic ray cloud chamber, space-craft models, and other exhibits, permanent and changing. In another hall are a set of weight scales that show how much visitors would weigh on the moon, Jupiter, Mars, and Saturn. Tours are given at regular intervals.

The bookshop on the main floor carries astronomy slides, a small selection of related books, star-finders, charts, posters, and souvenir items.

Knott's Berry Farm
8039 Beach Boulevard
Buena Park   (714) 827-1776

Knott's Berry Farm is the Horatio Alger of amusement parks. It has grown from a Depression era berry patch and roadside stand to the present 150-acre valhalla of wholesome, countrified family entertainment. It's the third largest theme amusement park in the country, and the oldest. Dedicated to preserving California's heritage right along with an annual harvest of one million pounds of boysenberries, the Knott clan has developed a squeaky clean, homey mosaic of thrill rides, nostalgia, live performances, dining alternatives, and endless emporia of every imaginable specialty. The park is festooned with flora of all kinds, and it is difficult not to get caught up in the cheerful innocence of the place. Visitors should try to come as early as possible, not so much to get a jump on the weekend crowds (over 20,000) as to get around to all the attractions.

Knott's comprises three themed areas, best encountered at a random stroll:

Old West Ghost Town is a fey reproduction of an 1849 mining town that is part movie set and part museum. Whether one is riding the restored 1881 Calico Railway train or a Wells Fargo stagecoach, a mock armed holdup will be staged to delight the kids. There's a hokey ride through a synthetic gold mine complete with robotic miners and near cave-ins. There's a sluice box from which to pan for gold ($100,000 is "discovered" annually, we're told). There are innumerable backdrops against which to shoot pictures, including a fully regaled Indian chief and a bona fide blacksmith fabricating horseshoes at an astounding rate. The streets are lined with a rib-tickling array of peek-in-window wax figure tableaux, such as a coyly arranged wild west brothel, a Chinese laundry, and a jerk-water jailhouse's sullen boarder. It's all goofy, but it's irresistible to the voyeur in us all. An exuberant revue of high-stepping cancan girls can be seen at the Calico Saloon, while the Birdcage Theater offers affecting hiss-the-villain melodramas. It is precious stage Americana, a dying genre, accompanied by old-timey piano.

Fiesta Village is a collage of Early California Hispanic culture. It is a colorfully distracting succession of parades, piñatas, wandering mariachis, and still more bit players from Central Casting. The quarter includes open-air mercados, arcades, Animal Farm with hundreds of barnyard beasts for city kiddies to pet, all the enchiladas you can eat, and El Cinema Grande, a 180-degree projection theater that runs breathtaking you-are-there aerial footage. And don't let your kids miss the marionette theater, one of the best around.

Roaring 20's Area and Airfield is supposed to evoke the jazz era, but its miniature classic auto ride isn't enough to do the trick. Aside from its two teenage discos, its character is pure carnival: shooting galleries, thrill rides, hot dogs and Pepsis at every turn, interminable lines. It is good, clean fun at a frenzied pitch.

A giddy counterpoint emerges between Knott's historic motifs and the anti-gravity technology that rises up in every direction. It's unnerving how so many people can consume so much food and immediately thereafter throw themselves on the mercy of careening roller coasters, revolving cages, log-bearing rapids, and lurching burros. Montezooma's Revenge, located next to Fiesta Village, shoots paying customers through a 360-degree loop at fifty-five miles per hour and returns them backwards—in less than thirty seconds. As many as 1,500 souls *an hour* queue up for this one. The Log Ride, located in the Ghost Town, is available to the more faint-hearted: its challenge lies in drying off afterwards. The rest of the thrill rides, located in the Roaring 20's Area and Airfield, include the Corkscrew, whose finale is a fearsome double-twist helix, and the Sky Jump, our favorite. It's a simulated parachute drop from a twenty-story tower, and the view at the top is magnificent, fear and trembling notwithstanding.

Although there are some twenty eateries at Knott's (all dry), this excursion wouldn't feel quite complete without feasting at the Chicken Dinner Restaurant. Cordelia Knott began selling this homemade fare in 1934 to bolster strained family income, and they're now serving half a million chickens a year. The spartan decor is absolutely appropriate to the hearty simplicity of the restaurant's single entrée.

Bring money. Situated throughout the park are shops where it is possible to find, among the usual trinkets, baked goods, Western and Mexican clothing, while-u-wait pastel portraits, religious miscellany, collector dolls, antique guns, magic tricks, and of course, Knott's renowned preserves.

The Knott family takes the summer season very seriously. They book names like Marcel Marceau and the Joffrey Ballet, the best bluegrass musicians alive, big bands, stunt shows, square dancing, film series, and more. Their annual country fair in April is a rustic revel where one can realize one's ambitions of greased-pig catching, wheelbarrow-jousting, cow-milking, banjo-picking, or arm-wrestling.

Lion Country Safari
Irvine Center exit, San Diego Freeway
Laguna Hills   (714) 837-1200

Orange County may seem a tame, hospitable place, but situated at its heart is a 500-acre African wildlife preserve teeming with animals that would as soon have you as an hors d'oeuvre as look at you. Noting the popularity of wild game preserves in Africa, conservationist Harry Shuster created Lion Country Safari as a transplanted habitat of lions, zebras, giraffes, elephants, and countless other species normally found on the African veldt. It's really eight preserves in one, separating the more incompatible beasts so that propagation of rarer species is maximized.

Lion Country Safari is the best that a zoo can be: the animals roam freely while the visitors remain "caged" in their vehicles and drive through at their own pace. Gaping at animals behind metal bars is really not quite the same as winding along miles of safari trails and watching big game come right up to the car to give you the once-over. It's *their* turf you're on, and they appear nobler for it. Thanks to a much-praised preservation program, it is possible to see some rare and extraordinary creatures, such as the Persian gazelle and the white rhinoceros.

Included in the main-gate ticket price is Safari Camp, an African theme-park in a semi-tropical landscape filled with exotic trees, shrubs, and flowers from around the world. There's live entertainment at the Bubbles (the Hippo) Memorial Theater, a bird revue called "Feathery Follies" at the outdoor Afritheater, a cruise on the Zambezi River, a ride on the African Express or a rented hippo pedal-boat, African-style architecture, and exquisite wild birds aplenty.

Over in the Petting Village, the kids can feed and coddle baby animals until dusk, when the park closes.

Watching all those animals during feeding time may or may not give you an appetite. If it does, the scenic Rondavel Restaurant offers dining on the shore of Lake Shanalee. There are also refreshment kiosks and cool, shaded picnic areas.

Trader Robbie's offers a selection of authentic African artifacts, fashions, and curios, along with souvenirs, toys, and film. You'll want to take lots of pictures in the preserve.

The best time to go out to Lion Country Safari is when it's raining or just generally cooler, because the animals aren't very active in midday heat. Convertibles are not allowed in the preserve, but air-conditioned automobiles are available for renting.

The people who created Magic Mountain used a simple formula: more is more. This 200-acre family amusement complex has everything a cabin-fevered mom and pop could hope for to work off their kids' surplus energy. While Disneyland offers the best of fantasy attractions to its patrons, Magic Mountain has concentrated on thrill rides, delivering the most thorough selection of white-knucklers available anywhere. One goes to Magic Mountain to have one's senses soundly thumped, glutted, and numbed. A full day's immersion in the park's hurly-burly atmosphere will cure the most acute doldrums, with the gusto of a Fourth of July celebration.

Magic Mountain
Magic Mountain Parkway exit,
Golden State Freeway
Valencia   (805) 255-4100

Located in the rolling hills and arroyos of Valencia, a tidy if unexciting planned community thirty minutes north of Hollywood, Magic Mountain gives you some seventy-five rides and attractions for a single admission price, so there's no bother with tickets to this and that. The best initiation to the park is via the encircling smooth-as-silk monorail, called The Metro, at Whitewater Lake Station, a short walk from the entrance. It's a great way to get acquainted with the layout of the place and see from above just how nicely landscaped it is.

Magic Mountain is particularly cherished by the kind of pleasure-seeker who prefers his high jinks at high speeds. For starters, the park has five roller coasters. The recently erected Colossus, the largest, fastest, highest, and steepest wooden roller coaster ever built and the first to offer two descents in excess of 100 feet, is unquestionably the star of the show. It has two sets of parallel tracks so that coasters can "race" each other at up to 65 mph along 9,200 feet of track in 3½ minutes worth of gravity-throttling terror. The Revolution is the world's longest steel roller coaster, whose tour de force is an exhilarating 360-degree vertical loop. The ride, 113 feet at its highest point and 60 mph at top speed, is a long-playing version of Knott's Berry Farm's Montezooma's Revenge. There's also the Gold Rusher, a harrowing "runaway" mine train, and The Mountain Express, a twisting European import.

Any critique of Magic Mountain's thrill quotient would belie the fact that people have different viscera. But it's safe to say that there is something for every stomach. The Scrambler, which is an effective variation of the time-honored whipping disc ride, snaps riders around at the outermost point of a continuous spin-within-a-spin. The Electric Rainbow is set up so that riders become glued to the metal-mesh wall of a large revolving drum by sheer centrifugal force while the drum slowly lifts into a Ferris wheel position. This one is gorgeous to watch from either on board or down on terra firma. The Enterprise, our nomination for the Sustained Nausea Award, is like the Electric Rainbow, with the added jolly of sitting in hinged cars that swing out from the wheel. The Log Jammer is a sort of aquatic roller coaster with log-shaped boats rushing through a watery maze of chutes. Other ride names hint at the immense variety of locomotion here: El Bumpo, The Sand Blasters, The Swiss Twist, The Crazy Barrels, Himalaya, Jet Stream. . . . Don't miss the spectacular views to be had from the Eagle's Flight Tramway, the classic forty-degree inclined Funicular to the summit of Magic Mountain, and the 384-foot Sky Tower. If these don't bring on acrophobia, you should also try The Galaxy, the highest double-arm Ferris wheel in the world.

Despite its high-powered ambience, Magic Mountain is by no means short on nostalgia. The Grand Carousel, a beautifully restored classic merry-go-round, has its original wooden horses, chariots, and hurdy-gurdy organ. The Grand Centennial Excursion is a train ride into an antique California landscape dotted with buffalo, longhorn cattle, and elk. Spillikin Corners is a theme village where sixteen traditional American crafts are demonstrated by master blacksmiths, glassblowers, potters, dollmakers, and so on. This area, which also boasts an amphitheater and an arboretum, is especially welcome at the point when you're too wobbly to go on another ride.

For the kiddies too young to rollick at high velocity, there's a whole fun-ground just for them. Children's World features pint-sized rides like Clown Coaster and the Red Baron's Airplanes. Animal Farm has gentle, pettable creatures from lions and llamas to chimps and chickens, along with a Pennsylvania Dutch barn. Wizard's Village is an acre of climbable kidstuff. The Trollywood Steam Train has scheduled runs to the home of the park's mascot trolls. These ever-present hairy little guys are the signature of the park's elusive theme, something like Mickey Mouse in a gorilla suit. These and a seven-foot itinerant wizard.

The food at Magic Mountain is various and plentiful, from the standard carnival hot dog on up to the cordon bleu Four Winds Restaurant perched at the peak of the mountain. Das Alpenhaus serves German cuisine in pseudo-*bierhalle* decor, La Cantina serves Mexican food, the Valencia Terrace serves farmstyle breakfasts and the Deli serves huge sandwiches, salads, and fruit juices. Quality varies.

A round of gift shops like Wizard's Wares, The Portal House, and The Square Bear offer jewelry, clothing, and souvenirs gathered from around the world. Shops in Spillikin Corners sell handcrafted items.

Summer night entertainment is presented in the Showcase Theater with talent like the Pointer Sisters, the Temptations, Sha Na Na, and Jose Feliciano. Live rock bands perform at the Jungle Disco, and the Rainbow Street Theater provides mime, magic, and juggling.

If this is your first visit to California and you've never seen the Pacific Ocean before, you should proceed directly to Marineland. This seaside theme park offers a pristine 180-degree vista of Catalina Island and the Pacific that beats anything south of Big Sur. From the park's Cliff Walk there's a spectacular view of the northern coastline and the Point Vicente Lighthouse Station. But Hanna-Barbera, who has renovated and newly landscaped its recently acquired park, also means for you and the kids to be entertained.

There's a continuous schedule of live shows that star remarkably well-trained sea animals and birds in a number of specially-designed open-air amphitheaters. Some of these shows are decked in fanciful theatrical backdrops and are narrated by ebullient,

Marineland
6600 Palos Verdes Drive South
Rancho Palos Verdes   377-1571

Joe Barbera, Bill Hanna, and famous Marine-land attractions.

tanned youths who chatter like disc jockeys. But we learn from them, for instance, that the leads in the Killer Whale Show, named Corky and Orky, are the largest calf-bearing killer whales in captivity and that Corky (or is it Orky?) weighs in at 14,000 pounds and stands twenty-five feet in his stocking feet. Their stunts, like leaping eighteen feet out of the water to grab a fish from a trainer's teeth, show off the animal's intelligence, gentleness, speed, and strength. A designated five-row "splash zone" warns visitors that these are very wet acts indeed.

Huckleberry Hound's Sea Lion Pirate School is aquatic burlesque at its most amusing. For a morsel of fish, trained sea lions do anything their pretty ship's captain commands, including walking a tightrope, a gangplank, and on water. Dolphin Island poses two emcee-surfers stranded on a bogus tropical island with six uncanny bottle-nosed dolphins. The finale finds one of the lads "waterskiing" on the backs of two dolphins. An act with Bubbles The Whale, the park's senior animal performer, partnered with two other dolphins is just more splashes and virtuoso leaps. Polly In Paradise is a new show starring ten colorful military macaws engaging in predictable feather-brained antics.

There's plenty of dry entertainment, too. The Land of Happiness Show is a perky stage production featuring a cast of Hanna-Barbera characters like Yogi Bear, Pixie & Dixie, and Snaggletooth. Singing To The World is a fast-paced musical revue with eight singer-dancers and a talented group of instrumentalists, seen in the Showplace-By-The-Sea amphitheater every day except Monday. Pets and Pirates is an energetic comedy band that roams through the park, as do several stray Hanna-Barbera critters who offer a paw-shake here and a photo pose there. Your kids will love most all of these amusements.

The most fascinating aspect of Marineland is its collections of sealife. Encyclopedia Britannica has set up a wondrous exhibit called Passages Beneath the Sea, filling thirty aquaria with the most beautiful, bizarre, and lethal undersea creatures imaginable, separated into the ocean's various zones. There's an open habitat pool with live sharks at the end of the exhibit.

Elsewhere in the park is a five-level viewing tank with schools of fish ogling the humans, and there are ponds stocked with oversized goldfish. Another viewing tank reveals a family of walruses, adorably immense, bewhiskered and betusked.

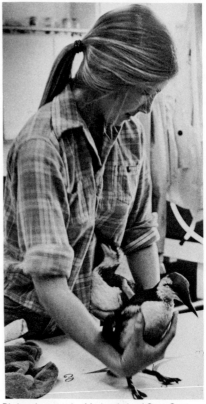
Bird patients at the Marine Animal Care Center.

At the Marine Animal Care Center, visitors may observe through large windows the care and cure of sick, wounded, and orphaned sea creatures. There are two-way microphones with which to ask questions of the lab technicians. This behind-the-scenes glimpse of Marineland's caretaking activities proves the place has a heart. Seaside Courtyard is a landscaped area that displays giant sea turtles, Japanese Koi fish, and California Harbor Seals. Over at Sea Lion Point, visitors may venture within twenty yards of crashing surf and observe the only colony of wild sea lions in Southern California.

The newest attraction, and easily the most exciting, is Baja Reef. It's the world's first man-made swim-through aquarium. For $2.75 visitors may don a wetsuit, snorkel, mask, and fins and venture along an eighty-yard, twelve-foot-deep course populated with some 2,000 fish. The attraction is designed to duplicate the area of Baja coastline between Ensenada and Cabo San Lucas, and it comes complete with Calico bass, garibaldis, leopard sharks, bat rays, turtles, to name a few species. For those who don't want to get wet (even though the water is a comfortable seventy-two degrees), there are underwater viewing ports.

When the kids need to work off some restlessness, there's Fred

Flintstone's Fun Factory, located on the cliffs. It's a playground with swings, slides, and an assortment of climbing, crawling, and jumping apparatuses that'll tire any kid out in short order.

Be sure not to miss the Sky Tower, a circular elevator ride up 344 feet above the sea. It offers a panoramic view along the coastline and out to sea for some twenty miles.

Movieland Wax Museum
Palace of Living Art
7711 Beach Boulevard
Buena Park   583-8025

Lawanda Page poses with wax double of herself and Redd Foxx.

From the annual Academy Award ritual to the cement impressions in front of Grauman's Chinese, Southern California has always hallowed its most compelling industry—Movies. It was inevitable that a temple should be erected in the name of the Silver Screen. And as any cross-breeding of contemporary religion and mass tourism will, Movieland Wax Museum attains a high kitsch that you must go a ways to surrender to, especially if you're the sort that finds waxworks "creepy." But it's worth it.

Behind an expansive, neon-crested facade are the life-size figures of over 200 television and film stars poised in more than ninety minutely replicated scenes. Gloria Swanson in *Sunset Boulevard*, Judy Garland in *The Wizard of Oz*, Basil Rathbone as Sherlock Holmes, Sophia Loren, Greta Garbo, Clark Gable, the Marx Brothers, et al. Some are dressed in the original costume. Most look convincingly like their subject, if occasionally woodenly posed or unflatteringly complexioned. Often, lavish sets have been devised to heighten drama, as with the *Ben Hur* chariot race scene and the twisted wreckage of *The Poseidon Adventure*.

This is illusion feeding on illusion, mere wax canonizing flickering light. It's appropriate that these film gods and goddesses should be housed next door to wax depictions of the *Last Supper*, the Crucifixion, the *Pietà*, and *Moses*. Movie stars inspire the closest thing to idolatry this secular century has produced.

The presentation is wholly apt. The winding labyrinth that visitors must follow is of the nature of a twisting thread of story. The ubiquitous mirrors represent the particular vanity of film, that unreal and fleeting reflection of ourselves. The darkness of the corridors punctuated with brightly spotlit vignettes gives the sense of illuminated visions in a darkened theater. Soundtracks, borrowed from the actual scenes portrayed, complete the self-contained frozen shards of film history. The overall effect can be intimate, devotional, haunting—infinitely more moving than if the exhibits had been amassed in a couple of large, undelineated halls, behind glass, silent.

It's amusing to speculate what future archaeologists will make of these effigies. Long after all celluloid record has decomposed, what could anyone think of a still-life Bogart and Hepburn in a rowboat behind a clapperboard that said *African Queen*? Or a menacing Edward G. Robinson beside a bullet-riddled storefront window and another clapperboard that said *Little Caesar*?

The museum doesn't rest on its Oscars; additions to the celebrity list are made all the time. Recent creations include Christopher Reeve as Superman, Barbra Streisand in *Hello Dolly*, the cast of television's "Star Trek," Burt Reynolds in *Deliverance* and Henry Winkler as the Fonz. Somehow the facsimiles of these newcomers aren't quite as satisfying, like homage before its time.

Very few film greats escape the wax treatment. In the Western genre alone, the museum spotlights early white hats like Tom Mix and William S. Hart, Will Rogers, John Wayne, Gary Cooper in (what else?) *High Noon*, Alan Ladd, Ward Bond, Robert Redford and Paul Newman in *Butch Cassidy and the Sundance Kid*, the entire "Bonanza" cast, Chuck Connors, and Roy Rogers. We did miss the Lone Ranger and Hopalong Cassidy.

Adjacent to Movieland and included in the price of admission is the Palace of Living Art. Visitors are confronted with a collection of life-size, three-dimensional wax interpretations of famous paintings, along with reproductions of notable sculptures. We had a harder time swallowing the rationale for these imitations. There's something cloying about translating pictorial masterpieces into pop-out versions of themselves. Whatever it is that makes the *Mona Lisa*, *Blue Boy*, and *Whistler's Mother* great is lost in this slavish technical feat.

A recently unveiled wax figure of Lawrence Welk.

Across the way from the wax complex is the new Haunted House, a fun specimen of hodgepodge ramshackle architecture. The "enter at your own risk" disclaimer might apply, if you scare easily. Once inside, you will encounter about six actors in full ghoulish uniform who will try their damnedest to give you cardiac arrest. Enough said.

At strategic points on your way around Movieland there are two walk-up restaurants, one a small cafeteria inside the museum and the other, the California Plaza, a beautifully landscaped outdoor affair in a tiled Early California motif. It's good for soups, salads, and sandwiches and carries beer and wine. There are also four different gift shops on the grounds, two photo stands, two photo galleries that offer shots of you and yours with your favorite monsters, and a studio where you can have pastel portraits made on the spot.

Queen Mary
Southern end of
Long Beach Freeway
Long Beach 435-4747

In 1967, after thirty-three years of illustrious service, the *R.M.S. Queen Mary* was permanently docked in Long Beach Harbor. The much-revered vessel was refurbished and made into a sightseeing attraction that will warm the heart of anyone who has ever voyaged on her, and amaze anyone who hasn't. She is an Art Deco jewel, on an extraordinary scale, an awesome combination of engineering prowess and thirties' design elegance. Her 81,000 tons of nostalgia harken back to a more opulent, civilized, stylish mode of travel.

Visitors will find that most of the tour is an unguided but easily followed course through the Queen's innards. There's a large hall featuring displays that illustrate the ship's checkered career (with a rousing account of her wartime role as a troop carrier and hospital ship) and a museum's worth of mementos and lovingly preserved settings. From her gym and barber shop to her most soigné salons and restaurants, the "Mary" is showcased in such a manner that one feels this mass of raw steel and dated interiors has a soul.

As you descend into the engine chambers, recorded voices explain the turbine workings that powered the behemoth. These and other specifications read like "Ripley's Believe It or Not": the liner got thirteen feet per gallon on as much as 240,000 horsepower, it cost $70,000 a day to keep her running, the four propellors weigh a total of 140 tons, it takes thirty tons of paint to cover her million-square feet of exterior, and endless other mathematical bogglers.

On another of the Queen's twelve decks, the Hall of Maritime Heritage houses a fascinating collection of detailed ship models, from centuries-old galleons up to a five-foot replica of the *Queen Mary* herself. Farther on, there is Jacques Cousteau's "Living Sea" exhibit, an appended theme museum that celebrates and explains the Earth's undersea environment. Through a round of films, electronic display gadgetry, and various aquaria (one contains a couple of sharks), visitors get a sizeable but digestible helping of marine biology. The living tidepool at the end is a big hit with children; they can pick up live starfish and urchins, and study them closely.

Just beyond the luxuriously tiled first-class swimming pool, visitors enter a spartan third-class dining room where they are grouped and guided up through prototypical cabins, then up onto the bow and occasionally up into the bridge. As lofty a perch as this provides, Long Beach offers a less than spectacular vista. Still, it is thrilling having this venerable giantess under one's feet.

Back down on the Promenade Deck, and self-paced once again, visitors may enjoy a boulevard of shops, from tobacconist to hobby outlet, and the Observation Lounge in rich period decor. Restaurants on this deck include Lord Nelson's, Lady Hamilton's, and the Queen Mary Dinner Playhouse. If these aren't enough, there is Sir Winston Churchill's on the Sun Deck and the Capstan Coffee Shop on A-Deck. A fifty-cent boarding fee will allow one access to these establishments after hours. The shops are generally open until about 10 p.m., the lounge until about 1 a.m.

Out-of-towners in need of lodging might well consider the Queen Mary Hyatt Hotel. Guests stay in the original ship's staterooms and have the rest of the Queen as their playground. Call 435-3511 for further information.

Adjacent to the *Queen Mary* is Mary's Gate Village which sports shops, a pub, and a spate of small eateries. The Jazz Safari serves live jazz with its lunches and dinners. Private guided tours of the vessel for twenty or more persons may be arranged ten days in advance.

Anyone who's ever seen a movie and wondered how it was put together will enjoy Universal Studio's tour package. The world's largest film and television production complex, Universal has handily cashed in on the public's fascination with screen entertainment. They've developed a glamorized, "behind-the-scenes" pastiche of studio sleight-of-hand that would have made Cecil B. De Mille proud. Each year over three million people are shuttled in candy-striped open-air trams through the 420-acre lot, past wardrobe and make-up departments, stars' dressing rooms, sets, sound stages, props, and countless other corners of the glitter factory.

The tour is divided into a two-and-a-half-hour guided meander through the studio labyrinth and several hours in the Visitors' Entertainment Center, which features four live shows, exhibits, shops, and restaurants. The tour guides on the trams all seem to be hopeful young comics, sprinkling the carnival barker spiel with their own humorous material.

The one stop on the guided portion is at Sound Stage Thirty-Two, which contains three different sets. On the first, there are demonstrations of rear-screen projection and matte process photography, nuts 'n' bolts stuff about production that reveals the flip side of movie magic. On the second set, visitors find themselves inside a replica of the Bionic Woman's apartment, where they are shown less than remarkable lighting and sound gimmickry. The third set is called the Bionic Testing Center. To visitors age ten and younger, audience volunteers appear to be rendered temporarily "bionic"

Universal Studios Tour
Universal City exit,
Hollywood Freeway
North Hollywood   877-2121

"Family" and friends at the tour center.

A green greeting from The Incredible Hulk.

View from Prop Plaza, *one stop on the Universal Studio Tour.*

An encounter with aliens from the Battle of Galactica.

and to demonstrate feats of superhuman strength. To everyone else, these same volunteers appear to be the unwitting foils of thinly disguised studio technology. But that's okay; trickery unveiled is what this tour is about.

Trams reboarded, visitors are conveyed through a maze of ersatz locales: Colonial Street, New York Street, Six Points Texas, and other false-front strips that stir intense déjà-vues for all the movies that have been shot there, going back to Tom Mix in 1918. Our favorite setting en route is the mansion used in Hitchcock's *Psycho*, gloomily perched high on a hill. With a straight face, the tour guide dubs the road leading up to it the "Psycho Path."

What follows is a succession of special effects which, for all the hype that has been lavished on this part of the tour, are embarrassingly anticlimactic. One particularly epic disappointment is a facsimile of the infamous *Jaws* shark that thrusts up at the tram in lunatic repetition, huffing noisily and looking much too synthetic. There is also a collapsing wooden bridge that doesn't really, a nine-ton runaway locomotive that stops in the nick o' time, a flash flood, and The Parting of The Red Sea. This last phenomenon is not so much a dramatic wonder as an electronic one, being neither tidal in scale nor Biblical in vehemence. The closest thing to a thrill ride is the Doomed Glacier Expedition. The tram enters a simulated ice cavern that is set up to revolve in a way that suggests an Alpine

The Shark from Jaws *cools off summer visitors.*

avalanche, sort of. The real effect is the vertiginous illusion that the tram is teetering onto its side, an optical trick that leaves one quite breathless.

Prop Plaza is the kind of attraction that appeals to people who think big. An oversized table, chair, camera, knife, telephone, and scissors have been rummaged from flicks like *The Incredible Shrinking Man* to create a surreal landscape. Visitors may also poke around a Western jail, a stagecoach with a looped moving background, portable palm trees, the John Wayne "war wagon," and other prop department clichés. There is a snack bar at this point and a picnic area that commands a view of the San Fernando Valley and Lakeside Country Club.

The live shows that await visitors at the Entertainment Center are among the high points of the day. A live stunt show features a brawler disappearing into a quicksand pit and gunfighters being shot off high roofs. The Land of a Thousand Faces is a make-up show in which volunteers are transformed into Frankenstein and his Bride by the miracle of cosmetic science, only to be assailed by The Incredible Hulk. It's kid stuff, but it's great. In the Screen Test Theater, a few intrepid tour guests become actors in underwater scenes which are filmed and intercut with actual footage from *Airport 77*, then instant-replayed. In terms of capturing the spirit of moviemaking, of turning the previous displays of gadgetry and masquerade into film action, this is the day's payoff. Unless, of course, one gets a glimpse of some of the in-the-flesh stars at large on the lot at any given time.

There are dining areas and gift shops galore in the Entertainment Center, and it seems that camera film is sold at every turn. In fact, if you forget to bring your camera, they will rent you one. They are dying for you to take pictures. The Tour is nothing if not photogenic.

Universal has opened a new attraction based on its *Battlestar Galactica* series-to-motion picture. Tour trams are driven into the midst of a live-action laser battle and ushered into a giant space vehicle by Cylon warriors. For sheer array of hardware and special effects, this is great fun.

If you've been searching all over the country for a single-wattled cassowary and you're about to give up, don't. The Los Angeles Zoo has them. They also have emperor tamarins, mountain tapirs, red-flanked duikers, and several other species available for viewing nowhere else in the United States.

The zoo is divided by area of origin: Africa, Australia, Eurasia, North America, and South America. In the two to four hours that a complete tour of the zoo takes, visitors may also look into the aquatics section, alpine animal hillside, Children's Zoo, Reptile House, Aviary, and the large walk-through flight cage. There are about 2,000 creatures in all, representing some 500 species.

Topatopa, the only California condor in captivity, resides at the Los Angeles Zoo.

Los Angeles Zoo
Junction of Ventura and
Golden State Freeways
Los Angeles   666-4650

Sure, there's your basic lion, elephant, and crocodile. But that's kidstuff. Any zoogoer worth his salted peanuts should be able to identify the following: gerenuk, bongo, harpy eagle, Arabian oryx, Japanese serow, golden-lion marmoset, springbok, binturong, and Przewski horse. Extra points for finding the Tasmanian devils. Markhors and brindled gnus get half.

An outstanding botanical garden complements the resident fauna. Thousands of flowers, trees, and shrubs from all parts of the world are planted throughout the 113-acre facility, usually reflecting the clime of each represented region of the world.

Snack stands, gift shops, and two large picnic areas are available on the zoo grounds. Trams provide transportation around the perimeter of the zoo, running approximately every twenty minutes.

Trainer Scott Riddle puts Joyce, an Asian elephant, through her paces as part of her training program.

California chic at So Much & Co.

SHOPPING:

Clothes, Books, Antiques, Markets and Butchers, Bakeries, Delis, and Bargains.

By Anne Gilbar,
LOS ANGELES MAGAZINE

I love to shop.

It's not so much that I love to own things; it's not having a closet full of clothes or a cupboard full of antiques that gives me that high. It's seeing the variety of beautiful, well-designed, wonderfully clever items that are available nowadays.

My friends always say I'm the kind of shopper who can go into a store where the shelves are lined with enticing objects that dazzle and confuse the eye, and can immediately focus on the shirt that is imported French silk, hand-finished, and costs four times as much as anything else in the place. But I'm also the kind of shopper whose greatest satisfaction is buying those two enormous black glass vases for $200 at Kreiss Imports when Neiman-Marcus has a similar version priced at $500 for one, then forever reveling in the smug knowledge that my two look much better than their one.

For me, Los Angeles is a shopping paradise. Take it from a seasoned shopper—I've lived in New York and in Paris, spent time in London and Buenos Aires, San Francisco and Rio de Janeiro, Tel Aviv and Rome—and dropped money in all those places. But today, Los Angeles, with its range of neighborhoods, the varied heritage of its residents, the pervasive "let's try it" attitude rather than "it can't be done"—and the money and talent available for designing, for buying and selling—is indeed a shopper's haven. Whether it's looking for antiques along Melrose Avenue, hopping into the furniture showrooms along Robertson Boulevard, gazing in amazement at those dazzling stores (and inevitable movie stars) lining beautiful Rodeo Drive, or smiling in delight at the many novelty shops lining the streets of Venice—you can find it all in Los Angeles.

Before setting out to become acquainted with the shopping market in L.A., better give in and realize that you need a car. Especially for those used to shopping in cities where taxis and subways are always just around the next corner, it seems hard to believe that very little public transportation is available.

The city of Los Angeles is only one area in Los Angeles County; there are other shopping districts in and around L.A. proper, like Santa Monica, Venice, Sherman Oaks, and the queen of them all, Beverly Hills. Often referred to as a "conglomeration of suburbs," L.A. is made up of small communities, each adjacent to the next and each carefully guarding characteristics of its own. Thus, each small area will have its own markets, clothing stores, beauty salons, and varied specialty shops. The trick is in knowing those unique stores in each neighborhood, and allowing time to spend walking around. Moreover, some areas specialize in certain kinds of stores. For example, Santa Monica's Main Street is lined with antique stores and current specialty shops. The area around Robertson Boulevard in West Hollywood abounds in furniture showrooms. Sunset Plaza, also in West Hollywood, has lovely, smaller stores carrying anything from silver and kitchen accessories to gifts and chic dresses. Sunset Boulevard in Silverlake has a block of stores carrying imported novelty items and gifts; La Cienega Boulevard is known for its art galleries, Sawtelle Boulevard for Japanese nurseries and gift shops, and the *crème de la crème*—Rodeo Drive in Beverly Hills— has a variety of everything except quality and price, both being consistently high.

Before we begin our discriminating survey of selected boutiques around Los Angeles, a word about the virtues of department stores. If you still have the view that these enormous warehouses for anything your heart desires only carry mediocre and ordinary selections of merchandise, forget it. Department stores, especially in Southern California, have entered the market of high class, designer, and avant-garde clothing, furniture, and accessories. Many chain stores now carry, in one place, a variety of items you would have found only at various boutiques around the city. For example, Bullock's has some of the best accessory departments anywhere. From the latest in jewelry designs, to hair combs and barrettes, to bags, hats, leotards, and the like, Bullock's buyers have come of age, with these departments carrying a large selection of colors, sizes, and varieties at reasonable prices. Neiman-Marcus also has terrific accessory deprtments (they are dispersed throughout the stores so you have to be sure to try every floor), with imported Chinese, Indian, and European gifts leading the list. But since their collection tends to rely more on well-known designer items, the merchandise here is generally more expensive than in other places. Robinson's has revised all their stores—their shoe departments are super, as are Neiman-Marcus'. The Broadway, Sak's Fifth Avenue, I. Magnin's (especially that lovely store in the center of Los Angeles), all have growing departments that carry the latest in everything. Another chain store, Judy's, is a terrific place to get inexpensive items that are copied from current styles in major fashion magazines. And new arrivals to Southern California, the Ann Taylor shops, bring to the West great clothes and shoes at reasonable prices.

In this chapter you will find stores listed under categories rather than areas. If you are intending to go to a certain area and want to cover all the stores there, just check the location of each store and make a list of all those in that neighborhood. Only one area—Rodeo Drive in Beverly Hills—is covered as a whole. I have listed the most unusual stores in this haven, but the best advice is to walk along every street and go into those shops that are enticing to you.

RODEO DRIVE

Rodeo (Ro-dáy-o) Drive has to be the only street in the world with its own public relations firm. This well-known company which regularly represents those in the movie industry is eager to disburse a beautifully printed folder about the area, including a packet complete with testimonials (says Andy Warhol, "Rodeo is a giant butterscotch sundae, deliciously edible, including the nuts"; adds Halston, "One of the most magical streets of America").

Please note that the shopping area in Beverly Hills is not limited to Rodeo Drive. In fact, terrific stores are located in an area encompassing Rodeo, Beverly, Camden, and Bedford drives, and Brighton Way. Below is a list of my favorite stores here. Some made it because they have fabulous merchandise; others for the audacity of their prices and decor; still others are, simply put, an experience, and have merchandise you'll be hard put to find anywhere else.

Giorgio

Star of the novel *Scruples* is Giorgio, one of the largest, fanciest, most service-oriented stores on Rodeo Drive. Owned by long-time Beverly Hills resident Fred Hayman, this beautiful store boasts a bar (complete with bartender) dispensing anything your heart desires on the house, a pool table, very specialized service, and an array of clothing and accessories for men and women. It is like a classy, small-scale department store designed in glorious living color. You'll find all designer-name clothing, other classic odds and ends, a complete shoe department (with reasonable prices), and more.

Right Bank Clothing Company and Tea Room

Up the street is the Right Bank Clothing Company and Tea Room, owned by Donald Pliner (who also owns the Right Bank Shoe Company on Camden Drive, one block west). The Tea Room, run by Sheila Ricci, is a tiny, lovely, private terrace with a limited menu where everything is freshly made, superbly served, and tastes delicious. The store itself carries trendy, outrageous, and fanciful designs at prices that are sometimes equally outrageous, although every now and then you can find a unique and more reasonably priced item that is the perfect accent to your wardrobe. Next door

Gunn Trigère

is Gunn Trigère, carrying expensive imported clothing and a unique line of silver jewelry. My favorite item here is a small, silk camellia that costs fifteen dollars and looks real enough to water.

Jerry Magnin

Jerry Magnin has the best collection of men's clothing, from the finest (and most expensive) and most elegant clothing to more casual and less-expensive sporty items. Jerry always has the latest merchandise—the latest shoes, beach bags that turn into blankets, belts with ceramic buckles, shirts boasting your favorite car's name, and sweaters hand-knit with your favorite phone number.

Gucci; Hermès; Céline; Van Cleef and Arpels

Farther up the street are Gucci, Hermès, Céline, Van Cleef and Arpels—all expensive stores that carry price tags to boggle most minds. Visiting them is an experience. Unfortunately, unless you are a regular customer or are obviously rich, you may find the reception at these stores less than cordial. Also on Rodeo is a

Theodore

favorite of mine, Theodore, an avant-garde shop where you'll find a large selection of cotton T-shirts, silk shirts, pants, blazers, and the trendiest items with well-known labels (especially DBA, designed by the store's owner, Norma Fink). My favorite part of Theodore is Pepi's, a jewelry counter that surpasses most in the simplicity and elegance of its gold jewelry. Next door is Theodore

Theodore Man

Man which has a well-stocked line of men's imported sportswear.

Williams-Sonoma

Williams-Sonoma is a lovely kitchen supply store and is also listed under that section.

On Brighton Way are some terrific, unusual shops. Alan Austin and Company is a women's shop that offers tailored, well-made, beautifully designed clothes in the latest fashions, colors, and fabrics. You can always count on Austin's clothes to not only fit well but to be wearable for years. The prices are high—but at this shop you are getting what you pay for. JAG started out as a jeans cavalcade, but lately has also been carrying a line of clothing in the newest fads. Dinallo, which carries its own label, is best known for its line of evening gowns that are considered some of the most fashionable around.

Alan Austin and Company

JAG

Dinallo

On Camden Drive you'll find The Rainbow (we list it under unusual shops, too) which has toys, children's clothing, and accessories in a lovely store, especially meaningful since all proceeds go to the Amie Karen Cancer Foundation. The Right Bank Shoe Company and Dorso's (which carries couturier men's and women's clothing) are nearby. Charles Gallay is well-known for carrying many French and Italian imports at couturier prices, as well as many respected California designs. Across the street is S.H. Platt and Company, which copies famous jewelry designs at well-below other stores' costs. On Bedford Drive you'll find Harold's Place, a virtual fantasy of anything you can think of, a tiny shop which has fur coats, Art Deco dishes (the real thing, folks), hundreds of pins, combs, barrettes, toys, and novelty items. Prices range from ridiculous to reasonable.

The Rainbow

Right Bank Shoe Company
Dorso's
Charles Gallay

S.H. Platt and Company

Harold's Place

In this section, we have by no means covered the entire area. There are many other stores, well-known and not so well-known, that are worth going to. You will enjoy stores like Glass Menagerie (for a large assortment of glassware and gift items), The Price of His Toys (outrageous and fun men's gifts and gadgets), and Kaleidoscope (traditional housewares and accessories).

Glass Menagerie
The Price of His Toys
Kaleidoscope

ANTIQUES

Under this heading you'll find a selection of antique stores in several areas. Please remember that there are hundreds of antique stores in Los Angeles, most located in clusters in different neighborhoods. Good streets to walk on for antiques include Washington Boulevard in Venice, Melrose Avenue in Hollywood, La Cienega Boulevard in West Hollywood, Main Street in Santa Monica, and Colorado Boulevard (and adjacent side streets) in Pasadena. Our favorites include the following (you'll find others listed under our furniture and accessories categories).

In twenty-five thousand square feet of space you'll find the largest inventory of imported antiques on the West Coast. There are tables and chairs (even in banquet sizes that are usually hard to find), armoires, mirrors, couches, roll-top desks, beds, buffets, and roomfuls of accessories. There is a separate section for the largest collection of stained glass in L.A., a room for Chinese accessories, one for

Antique Guild
3225 Helms Avenue
Culver City   838-3131

antique jewelry, dishes, clocks, etc. The Guild has shipments of foreign (mostly English and French) antiques arriving nearly every week, so the inventory is constantly changing. It's an enormously popular place, mainly because they have such an amazing collection, and because their service includes financing plans and delivery of even the largest and most difficult-to-pack pieces.

Beverly Antiques
8827 Beverly Boulevard
West Hollywood   271-8517

Here you'll find the most unbelievable collection of rare silver you're likely to see anywhere. There is a good selection of Georgian silver, including varied pieces in obsolete patterns. Just bring in a piece from your own set or one you want to match and chances are you'll find the matching piece you've been looking for.

Coleman's Antiques
1015 Montana Avenue
Santa Monica   395-7541

What a vision—lines of lovely pieces of French china from the 1850s to the 1940s (even Price Haviland pieces). Hard-to-find items may show up in their collection (you can call with your needs and they will look up which pieces are in stock). You'll also find many lovely pieces of American cut glass, both old and new.

Cricket Antiques
2025 Pacific Avenue
Venice   396-5922

This is a large, popular shop specializing in country French and English seventeenth- to nineteenth-century pieces. You'll find a little bit of everything here—that set of dishes that matches those your aunt left you, that dresser you've always wanted, accessories galore. There's a fabulous French armoire that is still available for $20,000, a wonderful set of table and chairs for $500, and lots of small pieces, including some samples of old stained glass. This place is truly fun to browse in.

Fantasy Lighting
7126 Melrose Avenue
Hollywood   933-7244

Owner Harry Miller has put together a visual fantasy you won't believe. Rows of antique-replica lamps, including a large selection of Tiffany shades, just dazzle the eye. Harry, who also does terrific custom work, carries his own glass designs that are not only lovely but very well executed. The enormous selection of beaded trim will entice you to design your own lamps. There are also old-fashioned silk lamps, newer glass models—and remember, Harry will make any design you bring in.

Hopkins Antiques
1434 Lincoln Boulevard
Santa Monica   393-8866

Bob Hopkins selects everything himself, and his delightful quality shop shows it. Although Bob specializes in silver and primitive American Indian antiques (his silver spoon selection is enchanting), you'll find other hand-selected items that won't appear anywhere else. There are Northwest Coast Indian relics, lots of scrimshaw pieces, unusual Indian pieces, and more.

London's Lair
427 North Cañon Drive
Beverly Hills   276-5466

Irene London means business—each and every one of the antique accessories in her store is especially selected and lovingly displayed. You'll find quality silver, crystal, and china pieces, wonderful enamelwares, unusual furniture from all over the world —the traveling Mrs. London is constantly surveying foreign markets to bring back the most fantastic objects. She also believes that her customers like to see a range of items—which explains the

Quality antique accessories on display in London's Lair.

occasional Plexiglass contemporary tray, some wood accessories, and one-of-a-kind ceramic pieces that she includes on her shelves.

Main Street, USA
2669 Main Street
Santa Monica   392-6676

This lovely and popular shop carries objects from the early 1900s. You'll find country store items like ice cream makers, many tins and medicine bottles, match containers, mini banks, and an enormous selection of old advertising graphics. Although this is really not a furniture store, you will find some smaller collector's pieces.

S.P.O.T. Antiques
511/513 North Robertson Boulevard
Beverly Hills   274-9530

Owner Giselle Dorf wanted a store which carried unusual, one-of-a-kind items that discriminating shoppers value. The result is a charming shop carrying a range of antiques, including many pieces Dorf brings back from her trips to England. You'll find items that belong in collections—like contraceptive boxes, match holders, mirrors, vases, and other accessories. There are Chinese pieces including tapestries and china. There's an antique highchair that turns into a cradle and rocker, tables with chairs with unusual carved backs, armoires, and hat racks. Though her selection changes daily, you can always count on Dorf to have lovely items ranging from the very bizarre to the precious.

CLOTHING

Brown's
68A North Venice Boulevard
Venice   399-0181

For those discriminating shoppers who would no more consider going bareheaded than barefoot, here is a true find: a hat collector's paradise, full of well-made, perfectly fitting hats. You can find some of these hats at various department stores, but at this, their home base, you'll find all the latest styles, colors, and sizes. Hats start at about fifteen dollars. From the most classic of brims, to berets, bowlers, and beanies, this is really the hat-lover's haven.

Camp Beverly Hills
9640 Santa Monica Boulevard
Beverly Hills   724-8317

Strange name for a store? Maybe, but some of the merchandise you'll find inside is stranger still. And fun. Here is a selection of shorts in cottons and satins to rival any in town; jeans galore; men's shirts that graced many a prisoner's back at one time and are currently covering the hippest bodies in town. Accessories abound—this jumping, fun shop carries any latest fad in clothing for men and women. Prices vary—some shirts and pants are bargains, others are expensive. But if you want to be the first in your house to wear the latest (and the craziest) fashions—pay this shop a visit.

Clothing Gallery
2909 Main Street
Santa Monica   399-0841

For a lovely, artistic experience, as well as a trip almost guaranteed to result in unusual, exciting finds, this stylish shop offers it all. In a gallery-like setting, where clothes are framed like the fine paintings gracing the walls, you'll find the latest avant-garde clothing from young California designers. The collection varies almost weekly, with the newest in women's fashions constantly arriving. You'll find a large array of clothing made from natural fibers— cottons, linens, silks—as well as a nice selection of swimwear. This attractive store is really a delight to spend time in.

Diamond Clothing Company
903 North Fairfax Avenue
West Hollywood   654-3708

It looks like a bargain hunter's dream; and it is. In a tiny shop, with walls lined with every color of cotton imaginable, with tiny, makeshift dressing rooms and a mirror or two, you'll find a huge inventory of gauze clothes in every size and color. Here, at a fraction of the price, are those styles you see in all the stores. There are drawstring pants, a dozen different shirt styles, shorts, skirts, jackets, halter tops, dresses, robes, and the cutest children's outfits around. As you gaze in wonderment at all the clothes you've seen everywhere else, your bill will also reflect the fact that Arnie Diamond charges about forty percent less than other retail stores. Tops run as little as five dollars, pants for ten—it's really the best bargain for any gauze clothes.

Love the Dodgers? Adore the Angels? Just never miss a Rams game? Well, sports fanatics, if you always wanted to sleep in a Dodgers uniform or have lunch in the Rams getup, here's the place that makes it all possible. This shop carries copies of these teams' uniforms and accessories, plus equipment for baseball, football, hockey, and basketball (made for both men and women). For example, if you want a complete baseball uniform, Goodman's can outfit you from cap to shoes. You can even get a bat. For costumes, or for serious public wear, Goodman's is really fun to visit.

W. A. Goodman and Sons
1421 South Lawrence Street
Los Angeles   749-8333

Did you see that shirt the guy next door was wearing, saying *"Je suis Américain"*? Want one like it? Just go to this shop and order your favorite shirt with any saying, name, logo, or decal on it. Boasting one of the largest selections of decals anywhere (they are catalogued by number, size, and subject), this shop also carries well-made T-shirts in many styles, cotton dresses, jackets—all ready for imprinting with your favorite saying. It's a great gift shop for special occasions—personalized service is guaranteed and usually delivered.

The Great American Sweatshirt Company
9635 Santa Monica Boulevard
Beverly Hills   273-1087

Greta has super taste. Whatever is new, well-made, and beautifully designed is likely to be in her shop. From the latest in foreign imports to the best of the California designers, Greta has a way of buying just the right items, in all sizes and colors. The salespeople are gracious and eager to please—if you need help in putting a wardrobe together, they know all that's available and can teach you the latest gimmicks. Besides clothing, Greta has a terrific selection of shoes, including hard-to-find sizes and widths (being a triple A, I really appreciate a store that carries the narrow widths). Add some jewelry, bags, belts, sunglasses, and hand-made, custom items, and you have a terrific boutique that carries clothing for every occasion.

Greta's
141 South Beverly Drive
Beverly Hills   274-9217

Are Hawaiian shirts in? How about oversized blazers? If it's in and if it's new, you are guaranteed to find it in this lovely shop. Originally conceived as a men's shop, Hardware has become so popular with women that the owners carry a good selection of clothes in smaller sizes just to accommodate their female customers. Here you'll find a good selection of New York designer clothes and some custom designs—all fashionable and unusual. Accessories are also carefully chosen to highlight the latest (there's a good selection of sunglasses). Chances are you'll bump into a movie star or two, but the real stars are the newest clothes and accessories that the owners always manage to have on hand.

Hardware
8620 Melrose Avenue
West Hollywood   659-4881

Owner-designer Alex Wilson has established a delightful store specializing in custom-made, one-of-a-kind hats. You may think that he is indeed the mad hatter, and some have called him that, but you can always count on Alex to have on hand the most unusual, well-fitting hats. Prices range from twenty to forty-five dollars, although special customized and elaborate orders may run higher. Alas, he only designs hats for women—although I always have the feeling that one could convince Alex to do anything.

Hats on Third
8028 West Third Street
West Hollywood   653-6462

Isabel, Too
12134 Ventura Boulevard
Studio City   760-2788

This is probably the tiniest clothing shop you've ever been to—and the fullest. Specializing in the newest designs for women, the shop carries the best of everything, from sportswear to evening wear. Whereas in other stores you have to go from department to department trying to put together outfits from various designers, here the gracious and knowledgeable salespeople will put together an entire wardrobe for you simply and easily. The buyers know what to stock —from the newest sweaters, pants, belts, and bags, to the latest in dresses and complete outfits. There is a terrific collection of matching separates from such designers as Carol Horn, Bis, New Man, and many other California and foreign designers. It's worth a trip to this delightful store—you'll find terrific clothes at prices much lower than many other boutiques.

King's Western Wear
6455 Van Nuys Boulevard
Van Nuys   785-2586

Mr. King really belongs on a horse. Meanwhile, he runs a western-wear supermarket that carries anything you can think of related to cowboys and western life, from a large selection of boots for both men and women, to western suits that are guaranteed to make you proud to live west of the Mississippi. Suits are not cheap—they run from about $145 to $200, but they are well made and as authentic as you'll find anywhere. And if that's not enough, there are belt buckles and hatbands, Indian beads and square-dancing outfits, saddles, fancy jeans, and a terrific selection of children's clothing.

Maxfield Bleu
9091 Santa Monica Boulevard
West Hollywood   275-7007

You'd never know it from the drab outside, but inside Maxfield Bleu some of the biggest names in Hollywood—with the biggest checkbooks—just can't seem to wait to spend a fortune on the latest French and California designer clothes. There are beautiful, one-of-a-kind hand-knitted sweaters selling for upwards of $300, men's and women's shirts for $100 and up, a great selection of jeans, dresses, accessories. Even though prices are high and the service sometimes snotty, Maxfield Bleu does carry the newest European styles. And the chances are if you've seen it in *Vogue*, you'll find it here first.

Mister Frank
8801 Santa Monica Boulevard
West Hollywood   657-1023

This is one of my favorite clothing stores in L.A. Located outside Beverly Hills (thus saving an enormous amount on rent), Frank carries the latest imported and California styles for women at reasonable prices. His stock is large and well thought out—from gabardine suits and silk shirts to the latest, most avant-garde clothing. Accessories abound—there's a terrific selection of unusual jewelry, sunglasses, belts, bags, and scarves. You can walk into Frank's and walk out with a new wardrobe. A big plus—the salespeople are always gracious, and when they say they'll call you when something comes in, you can count on it. With a tailor on hand for alterations, Frank's becomes a truly complete store.

North Beach Leather
8514 Sunset Boulevard
West Hollywood   652-3224

You thought leather meant suede blazers and leather jackets? Forget it. Michael Hoban, together with designers Clifford Olsa and Gary Saxed, have assembled the most outrageous and courageous clothing in leather you'll find anywhere. Unique Indian designs, bizarre Hollywood creations made especially for the likes of Cher and Elton John, and other custom and stock items will dazzle the eye (and shock your wallet). From briefcases to pants, jackets, dresses with beads and fringe, to just about anything you can think of—they've got it.

"My customers know what they want," says Anna Lindstrom, who opened her well-designed women's clothing boutique last spring and stocked it with local designers' clothes, "and I give it to them." What she gives them is a lovely selection of colorful, cleanly designed sportswear and accessories at reasonable prices. All the clothes—shirts, pants, cotton and linen skirts, knit dresses—look like they came from the most expensive Beverly Hills shops. The lines are clean, the clothes well made and well fitting, and the designs the newest around. Lindstrom carries colorful clothing even when others are resorting to those boring beiges and browns. It's worth a trip to visit this unusually sophisticated shop.

O.M.A.
8361 West Third Street
Los Angeles   653-8228

This eclectic shop is most enticing for lovers of recycled clothing from 1860 to the 1950s. There's a huge selection of men's clothing guaranteed to bring back your fondest memories, and some women's clothing that is really lovely. Everything is in excellent condition—this is no junk shop, but a quality store carrying well-preserved and cared-for clothing.

Repeat Performance
7621 Melrose Avenue
West Hollywood   938-0609

Brandon Wolfe revels in his lively shop. The classiest shoppers in Hollywood are said to grace his dressing rooms and look through his many shelves and baskets searching for his latest imports. Because his shop is not in Beverly Hills, Wolfe can afford to sell popular designer clothing at less-than B.H. prices, thus assuring his popularity with the classy yet money-smart crowd. You'll find a terrific selection of silk shirts and the latest in pants (whether they are wide-legged, peg-legged, pleated, or straight, you can bet that Wolfe will have them in a variety of fabrics, sizes, and colors).

Savage Space
7623 Melrose Avenue
West Hollywood   655-7091

When Sylvia Stevens had surgery for breast cancer in the early 1970s, an unfruitful, humiliating search for comfortable and attractive clothing convinced her to open a store specializing in attire for mastectomy patients. Stevens, who designs clothes made specifically for these women—including bathing suits, nightgowns, robes, and outdoor clothing, also carries a large line of clothes becoming to women who have special figure problems.

Sylvia Stevens
321 South Robertson Boulevard
Beverly Hills   652-4150

What can you say about a shop that specializes in lingerie guaranteed to make mother blush and boyfriends, lovers, and husbands beam with anticipation? Well, you can say that Mitch Shrier, owner and designer, has amassed an unbelievable collection of slips, negligees, and the like. You can say that he carries mostly small sizes, that his range of colors strains the rainbow, that his styles are, well, sexy, and that there is no way a woman can go into his store and not be enticed by at least some of his many items.

Trashy Lingerie
402 North La Cienega Boulevard
West Hollywood   652-4543

Kids' Clothing

Auntie Barbara's
251 South Beverly Drive
Beverly Hills   276-5437

Both my daughter and I are addicted to Auntie Barbara's. She loves the apple juice that comes out of a tree, the puppy and bird that relish her attention, and the many enticing toys that lie about. I love the fantastic selection of the newest in children's clothing, from tiny espadrille shoes to string bikinis to Hawaiian print shirts to satin baseball jackets to sweatshirts embroidered with alligators to Raggedy Ann socks and shoes to baby clothes in the brightest colors and most outrageous designs you've ever seen. If you want Oshkosh overalls, Barbara's got them in any color, any pattern. There are imported French designer dresses (Cacharel, Christian Dior, Petit Bateau, Absorba) that are delectable (if a bit expensive), infant outfits that will make the most cynical of us smile, blankets, wall hangings, and a large selection of socks (don't laugh; ever try to find socks in colors other than blue and white, in sizes other than eight and ten?).

Babytown
12110 Ventura Boulevard
Studio City   762-6123

The outside of this large store looks like any bargain-basement shop. But enter and you'll find a tremendous, well-thought-out selection of moderately priced children's clothing. My favorite attraction is a boutique in the back called, appropriately, the "Backyard Boutique." Here you'll find the newest, imported, avant-garde clothing for kids. It's really a terrific place to find items—children's sunglasses, belts, bags, hats, fancy dresses, bikini panties, and more.

Bear Threads
2521 Wilshire Boulevard
Santa Monica   828-6246

This constantly expanding store carries the newest in clothing, toys, and shoes for kids. From velvet jackets to hand-knit sweaters, from an enormous collection of Absorba baby's clothing to growing girls' imported dresses, Bear Threads has got it. Prices are relatively high, and, unfortunately, service sometimes leaves a bit to be desired (their return policy is, to say the least, unfriendly). Still, I recommend it because you will find items there that you may not see at other places.

Bonnie's Wee Shop
11973 San Vicente Boulevard
Brentwood   476-5450

One of the most delightful children's shops in Los Angeles, this chock full mini-department store has a large variety of imported, highly designed clothes for infants, toddlers, all the way up to teens. Besides the French and Italian imports, including fashionable and tailored clothes, Bonnie's carries well-known American brands of the highest quality. And, if you don't find what you want, they'll make it for you. Bonnie's seamstress can copy any dress in any fabric you want. It's really a terrific place for those hard-to-find items—winter coats (remember that pea coat from back East?), long evening dresses for the very young, bathing suits, shoes, and more.

Los Feliz Dancewear and Kids' X-Change
1943 Hillhurst Avenue
Silverlake   666-0961

Owner Francis Miller carries the largest selection of Oshkosh clothing that I have found anywhere in Southern California. Ranging from sizes one to forty-six, they come in every color you can imagine. You'll also find a large selection of stuffed animals made just for the shop by local designers. There are elbow puppets, kites galore, and lots more. Francis has also put together a tremendous selection of dancewear in all sizes (plus seconds in nearly every style). This shop is really fun to visit, and you are guaranteed to come away with well-priced merchandise.

While this shop carries primarily girls' clothing (sizes one to fourteen), you will find a variety of children's clothing at terrific prices. You'll be astonished at the popular name brands you'll see marked down.

Ridiculous Discount Shop
5232 Laurel Canyon Boulevard
North Hollywood   761-8466

Although this is a very small shop in size and in quantity of merchandise, what they have is unique. Custom-made jackets, pants, and dresses are beautifully designer crafted—items you'll see in no other store. Kathy Hodge's one-of-a-kind masterpieces are snapped up by the most stylish kids in town.

Spilt Milk
8471 Melrose Avenue
Hollywood   651-3301

Brigitta Thornton and her sister Marga are expert embroiderers. What you'll find in their shop is the largest selection of hand-embroidered children's clothing anywhere. You'll also find unusual items like theme shadow boxes, stage-set planters, hand-made stocking dolls, wall hangings, pillows, and quilts.

Stitches
2824 South Robertson Boulevard
West Los Angeles   559-1191

UNUSUAL SHOPS

Remember the Saturday cartoons? Sure. But did you know that there is a store in town that specializes in merchandise dealing only with such cartoon characters as Superman and Mickey Mouse and Donald Duck and Porky Pig and Woody Woodpecker and the Pink Panther and more and more and more? It's Bill Uglow's emporium where you can find Popeye's spinach, Snoopy's dishes, Mickey Mouse radios. . . .

The Character Company
561 Fashion Plaza
West Covina   960-4533

Got something you don't need anymore? Tired of running your own garage sales? Just bring anything you have down to this shop and they'll take it on consignment—you get seventy percent, they get thirty percent. And for a shopping spree this place is terrific. You'll find all kinds of furniture and accessories at true bargain prices.

The Consignment House
5654 Van Nuys Boulevard
Van Nuys   786-7860

Adam Boserup has a philosophy: If you have to have a cane, make it a beautiful support that will make walking a pleasure. To back up his beliefs, Adam owns a shop specializing only in canes—over 1,600 varieties, ranging in price from $6.50 to $2,000.00, with ivory and gold and jade and animal heads. Does he do custom work? "Not really," says Adam. "With over twenty thousand in stock, I've got any cane you would want." To add to it all, Adam will teach you how to use this accessory (whether it's a necessity or an affectation).

Boserup's House of Canes
1636 Westwood Boulevard
West Los Angeles   474-2577

Jolly Wall Graphics
7549 Melrose Avenue
West Hollywood   852-1240

A truly unique store, Jolly Wall Graphics has a collection of masks and spectacular one-of-a-kind furniture. Each piece is hand-crafted and is a fantastic work of art. The shop may be small, but the variety makes it well worth your while.

Mitsuru Children's Shop
41 First Street
Downtown   485-8391

If your kids are fascinated by or addicted to Japanese toys—especially those mesmerizing robots—you must visit this enchanting shop. Carrying all kinds of mechanical and one-piece toys, it is a wonderland for both adults and kids.

The Rainbow
434 North Camden Drive
Beverly Hills   271-5384

The Rainbow was founded several years ago in order to raise money for the Amie Karen Cancer Foundation, a research organization to help fight childhood leukemia. The store has become a huge success, carrying the most beautiful children's toys, hand-crafted items, clothing, books, candy, and jewelry. The Rainbow is lovely, with an enchanting atmosphere; the volunteer sales people are helpful and the merchandise is enticing and attractive.

The Real Thing
11650 Riverside Drive
Studio City   980-3444

Coca-Cola lovers—here it is! Coca-Cola heaven—a collection of memorabilia and accessories as complete as you've ever seen. There are those old trays with the Coke lady, coasters, posters, bottles, Coke machines—you name it, they have it. It is really a playland—whether or not you're collecting the stuff. It's a terrific place to buy novelty gifts and to experience the nostalgia these items instill.

School Days
973 North Main Street
Downtown   223-3474

Wholesale school furniture? It sure is, including desks, reading tables, metal chairs (in both regular and special tiny sizes), blackboards, cabinets, and other schoolroom accessories. It's all in this terrific warehouse, and also in a catalogue put out by this bargain basement store. Don't miss it—it's an affordable way to furnish many a child's room.

Shatsky and Shapiro
8936 Santa Monica Boulevard
West Hollywood   655-7808

This is what five and ten cent stores were really like—small, crowded, general stores that had everything. Whether it's trendy clothing, sportswear, gift boxes, toys, combs, jewelry, novelty items, kitchen supplies, cards—it's all here. The people are great and the variety is astounding. You just won't believe the number of things that are in this store! And half the fun is looking through the shelves and tables full of anything and everything you might ever need.

Treehouse Bookstore
17322 Ventura Boulevard
Encino   986-7374

Estelle Fenenbock always loved miniature toys and doll houses, so when she opened her combination bookstore and toy store, she made sure she had lots of doll houses around so she could fill them with furniture. Estelle has the most amazing miniature collection for sale—everything from Tiffany lamps to breads, wallpaper to player pianos, canopy beds, bathtubs, baby carriages, and more. She will also make custom order reproductions of your own house, or your doctor's office, or your favorite general store. Prices depend on the individual piece, but stock doll houses run from $40 to $350.

This famous Hollywood landmark has been renting costumes to movie companies for about seventy years. It is housed in an enormous warehouse containing thousands of costumes available to both movie studios and regular people who just want to dress up. Want a Scarlett O'Hara from *Gone with the Wind?* You got it. How about a scarecrow? That, too. Anything from butlers to bunnies, from can-can girls to Zorro. It's all here for you to browse through. Take a trip to this wonderland—you will be amazed at the number and variety of costumes on hand.

Western Costume Company
5335 Melrose Avenue
Hollywood   469-1451

Hugh Gundry makes wooden toys. Not just any wooden toys, but fine hand-crafted toys ranging from stock cars to rocking horses, from chairs to trains. Gundry's skill and imagination make for a fascinating collection, truly worth seeing.

Whimsical Woodcrafts
203 South Fair Oaks Avenue
Pasadena   795-0145

ACCESSORIES

Owned by Judy McKee, this lovely gift shop has a tremendous inventory of gifts from all over the world. Their collection includes lots of antique and new baskets, examples of some of the finest folk and contemporary crafts, ethnic pieces including jewelry and small one-of-a-kind gifts (the contemporary jewelry collection is astounding, including pieces you have never seen anywhere else). It's the perfect shop to find unusual and exciting gifts.

Alison's Gifts
11658 San Vicente Boulevard
Brentwood   820-4537

For those of us who have always wished L.A. would have a spectacular showroom with the latest European designs for the bathroom and kitchen, Altman's is paradise. I have never seen, in one place, a more thorough, beautifully displayed array of bathroom accessories. There are marble bathtubs larger and deeper than ordinary American baths, toilets and bidets in the most beautiful, sculptural shapes and luscious new colors. Bath accessories and hardware are fabulous—from the most modern faucets to those traditional more ornate designs—it's all here. And the kitchen cabinets are clever and sleek, and beautifully designed. It's a terrific place to browse and see not only the latest in designs but to get ideas that can be adapted to your own home.

Altman's Il Bagno
8919 Beverly Boulevard
West Hollywood   274-5896

For modern linear truly sleek pottery and outdoor furniture, there's no place like Architectural Pottery. Long a respected design firm, Architectural Pottery has lately been open to the public; it offers substantial discounts. Here you'll find a tremendous collection of pottery, ranging in sizes from small pots to enormous tree-size ones. Their line of outdoor furniture includes futuristic fiberglass designs that are modular-looking, sturdy, and truly beautiful. It's a wonderful place to visit, and a great alternative to the world of plastic pots.

Architectural Pottery
3601 Aviation Boulevard
Manhattan Beach   679-1103

Art Services
8221 Melrose Avenue
West Hollywood   653-9033

Considered one of the best framing shops in Los Angeles, Art Services will custom-frame paintings or other art objects of any size and shape. Since they build everything from scratch, you can bring in the most unusual works of art and they will create showcases. They also make a variety of objects (such as furniture) from Plexiglas.

Bag Ends
616½ Venice Boulevard
Venice   821-7676

Marie Holman sews—does she ever! No dresses or T-shirts for this lady—her forte is making bags, and the results are fantastic. Holman's shop carries an entire line of machine-washable Cordura bags and luggage, in all sizes and colors. Holman will create bags to meet your custom needs. Located in the Venice Studio Village, the store is a supermart for luggage lovers.

Belgravia
8650 Melrose Avenue
West Hollywood   652-5383

Michael Ernt's shop carries antique accessories made out of brass. Here you'll find fireplace fixtures, lamps, bases, hardware in all styles and sizes, and unusual pieces you probably have never thought of. Many are from England; some are newer home-made models. It's a good source for anything made from brass.

Bon Voyage Bazaar
348 North Beverly Drive
Beverly Hills   274-7237

A leather lover's heaven, this luggage shop carries an enormous selection of imported and American luggage. There are various pieces in stock, in each style, and the assortment of accessories is quite complete. There are leather gift items (wallets, smaller bags, picture frames, date books, key chains) and also a well-respected and reliable repair service.

Boyd's of Madison Avenue
427 North Camden Drive
Beverly Hills   550-0382

For some of us the first stop on trips to New York is at Boyd's Chemists to get the latest in make-ups, bathroom accessories, perfumes, soaps, brushes, bath oils—anything your heart could wish for in the way of beauty products. Now Boyd's has opened a shop in Beverly Hills, chock full of those favorites—lots of lipsticks and glosses, special face brushes (over twenty different sizes), imported bath oils, make-ups in shades you won't believe, nail polishes, and more.

Burbank Saddle Sales and Exchange
828 South Victory Boulevard
Burbank   841-0900

Here is a large collection of English riding clothes and accessories, such as boots, saddles, hats, pants, and jackets for both men and women. You'll also find complete outfittings for horses—western and English saddles, both new and used rigs at low prices. And there's a large selection of equipment for driving horses, buggies, carts, and harnesses.

The Card Factory
8908 Santa Monica Boulevard
West Hollywood   652-0194

This is a lovely shop with a tremendous assortment of cards. Now understand that there are no cards for kids here. You'll find artistic cards, very humorous cards, X-rated cards, and a large selection of lovely stationery. The shop carries many exclusive lines you won't find in ordinary stationery stores.

The Margaret Cavigga Quilt Collection

This charming, unusual shop includes over 400 hand-quilted antique and new quilts, from 1805 through today. The patterns are dazzling, the colors absolutely astounding. You'll find crib sizes, king sizes, some found years ago, others made today by senior citizens. Each quilt is individually hand-quilted in the quilter's home; thus no quilting bees or groups are used. You can also order a pattern of your choice. The shop offers quilting lessons, appraisals, decorating help, custom designing, rental and leasing of quilts, and quilting of pre-pieced tops. It's a lovely shop and worth a visit.

8648 Melrose Avenue
West Hollywood   659-3020

Chadwick-Ling Studios
7969 Melrose Avenue
West Hollywood   658-8463

Owners David Ling and Bill Chadwick are painters who just happen to paint with glass. What you will find here are the most beautiful stained-glass lamps you've ever seen—new lamps that look just like watercolor originals. The owners buy glass all over the world, bringing back even the tiniest of pieces to use in their fantastically intricate and beautiful mosaics. Their work is truly fine art, and the results will astound you. Prices are $2,000 and up.

Wayne James is a bit of an eccentric. His all glass, all white shop is only open at his whim; his gift boxes are gone now and he refuses to order any more, hating to wrap his merchandise. But, his idiosyncracies notwithstanding, James has a large selection of anything you can imagine made out of glass, Plexiglas, crystal, white glass, and a few pieces of precious black glass. There are glasses, vases, bowls, accessories, tables, lamps, and paintings. It's really the place for buying gifts for friends—if you can figure out how to wrap them.

Clear White
7617 Melrose Avenue
West Hollywood   653-9990

F.O.B.
1917 Westwood Boulevard
West Los Angeles   475-1497

Vicky and Jacki collect Thai gifts. Now they've made their collection public at their twin stores. You'll find a wide selection of unusual gift items—soaps, hats, cards, wallets, and many one-of-a-kind gifts.

Geary's North
437 North Beverly Drive
Beverly Hills   272-9334

Geary's is not sure if it wants to be an art gallery, a crafts shop, a novelties boutique, or the trendiest shop in town. Unlike its mother shop down the street, which specializes in china, silver, crystal, and the more prosaic accessories that fill traditional homes, the "annex" is filled with graphics, ceramic dishes and art works, the latest novelties and fad-related objects and gifts, stuffed pillows, and many interesting, fun, and well-designed accessories. It really is a terrific gift shop for those who want whatever is new. I have always found the staff to be very helpful, courteous, and eager to help customers find that special and perfect gift.

Gemstones
11274 Ventura Boulevard
North Hollywood   985-2445

For true hobbyists, this is a find. Gemstones carries a large selection of precious and semiprecious stones. You'll find lots of cut and polished amethyst, lapis shaped into butterflies, rough minerals, Chilean azurite, and a complete line of lapidary supplies. They don't set stones, but if you're looking for raw materials in huge supply, this is the place.

Glass Menagerie
9646 Santa Monica Boulevard
Beverly Hills   272-3724

Glass collectors, gift buyers, and plain old accessory lovers—this shop has an interesting and wide selection of glass objects. Animals, vases, glassware, and the unusual, one-of-a-kind pieces are in abundance here. The service is terrific—phone orders are handled promptly, as are gift items being sent out of state. The people are friendly and helpful. Even if you are looking for run-of-the-mill glassware, this store will handle your order faithfully.

Harold's Place
420 North Bedford Drive
Beverly Hills   275-6222

Kimonos, fur coats, Art Deco glass (the real thing), Chinese jewelry, combs galore, toys, novelty artifacts—you'll find it all in this jam-packed fun-filled shop. Prices vary from ridiculous to very reasonable. You'll just have to go through the piles of enticing finds to locate something you probably have been looking for forever.

Homeworks
2913 Main Street
Santa Monica   396-0101

This is one of my favorite stores, mostly because it's as close to a classy mini-supermarket as you'll find. Owner Annie Kahn has laden her shop with lots of goodies—accessories for the house (dishes, trays, flatwear, decorative items) in contemporary, Chinese, and eclectic variations. You'll find mats, jewelry, unusual clothing, and fun items like masks, boxes, and tiny toys. It's really a lovely shop, putting together in one place merchandise you're likely to find scattered in many other boutiques.

Julian
3716 Sunset Boulevard
Silverlake   660-6350

Julian's is a fantasy-come-true for lovers of custom-made pillows, linens, comforters, and clothing. Silks and satins predominate; patchworks are favorites. Prices range from twenty-six to thirty-two dollars a pillow. Prices of comforters vary.

What a find! This shop is packed to the hilt with the most enchanting merchandise you've ever seen. Any novelty item or home accessory that is in vogue is on Bobi's shelves. There are baskets galore from all over the world, in sizes you've never imagined. Leonard has silk flowers made especially for the shop; they are glorious duplications of the most extraordinary blossoms. You'll find combs, boxes, vases, and other accessories. Moreover, Bobi also runs an interior design service.

Bobi Leonard
2801 Main Street
Santa Monica   399-3251

Margo and Victoria Levee, mother and daughter, established this out-of-the-way wonderland of Chinese accessories in 1974 and have been going strong since. On annual trips to the Orient they bring back some of the most beautiful and unusual pieces you'll see—antique porcelains, baskets, scrolls, exotic brooms, wood carvings, plates, and jars. You'll never tire of coming back to this unusual shop—there are always new finds to entice the eye.

M. Levee and Daughters
8437 Clinton Avenue
West Hollywood   855-0269

While this shop is mainly a clothing store for women, I go there specifically for their large selection of casual earrings, hair combs, and barrettes. While you may find these items in many other stores, here they are all together in one place, displayed so you can see the many different styles and colors. It's worth the trip!

Mihitabel
3707 Sunset Boulevard
Silverlake   666-7748

Better beware before you enter this supermarket of accessories and stationery goods—just the amount of items on hand will make you dizzy. An enormous crafts department (the largest I've seen anywhere), candles galore, party goods by the thousands, cheap accessories for parties (center pieces, vases, favors), silk, plastic, and dried flowers in droves. And when the holidays come, be it Easter or Christmas or Halloween, the place becomes a virtual wonderland of accessories and toys. The best way to shop at Moskatel's is go once every few months and load up. (I bought six dozen candles here several years ago and haven't bought one since.) Wrapping paper is a great buy, as are the ribbons to go with it. Load up—and enjoy!

Moskatel's
733 South San Julian Street
Downtown   627-1631
Check phone book for
neighborhood branches.

Owned by Peggy and Dennis Day, this unusual shop carries specially made layettes, children's clothes, antique accessories, all set in a very old house. Every inch of the charming home is full of accessories. It's a delightful place.

The Old House and Poupees and Polliwogs
528 Colorado Avenue
Santa Monica   394-7401

Besides carrying anything you've ever seen made of plastic, this shop has in stock a large inventory of Plexiglas sheets in a variety of sizes and colors. This allows the Plastic Mart to provide custom order service at the drop of a hat. If you need any tables made, plaques designed, accessories copied or repaired, this shop will do it on time, well, and for a reasonable price. They also have a do-it-yourself department and will gladly advise you as to the hazards and special features of working with Plexiglas.

Plastic Mart
2101 West Pico Boulevard
Santa Monica   451-1701

If you wake up at eleven at night and suddenly remember you need to buy that special gift, never fear. Propinquity, a gift lover's paradise, is almost always open late so you can hop in, browse, and

Propinquity
8915 Santa Monica Boulevard
West Hollywood   652-2953

buy to your heart's content. It's the best place to find bizarre items (cups in the shape of ducks, pins in the shape of cups), novelty gifts, trendy and funny accessories. They even have their own catalogue so you can order without ever leaving your home.

H. Savinar Luggage
4625 West Washington Boulevard
Los Angeles   938-2501

I've been buying my luggage here for years. The selection is terrific, the prices are way below those in retail stores, and the service is impeccable. If you see an ad with your favorite luggage in it, just call one of the Savinars, father or son, and they'll track it down for you. Handbags, briefcases, hand luggage, dress bags, wallets, and other accessories are all available at reduced prices.

So Much and Company
8669 Sunset Boulevard
West Hollywood   652-4291

Owners Fran Schaen and Phyllis Factor run one of the nicest, prettiest, and most complete gift shops in Los Angeles. Fran, who has been designing jewelry for years, carries her delicate, simply elegant designs, ranging from the most contemporary to copies of antiques, in both silver and gold. And that's only the beginning. You'll find snakeskin evening bags, suede belts, hand-knit sweaters, silver combs, extraordinary beaded giftware, mirrored day books—so many one-of-a-kind items that just mentioning them doesn't do the store justice. It's really the perfect boutique—if you need a gift, for a friend or for yourself, you're almost guaranteed to find something you like at this darling shop.

The Soap Plant
3720 Sunset Boulevard
Silverlake   665-7349

If I even attempted to begin to list the gift items carried in this store it would sound like a catalogue out of "what's new on the market." Here is an array of soaps the likes of which I have never seen. There are also oils, fragrances, a large card selection, masks, boxes, paper flowers, fans, pins, earrings, baskets—nearly every imaginable new and trendy gift item. It's a crowded chock-full-of-goodies type of store that entices you to buy things you never thought of. Don't miss it—it may not be on your way, but take the time and pay this shop a visit.

Wonderful Things
2827 Main Street
Santa Monica   399-1931

Peggy Margulies has a wonderful collection of Indian, Thai, and Afghanistan ceremonial pieces on sale at her lovely shop. There is ethnic jewelry from all over the world, unusual one-of-a-kind pieces that are intricate and beautiful. Peggy has a collection of old and reproduction silver frames, Russian lacquer boxes, and other craft items. It's a good place to pick up that extra accessory that will make your room or your day.

Yamaguchi
2057 Sawtelle Boulevard
West Los Angeles   479-9531

For Japanese accessories, gift items, entire outfits—this is the place. You'll find baskets, dinnerware, cooking equipment, men and women's cotton kung fu and kimono outfits, and flower arranging supplies.

Kitchen Supplies

The Cookstore
13016 San Vicente Boulevard

These selected shops carry complete, unusual, and attractive new and fashionable kitchen accessories. Prices may vary slightly at

Brentwood   395-4777
8634 West Sunset Boulevard
West Hollywood   657-1555

Pottery Barn Stores
in Westwood, Century City,
Marina del Rey, and many
other locations.

Williams-Sonoma
438 North Rodeo Drive
Beverly Hills   274-9127
333 Bristol Street
South Coast Plaza
Costa Mesa   (714) 751-1166

Fashionable kitchen accessories at The Cookstore.

each, but you can depend on good service and tremendous selections at all. Each has its specialty—Williams-Sonoma has a great line of gourmet pots and spices, as well as mechanical gadgets. The Cookstore gives cooking classes as well as selling accessories of every kind, including fine dishes and pots, placemats and napkins, and tables. Pottery Barn stores are the supermarkets of kitchen suppliers. They handle gadgetry, pots, a tremendous line of dishes, some furniture, those wonderful plastic accouterments, napkins and placemats galore, and a terrific collection of every kind of glass imaginable.

FOOD SHOPS

Bakeries

Authentic British pastries are their specialty, including Madeira cake, Dundee cakes, princess and Banbury tarts. You can also order ahead for large quantities.

Bailey's Bakery
414 North Cañon Drive
Beverly Hills   276-6102

For traditional tortes—sacher torte, linzer torte, pichinger torte, come around.

Viktor Benes' Continental Pastries
8718 West Third Street
Los Angeles   276-0488

This terrific little bakery is famous for the delicious carrot cakes that make the rounds in town. You can even order one for fifty people, if you so desire. Bubbles also makes a traditional noodle kugel for take-home addicts.

Bubbles Baking Company
15215 Keswick Avenue
Van Nuys   786-2181

The Buttery
2906 Main Street
Santa Monica   399-3000

When you drive by this shop and see the people lined up outside waiting to get in, you know you must be in for a treat. And indeed you are, what with an assortment of fabulous cookies, cakes, breads, chocolate croissants, and other wonderful treats. Owned by Richard Mynatt, a some-time computer analyst, the bakery is a treat for dessert connoisseurs.

Cake and Art
8709 Santa Monica Boulevard
West Hollywood   657-8694

For those of us who are still fascinated by cakes in the shapes of hamburgers, castles, hot tubs, and the like, Cake and Art is a find. Willing to design cakes in the shape of almost anything, these artists are cooperative, sometimes courageous (my friend's cake in the shape of a hot tub, complete with a likeness of her dog was super!), and always talented. Prices vary depending on the complexity of the design.

Miss Grace Lemon Cake Company
443 South Robertson Boulevard
Beverly Hills   274-2879
16733 Ventura Boulevard
Encino   995-1976

I have never tasted a lemon cake to compare with the one baked here. Tangy and light, it is a superb dessert. Also available are fruit mousses, cookies, and a variety of special cakes.

Hansen Cakes
1060 South Fairfax Avenue
Los Angeles   936-4332
193 South Beverly Drive
Beverly Hills   878-0433

A legend in Los Angeles, this huge bakery specializes in creating custom-designed cakes of any shape or size. If you've ever had those delicious butter sheet cakes at a birthday party, decorated with "Sesame Street" characters or a special three-dimensional number, chances are it was from Hansen's. The first to create these look-alike cakes, Hansen's is still going strong. Be sure to go in and look at Bob Hansen's book of photos of cakes he's designed—and then go to it!

Jelato
8678 West Pico Boulevard
West Los Angeles   659-2435

For some of the best naturally flavored and homemade ice-creams in the city, visit this enticing shop. With flavors ranging from espresso to blackberry to papaya to avocado, your taste buds will be in heaven.

L.A. Desserts
8249 West Third Street
Los Angeles   653-6782

Whenever I serve the marjolaine made by Richard Irving, my guests are speechless, and then promptly ask for more. It's a fabulous chocolate, hazelnut, and praline dessert-cake that you will never forget. For those truly devoted chocolate freaks among us, you must try the double chocolate cake and the most delicious chocolate chip and nut cookies you've ever had. About that marjolaine—don't be put off by the price (twenty-two dollars each). A full marjolaine will serve at least twenty people, because you must slice it thinly (it is rather rich); but for smaller appetites or parties, buy a half (eleven dollars).

Mamola's Bakery
12027 San Vicente Boulevard
(In San Vicente Foods Market)
Brentwood   476-3200

Everything you'll find here is delicious. Amazing for a bakery at a larger market, the desserts and baked goods are always fresh and very good. Their own recommendation: cheesecake, both traditional and in choice flavors.

Like Napoleons? How about a Napoleon cake? It's wonderful, and you can order one big enough for fifty people. You'll also find traditional Italian pastries and cookies that will make your mouth water.

Well-known for its excellent pastries and desserts, Richard caters and also runs a tiny restaurant complete with outside cafe. Try the raspberry cream cake, peach pie, elaborate chocolate desserts, and more traditional Napoleons, eclairs, and fruit tarts.

These desserts may look like they have a thousand calories each, but the truth is that they are all sugar-free and made from low-sodium ingredients. It's a wonderland for diet-conscious folks who still like the idea (and taste) of traditional desserts.

Nicolosi's
17552 Ventura Boulevard
Encino   789-0922

Michel Richard
310 South Robertson Boulevard
Beverly Hills   275-5707

The Thinnery
6280 West Third Street
Los Angeles   936-8877
(Also in Encino, Woodland Hills, Torrance, North Hollywood, and Arcadia.)

Small Markets

Long known as a reliable market that carries only top meats, Brentwood Foods has daily selections of prime beef, veal, lamb, chicken, and fish.

People travel from all over Los Angeles to buy the finest veal. Here you'll find chops, roasts, scallopine cut to order, chicken breasts already skinned and boned. You can call in your order in the morning and find it ready at night. Hugo's is a truly traditional butcher.

The Premier has long been frequented by Beverly Hills residents who like the convenience of a smaller market with a large variety of goods, a fresh meat counter, and deliveries right to your door. You'll find a collection of imported goods, a bakery counter, and a liquor and wine section. Their fresh fruits, whatever is in season, are always excellent.

For lovers of Japanese foods, store up at this enchanting market carrying Japanese, Chinese, and Hawaiian specialties. There are meats and seafoods (they'll cut them in the traditional Oriental style), dry goods, canned foods from various countries, cooking utensils, and accessories.

Brentwood Foods
11630 Barrington Court
Brentwood   472-1203

Hugo's Fine Meats
8401 Santa Monica Boulevard
West Hollywood   654-3993

Premier Market
425 North Cañon Drive
Beverly Hills   278-1222

Safe and Save Market
2030 Sawtelle Boulevard
West Los Angeles   479-3810

Delicatessens

Enter and you feel like you're in a different country, probably Hungary or Yugoslavia, because this ethnically delightful market specializes in Hungarian and Yugoslavian foods, crafts, books, records, and kitchenware.

Most surveys rate this deli as the best. I'm not sure it is, but it certainly has a great selection of traditional deli foods, including pastrami sandwiches that seem to reach towards the sky, stuffed

Al's Hungarian Deli
1055 North Vine Street
Los Angeles

Art's
12224 Ventura Boulevard
Studio City   769-9808

cabbage, tongue, boiled beef, and chicken soup (not my favorite here). Their sandwiches are terrific, as is the service at the take-out counter. Art is a charming and personable host, and his delicatessen has been at the same location for twenty-four years.

The Bagelah
22233½ Pacific Coast Highway
Malibu   456-3635

In addition to the more traditional deli sandwiches and plates are health-food meals like avocado sandwiches and zucchini salads. But bagels predominate. This small deli has an enjoyable outside eating area.

Junior's
2379 Westwood Boulevard
Westwood   475-5771

Terrific chicken soup, pickles on each table, a large take-out section featuring fresh bagels and lots of lox, what more could you ask for? Besides, their hot chocolate is perfect, their whitefish and tomato plate is scrumptious, and their triple and quadruple decker sandwiches are enough for a week-long meal.

Langer's
704 South Alvarado Street
Downtown   483-8050

There are some deli lovers who don't live on the West Side. For them, and for those who work around the mid-town area, Langer's is a real treat. Terrific pastrami and corned beef sandwiches, great blintzes and potato pancakes, and a large selection of unusual combination plates and sandwiches.

Nate 'n Al's
414 North Beverly Drive
Beverly Hills   274-0101

I think their chicken soup is the best (I buy it by the gallon and freeze it to be used later with noodles or as a base for my homemade soups). But I also love their hard salami, their imported Brie cheese, and their potato pancakes that look more like overblown fries. This is an especially exciting place to eat for star gazers; among the pastrami sandwiches and matzo ball soup you may see James Caan, Doris Day or Danny Thomas. The counter has every deli item you can think of, and is usually packed with people lined up to take home the goodies. Try calling ahead and ordering what you want—they'll have it ready when you arrive.

Quality Food Company
7703 Melrose Avenue
West Hollywood   653-1034

A terrific discount deli, this shop carries Hebrew National products at wholesale prices.

Label's Table
9226 West Pico Boulevard
West Los Angeles   276-0388

Discount deli at its best—you'll find quality meats and cheeses discounted as much as forty percent here. And it's no ordinary collection of foods—there's Brie, Jarlsberg cheese, salami, pastrami—and all the rest. And the crowd is a treat—devoted customers who have been enjoying Label's food for many years.

San Remo Deli
3814 Sunset Boulevard
Silverlake   666-1201

One of the best things about Los Angeles is our variety of nationalities. Besides resulting in a wonderfully heterogeneous population, this flow of immigration has brought a myriad of ethnic restaurants and markets to L.A. San Remo is one of the most intriguing because its products—all South American—are so unique. You'll find those rare maté teas, delicious sweet desserts (sweet and sour coffee cake is a treat), all kinds of deli meats and cheeses, and a good selection of South American wines (yes, Virginia, wine does come from countries other than France). If you have any questions about preparing South American foods or how to use their spices and delicacies, don't hesitate to ask José Delgado, the eager-to-please owner.

Large, crowded both with people and lots of tasty delicacies, Saul's serves enormous portions of all your favorites, plus free pickles waiting on each table. The food is always fresh (never, God forbid, reheated) and nicely served. Be sure to order their herring, chopped liver, chicken soup, and hot pastrami. The best!

Saul's
16358 Ventura Boulevard
Encino   788-5010

The best thing about this bustling deli is that it is always open. Some other delis in town just don't understand that one can get a craving for a hot corned beef sandwich at five in the morning. There's also a take-out counter offering almost everything that appears on the large and varied menu. Try the combinations—they are inventive and good.

Zucky's
431 Wilshire Boulevard
Santa Monica   393-0551

Gourmet Takeouts

For those of us who sometimes don't feel like cooking gourmet food at home, especially just for two, Bagatelle has a large variety of delicious frozen entrées and desserts that may make you an addict of French food. Usually packaged in cartons for two, the meals are always seasoned just right, come with rice and sometimes a vegetable, and may be heated in half an hour. You'll find wonderful coq au vin, charcuterie, chicken in truffles, salmon mousse, sole veronique, and many more. There is also a food counter serving chocolate mousse, various pâtés, and French cheeses. For an extra added attraction, there is a superb restaurant next door.

Bagatelle French Gourmet Deli
8690 Wilshire Boulevard
Beverly Hills   659-0782

A delightful, pretty restaurant and take-out Italian deli serving delicious foods is currently the rage in this West Los Angeles community. You'll find such favorites as manicotti, lasagna, veal in various sauces—all ready to take home and heat. There are wonderful daily made soups, sandwiches galore (remember how good a meatball sandwich can taste when it's made right?), and desserts like crème caramel, chocolate mocha mousse soufflé, and those popular cannolis.

Gourmet Italia
11620 San Vicente Boulevard
Brentwood   820-6619

Robert Wemischner and his sister Marge Levine run a tiny take-out shop featuring wonderful dishes. Some are expensive, and the portions are not always as adequate as you might like (be sure to check the amounts—you might need two packages rather than one), but the food is as tasty as you'll find anywhere. My favorite is chicken in mustard, but the variety of veals and fish is overwhelming. Plus there is always a counter full of freshly baked cakes and cookies, just-made salads (the green beans and the mushroom salads are superb), a selection of mustards and breads, and even frozen desserts. At various times during the year Le Grand Buffet also prepares box lunches and sandwiches, often made with one of several pâtés they have on hand.

Le Grand Buffet
9527 Santa Monica Boulevard
Beverly Hills   278-4674

FURNISHINGS

A large part of this category is covered under accessories and antiques because often these are interchangeable with what is commonly meant by furnishing a home. In this section we have chosen a few unique and valuable sources for more modern, contemporary furnishings and accessories, plus some unique shops that carry a variety of styles. Let us not forget to mention, however, the building we refer to as the "Big Blue Whale"—the Pacific Design Center in West Hollywood (it's hard to miss—you'll find it on the corner of Melrose Avenue and San Vicente Boulevard). This enormous building houses scores of furniture and accessory showrooms. You'll find carpets, tiles, furniture, window coverings, accessories—anything your home could possibly need. There are famous-name showrooms like Kneedler-Fauchère, Knoll, I.C.F., Stendig, and the other standard lines, as well as newer, smaller places such as Janus et Cie and Forms and Surfaces. It's a wonderland for anything you ever wanted to know about furniture but were afraid to ask. Please remember, though, that most of the showrooms will only allow you to enter if you are accompanied by an interior designer (or sometimes your architect). And not all furniture showrooms are represented in this building. The best advice I can give you is to go with someone who knows the place and has admission to the showrooms, survey the newest goings on in the field, and then proceed to other establishments in the nearby Robertson Boulevard area to finish off your decorating course. Here, then, are our choices outside the design center (with the exception of Palmer Garland which has some special features we recommend).

Mel Brown
5840 South Figueroa Street
Downtown   778-4444

The best in contemporary furniture, both famous designs and the latest and more trendy pieces can be found at this large store. Lighting, accessories, the more traditional pieces (couches, bedroom and dining room sets), and wall coverings fill the many rooms. Brown's has a good collection of furniture, at prices you'll find in other stores. Here it's the size of the inventory that is the prize. If you haven't surveyed the market lately and need to know what is new and what designers are doing, this is the place to go.

Danica
9244 Wilshire Boulevard
Beverly Hills   272-3757
260 West Twenty-second Street
San Pedro   831-1235

Full of contemporary and Scandinavian furniture, lighting, and accessories, both Danica stores have a large selection of designer pieces for your home. Lots of chrome and glass, modular units for couches, cubes galore, modern lighting fixtures, bar stools, and a good selection of children's furniture. The San Pedro warehouse has bargain products that are as new as the other store's merchandise but for various reasons are put on sale. I think Danica's is especially reliable for the variety of dining room furniture, and for the design advice they give to people who are amateurs at the decorating game.

Donghia
8715 Melrose Avenue

Named for famed interior designer Angelo Donghia, who has been designing some of the most exciting modern furniture anywhere in the world (and who has showrooms in other cities and has recently designed furniture sold at retail department stores), this absolutely beautiful showroom is run by Jerry Gallagher, a responsible, helpful, and talented manager who always makes certain that the showroom is full of the most breathtaking and exciting designs anywhere. From wallpapers to fabrics, couches to accessories, bathroom fixtures to rugs, Donghia's selection is tremendous. Please note that you can only buy here through an interior designer, and that the furnishings and accessories are not cheap. But, if you can't get in or afford the prices, at least go by the store. Donghia's windows have the most beautiful and different displays you'll see anywhere in Los Angeles.

West Hollywood   657-6060
Entrance with
Interior Designers Only

Several years ago Jim and Penny Hull started their small furniture store with a few cardboard pieces that were well designed and contemporary, at that time a rarity. These days Jim has several factories, a line of furniture, both adult and children's (their famous bunk beds made of two cylinders are well known by now), some bathroom accessories that are futuristic and well designed, a chain of stores, and customers that keep coming back for more. It's a really lovely shop with ultra-modern pieces that are unusual and exciting. You'll also find many pieces that you can assemble yourself.

H.U.D.D.L.E.
10918 Kinross Avenue
Westwood   478-1112

At these two large and well-stocked showrooms you'll find a tremendous selection of any kind of tile you can imagine. From traditional Spanish tiles to the most modern designs, from the now boring but still popular pastel shades to the most vibrant deco blues and reds, this shop has got it all. You'll also love the displays of bathrooms already made up so you can get ideas about how to use their many tile designs. Owner Gloria Malloy is very helpful and knowledgeable, so don't hesitate to ask her for advice on using her tiles.

International Tile
1288 North La Brea Avenue
Hollywood   931-1761
9324 Corbin Avenue
Northridge   886-8811

Deco and moderne furniture at reasonable prices? Yes, and in an attractive store, chock full of lamps, tables, couches, in the loveliest colors and styles. Add to these, dresses, accessories, period clothes, and furnishing pieces, and you're in for a delightful experience.

Jadis
2701 Main Street
Santa Monica   396-3477

No reproductions here, no cheap replicas—only original museum-quality deco pieces designed by Lalique, Cartier, and Tiffany. Owners Walter Yows and H. Frank Jones keep rather irregular hours and keep changing their phone number, but try to catch them in because it's really worth a trip to see these exquisite objects.

H. Frank Jones
8101 Melrose Avenue
Hollywood

The Kreiss family runs this supermarket of furniture and accessories. But don't let the term supermarket fool you. It's true you'll find a tremendous collection of glassware, trays, baskets, flatware, and vases at pretty cheap prices, but there is also the "collections" showroom full of lovely furniture, from well-made and designed wicker furnishings to overstuffed chairs and sofas in the latest designs and colors. Be sure to visit the back room at the furniture store. There are always seconds and extra pieces on sale there.

Kreiss Ports of Call Imports
8409 and 8445
Santa Monica Boulevard
Hollywood
654-4142 (accessories)
656-1606 (furniture)

The 1900's Company
12406 Ventura Boulevard
Studio City   769-1900
8819 National Boulevard
Culver City   204-0436

This accessory and furniture store carries reproductions of early-American oak furniture. There are huge tables, tiny mirrors, lots of dining chairs and dressers and roll-top desks and anything your heart desires—at reasonable prices. The huge inventory includes many pieces from a variety of manufacturers, so a survey of these two shops will insure that you have covered a large portion of the early-American furniture market.

Palmer Garland
8687 Melrose Avenue
Pacific Design Center
West Hollywood   657-7101

Paul Palmer loves great designs, and his showrooms show it. Handling such famous names as I.C.F., McKintosh, Eames, and the like, his collection has wonderful, classic furniture, lighting, and accessories. Ever looked through a book on modern furniture—the great designs? Well, Palmer has them all, plus the newest in both furniture and accessories. My particular favorites are his bathroom accessories, from the Fearless Faucets collections of brightly colored, enameled faucets and shower heads, to the Ironmonger handles and pulls for cabinets and doors (also in the brightest colors of the rainbow), to other pieces in chrome, brass, enamels, and more. It's all moderne or contemporary, and only the best quality and designs. Remember, you must buy through an interior designer at Palmer Garland.

Rapport Company
435 North La Brea Avenue
Hollywood   933-7211

Remember all those famous designs you've seen in showrooms and magazines? Well, Rapport has them all—if not the real thing, then in perfectly good reproductions at a fraction of the cost. And the inventory is astounding—rooms full of dining chairs, bedroom sets, couches, armchairs, outdoor furniture, lamps, and other accessories—anything your home would need. The floors are crowded, the collection overwhelming in scope. But if you take your time and shop carefully, chances are you'll find the pieces you've always wanted at prices quite a bit cheaper than other retail stores. And the inventory keeps changing: what you may not find one week is worth waiting for, because chances are that by the time the next shipment of bargains arrives, they'll have what you want.

BOOKS AND RECORDS

They say a thirsty person will go anywhere for a drink of water. I feel that way about books and records. I will travel as far as need be to find the collection I want or just to browse. Los Angeles is full of enchanting shops, both specialized and general interest. The following is a list of a few of them, with brief descriptions.

Book Soup
8868 W. Sunset Boulevard
Los Angeles   659-3110

Owner Glen Goodman provides personal service at this small, cozy shop. There is a terrific selection of books, particularly movie and music literature for the Sunset Strip habitues. Will special order!

Brentano's Book Stores
Several locations. Check phone book for nearest branch.

This classy chain is more than a book store. Although you'll find the latest novels, art books, and nonfiction of the bestseller variety, you'll also find less-well-known volumes, calendars, games, toys, jewelry, and salespeople who are truly helpful.

In addition to a good general collection, Chatterton's have concentrations in contemporary and small press literature, gay writing, and drama.

Chatterton's Bookshops
1818 North Vermont Avenue
Hollywood   664-3882
520 East Colorado Boulevard
Pasadena   681-6803

This chain's Hollywood branch is a favorite old standby, having the largest selection of new books, easily identifiable in specially marked subject sections. Their children's, psychology, and history sections are very complete.

B. Dalton Bookseller
Many locations. Check phone book for nearest branch.

For a large chain, Doubleday's service is excellent. The shop in Beverly Hills has on many occasions located books for me that everyone else swore were no longer available.

Doubleday Book Shops
Several locations. Check phone book for nearest branch.

In addition to books—new, used, and antiquarian—Dutton's has lovely prints, etchings, lithographs, and illuminated manuscripts.

Dutton's Books
5146 Laurel Canyon Boulevard
North Hollywood   877-9222

Fowler's general collection is augmented by a good selection of foreign maps.

Fowler Brothers
717 West Seventh Street
Downtown   627-7846

In addition to general books, Hall's is strong on black history and literature.

Hall's Bookmart
4004 West Santa Barbara Avenue
Los Angeles   294-0260

Five miles of books, new and used. Even Evelyn Wood would be satiated by their collection.

Hollywood Book City
6627 Hollywood Boulevard
Hollywood   466-2525

Hunter's has a wonderfully complete children's section, as well as lots of cookbooks, art books, and paperbacks.

Hunter's Books
Several locations. Check phone book for nearest branch.

Great for late-night browsing, this store features contemporary literature and politics. They also publish an excellent literary magazine, *Bachy.*

Papa Bach
11317 Santa Monica Boulevard
West Los Angeles   478-2373

Located near the beach, Small World offers a good selection of children's books, magazines, and poetry.

Small World Books
1407 Ocean Front Walk
Venice   399-2360

Craig and Pat Graham carry a wide collection of literature, with emphasis on the twenties and thirties.

Vagabond Books
2076 Westwood Boulevard
West Los Angeles   395-8811

A general interest bookshop with terrific individual help.

Valley Book City
5249 Lankershim Boulevard
North Hollywood   985-6911

Vroman's Bookstores
Four locations. Check phone book
for nearest branch.

Started by A. C. Vroman, noted photographer of the Southwest, these stores feature money-saving sales and exceptionally helpful staffs.

Walden Books
Several locations. Check phone
book for nearest branch.

This chain offers a good general selection with emphasis on current bestsellers.

Westwood Book Store
1021 Broxton Avenue
Westwood   473-4923

Located near UCLA, this excellent college store has academic and general books and friendly browsing. Open evenings.

Antiquarian

Bennett and Marshall
8214 Melrose Avenue
West Hollywood   653-7040

Rare books and manuscripts, medicine, and early Americana are in abundance here.

Caravan Book Store
605 South Grand Avenue
Downtown   626-9944

You'll find a terrific selection of military and naval history, western Americana, and other rare books.

Cherokee Book Shop
6607 Hollywood Boulevard
Hollywood   463-5848

Crowded into a seemingly small shop are thousands of out-of-print books, children's books, first editions, and more.

Dawson's Book Shop
535 North Larchmont Boulevard
Los Angeles   469-2186

You'll find a large selection of printing books, rare art and literature, and old western Americana.

Heritage Book Shop
847 North La Cienega Boulevard
West Hollywood   659-3674

Lots of first editions, early travel, and other old finds.

Krown and Spellman, Booksellers
1945 Westwood Boulevard
West Los Angeles   474-1745

A large collection of classical books lines these shelves, but you'll also be amazed at the medieval and Renaissance finds.

Lennie's Book Nook
8125 West Third Street
West Hollywood   651-5584

A collection of scholarly out-of-print books lies hidden among biographies and volumes on theater and history.

Needham Book Finders
2317 Westwood Boulevard
West Los Angeles   475-9553

If you're trying to find a book and have gotten nowhere, Stanley Kurman will get it for you through his search service.

The Scriptorium
427 North Cañon Drive
Beverly Hills   275-6060

The Scriptorium is a fascinating shop just to browse in. Owner Charles Sachs is also a respected buyer and seller of autographed letters, manuscripts, and documents. If you have what may be valuable letters, bring them in for appraisal.

Jake Zeitlin in front of his "Red Barn" on La Cienega.

This beautiful shop specializes in arts and graphics, science and medicine.

Art and Architecture

This new shop and gallery features the cutting edge of contemporary art books, many of them hand-made by the artists.

Artworks
66 Windward Avenue
Venice   392-4203

Hennessey and Ingalls
10814 West Pico Boulevard
West Los Angeles   474-2541

Helen Hennessey knows her stuff. There isn't an art book published that she has not seen or heard of. Since they moved into a larger, more spacious store, Hennessey and Ingalls truly has become the best art store around. You'll find the most beautiful art books, some published abroad, and a host of do-it-yourself soft-cover books.

Norton Simon Museum
Colorado and Orange Grove
Boulevards
Pasadena   449-3730

Because this museum is a nonprofit organization, the book shop, which has a large selection of art books, sells them at about forty percent less than other stores. It's really a terrific place to get those otherwise expensive books you have always wanted.

Cinema, Science Fiction, and Comics

Bond Street Book Store
1638 North Wilcox Avenue
Hollywood   464-8060

A large selection of comics, movie books, and science fiction.

Book Treasury
6707 Hollywood Boulevard
Hollywood   466-6527

Lots of science fiction and fantasy books, plus detective novels galore.

A Change of Hobbit
1371 Westwood Boulevard
Westwood   473-2873

Preferring to call it "speculative fiction," Sherry Gottlieb runs a very popular and well-stocked bookshop.

Collector's Shop
1063 North Spaulding Avenue
West Hollywood   650-0973

Movie books, westerns, comics, magazines, old records, and selected Disney items are just a few of the treasures at this enticing shop.

The Comic Vendor
Old Town Mall
19800 Hawthorne Boulevard
Torrance   542-9040

Comic book lovers are fanatics. If you don't believe that, you ought to take a trip to this comic collector's paradise and see the browsers and buyers revel in their finds. Lining the shelves you'll see famous old editions of Superman, Batman, Wonder Woman, Spiderman, and more.

Larry Edmunds Book Shop
6658 Hollywood Boulevard
Hollywood   463-3273

This Hollywood landmark offers cinema and theater books, photos, and posters in an atmosphere rich with nostalgia. (See Tours, p. 000.)

Mystery and Suspense

Boulevard Bookshop
10634 West Pico Boulevard
West Los Angeles   837-1001

A good selection of mystery detective books.

Scene of the Crime
13636 Ventura Boulevard
Sherman Oaks   981-2583

Even if you aren't a mystery buff, you must visit this wonderful shop. Designed like someone's study, the room is lined with famous and not-so-well-known mysteries. Readings by writers and other personalities are given.

International

Books and tapes on world-wide Chinese culture.

China Cultural Center
970 North Broadway
Downtown   489-3827

Translated as The City of Books, this shop carries French books, records, and magazines.

La Cité des Livres
2306 Westwood Boulevard
West Los Angeles   475-0658

German books head the list, but other countries are also represented here.

Los Feliz International Bookstore
1767 North Vermont Avenue

Spanish and Latin American books.

Bernard H. Hamel
2326 Westwood Boulevard
West Los Angeles   475-0453
Hollywood   660-0313

A wonderful collection of Russian books, records, and folk art objects.

Victor Kamkin Bookstore
2320 Westwood Boulevard
West Los Angeles   474-4034

Japanese books, magazines, records, and tapes.

Kinokuniya Bookstore
110 South Los Angeles Street
Downtown   687-4447

Specialty

Books, records, and films on the Asian-American experience.

Amerasia Bookstore
338 East Second Street
Downtown   680-2888

A fine selection of metaphysical and spiritual books, magazines, and accessories.

Bodhi Tree Bookstore
8585 Melrose Avenue
West Hollywood   659-1733

This pleasant neighborhood shop features politics, ecology, and nonsexist children's literature.

Book Shop in Ocean Park
2915 Main Street
Santa Monica   396-3659

You'll find over 1,500 cookbooks published by some of the most obscure and valuable organizations and groups in the world. Note: you can't check out any of the books. This means that you don't need to buy a UCLA library card. Just go to the information desk on the main floor and the librarians will issue you a one-day card which will entitle you to use any of the books in this section.

California Cookbook Collection
UCLA Research Library
Westwood   825-1323

I am a magazine addict. I love this stand. They carry magazines from all over the world and foreign newspapers you haven't seen in years. They always have the latest issues on the stand, and will try to get for you any you may have missed. It's a terrific place.

Century City Magazines
Century Square Shopping Center
Century City   277-5509

Theodore Front
155 North San Vicente Boulevard
Beverly Hills   658-8770

Anything and everything you ever wanted to know about musicology.

Gilbert's Book Shop
6278 Hollywood Boulevard
Hollywood   465-4185

Serious works on astrology and the occult are featured at one of Los Angeles' oldest bookstores.

Intellectuals and Liars
1028 Wilshire Boulevard
Santa Monica   451-1842

This new store offers contemporary fiction and poetry from major publishers and the small presses, in addition to readings and discussions on modern literature.

Monterey Book and Card Shop
2330A South Atlantic Boulevard
Monterey Park   728-4496

Chicano studies lead the list here.

George Sand Books
9011 Melrose Avenue
West Hollywood   858-1648

Books and magazines on all aspects of the fine arts are available at this helpful store. Check out the stunning European graphics magazines.

Sandpiper Books
1520 Washington Boulevard
Venice   396-7600

This small shop is devoted to first editions of twentieth-century literature.

Sisterhood Bookstore
1351 Westwood Boulevard
Westwood   477-7300

Truly a one-of-a-kind bookstore, this wonderful shop specializes in feminist literature and records. You'll find a selection of books and calendars not available in other shops. There is also an invaluable children's section that carries nonsexist literature.

Scientific-Technical Book Center
17801 Main Street
Irvine   (714) 557-8324

Maire Walter owns this amazing technical bookstore that carries an enormous selection of hard-to-find books (and those regular bookstores are not interested in carrying). If you can't travel to Irvine, just call her and she'll be delighted to send you any book she has.

Treehouse Bookstore
17322 Ventura Boulevard
Encino   986-7374

Also listed under our unusual shops category, this store has an invaluable collection of children's books, where kids can look and touch as well as buy.

Many bookstores specialize in Hebrew and Jewish books, records, and folklore accessories. They line the streets of Fairfax Avenue in West Hollywood. Since there are so many, we have avoided listing all of them and simply urge you to walk along Fairfax Avenue between Third Street and Melrose Avenue and try them for yourself. It's worth the time.

Used Books

Acres of Books
240 Long Beach Boulevard
Long Beach   437-6980

Although many of the bookstores we have mentioned carry used books, for a truly heavenly experience you must visit the queen of them all. The huge warehouse is lined with thousands of books, most costing about three dollars apiece. You'll find books about anything and everything. It's really a wonderland for book lovers.

Records

Balfour Barton has the largest collection of reggae, soul, and calypso records in Los Angeles. He also carries gifts from the Caribbean, sells concert tickets, and will bring back from his many trips abroad any record he doesn't have in stock. And what's more, you can even listen to records here!

Barton's Record and Gift Shop
4018 Buckingham Road
Crenshaw District   296-9166

As the name implies, you will find only classical records here— eighteen thousand of them. The staff is knowledgeable and helpful.

Classical Record Shop
366 South Maple Drive
Beverly Hills   275-7026

Mary Aldin's shop offers a rich selection of blues, jazz, vintage rock, ethnic, and folk music as well as books and magazines.

Muskadine Music
212 Pier Avenue
Santa Monica   392-1136

The selection at this chain of stores is hard to beat. If it's been recorded, chances are they'll have it. Sometimes, however, the staff plays zombie rock at volumes that make browsing unpleasant. The main branch on Sunset Strip is frequented by musicians who perform in the nearby clubs. The classical annex across the street is a good bet for the symphonically inclined.

Tower Records
Several locations. Check phone book for nearest branch.

If you are feeling nostalgic, Music & Memories is the place to go, whether you prefer rock 'n' roll, jazz, show tunes, or movie music. This store specializes in musical memorabilia, including posters. Located one block east of Vineland.

Music & Memories
10850 Ventura Boulevard
Studio City   761-2126

Point Vicente on the Palos Verdes Peninsula.

BEACHES AND SPORTS:

Including Surfing, Water Sports, the Rose Bowl, and Major College and Pro Teams.

By David Lees, LOS ANGELES MAGAZINE
And Anthony Squire

T he Beach.

Those two words, along with one more—Hollywood—pretty well conjure up what most people think Los Angeles is all about. After all, the orange groves are gone, smog stains many of the once-famed sparkling sunny days, and gas shortages can take the fun out of cruising for burgers.

But The Beach remains. A piece of the world away from the world, where the smell of sizzling suntan oil, the tang of seaweed iodine, and the occasional, unmistakable, odor of overcooked French fries come together in an olfactory evocation worthy of Proust.

The Beach is a place where time is measured by how high the sun stands in the sky—the way the Indians used to do it. A place where people, who are themselves mostly warm salt water, come to be close to a large body of warm salt water.

Sand and sea, sea and sand. In Los Angeles, it's the same sea, euphemistically called the Pacific, that the Spanish fleet used as a freeway to colonize California. It's the same sea that farther north drew John Steinbeck and Robinson Jeffers to its shores. And it's the same sea, the same Beach, that Hollywood got hold of in the mid 1960s to create once and for all the beach blanket image of shoreline recreation in Los Angeles.

People go to the Beach for all sorts of reasons, but the chief one nowadays is fun. The more vigorous do battle with the waves on surfboards, inflatable canvas rafts, strange flexible "boogie boards," or with feet and fins. Others paddle along happily, content to bob up and down beyond the surf line. Some arrive at the Beach just to get away from it all for an afternoon. Some go to drop a hook, others to explore the flora and fauna, others to experience the mystique of the ocean coast. Still others go to look, and be looked over. Introverts commune with the ocean, extroverts with each other. They come to work on a tan, or to work on growing up.

This guide to the beaches near Los Angeles is by no means objective. A good beach, these days, is hard to find, if by "good beach" you mean a place that isn't obsessively organized into too many parking lots at the expense of sand space, cluttered by concession stands, or in other ways just about totally wrecked by the one thing, above all, you want a break from at the beach—civilization. On the other hand, some parking is a good idea, lest your sunny day be spent broiling in the car. And, restrooms, we are forced to admit, are sometimes necessary.

By and large, we go to the beach to get away from people. Singing along with this misanthropic refrain are two leitmotifs: the worst time to go to the beach is on a Sunday and the worst time to ignore it is during the winter. In wintertime, the play of light on the heaving ocean is beautiful. The absence of crowds is delightful. And the water is, well, bracing.

This guide is the result of months of intensive, though hedonistically happy, research, supplemented by years as a dedicated beach rat. It is based on weekday, and, yes, weekend observations. It is intended to give you an impression of the diversity of delights available at the coastal plains of the Los Angeles tidal basin.

We have put the entries in a south-to-north geographical organization, using Pacific Coast Highway as the backbone. Unless you happen to live near the beaches we mention, Pacific Coast Highway is not the fastest way to get to them. But all roads and most off-ramps eventually end at what local residents call "PCH," so it was selected as the best common reference point. We have generally described each beach, pointed out the most convenient way to get to it, and catalogued facilities and services available. "Journeys to the East" is a thumbnail guide to sights worth seeing a few blocks inland from the sand.

Now to The Beach.

It offers unlimited opportunities for people of any age, alone or with families; it promises a treat for those of any income or political persuasion. We have tried to sketch some of those treats here. Still, the best way to know . . . is to go.

We begin in the south, at Dana Point, home of Hobie Alter, inventor of the fiberglass and foam surfboard and the Hobie Cat sailboat. Ironically, his boards are now useless here, because Dana Point is, thanks to a boat harbor, flat these days as far as waves go. Permanently.

But in place of the legendary Blood Reef and other breaks is Dana Point Harbor, a recreation complex that has opened the area to a range of family activities that center on the water. There are small piers for fishing, a tastefully landscaped bike path for pedallers and joggers, and a lovely pocket-size swimming lagoon whose unrippled surface and shallow bottom make it a joy for families with small children. The harbor, Dana Point Marina, is an anchorage for a moderately impressive armada of pleasure craft. Although the breakwater has wiped out the surf, a perfectly respectable beach remains at the northern edge of Dana Point Harbor.

Moving north between Dana Point and Laguna Beach, you'll find two more well-planned beach parks which seem to cater primarily to families with children.

Niguel Beach Park is a clean well-manicured beach area with wide, raked nature trails. It used to be a famed surf spot called Salt Creek. Swimming and body surfing here are still enjoyable, although it somehow seems to lack the punch it used to have for boarding.

Aliso is a new favorite of fishers because of a concrete pier recently constructed for the hook, line, and sinker bunch. A wide, sandy beach and gentle combers make this another great place for the kids.

Dana Point Harbor
Parking: Adequate.
Facilities and services: Lifeguards, restrooms, showers, drinking fountains. No concession stands in Dana Point Harbor recreational site, but there is a collection of cafes in Dana Point Village, a blight of shiny shops which forms the border between Dana Point Harbor and Doheny State Beach.
Access: Pacific Coast Highway to Del Obispo Street (south entrance) or Street of the Green Lantern (north entrance).

Niguel Beach Park
Parking: Adequate.
Facilities and services: Lifeguards, restrooms, drinking fountains.
Access: Pacific Coast Highway, west on Crown Valley Parkway.

Aliso Beach Park
Parking: Adequate.
Facilities and services: Lifguards, restrooms, drinking fountains.
Access: Pacific Coast Highway, two parking lots on both sides of the highway.

Laguna Beach

There really isn't a Laguna Beach. Instead of just one stretch of sand, you'll find a succession of small coves which amble their way invitingly northwards within the city limits of this affluent, conservative town. Each cove is a pocket paradise, with clear, azure water, abundant sea life and clean sand. The trouble in this paradise is parking. Turn west almost anywhere off Pacific Coast Highway and you'll find a cove worth stopping to see—that is, if you can find a place to put your car. Moving north through Laguna, some of the highlights are:

Moss Street has the drawbacks of a narrow beach, tricky currents, and a treacherous bottom. It's too rough for swimming or body surfing and too hacked up for surfing.

Moss Street Beach
Parking: Inadequate. Moss Street itself is narrow, and usually

filled up. Scouting along the streets a few blocks east of Pacific Coast Highway will usually yield results.

Facilities and services: None.

Access: Pacific Coast Highway to Moss Street.

Why go?

The tidepools. The pools here and just to the south are always captivating, in any season. The Moss Street tidepools feature a natural stone arch and a partially submerged cave at their northern entrance, a subtly spectacular preview of the sea life just ahead. Starfish, sea anemones, sea urchins, small crabs, and scads of mussels abound here, as they do in other Laguna tidepools. Any time you plan to go tidepooling, bring along a pair of tennis shoes for protection as well as traction. And, please, leave the sea creatures right where you find them.

Brooks Street Beach

Parking: Inadequate. The same reasons and the same strategies apply here as for Moss Street. But, since for nonsurfers, the primary attraction is the view, parking the car in a red zone and getting out for a quick look can be satisfying.

Facilities and services: None.

Access: Pacific Coast Highway to Brooks Street.

Brooks Street is one of the most famous surfing spots in Southern California. It has a unique reef formation off shore that makes for a long, cylindrical wave. If you're an experienced surfer, the shape and consistency of the place recommend it. If not, remember it's a full mile of paddling, each way, out to where the waves form. No tidepools; the beach itself is narrow and usually packed with surfers and drying strands of ropy seaweed. Brooks also offers a fine view of the curve of the coastline.

Oak Street and Thalia Street, two more surfing beaches whose reputation is built on a reef break, each share the characteristics of Brooks Street. For some reason, though, parking is less of a problem. A car space can be had by driving east along Oak Street, across Pacific Coast Highway. There are no services or facilities at either beach. Access is Pacific Coast Highway to Oak or Thalia Street.

Main Beach has volleyball nets, a lifeguard tower, and a few picked-over tidepools at its northernmost point. An overly organized spot, in our opinion, with bright new grass encircled by a brand new boardwalk made of planks that are preweathered to look old. Its usually gentle surf and sloping bottom make it a good place for families, though.

Laguna Main Beach

Parking: Inadequate. But it's better than the coves, since metered parking and a small municipal lot in town—ten yards away—provide some relief.

Facilities and services: Lifeguards, restrooms, drinking fountains. No concession stands on the beach, but a short walk across Pacific Coast Highway yields a variety of things to eat, from charburgers to organic smoothies.

Access: Pacific Coast Highway, between Forest Avenue and Broadway.

Shaw's Cove is a breathtakingly beautiful spot, long a favorite of scuba and skin divers. It has a rocky beach, which is a sunbathing drawback for some, but its plentiful tidepools and gentle bay delight children.

Shaw's Cove

Parking: Inadequate, but try parking along Cliff Drive or three very steep blocks east of Pacific Coast Highway, on Monterey Drive.

Facilities and services: None.

Access: Pacific Coast Highway to Fairview.

Crescent Bay Beach

Parking: Inadequate, but see Shaw's Cove, above.

Facilities and services: Lifeguards, restrooms, showers, drinking fountains.

Access: Pacific Coast Highway to Cliff Drive.

Crescent Bay is right next door to Shaw's Cove, connected by a shared tidepool system. It's our favorite spot in Laguna. Although its sandy beach is narrow, it is long enough to accommodate all but the most massive crowds. Crescent Bay has two rich tidepooling patches at either end of the beach. The surf is just right for an enjoyable day of relaxing, body surfing or swimming. The volleyball net is usually the center of a fast and fearsome all-day contest between teams of local teenagers.

The flora, surf, and varied shoreline of Laguna Beach.

Journeys to the East. Laguna is a quaint, tiny town whose narrow streets are usually jammed with traffic. If you can manage it, the coves are best visited in the late afternoon. Then, a leisurely stroll in the early evening will show the town off at its best. The Vorpal Gallery, 326 Glenneyre Street, is the Southern California gallery representing the works of M.C. Escher. The gallery itself is as intriguing as the art displayed on the walls. We recommend a restaurant called The Place Across the Street From the Hotel Laguna, 440 South Pacific Coast Highway, for its salads and mild Mexican food. The Penguin Malt Shop, 981 South Pacific Coast Highway, makes what are perhaps the best chocolate malts in Southern California.

Treasure Cove

Moving on up the highway, Treasure Cove is a once-private preserve that is now open to the public. It has a wide beach, tidepools, and a stable perched near its entrance. Parking is adequate (most people think the cove is still private).

Corona Del Mar

Corona Del Mar is a pretty village between Laguna and Newport, just the other side of the channel from Newport Harbor and its infamous body surfing spot, "the Wedge." A roomy triangular beach offers lots of protected family bathing and a soothing view of the gilt-edged Newport pleasure boat fleet.

If you happen to be an ornery type who is doing the beaches we talk about here from north to south, you're in for a treat: the drive between Corona Del Mar south along Pacific Coast Highway to Laguna is one of California's most beautiful tours. Good on bikes, too.

Newport Beach

Newport Beach has long had a reputation as the land of Porsches and the people who can afford to lease them. An affluent, upwardly mobile community, its citizens find their recreational opportunities in boating, beachgoing, and voting Republican.

Narrow streets, strictly enforced regulations on severely limited parking, and a lack of clear signs are either a problem or a partial solution, depending on your vantage point as tourist or resident. At any rate, if you turn off Pacific Coast Highway at the sign that says "Balboa Peninsula" you will discover a series of numbered streets running perpendicular to the road you're driving along. Each of these dead-end at dazzling patches of wide, white beach, with wave action suitable for board or body surfing. Farther out on the Peninsula is "the Wedge," whose inverted-V shaped waves will give you a modern day Christians and lions show, as foolish body surfers play the odds at bone breakage for the honor of having dared the sea.

A detailed catalogue of each beach, at each street, would be tedious. They are all well-equipped with lifeguards, but restrooms can be a good hike from where you are. Parking is scarce.

Journeys to the East. The Crab Cooker, 2200 Newport Boulevard, serves the best clam chowder in California from a huge pot that never stops bubbling. Charlie's Chili, 102 McFadden Place, near the Newport Pier, is justly renowned for its spicy delights.

Although they've taken out the ratty old fun zone and slipped in a fake-Spanish mall at the end of Newport, the ferry ride to Balboa Island—ten cents if you're walking, twenty-five cents in a car (but leave your car)—is worth taking.

Once on Balboa Island, you can get a Balboa Bar, a concoction of vanilla ice cream on a stick hand-dipped in chocolate and sprinkled with nuts. Or try a frozen banana, a Balboa Bar which stars fruit instead of ice cream. Three or four places claim to have invented these culinary breakthroughs. Then, chomping and munching, you can take a pleasant one-hour stroll along the island, looking in the confidently undraped windows of the wealthy. Everybody does it; sort of an "Affluentland" if Disney had designed it. All of this high calorie Peeping Tom-ism is most enjoyable at dusk.

Balboa Island

A last note before we approach the Los Angeles County limits: the Dana Point to Balboa stretch is to be avidly avoided during Easter vacation. These places are the Fort Lauderdale of California, with the usual excesses of youth multiplied by a rather large coefficient of parental wealth.

Oh, and if you haven't taken the hint as yet, on a summer Sunday, the traffic through these places is bumper to license plate bracket. Try for a week day. You'll have a much better time.   a week day. You'll have a much better time.

Huntington Beach

Try as they may, the city fathers of Huntington Beach haven't been able to do much damage to the affably scruffy ambience of their town. It is actually three locales: Huntington Beach, the state beach which also bears Henry Huntington's name, and Huntington Pier.

Huntington Beach, with low rents and good surf, became a mecca for pioneering surfboard designers in the early 1960s. On Main Street and around it, you can still find a dozen or so surfboard shops. While the pungent, sweet and sour smell of resin and fiberglass has been replaced in the shops by the smell of clean carpet, it's good to know they're still around. And the Surf Theater, 121 Fifth Street, still plays a surf film every Wednesday and a year-old feature the rest of the week. After dark, Huntington can be a bit rough; as of this writing, it's beginning to get a biker image.

Except when big surf rolls through, bringing rip tides, Huntington offers crowded surf that's nearly ideal for body surfing and just about perfect for getting the hang of board surfing. You can walk out past where the waves break, still touching bottom. As for the beach itself, it looks like a beach blanket movie come to life. The highest age is about sixteen. If you can manage to relax despite the noise of transistor radios and shouted, casually obscene greetings, it's a sure bet that the outdoor speakers at an on-beach burger palace called Snuffy's will keep you nicely on edge.

Huntington Beach Pier
Parking: Adequate.
Facilities and services: Lifeguards, restrooms, showers, drinking fountains, concession stands.

The home of the national championships in surfing, held each year on the left side of the pier as you face the ocean, the Huntington Beach Pier has the same adolescent aura as its neighbor next door. The pier offers fishing and a good gallery view of the surfing. There are three fast-food shacks, also, one with a notice reading "25 cent purchase required to occupy a seat at the window." The establishment at the end of the pier serves a quasi-delicacy you might not otherwise sample. Called "strips," these thick, Frito-like munchies are to be dipped in the mix of salsa sauce and ketchup that comes with them. Definitely an accessory for looking, uh, "cool" on the pier.

Huntington State Beach
Parking: Adequate in the beach lot. For the foolishly adventurous, there is also parking along Pacific Coast Highway. Not recommended unless saving a dollar and a half means more to you than getting run over.
Facilities and services: Lifeguards, park rangers, restrooms, showers, drinking fountains.

The state beach has a very different feel from Huntington Beach. It is less crowded, and is firmly oriented towards the family and beach chair set. Huntington State Beach features snack shacks and lifeguard stations with roofs of Spanish tile. Its waves are usually good for a day of body surfing or swimming.

Huntington is only the first of a string of state beaches which run from the border of Orange County to the outskirts of Long Beach. Bolsa Chica State Beach is a paradigm of ocean recreational development. It used to be known as Tin Can Beach, a reference to its shady status among surfers and other beach addicts as the dirtiest beach in the state.

Bolsa Chica State Beach
Parking: Adequate, with easy access to and from Pacific Coast Highway and understandable signs.
Facilities and services: Lifeguards, park rangers, restrooms, showers, drinking fountains, picnic tables.

My, how it's changed. It's now a broad, clean beach, sloping gently to the shores of a good break for swimming or body surfing. Plenty of restrooms, picnic tables, and parking, with an absence of concession stands, make it the best of the southern state beaches. Good for families, kids, and teenagers.

Surfside, located near Huntington Harbor, is a small beach town slowly being eroded by the onslaught of development projects. There is virtually no tourist parking, but some swear by its gentle surf and quiet family beach atmosphere.

A solidly middle-class suburban town, Seal Beach offers good surfing, swimming, and body surfing on beaches whose width cuts down on crowding—even on a summer Sunday. Although some evidence of the ubiquitous shopping mall has crept in (a placed called the Coffee Nook would have been laughed out of Seal less than a decade ago), the community remains a relaxed place which attracts families with 2.5 kids, as well as college students from nearby Long Beach State.

Seal Beach

Parking: Marginally adequate.

Facilities and services: Lifeguards, restrooms, drinking fountains. Concession stands on the pier, which is otherwise less than noteworthy.

Access: The best of Seal Beach are the numbered streets which intersect with Seal Beach Boulevard. Parking is either elusive or nonexistent on these tiny avenues, but you can park in a city lot and hoof it.

Long Beach Marine Stadium.

Long Beach

Long Beach is billing itself as "the International City" these days, part of an effort by the people who live there to revitalize the economy of a place most people would rather drive through than stop in. The truth is, Long Beach has always had plenty going for it—along its coastline.

Unfortunately, the first glimpse of the water you'll see as you drive north into Long Beach on the Pacific Coast Highway is not especially invigorating. The Long Beach Marina has none of the recreational opportunities, except boating, offered by the well-planned facility at Dana Point. While Seaport Village in the marina makes a stab at being picturesque, its specialty shops are not very special.

Moving farther north, though, things pick up. Long Beach Marine Stadium, home to all kinds of boat races, rates a recommendation for its attractive manmade beach, safe swimming lagoon, and collection of facilities, all of it adding up to a good place for a family day excursion.

Continuing north, along Bayshore Avenue, the wide blue canals and expensive homes of Naples beckon invitingly. But there is no beach here, and access is restricted to residents.

Alamitos Bay

Parking: Inadequate. This time, we have no ready solutions. Perhaps simply getting there early?

Facilities and services: Lifeguards, restrooms, drinking fountains, basketball and handball courts.

Long Beach

Parking: Parking is sort of a "good news—bad news" joke in Long Beach. The bad news is that the best beaches are located on narrow streets which must also accommodate residential parking. The goods news is that the beaches towards downtown have adequate parking in city lots . . . but the bad news is that the beaches aren't as appealing.

Facilities and services: Depends on the beach you pick, but all offer restrooms, drinking fountains, and showers, and some have volleyball nets. Long Beach is known for its competent, courteous lifeguards, who still use big paddleboards to effect rescues.

Alamitos Bay, next to Naples, looks all right at first. A closer look reveals a gnarly parking problem and an overcrowded beach. For people who actually take pleasure in rubbing elbows, it is ideal. Since it is a bay, safe swimming is afforded. And you can watch the Hobie Cat people glide serenely back and forth.

The stretches of sand making up the "long beach" that gives the city its name all lie at the foot of sequentially numbered streets which intersect with Ocean Boulevard. The beaches here are a pleasant surprise. They are not only clean, they're wide, which takes care of crowds. Body surfing and swimming are uniformly good.

The best areas are from Fifty-fifth Street south. Belmont Shores, Fifty-fourth Street north to Belmont Plaza (a sparkling city recreational swimming complex), is perfectly fine, too, but it seems more crowded, as does the sand between Belmont Plaza and the Long Beach Pier. The spectacle of pole to pole fisherfolk on the pier has its urban-arcadian charm. Great greasy food emporiums, too, for aficionados of that kind of thing.

After all this sandy splendor, the downtown beaches seem a bit depressing. They are set off from the older sections of the city by wide patches of grass, but the groomed introduction can't make up for their oily waters. The view of harbor activities is continually interesting, especially on a foggy spring day.

Journeys to the East. The subject of what to do in the city of Long Beach really deserves a guidebook of its own, but here are our highlights. The Long Beach Museum of Art, 2300 East Ocean Boulevard, 439–2119, features a steady schedule of outstanding exhibitions by important modern artists. Cherry Avenue Park, at the corner of Cherry Avenue and Ocean Boulevard, hosts a series of days dedicated to the city's mixture of ethnic groups. Free food and a festive air abound. Call the Long Beach Department of Recreation at 432–5931 for details.

Long Beach has always been a major port center; it and San Pedro make up Los Angeles Harbor. Although there are no beaches in San Pedro—Cabrillo Beach was wiped out by the "yo-ho, yo-ho" sailor shtick of Ports O' Call Village—the sprawling city rates a look. The harbor area, with berths for huge luxury liners and slips for commercial fishing trawlers, is an excellent wandering ground on a quiet Sunday. You can park your car in the Ports O' Call lot, use the Ports O' Call restrooms, and take yourself and your camera for a picturesque promenade away from Ports O' Call.

Just down Harbor Boulevard, you will find the Thomas Bridge, connecting San Pedro with Long Beach. A quarter toll per car each way buys a spectacular view of L.A. Harbor. For a closer look at harbor happenings, pick up your complimentary tickets for a harbor tour by tug at the public relations headquarters for the harbor. They are located in room 708 of the Pacific Trade Center in San Pedro, 255 West Fifth Street. Hours are eight to five, Monday through Friday. Yes, you have to show up in person, they will neither take nor make reservations by phone—unless you're with a school or organization.

Palos Verdes is a posh community elegantly planted next to the working harbor city of San Pedro. Most of its beautiful cliffs and coves are private, but there is almost always a lovely view to be had along the curves of Palos Verdes Drive. On one side, you'll see gently sloping hills, suddenly hacked off into sheer cliffs plummeting into the sea. On the other side of the car are open green fields of nasturtiums and wild mustard. Once you reach Palos Verdes Estates, whose Spanish tile roofs (mandated by city law) keep the rain from falling inside homes that start at $450,000, the driving tour is improved with several scenic vantage points.

Just off Palos Verdes Drive is the well-cached Palos Verdes Estates Shoreline Marine Preserve. The preserve is a magnet for scuba and skin divers; its reef and beach breaks lure surfers—but watch the rocks! Its area covers two sea spots, Lunada and Malaga coves. Of the two, Malaga is more to the taste of the casual visitor. The walk from the parking lot to the beach is incomparably easier than the interminable hike on a steep dirt road that you are confronted with at Lunada. And the beach at Malaga Cove is neither as narrow nor as rocky.

Palos Verdes Estates, including a walk down to the marine preserve, can be seen by car in about an hour, done at a leisurely pace.

Those who happen to fancy either Torrance or Redondo beaches may burn this book, but we look in vain for a reason to go out of your way to visit either of those two towns. Although both offer broad, sandy beaches, good swimming and surfing, and do a good job with parking, lifeguards, and facilities, neither is as interesting as the two other beaches in the South Bay, Hermosa and Manhattan.

Palos Verdes Estates Shoreline Marine Preserve

Parking: Adequate, but access is tricky.

Facilities and services: None.

Access: Somebody, somewhere doesn't really want you to find the marine preserve. But here's one way to do it: once you pass the signs on Palos Verdes Drive that let you know you're in the plush terrain of Palos Verdes Estates, slow down. Just before the turn off to Pacific Coast Highway, directly across the street from a (what else?) Spanish-style shopping mall, is Via Almar. Turn west, toward the ocean, then left on Via Arroyo, to Paseo del Mar, which takes you straight to the parking lot for Malaga Cove.

Hermosa Beach

Parking: Inadequate, but they're trying. Meters along Hermosa and Pier avenues as well as city lots east of Pier Avenue give at least the impression of progress.

Facilities and services: Lifeguards, restrooms, showers, drinking fountains, volleyball nets. Concession stands on the Pier, casual restaurants on Pier Avenue.

Hermosa, we think, is one of the best of the Los Angeles beach towns. Its central stretch, Pier Avenue, is nearly impassable in summer and parking is a Kafkaesque undertaking. But the town and the beach have a ragamuffin, relaxed ambience. Numbered streets which meet Hermosa Avenue lead you to the sand between solidly compact wooden homes that are now having to share the neighborhood with condo conversions and ritzy remodels. The Strand, between sand and the terminus of each walking street, comfortably accommodates roller skaters, skateboarders, joggers, and cyclists. The beach is a good spot for body or board surfing. It is well-watched by lifeguards, too, a benefit enjoyed by the families with young children who live near the sand.

Hermosa's numbered streets end at the pier. Fishing and fast fooderies are the main attractions on the pier, but a stroll up Pier Avenue yields an impressive concentration of delights (see below). Surfing is only allowed south of the pier.

Venice Beach.

Journeys to the East. Even if you can't stand the beach (what are you doing reading this, then?) you'll enjoy Pier Avenue in Hermosa Beach. Its highlights:

Bill's Tacoburritos, on the corner of Pier Avenue and the Strand. Go on in. It's raucous and almost clean, like its clientele, who are waiting for that take-out sensation and culinary treat, the tacoburrito.

Just Desserts, 29 Pier Avenue. We are ice cream junkies, and we give Just Desserts the nod for its orgasmically delicious ice creams and yogurts, made on the premises. You can load these up with crumbled cookies, M & M's, and other sugar modifications for a true debauch.

The Lighthouse, 30 Pier Avenue. This joint is billed correctly as "L.A.'s oldest jazz club and waterfront dive." Good sounds from jazz greats new and old dance out over the pier almost any night. (See Going Out, p.184 .)

El Yaquil, 118 Pier, is recommended for veterans of Mexican food. The fare is hot, authentic, and in a word: hoo-ha!

Either/Or Bookstore, 124 Pier. This shop is a demonstration that beach freaks actually do read. One of the best bookstores in Southern California, its four octagonal rooms display a dizzyingly thorough collection. Classics, best sellers, how-to's, and just about anything else.

The community of Manhattan Beach is made up of two groups of residents, segregated by choice. Families with children live away from the beach, on shady streets with arboreal names like Elm and Pine. These folks, called "tree people," don't have much to do with the hectic hedonists who hang out at the beach. Those Manhattanites are the "sand people."

That's the prevailing mythology, anyway. Fact is, everybody goes to the beach.

Small wonder, either. Like the town, with its small shops, carved wooden signs, and curiously conical roofs, the beach is clean and orderly. It is broad with many volleyball nets and lots of room for all age groups to play. The surf can be a bit rough at times, though, so a warning to inexperienced body or board surfers is in order.

The Strand in Manhattan Beach, like its cousin in Hermosa, is a traffic artery for all manner of vehicular locomotion. Bicycles are assigned to a separate bike path, just below the Strand.

Journeys to the East. Not too much goes on in Manhattan Beach, which is OK by us. However, Sloopy's, 3416 Highland Avenue, makes burgers and strawberry shakes that are deservedly legendary.

Manhattan Beach
Parking: Inadequate. You can find it along the main street (Highland Avenue) only if you're lucky. Parking on streets east of Highland will work, but there's a hitch. After you smugly park and lock your car, consider the walk *back* up the steep streets. (One regular visitor told us, "You're so tired from the walk up here, you need a beer to get ready for the drive home.") Our advice, meager as it is: get to Manhattan Beach early. A small city lot just doesn't help much.
Facilities and services: Lifeguards, restrooms, showers, drinking fountains, volleyball nets.

Dockweiler State Beach
Parking: Adequate.
Facilities and services: Lifeguards, restrooms, drinking fountains, concession stands, fire rings.

Dockweiler is a long, wide, oily beach that slinks north from the city limits of El Segundo into Playa del Rey. It is quite popular with lots of Southern Californians. There are fire pits and plenty of parking; concession stands, too, selling everything from phosphates to firewood. The fire rings on the beach mean a picnic after dark.

Well, Dockweiler has all those amenities and conveniences, all right, but it has something else: constant noise pollution. The place is a veritable symphony in the *musique concrète* idiom, fully orchestrated with hot rods, outdoor speakers, and jets in full song as they arrive and depart from Los Angeles International Airport. All of that noise can put a large dent in what should be a quiet time at the beach.

During the day, the landscape is blotted out by the Hyperion steam generating plant, a hulk of green metal that squats across from the beach on Pacific Coast Highway. The silences between jet take-offs are punctuated with the sound of Hyperion employees being paged through gigantic squawk boxes.

The one redeeming feature of the whole set-up is its unofficial status as a center for hang-gliding in Southern California. So, bring earplugs, and watch man fly.

Or just keep driving.

Playa del Rey
Parking: Our only knock against the place. We estimate the number of official parking spaces for both the beach and the lagoon to be fewer than 200.
Facilities and services: Lifeguards, restrooms, showers, drinking fountains, basketball courts, picnic tables, barbecues.

Playa del Rey is a compact beach town that is refreshingly free of the lumbering attempts at "beautification" that threaten some seaside communities.

You can still get a quarter-pound whaleburger here.

The beach is wide and pleasant. On calm summer days, the surf is gentle, but when the waves approach any size, a vicious rip tide is in evidence, too.

Del Rey Lagoon is a surprise treat. Located about ten yards from the sand, this spacious semicircle of green grass set around a small pond offers picnic tables, basketball courts, barbecue facilities, and a full year-round recreation program.

The northern edge of the beach at Playa del Rey borders one of the channels feeding Marina del Rey. One intrepid fisherwoman we know, a veteran of many seasons, claims that perch is a reliable catch here. And you can watch the boats.

Marina del Rey, the largest manmade boat harbor in the world, is also the Southern California focal point for the swinging singles scene. Its one beach is a crescent that reaches along the Marina's "restaurant row" on Admiralty Way. We like it a lot. Its sheltered surface, free of even the hint of a wave, and its shallow bottom make it an excellent place for children. Parking is adequate. In the midst of the high-rent highrises, a bike path through a wildlife sanctuary provides surcease for humans as well as for birds.

Over the years, Venice has been many things to many people—but never the same thing, to the same people, at the same time. Some saw it as a scummy backwater during the 1950s, while others, like the beat poets, wintered in the Gaslight Cafe on Windward Avenue. During the next decade, Venice was perceived as either hippy heaven or heaven on earth, depending on who was doing the perceiving. Today, at last, there is general agreement on a unifying characteristic for Venice, a unique community whose five sluggish canals are all that's left of the dream of Sweet Caporal cigarette magnate Abbot Kinney to turn Venice, California, into a stateside replica of Venice, Italy. Everyone agrees, finally, on what Venice is all about: prime real estate. Property values have soared, and bohemian funkiness is giving way to chic renovation.

Developers haven't hung raw wood paneling and ferns on the beach, however; it remains one of the best in the state.

The first thing you'll notice before you set foot on the sand, though, is that your foot has been nearly run over a dozen times. Ocean Front Walk, an asphalt and concrete pathway, is the beach roller-skating capital of the United States, as well as a favorite bicycling track. It provides a sidewalk spectacle all the way to Santa Monica. You can fill your eyes with the panorama of huge wall-sized murals, watch a fast game of paddle tennis, gaze with admiration or amusement on the muscles rippling at the only beachfront weightlifting club in California, or play a game of pickup basketball. There is a boutique and a bookshop, a couple of trendy eateries and a sidewalk cafe, too. Indeed, Ocean Front Walk is the only beach activity we're going to *recommend* you do on a Sunday. (See Tours, p. 115 .)

Down on the sand, Venice Beach is a straight carpet of sand with lifeguard stations every eighth of a mile—progress indicators that make it popular with joggers. Surfing is generally respectable in north Venice, although the beach break is inconsistent in summer and only occasionally overhead in winter. Body surfing and swimming are good all along the beach, but the surf near Venice Pier can sometimes be dangerous.

Venice is also a big deal with two kinds of people who trust to luck and a line: kite flyers and fisherfolk. Surf fishers dot the coast in the early morning, while kite flyers play with the wind in the afternoon.

Journeys to the East. Handling all the happenings in Venice in the space of a few paragraphs is a doubtful undertaking, but Washington Boulevard, just northwest (left) off South Venice Boulevard has many good restaurants and intriguing shops. (So does Washington Street near the pier, but it is more on the beaten track.)

Venice
Parking: Adequate, but tight on Sundays.
Facilities and services: Lifeguards, restrooms, drinking fountains, concession stands, basketball courts, paddle tennis courts, volleyball nets, children's play area.

Merchant of Venice, 1349 Washington Boulevard, is an old standby, known for its beautiful refinishing of fine antiques and the stellar soups served six days a week in its small restaurant. Chez Hélène, 1029 Washington Boulevard, serves hearty, excellent French food at realistic prices. Reservations are needed here. Harry's Open Pit Barbecue, 1627 Washington Boulevard, is spicy and good.

The Brass Rubbing Center, 1142 Washington Boulevard, has everything you need, including authentic medieval brasses, to do a rubbing. It's inexpensive, and the people who work there are always helpful. Ted Cavagnaro, 68 North Venice Boulevard, proves that fine craftsmanship isn't a lost art in Venice with his handmade jewelry of silver and gold.

A brisk winter afternoon on the beach of Santa Monica, 1897.

When local headlines read "Million at beach this weekend," the beach everybody is at is Santa Monica. Its width and length, and its location at the end of the Santa Monica Freeway, have long made it a popular tourist beach. A shallow, sloping ocean bottom makes it almost always safe for swimming and good for body surfing. Lifeguard station number eighteen is the spot for surfing, although waves tend to be small.

Volleyball nets and the usual restroom facilities are available, too. It's a good place to bring the family, although the crowds can get to you after a while. But then, you can always work off your frustrations on the ring sets and bars near the pier, a token remembrance of the days when this was "Muscle Beach."

Santa Monica Pier may be best known nationally as the location for much of the movie "The Sting." The pier and its carousel provided the backdrop for many of the early adventures of Messrs. Newman and Redford. And, although it was never identified as Santa Monica in the film, the pier has a seedy atmosphere that must have struck the location scouts just right. It is an old time honky-tonk sort of pier, a gallery of arcades, bumper car rides, corn dogs, lemonade, and excellent people-watching. Do not miss the homemade French fries at Fish and Chips, an establishment with no regular hours.

Leo Carillo State Beach is actually three distinct areas, each sharing about one third of the sand. Two of these segments of sand have no name that is known to us, but the southern section is a fabled board surfing ground called Secos.

Leo Carillo offers a full range of recreational opportunities. Camping is permitted on part of the beach; body surfing and swimming, too, in addition to the aforementioned board surfing. Leo Carillo is even equipped with a few rocky caves for crawling through or exploring, depending upon your age or your height. The kelp that keeps wave conditions shapely for surfers also draws scuba divers in search of sea life.

Snaky piles of rocks form the borders of this trio of areas. The rockpiles sometimes slink up onto the beach itself, carving out natural windbreaks. These charming secluded spots, with green hills behind them, make for a perfect day at the beach.

County Line Beach is a living dinosaur, a reminder of what most Southern California beaches looked like before they were developed. It starts about a quarter of a mile past the Ventura County line, but no identifying signs or markings of any kind let you know you are there. A collection of motor vehicles of all costs and vintages, parked along Pacific Coast Highway, serve as the only clue. The parking lots are two patches of soft, deep brown dirt.

Its narrow, rocky beach has neither lifeguard nor loo; the boulders

Santa Monica
Parking: Adequate.
Facilities and services: Lifeguards, restrooms, drinking fountains, concession stands, showers, volleyball nets, swing sets.

Leo Carillo State Beach
Parking: Adequate.
Facilities and services: Lifeguards, restrooms, showers, drinking fountains, concession stand, campground.

on the sea bottom erase any hopes of body surfing or swimming. And the beach—ah, rapture—even has a few rusty beer cans. Only surfers at the low end of the sixteen- to twenty-five-year-old demographic group hang out here.

County Line Beach

County Line is a friendly, albeit scummy reminder that just you and the beach can often be the only ingredients you need to cook up a good day.

Journeys to the East. Santa Monica's Main Street is a slightly better dressed version of Washington Boulevard in Venice. It's a mix of restaurants and shops, of varying quality. Among the best is the Pioneer Boulangerie, 2012 Main Street, an outdoor-indoor restaurant with good soups and stews and fine wines to enjoy there or take out. Dhaba India, 2104 Main Street, serves tasty curries at reasonable prices. The Oar House, at 2941 Main Street, is a scuzzy bar and club owned by Al Ehringer, a Western Airlines pilot who also owns most of Main Street. Despite the expanding activities of its owner, the Oar House still serves large burgers and good sized pitchers of beer. One of the most interesting shops in Los Angeles, Colors of the Wind, 2900 Main Street, designs and sells custom silk and nylon flags for homes, shops, or whatever you please.

Will Rogers State Beach
Parking: Adequate.
Facilities and services: Lifeguards, restrooms, drinking fountains, swing sets and playground equipment.

Located just north of Santa Monica, the long arm of Will Rogers State Beach curves around the coast as far as Malibu. Its usually calm surf and relatively flat bottom make it attractive to families with children. An array of swing sets, jungle gyms, and other iron-workings take care of juvenile jumpiness. Relaxed body surfing is a daily happening at Will Rogers; passable board surfing conditions can be found only at the section of the beach near Sunset Boulevard. A popular beach, Will Rogers can get crowded.

Malibu
Parking: Awful. A dinky two dollar lot is supposed to corral all the cars for beach and pier. Parking along Pacific Coast Highway is scarce and dangerous. If you're dying to see Malibu Beach, stop in a no-parking zone and take a look.
Facilities and services: Lifeguards, restrooms, showers, drinking fountains, concession stands on pier.

The very name Malibu calls up images of the California dream, seen through a Panavision lens. From high glamour to Gidget, from William Holden to Frankie Avalon, Malibu is a "setting." The beach isn't as good as it once was, but the town retains its mystique. Malibu Colony is still just as exclusive, still just as secluded. In fact, most of what used to be called Rancho Malibu is private, whether in the Colony or in the plots of land to the north.

For our purposes, Malibu will mean its one major public spot of sand, Surfrider Beach, located between Malibu Creek and the Malibu Pier. Surfrider, as its name wistfully implies, is a shifting point surf break which was once the laboratory for the radical new styles of surfing made possible by the invention of the lightweight foam surfboard. The surf rats in those days (late 1950s and early 1960s) were a pretty rambunctious collection of people. Surfrider is still OK for small surf with good shape, although its rocky bottom and usually crowded water conditions make body surfing a painful chore at best. Still, in all, the only reminder of the good ol' surfin' days is the Natural Progression Surfboards Shop above an instant printer on Pacific Coast Highway. (Surfing is presently allowed only on the right side of the pier.)

Malibu Pier hasn't changed much over the years. Oh, there's an overpriced restaurant at one end, but the pier is still fitted out for fishing. At the ocean end of the pier is a small seafood joint and a bait store. Fish to be had with a pole and a line (no guarantees) include halibut, sea bass, and barracuda. Freshwater sinks and plenty of benches outfit the pier, too. Deep sea fishing boats leave the pier daily in two half-day shifts, at 8:00 a.m. and 1:00 p.m. Nonfishers will enjoy the view up or down the coast. A new innovation well worth it for the staunchly nonqueasy is the water taxi that chops its way between Malibu Pier and Santa Monica Pier. As of this writing, it does not run on weekends, but two dollars buys a one-way ride from 6:15 a.m. to 5:30 p.m. on weekdays.

Corral Beach, just north of Malibu, is a narrow, coarse strand. Two portable toilets comprise the gamut of facilities and services, parking is dangerous and available only along Pacific Coast Highway. For all of those reasons, your chances of being more or less alone are pretty good.

Zuma Beach is a playground for families and other citizens of the San Fernando Valley. It can get crowded, but we find it to be one of the most impressive ocean recreation areas in Southern California. Zuma seems to go on forever, with body surfing and swimming available as far as the eye can see along its miles of sea and shore. Scuba diving is big at Zuma, too. Los Angeles County conducts training dives here, and teaches lifeguards their job. And, don't tell anybody, but Zuma's southern tip, past its most southern parking lot, is the location of an unofficial nudist beach—but leave your camera in the car.

Zuma
Parking: Adequate. Zuma's lots match its size. Parking also available along Pacific Coast Highway.
Facilities and services: Lifeguards, restrooms, showers, drinking fountains, concession stands.

UCLA's Bill Walton (32) signals for a high lob during the 1973–74 season.

SPORTS:

By David Lees, LOS ANGELES MAGAZINE
And Anthony Squire

For this generation's sports fan the standard fare is "pro" or, even more correctly, "televised pro." As usual, Los Angeles stands apart! We are the only city in North America where a college football team, the USC Trojans, outdraws its NFL rival, the Anaheim-bound Los Angeles Rams. Similarly, the National Basketball Association's Los Angeles Lakers have, for over a decade and a half, had to take a back seat to the UCLA Bruins' fifteen Pacific Conference basketball championships, including eleven national championships in the last sixteen years. Yes, eleven national championships, not ten as every NCAA press guide will tell you. Those press guides omit the UCLA women's basketball team's championship victory in 1978 for the national title.

It's not that L.A.'s pro teams are so bad. The Rams, with seventy-five wins to only twenty-five losses since 1973, surpass all other NFL teams; and the Baylor-West Lakers played bridesmaid for a decade to the greatest basketball team of all, the Bill Russell Boston Celtics. Our pro teams are usually in contention and frequently make their respective playoffs.

For spectator and participant alike, Los Angeles is a sports mecca of dazzling proportions and variety. No single star, team, or event can hope to dominate. However, there are priorities.

First, the basic facts. Los Angeles has the largest and best equipped interscholastic sports system anywhere, comprising 526 teams and 68 leagues from the City and CIF conferences. This network, combined

The shaky beginning of a great football tradition.

with numerous junior colleges, clubs, and amateur leagues, makes up the richest talent pickings in North America. The list includes football, baseball, basketball, tennis, swimming, track and field, volleyball, and water polo. Also available to the sports enthusiast are skate boarding, bicycle racing, and roller skating! There are more professional basketball, football, and baseball players from Southern California than any other metropolitan area in the nation. And not surprisingly, the U.S. Olympic squad draws more talent every four years from Los Angeles than any other metropolitan area. Consequently, it is only fitting that the Olympics are returning in 1984 to Los Angeles and the Memorial Coliseum—the site of the 1932 games. Only one other U.S. city has hosted the summer games, St. Louis in 1904. We are on our way to building an Olympic tradition.

And that's the next Los Angeles priority, tradition!

The pro teams—Dodgers, Lakers, and Rams—were born in such places as Brooklyn, Minneapolis, and Cleveland. Without the support of the Los Angeles fans, they might be considered by some rabid aficionados as "hand-me-down" clubs.

The Rose Bowl, the University of Southern California, and the University of California at Los Angeles are all h-o-m-e-g-r-o-w-n! They are made of Los Angeles gold. While our pro brethren have struggled val-

:t Tournament *East-West* Football Game
Jan. 1, 1902 - Michigan vs Stanford

iantly and with honor, USC and UCLA rate consistently as the best.

Unquestionably, the Rose Bowl, first and foremost, is not only the oldest and the grandest, but as the 1905 poster declares, it is "for all the people." And that's Southern California's sports tradition at its best. It comes down to community participation and excellence by and for the greatest number.

The Rose Bowl

The Rose Bowl was originally spawned by the Valley Hunt of Pasadena, who sponsored on January 1, 1890, a tournament and field sports day, including a twenty-minute football game before 3,000 spectators. By 1897 the "Tournament of Roses," as the event was christened by the local press, was demonstrating to the rest of the country the sunny climate, natural beauty, and athletic prowess of the region. In 1902 the first intersectional, post-season college football game was played in Pasadena when the "point-a-minute" Michigan Wolverines, led by Fielding Yost, defeated Stanford by an awesome score of 49–0.

From 1903 to 1915 chariot racing replaced football as the centerpiece of the tournament's several sporting attractions, which included track and field events, an ostrich race, and (if you can believe it) a race between an elephant and a camel. It had come to that. Apparently, no western football team was willing to risk Stanford's humiliation until 1916 when a brave Washington State team beat a tough, Ivy League,

Chariot Races in the Rose Bowl were part of 1911 Tournament of Roses celebration.

Eight thousand spectators at the first Rose Bowl watched Michigan defeat Stanford 49–0. The legendary Fielding Yost coached the famous "point-a-minute" Wolverines.

In the 1929 Rose Bowl, California's Roy Reigals recovered a mid-air fumble by Georgia Tech and rambled the length of the field only to be caught by Benny Lom who pushed Reigals back to California's one yard line. Reigals had run the wrong way and set up the Georgia Tech score that defeated California 8–7.

Brown University. From that New Year's day a tradition was born that has continued every January First since.

In that 1916 game Washington State's Carl Dietz set a Rose Bowl record of 237 yards in thirty-four rushes, a record broken on January 1, 1980, by Charles White of USC (thirty-seven carries for 247 yards) as USC defeated Ohio State 17–16 in one of the greatest bowl games of all time. The 8,000 attendance of the 1902 and 1916 games has grown to 106,000, and the Rose Bowl now draws the largest television audience for any football game except the Superbowl.

The Rose Bowl is situated in the spectacularly scenic Arroyo Seco, framed on the west by the San Rafael Hills and to the northeast by the magnificent snow-capped San Gabriel mountains. A few minutes drive northwest of downtown Pasadena, the stadium is located on the grounds of Brookside Park and Municipal Golf Course, which is bounded on the south by Route 134—the Ventura Freeway—and on the east by Route 210—the Foothill Freeway.

Each year the Auto Club of Southern California (746-3111) publishes an excellent brochure with maps and complete information regarding transportation and the time schedule for the Rose Parade. The Pasadena Tournament of Roses Association (449-4100) also provides plentiful information.

In 1970, 104,000 fans watch USC and Michigan. Michigan's Rose Bowl fortunes have lessened since 1902. Beginning with the 1970 game, Michigan has lost at all five of its Rose Bowl appearances. The Pacific Conference has won ten of the last eleven games, with Ohio State providing the sole Big Ten victory. USC won the 1970 game by a score of 10–3 and has won five other games since. USC is the all-time Rose Bowl champion with a 17–6 record.

THE COLLEGES

UCLA and USC, with two of the most outstanding college athletic programs in the country, annually contest for Los Angeles city bragging rights. (It's become an international matter. Many heads of state, children of royal families, and oil-rich Middle East sheiks have attended one or the other school. One Saudi is reported to have squared off against another in a mock battle and said, "You UCLA graduates messed up all the ministries until we USC men came along.")

From football to volleyball, the rivalry is fiercely competitive and while some Trojans and Bruins won't speak to each other during a contest, it's still a friendly fight. When the two teams do battle, old acquaintances from the local city and CIF sports systems face one another.

USC

The USC Trojans, regarded by some UCLA'ns as the best "professional" team in town, have indeed produced more NFL players than any other school. In fact, USC's football alumni are the only ones who could organize their own franchise from active NFL players and still have a few left over for trades.

USC has the country's best overall bowl record of nineteen wins to only six losses, which includes an amazing Rose Bowl record of seventeen wins to six losses. The Trojans can also boast to be the country's number one all around sports record holder with sixty-three NCAA team titles and 241 individual titles plus eight football national championships. The baseball Trojans have captured eleven NCAA championships while leading the nation in developing major league ballplayers. And in track and field they hold twenty-seven NCAA team titles plus countless Olympians. This tradition of excellence is also true for both swimming and tennis, with nine and twelve NCAA team titles respectively.

Whatever your sports interest you can get information from the USC ticket office at 741-2620, located in Heritage Hall on the USC campus. The football team plays in the Memorial Coliseum with five home games plus UCLA in 1980. Ticket prices range from five to ten dollars, with season tickets slightly over fifty dollars for five games plus a chance to buy a UCLA game ticket. The basketball team plays in the Sports Arena next to the Coliseum. North of the Coliseum is Heritage Hall with its collection of Heisman and other trophies.

USC's Tommy Trojan on the USC campus.

UCLA

While UCLA is number two to USC in football, the Bruins have plenty to offer. They have produced the most varied and successful men's and women's sports program for the last two decades. Not even USC can match UCLA's record thirty NCAA team titles during the seventeen-year tenure of recently retired athletic director J D Morgan. There is no single college sports dynasty and legend to match John Wooden's Bruins basketball teams and their ten national championships in twelve years, from 1964 through 1975.

Pauley Pavilion on the UCLA campus is the house that Wooden built. Hanging from its rafters are ten men's and one women's national basketball championship pennants.

Pauley Pavilion, home of the Bruins basketball team, has a capacity of 12,600 and was dedicated in June of 1965. Next to Pauley Pavilion on the UCLA campus is Drake Stadium, a splendid track and field facility first opened in the spring of 1969. It annually serves as host for the UCLA—USC dual meet and several national AAU track meets along with the Pepsi Invitational, usually held in May. Drake Stadium, named in honor of Alvin "Ducky" Drake, former track and field coach and now trainer, is a beautiful outdoor recreation center for track and field enthusiasts, as well as sun lovers. On a sunny Saturday afternoon it can't be beat.

Whatever your sports interest, information is available by calling the UCLA ticket office at 825-2106. The Westwood campus, situated near Beverly Hills and Bel Air, is a picturesque and delightful locale for all sports events.

In addition to UCLA and USC and their city rivalry, several other local college and amateur teams offer splendid performances. Pepperdine University excels in volleyball (national champions in 1978) and basketball. Long Beach State is noted for its excellence in basketball and track and field. Cal State Fullerton has great baseball and took the NCAA championship in 1979.

For sports information the Los Angeles *Times* has a calendar of local events, and the *Herald-Examiner* carries television and radio listings, plus the daily betting line.

THE PROS

Rooting for pro teams in the City of the Angels, well you have to be an existentialist. For no matter who—the Rams, the Lakers, the Dodgers—these teams personify that young chap in the Camus story. You know, the one who rolls the rock up the hill and—oops—down it comes. So he starts again. And again. And again. Well, it's like that in L.A. We push the rock of talent up the hill of victory, but, during the playoffs, we slip. So, we start again next season. And the next. And the next.

Anyway, should you want to see any of this almost-running in action (and the action is often first-rate), here's how:

Angels

This is the group that plays baseball out in Anaheim under the leadership of owner Gene Autry and manager Jim Fergosi. In 1979 the Angels won their first pennant and in 1980 they'll be going for their first World Series.

Anaheim Stadium, commonly referred to as the "Big A," holds some 43,250 baseball nuts. Anaheim Stadium is located just off the Santa Ana Freeway (Route 5) about forty-five minutes from downtown Los Angeles. Ticket information may be obtained by calling (714) 634-2000.

Aztecs

The soccer team for Los Angeles, they play in the Rose Bowl and are led by international star Johann Cruyff. Single seat admission ranges from $2.50 a seat to $10; a season ticket can be yours for $150. Although the Rose Bowl can accommodate more than 100,000 spectators, the Aztecs open up about 27,000 seats. Basic concession stands and beer are available. The season starts in early May and lasts until August. Need more ticket information? Call 795-7733.

Dodgers

Since their disastrous performance in the 1978 World Series and their collapse in the 1979 season proved that the Dodgers choke up on more than just the bat, Los Angeles has been living on hope fed by their late 1979 resurgence. Dodger fans pray 1980 will be *the* year.

Despite having taken it on the chin from the eastern sporting press and establishment for stealing their beloved Dodgers from Ebbets Field, Los Angeles has been good to the Dodgers by shattering attendance records in both good and bad years. In any case, perhaps the best thing about the artful Dodgers is where they play. Dodger Stadium is made up of virtually all good seats, which range from $2.00 for general admission to $6.50 for clubhouse and dugout seating. Children under twelve get in for a buck. Season tickets are $280, however availability is strictly limited.

Dodger Stadium holds 56,000 eternal optimists and is situated in beautiful Chavez Ravine, just off the Pasadena Freeway and only minutes from downtown Los Angeles. You can obtain more information on Dodger Blue by telephoning 224-1301.

Dodger manager Tommy Lasorda.

Kings A true hockey powerhouse, the Kings, like the Lakers, play their home schedule at the Inglewood Forum. For the hockey ice escapades, the Forum is fixed to seat 16,000 fans. Ticket prices range from $5.75 to $10. The Forum is at the corner of Manchester Boulevard and Prairie Avenue in Inglewood. More information may be gleaned by telephoning 673-4700.

Latkers The Lakers are a joy to watch—win, lose, or draw. Personalities and stars are in abundance at the Forum. Kareem Jabbar, another UCLA alumnus, leads the way. Magic Johnson gets the publicity, but if the Lakers win a championship it will be complete players like former UCLA star Jamal Wilkes who'll make it happen. The season starts around late September and runs until early April. For complete ticket stats, phone the Forum at 673-4700.

Rams The Rams, spearheaded by their cheerleaders, the Embraceable Ewes, went to their first Superbowl to climax their 1979 season. No one gave them much of a chance of upsetting the Pittsburgh Steelers, but the Rams refused to collapse and fought Pittsburgh gallantly. Despite losing their first Superbowl bid, the Rams gave their legion of fans the courage to hope again.

Jim Youngblood, one of the Ram's defensive leaders.

The Rams came to Los Angeles and the Memorial Coliseum from Cleveland in 1946, and are now moving to nearby Anaheim. The local sports community awaits with mixed feelings the possible arrival of the Raiders from Oakland. At least the Raiders would bring several former Trojans and a few Bruins back home to the Coliseum!

The Ram's move to Anaheim will be completed in time for the 1980 season opener. Georgia Rosenbloom is fully in charge and Ray Malavasi will continue on as head coach. They may even have an offense to go with their new move. UCLA grad Wendell Tyler supplies a breakaway threat, and the perennial quarterback debate continues—Pat Haden of USC versus Vince Ferragamo. Like Haden, Ferragamo is a product of the Los Angeles high school football program. You can find out more concerning the Rams and their new home by calling 277-4700.

Although it is definitely off the beaten track of sports, no thumbnail guide to arenas in Los Angeles would be worth much without a mention of the Olympic Auditorium. Wrestling there is an experience not to be believed, a passion play where "good" wears rhinestone trunks and "evil" a set of filed teeth.

Olympic Auditorium

Single seat admission to this uplifting entertainment may be yours for only $2.00 for adults and $1.00 for children on Wednesday nights; $3.50 to $5.00 for adults and $1.50 for children under twelve on Friday nights. More information on all this grappling action by calling 749-5172.

The Memorial Coliseum, site of the 1932 Olympics, and home of USC and UCLA football, seats 92,604.

SPORTS AND RECREATION INFORMATION

The fine climate and great variety of geographic conditions found in Southern California have combined to make it a wonderland for outdoor adventures. Skiing and surfing, golfing and gliding, running and rock climbing, sailing, scuba diving, fishing, flying, and falconry—in fact, nearly every conceivable sort of recreation can be found in or near Los Angeles. Information about most activities and facilities may be obtained from the offices listed below.

City of Los Angeles Department of Recreation and Parks

The city operates a system of over 200 parks, including amateur competition and facilities for golf, tennis, hiking, riding, and swimming. For information call the administrative office at 485-5515.

Watts Summer Games

The Los Angeles Junior Chamber of Commerce sponsors the Watts Summer Games. Started in 1968 and held during the last two weekends of June, the Games have become the largest high school athletic event in the country with over twenty-three events and 7,500 participants. The Games are held on the campus of East Los Angeles College at 1301 Brooklyn Avenue, Monterey Park. For information call the L.A. Junior Chamber of Commerce at 482-1311.

Los Angeles County Parks and Recreation Department

The county's eighty parks offer a wide variety of instructional programs and sports facilities. For specific information call the main office at 744-4211.

State of California Parks and Recreation Department

Incorporating over 800,000 acres, California has the country's largest state park system. Information about facilities, camping permits, and reservations in Southern California may be obtained by calling 620-3342.

The AAU, which supervises most amateur athletic competitions in the United States, can supply information about sports activities in the area. Call 877-0256.

Amateur Athletic Union

The UCLA track is a favorite, with music and film stars occasionally on the run. It is very popular, especially at peak hours mornings and evenings.

Jogging Routes

San Vicente Boulevard provides many local runners with a jogging path along the meridian. Major problem—traffic; you're running alongside a main thoroughfare. Don't let it stop you though; clinical studies prove that it is better to run in polluted air than not to run at all.

The Beach. Most Los Angeles area beaches have paths for runners and cyclists, as well as a challenging swath of sand.

Mulholland Drive, between Laurel Canyon Boulevard and Beverly Glen. Enjoy a great view of the San Fernando Valley and the surrounding mountains.

For the extremely hardy, or advanced runner, there is a growing phenomenon in the area: the ten-kilometer run (approximately 6.2 miles). Each race is sponsored by a well-known company with proceeds going to charity. To find out about upcoming races, contact your nearest running shop, or Phidippides, Manhattan Beach, 546-2481.

Bicycling in Los Angeles

Although bicycling for pleasure can be done nearly everywhere, we recommend the Los Angeles beach areas. The cool, clean air, flat terrain, and off-the-road bike trails create ideal conditions.

The Beach Bikeway runs almost ten miles round trip beside the sand of Santa Monica and Venice and through Marina del Rey. This is a very popular cycling spot—especially in the summer months—so begin early in the morning or in the evening for the cooler part of the day and fewer crowds. Route: start at the parking lot at Washington Street in Venice and travel south through Marina del Rey along the path, then curve back and head north as far as the Santa Monica Pier. Bike rentals are available at the Yankee Peddler on the corner of Via Marina and Admiralty Way in Marina del Rey, and at many places along the beach.

The Beach Bikeway
Santa Monica and
Venice Beaches

This bike path starts at the half-way point of the bay at Marina del Rey and takes the rider through Playa del Rey and all the South Bay cities to Redondo Beach. It is pleasant to have lunch at the Redondo Pier before starting back to Marina del Rey. This path provides twenty-two miles of flat, easy riding that is removed from traffic; it provides an excellent beach outing. The path is very easy to follow and it is all marked, except for a quarter-mile stretch through King Harbor in Re-

The Beach Cities
Playa del Rey to
Redondo Beach

dondo Beach. Proceed south from Playa del Rey all the way to Redondo. For a shorter, alternate route, begin at the intersection of Forty-fifth Street and Vista del Mar in Manhattan Beach. Pedal south to King Harbor in Redondo Beach and return via the same route. This is a flat 10.5 miles on a car-free path; the main traffic danger is stray children and aberrant roller skaters.

Sports Equipment Rentals Whether your choice of sport is bicycling, skating (on wheels or blades), skiing, horseback riding, sailing, or even auto racing, the best place to find a rental source is in the Yellow Pages. The Los Angeles Yellow Pages is the most complete of the Southern California regional phone books. Listings include facilities and rental services in outlying areas.

Marinas and Harbors

Los Angeles and Long Beach Harbors Los Angeles and Long Beach Harbors together form one of the biggest and busiest harbors in the world. Its piers and berths spread over Wilmington, Long Beach, and San Pedro. These adjacent ports are connected by Cerritos Channel. The harbor was developed on the site of a natural port first spotted by Juan Rodríguez Cabrillo in 1542. The port has been enlarged to its present size: two miles wide, ten miles long, with a nine-mile breakwater. Today it has facilities for nearly 200 ships, and handles over 70 million tons of cargo a year. It also offers many recreational facilities:

The *Queen Mary*, Pier J, Long Beach, 435-4747. Daily tours are available (See Family Entertainment, p. 238.)

Cabrillo Marine Museum, 3720 Stephen White Drive, San Pedro, 831-3207. Cabrillo Museum features ocean displays and historical ship exhibits.

Point Fermin Lighthouse, 805 Paseo del Mar, San Pedro.

Ports O' Call Village, Harbor Boulevard at berths 76–77, is built in the style of nineteenth-century New England and California towns, with shops, restaurants, and entertainment along gaslit streets. Open from 11 a.m. to 9 p.m. with restaurants open later. Tours of the twin ports and the surrounding area are offered at several places in Ports O' Call Village: Buccaneer Cruises, 548-1085; Ports O' Call Harbor Cruise, 547-2662; and Village Boat House, 831-0996.

Marina del Rey Marina del Rey is one of the world's largest marinas with over 6,000 slips for recreational boats. It is also new. Formal dedication of the marina took place on April 10, 1965. This is the closest marina to downtown Los Angeles and has a variety of recreational facilities. Marina del Rey has launching areas, six yacht clubs, fuel docks and pump-out station, a sailing lagoon for small craft, and facilities for visitors. In addition, Marina del Rey has many fine restaurants, nearly all with ocean views, sailing motifs, or other artificial means to remind you that you're on the coast. Along the main drag, Admiralty Way, there are an abundance of shops, commercial office buildings, hotels, and eighteen apartment complexes.

Points of interest in Marina del Rey: Fisherman's Village, off Admiralty Way, has shops and restaurants and a picturesque view of the boats sailing by; the beach bikeway winds through Santa Monica, Venice, and Marina del Rey; and Marina Beach is open to the public and recommended for children since there are no waves to bash them about. (See Beaches, p.296 .)

King Harbor

King Harbor is a recreational marina located along Harbor Drive in Redondo Beach. Four separate marinas, each with varying facilities, make up the complex. King Harbor Marina has 850 slips ranging in size from sixteen to eighty-three feet with most availability in the twenty-seven to thirty-three feet range. For information call 376-6926. Portofino Yacht Anchorage, 376-9494, has 340 boat slips as well as rentals, sailing lessons, yacht sales, and cruising clubs. Redondo Beach Marina is a complete recreation, dining, and entertainment center located on the waterfront of Harbor Drive. Information there can be obtained by calling 374-3481. Port Royal Marina, the last of the four, provides similar facilities and a charming beachfront environment. The phone number there is 376-0431.

Among the many excellent restaurants offered within the King Harbor complex are: Captain Kidd's Fishmarket and Restaurant, 372-7703; Blue Moon Saloon, 374-8481; Dirty Sally's Discotheque and Backgammon Club, 372-2131; The Landing, 372-8481. Other recreational facilities: Redondo Boat Rentals and Hoist, 374-4473, has rental skiffs and outboards for light-tackle fishing in the harbor, three boat hoists with five-ton capacity, and a fuel dock. Redondo Sport Fishing, 372-2111, offers a complete tackle shop, charter boat fishing, and whale-watching trips January through April. The Courts at King Harbor, 374-8187, has six championship night-lighted tennis courts and nine racquetball courts.

Horseracing

Regardless of whether you fancy yourself a betting man or not, watching Thoroughbred, harness, and quarter-horse racing at the tracks of Southern California provides some of the best excitement in spectator sport. The local tracks of significant note are:

Hollywood Park

A handsome 350-acre park located in Inglewood, Hollywood Park offers daytime Thoroughbred racing from early April to late July, and nighttime harness racing from August through December. The track address is 1050 South Prairie Avenue and the information line is 678-1181.

Arrochar Replica winning Gold Medal Stakes at Hollywood Park.

Santa Anita Race Track

Found in Arcadia and set against the San Gabriel Mountains, Santa Anita is a sprawling 500-acre park, and a showcase for the best in Thoroughbred racing. It's strictly a daytime track with the seasons running from December 26 through April 7, and for one month starting with the second week in August and into September. The address is 285 West Huntington Drive, Arcadia, 574-7223.

Los Alamitos

For day and night racing Los Alamitos offers the excitement of both quarter-horse racing and harness racing. The season runs from mid May to late August. The track's address is 4961 Katella Avenue, Los Alamitos, 431-1361.

Motor Racing

From the well-tuned reputation of the Ontario Motor Speedway to the newborn tradition of the Long Beach Grand Prix, Southern California provides a record-smashing backdrop for year-round motor racing. Of major notice are:

Long Beach Grand Prix

For one weekend in late March the streets of Long Beach become the setting for the roaring sounds and blurring speed of the internationally prestigious Long Beach Grand Prix. First run in 1976, the Grand Prix brings the best Formula One race drivers in the world into stiff competition. Information can be obtained by calling 437-0341.

Gilles Villeneuve's Ferrari collides with the "Shadow," driven by Clay Regazzoni in the 1978 Long Beach Grand Prix.

Ontario Motor Speedway

This famous track is host to four major races each year: the Datsun Twin 200 (stock and Indy cars) in March; the California 500 (Indy championship cars); the Winston World finals (drag racing) held in October; and the L.A. *Times* 500 (stock cars) in November. The track is also used for testing and several auto club events. On the track grounds visitors may tour the Victory Circle Hall of Fame. The address is 3901 East G Street, Ontario, (714) 983-5811.

Riverside International Raceway

A bit farther east, Riverside International also offers the motor racing fan the thrills of high-speed competition. The track is located at 2225 Eucalyptus Avenue in Edgemont, (714) 653-1161.

Briggs Cunningham Automotive Museum

For the museum and restoration buff, the Cunningham Museum has on display over 100 pieces dating from 1910 to 1980. Among the collection are many classic and antique race cars. Located at 250 East Baker Street in Costa Mesa, (714) 546-7660, the museum is open Wednesday through Sunday, 9 a.m. to 5 p.m.

The view from Griffith Park looking toward the city center.

SCENIC AND OPEN-AIR PLACES:

From Malibu Canyon to Mount Wilson, the Vistas, Mulholland Drive, Griffith Park, the Canyons, and the Places to Enjoy the Out-of-Doors.

By Anthony Squire
And Richard Kahlenberg

L os Angeles is an outdoor city. Blessed with a warm climate, long, sandy beaches, and rugged mountains, she offers elemental wonders of nature in the midst of a futuristic metropolitan culture. Los Angeles is a city of contrasts, of drama, of dazzle, and nothing is more dazzling than its natural surroundings. The greater Los Angeles area contains 454 square miles and over nine and one-half million people, over 200 parks and fourteen public golf courses. It also has mile after mile of untamed country populated only by wildlife hidden in the chaparral.

Contrasts abound in any description of Los Angeles. It rises from sea level at the Pacific to 5,710 feet at Mount Wilson. The annual rainfall is nearly fifteen inches—averaging three inches in February and one hundredth of an inch in July. The mean temperature is 63.6 degrees, but a thirty-degree temperature variation from afternoon to evening is not unusual, even in summer. The San Fernando Valley is often ten to fifteen degrees warmer than the breezy beach communities. Bathing suits as well as jackets are appropriate for most of the year.

Though the sun shines most of the time, there are subtle but distinct seasons. The flowers in bloom—and there are always lots of flowers in L.A.—are a good indication of the months. Poinsettias at Christmas, jacaranda trees in June—all radiate the beauty of nature that is never far away in Los Angeles. Take a tour of the area, and any doubts will melt away like the snow that faces the hills and mountains north of the city. Just above Pasadena, Mount Wilson, on the Angeles Crest Highway, receives forty-plus inches of snow a year. Wherever you choose to explore, the range of outdoor experiences is breathtaking—high mountain forests, deep winter snow,

A 1927 Tournament of Roses poster.

steep canyons, idyllic beaches. Los Angeles contains more mountains and hills than any other city, including her sister city, San Francisco. This rugged, semi-arid region is approximately the same latitude as North Africa—thirty-four degrees, three minutes, and fifteen seconds, to be exact.

THE CLIMATE

During the autumn and spring, Los Angeles is bright and clear with low humidity and moderate temperatures. The city shows her best face during these months. The skies are blue, and the hills, mountains, and gardens are alive with color.

From October through December windy storms fill the sky with dazzling cloud formations. These storms usually pass quickly, but if you travel to the top of Lookout Mountain or along Mulholland Drive between Laurel and Coldwater canyons—two great viewing spots—you might catch glimpses of a glorious gold-red-orange-blue-rainbow arching over the city. Clear skies and sparkling vistas follow the storms. In November you can see a stormy sky give way to bright sunshine and, in half an hour, enjoy warm sunshine splashing over the Palos Verdes Peninsula while a light rain falls on the Santa Monica Mountains.

THE CHARACTER

Mountains dominate the northern and eastern edges of Los Angeles. Outlined by the Los Padres National Forest to the northwest, the Angeles National Forest to the north, and the San Bernardino and Cleveland National forests to the southeast, the area contains a staggering variety of recreational facilities including Lake Arrowhead, Idyllwild, Big Bear, Angeles Crest, and Mount Piños. Many visitors are astonished to find several winter ski resorts within an hour of Los Angeles, when the temperature in the city is perfect for tennis, jogging, and swimming.

To the west, mountains and ocean together create a spectacular setting. The Santa Monica Mountains meet the ocean in Malibu, then rise up again farther north as the Channel Islands: Anacapa, Santa Cruz, Santa Rosa, and San Miguel. Just west of Long Beach, the Palos Verdes Peninsula juts out into the Pacific. From Palos Verdes one can see Santa Catalina Island, about twenty miles to the southwest. Palos Verdes and Point Dume in Malibu form the boundaries of the Santa Monica Bay, a long crescent of dazzling white beaches.

It is not surprising that such magnificent surroundings and inviting weather draw the people of Los Angeles to the outdoor life. Southern Californians from Malibu to Palos Verdes, from Pasadena to Laguna Beach, from the San Fernando Valley to Anaheim take their pleasure in the natural beauty of the outdoors. Today, even though the city has grown to a staggering size, metropolitan Los Angeles is interlaced with open areas, hills and greenbelts, and a freeway system (despite its bad reputation) that gives easy access to the rugged, scenic wilderness nearby. Though it may seem far-fetched to the visitor, even today, between City Hall and Universal City, between Sunset Boulevard and the San Fernando Valley, one can find stray coyotes and deer, and mile after mile of rugged hiking trails.

THE TRADITIONS

Right from the beginning, the residents took all this natural beauty and turned it into a colorful playground. The people of Pasadena and the Valley Hunt initiated the Tournament of Roses in the 1890s, and it quickly grew into a mid-winter floral celebration, complete with togas and chariot races. Today, the celebrated Tournament of Roses features a parade and a football game, which are nationally televised to an audience thrilled by the sight of brilliant sunshine in the middle of winter.

Laurel Canyon's electrified trackless trolley.

How did the world first hear of the charms of Los Angeles? The venerable Automobile Club of Southern California, founded in 1900, extolled the virtues of motoring and sightseeing from 1909 to 1932 in *Touring Topics* magazine with its "motor'graph" features. By 1923 the club had distributed seven million touring maps to members and visitors. Today the club continues its travel adventures in *Westways*, the successor to *Touring Topics*. For any visitor or resident, the Automobile Club and its publications are an invaluable resource.

Automobile Club of Southern California
2601 Figueroa Street
Downtown   741-3111

In the 1930s the Mountain League of Southern California published a quarterly, *Trails*. This magazine was sponsored by the Los Angeles County Department of Recreation and gave hikers, campers, and skiers plentiful information. The magazine advertised such wonderful early resorts as Mount Lowe and Valley Forge Lodge near the Angeles Crest Highway. The 1934 autumn issue of *Trails* carried this brief notice:

Angeles Crest Highway

New Section Opens November First
This splendid mountain road, now open to Red Box at the head of Arroyo Seco Canyon, makes easily accessible for one day or weekend trail trips, two mountain beauty spots which have long been favorites with those who hike the the back country, the beautiful forest and grassy slopes of Barley Flats and the West Fork of the San Gabriel.

There are three Trail Resorts and several Forest Service camp grounds in this area.

Mount Lowe advertisement in the autumn 1935 issue of Trails magazine.

Angeles Crest in winter.

Hikers can still find abundant trails not only in the surrounding National Forests and mountains, but also in the "center" of Los Angeles, in Griffith Park, off Mulholland Drive, at Point Vicente, in Topanga Canyon, and near Hollywood Reservoir. For every surfing and skateboarding and rollerskating Angeleno, there are hikers, joggers, and bicyclers who continue the longstanding tradition of exploring the hinterlands of Los Angeles. Others simply enjoy looking into the clear spring sky, following a cloud formation drifting from the sea over the city, or watching hawks effortlessly catching updrafts from the hillsides and canyons.

Whether the outdoors you love is rugged or sedate, solitary or social, challenging or contemplative, you will find it in Los Angeles. Variety and contrast, discovery and adventure are here to delight you in untold ways.

THE PLACES

Griffith Park

Main entrances on south side from Western and Vermont avenues. On north side off the Ventura Freeway and Forest Lawn Drive.

665-5188

Griffith Park is a 4,063 acre expanse bounded on the east by the Golden State Freeway, on the south by Los Feliz Boulevard, and on the north by the Ventura Freeway. To the west is Hollywood Reservoir, Mount Lee, and the Hollywood Sign. Only a few minutes from downtown and quickly accessible from the San Fernando Valley, Glendale, and Hollywood, this area offers five golf courses; twenty-eight tennis courts; mule and hiking trails; numerous picnic areas such as Crystal Springs and Mineral Wells off Riverside Drive; plus Griffith Observatory (see Family Entertainment, p. 226), the Los Angeles Zoo (see Family Entertainment, p. 242), and Travel Town. just off Zoo Drive on the north side of the park.

The picnic areas and the major attractions are well maintained, but the vast majority of this "park" is in fact a naturally wild area of rugged hills and trails. Dominated by Mount Hollywood (elevation 1,625 feet) and traversed by the twisting and scenic Mount Hollywood Drive, the park offers the inveterate hiker, bicyclist, or horseback rider ample territory for a full day's outing. All trails and entrances close at sundown. For a helpful guide to all the parks in the city of Los Angeles, contact the Recreation and Parks Department, 200 North Main Street, City Hall East, Los Angeles 90012, 485-5571, and ask for their booklet *Recreation and Parks in L.A.*

The Hollywood Sign

From the north—Barham Boulevard to Lake Hollywood Drive. From the west—off the Hollywood Freeway at Oak Knoll. From the south—Beachwood Drive to Durand Drive.

One of the most famous landmarks in Los Angeles is also one of the most inaccessible. The Hollywood Sign can be seen from many parts of the city, but how to get closer to it than the Hollywood Freeway is a well-guarded secret. Only a few persevering hikers and residents of the Hollywoodland (Beachwood Drive off Franklin Avenue) and Lake Hollywood (off Barham Boulevard) districts know the route. The sign, built in 1923 at a cost of $21,000 by a syndicate including the Los Angeles *Times'* own Harry Chandler, is located on the south slope of Mount Lee (elevation 1,800 feet).

Originally, it read "Hollywoodland," an advertisement for the delightful Hollywoodland residential area located in the Beachwood Canyon area below the sign. The years and the weather reduced the sign to just "Hollywood." Recently restored through individual donations (one per letter), the nine thirty-by-fifty foot letters cost more than $27,000 each (more than ten times the original cost).

Below the famous Hollywood Sign, an abandoned section of Mulholland Highway connecting Hollywood Reservoir with Mount Hollywood Drive in Griffith Park.

Hollywood Reservoir is located just southwest of the sign, and both can be approached by Lake Hollywood Drive, Mulholland Highway, and Durand Drive off Beachwood Drive. It's not easy to find, but don't be discouraged too quickly; it's well worth the adventure. The reservoir was built by William Mulholland, the well-known dam and highway engineer, and is surrounded by attractive jogging and biking paths. It looks out over Hollywood and the Capitol Records building—but don't worry, it's never allowed to reach more than one-half capacity (one of Mulholland's earlier dams in the Santa Clara Valley collapsed in1928, drowning many residents). Above the reservoir and below the sign is an isolated and mostly abandoned section of Mulholland Highway which can't be reached directly from Mulholland Drive. You can motor on it for about a mile, from the reservoir to Durand Drive, but from there on it's a hiking trail to Mount Hollywood Drive and Griffith Park. This is the best spot for viewing the sign and the best access to the steep trails up to it.

Hollywood Reservoir

Lookout Mountain
Approach from Sunset Plaza off Sunset Boulevard, or Lookout Mountain Avenue off Laurel Canyon Boulevard to Appian Way.

Looking downtown from Lookout Mountain.

Mulholland Drive and Highway
From the east off the Hollywood Freeway at Highland Avenue, and also off Cahuenga Boulevard, just south of Barham Boulevard. Also from the San Diego Freeway between Sunset and Ventura boulevards, and the following canyons. Nichols, Laurel, Coldwater, Benedict, Beverly Glen, Valley Circle Drive, Topanga, and Las Virgines Road (from north) and Malibu Canyon (from south).

Malibu Creek State Park

Malibu Lake

One of the most beautiful places to view Los Angeles is just above Blue Jay Way, which the Beatles made famous. This vantage point, a favorite for couples and photographers on balmy autumn and spring evenings, provides a panoramic view of the city from Malibu across the basin to East Los Angeles. The Lookout Mountain Inn was here in World War I. Tourists and residents came to view a far smaller Los Angeles, complete with oil derricks and trolleys. trolleys.

Dedicated to William Mulholland and opened January 1925, this roadway offers hundreds of scenic views over the San Fernando Valley, downtown Los Angeles, Hollywood, and all of West Los Angeles. It runs along the ridge of the Santa Monica Mountains as Mulholland Drive from the Hollywood Freeway (the Cahuenga Pass) to Valley Circle Drive (above Tarzana Street). It becomes Mulholland Highway about one mile east of Valley Circle Drive; you need to watch carefully for the sign for a left turn. The highway portion crosses Topanga Canyon, Las Virgenes Road, Malibu Canyon Lake, and follows a circuitous, rugged route to Leo Carillo Beach, just north of Malibu.

For hearty souls, it is a splendid drive. Be careful, because the final and most important signs are frequently covered by chaparral. From the Hollywood Freeway to Leo Carillo Beach is about one and a half to two hours. A few miles of Mulholland Drive just west of the San Diego Freeway (above Encino) are unpaved, heavily rutted, and dusty. Still, it's well worth the adventure and is a unique experience within the confines of a modern metropolis.

In the section from Laurel Canyon to Beverly Glen are several easily accessible hiking trails and rugged areas with coyotes, deer, small game, and numerous hawks circling above searching out a meal. One of the most scenic outlooks is at Bowmont Drive between Laurel and Coldwater canyons. In the winter one can see the snow-capped peaks of the San Gabriel Mountains to the east, the Tehachapi Mountains in the Los Padres National Forest to the north, the rocky Santa Susana range—setting for countless westerns—to the northwest, and all of the San Fernando Valley. The highway section, west of Valley Circle, is well paved and runs through a vast open wilderness area with access to countless hiking trails.

An absolute must for anyone wishing to explore this area is the ninety-page booklet *Day Walks in the Santa Monica Mountains* published by the Santa Monica Mountain Task Force of the Los Angeles Chapter of the Sierra Club. Among the hiking delights is the trail through Malibu Creek State Park near Las Virgenes Road and Mulholland Highway. Complete with the 700-year-old Mendenhall Oak and the set for "M*A*S*H," the trail winds from Tower Road along Malibu Creek to Malibu Lake. Wildlife is abundant and in past years so were filmmakers. Laurel and Hardy used the lake whenever a watery grave was needed for one of their ill-fated autos.

Looking toward Los Angeles from Lookout Mountain in 1914.

Malibu Lake is private property (Clark Gable's former hunting lodge overlooks the lake), and is a surprising and lovely oasis nestled amongst the craggy Santa Monica Mountains which range up to nearly 3,000 feet. In Baedeker, this trip, well worth a day's outing, would be five stars! We're more modest—three rosebuds. Be sure to pack a lunch and a good Zinfandel.

The Canyons

The steep hills and mountains in and around Los Angeles are covered with dense chaparral and deeply cut by ravines and canyons. The heavy winter rains and hot summer sun, and the dazzling array of plants and flowers introduced by hillside residents have made this area an enticing, but sometimes perilous place to live. The Santa Monica Mountains, in particular, are crisscrossed with deep canyons, a few of which provide the only roadways from West Los Angeles to the San Fernando Valley. Each of these canyons has its own history and character.

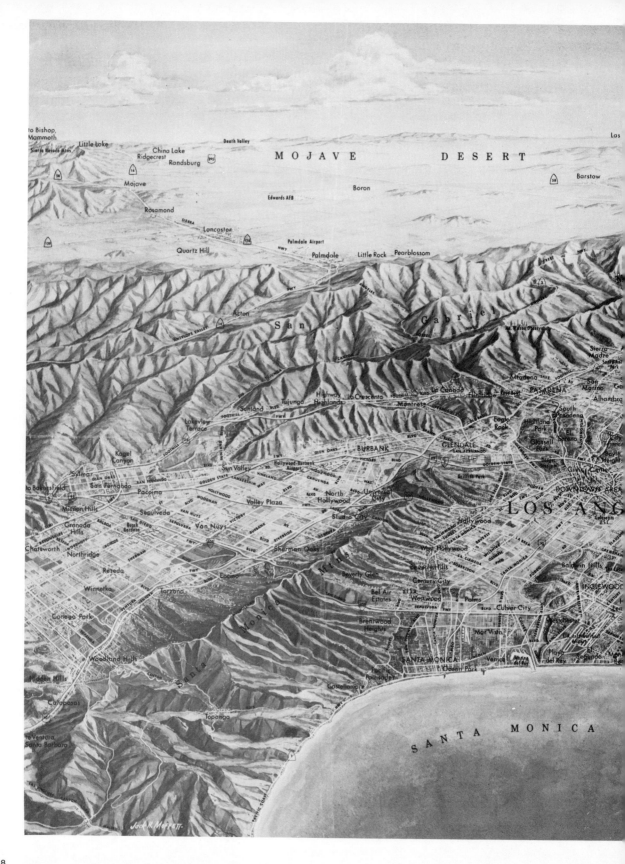

A canyon map showing the stretch of picturesque Mulholland Drive and Highway as it traces the crest of the Santa Monica Mountains from Griffith Park to Malibu.

Mulholland Highway near Malibu Canyon looking east over the former Diamond X Ranch of William S. Hart.

Beachwood Canyon
Beachwood Drive off
Franklin Drive
Hollywood

This is the home of Hollywoodland and the district which gave birth to the Hollywood(land) Sign in 1923. Picturesque residences—most notably, Tower Hill (or Castillo del Lago)—steep, twisting roads, and old-fashioned services (the local market delivers and puts away your groceries!) characterize Beachwood Canyon.

Nichols Canyon
Hollywood Boulevard

A charming still-rural and little-known canyon which winds steeply up from Hollywood Boulevard to Mulholland and Woodrow Wilson drives. It was named for John Gregg Nichols, Jr., who came to Los Angeles on New Year's Eve, 1849, after leading 100 wagons from Iowa over the Donner Pass.

Near the top of Nichols Canyon, close to Mulholland Drive, one can take Woodrow Wilson Drive, a twisting road which forms a figure eight with Mulholland between Laurel Canyon and the Hollywood Freeway. Woodrow Wilson Drive is full of architectural surprises and unexpected hiking opportunities.

Laurel Canyon
From Crescent Heights and Sunset
boulevards to Ventura Boulevard

The first canyon to be developed, we are told. A trackless trolley was in operation from 1909 to 1915 to encourage land development. Laurel's notorious reputation is justified. In the early days "photo-players" (movie stars to us) made it a hideaway, followed by today's musicians, writers, and television performers. The famous Laurel Canyon log cabins (formerly brothels) are still there, plus Fatty Arbuckle's home, Houdini's Castle (with a secret passage to his favorite "log cabin"), and the house where Robert Heinlein wrote *Stranger in a Strange Land*. On a balmy evening one can smell the

The Hollywood Reservoir in the 1930s, looking south from the Hollywood Sign.

night jasmine mixed with eucalyptus and oleander. Laurel sumac, California holly (or tayon), and dense chaparral cover the hillsides, and one can hear coyotes howling in the dead of night.

Coldwater Canyon
From the Beverly Hills Hotel and Sunset Boulevard to Ventura Boulevard

Coldwater Canyon is a bit more up-market and spacious than Laurel and Nichols. Just off the Canyon Drive, at 501 Doheny Road, is the very beautiful and grand Greystone Mansion and Park, now the home of the American Film Institute. Invent a reason to go for research, take a picnic lunch, and leave pen and paper at home.

Franklin Canyon

Franklin Canyon is just west of Coldwater and shelters the Franklin Canyon Reservoir. Coyotes roam these hills a few minutes from the Polo Lounge. Coldwater at Mulholland Drive is the home of Tree People, a hardworking and friendly conservation group located at a former fire station (12601 Mulholland Drive, 769-CONE). During a major flooding, they distributed 32,000 sand bags, and organized 800 volunteers and 100 four-wheel drive trucks, to assist 300 hillside families. They are also involved in organic gardening and landscaping. Their ten-acre park includes many outdoor activities and hiking trails.

The Tree People, a conservation group.

Rustic Canyon
From Sunset Boulevard off Amalfi Drive

Rustic Canyon, just west of Sullivan and Mandeville canyons and between Brentwood and Pacific Palisades, has a remarkable history which has been chronicled, complete with a dazzling array of photographs, in the 176-page book *Rustic Canyon and the Story of the Uplifters* by Betty and Thomas Young (Casa Vieja Press, Santa Monica). Few books give the flavor of early Los Angeles as well. this.

Will Rogers State Historic Park
14253 Sunset Boulevard
Pacific Palisades   454-8212

Will Rogers State Historic Park is near Rustic Canyon. Here you can enjoy a nostalgic visit to Rogers' home, view his collection of Charles Russell's western paintings, see the old polo field (now used for soccer) and stables, and hike to Inspiration Point, a favorite spot of Will Rogers himself. The point has a spectacular view of the city, the mountains, and the ocean. You can take further hiking trails from here into the vast adjacent wilderness area, Topanga State Park.

Topanga Canyon
Topanga Canyon Boulevard from Topanga Beach off the Pacific Coast Highway to the Ventura Freeway and Woodland Hills

The Topanga community centers around the villages of Fernwood and Topanga. Immediately east is Topanga State Park, and running northeast is Old Topanga Creek, paralleled by Topanga Canyon Road. This scenic and rural roadway winds along slopes of Topanga Lookout (2,469 feet) and Calabasas Peak (2,163 feet) to Calabasas Highlands where it intersects Mulholland Highway. Topanga is well worth a visit, not only for its natural beauty, but also for its unique history and contemporary rural lifestyle. Among its past residents are the most extensive Chumash Indian population in the Los Angeles area, Joaquin Murietta, Tiburcio Vasquez (the legendary Hollywood bandit of the 1870s), Woody Guthrie, F. Scott Fitzgerald, Cecil B. De Mille, and numerous rock stars including Linda Ronstadt and Neil Young. The adjacent Malibu Canyon area to the west is well described in the first chapter of *L.A. on Foot* by David Clark (Camaro Publishing Company, Los Angeles). The paperback is full of fascinating information on a fiercely independent and eccentric Topanga, as well as other unusual Los Angeles points of interest.

Rainstorms are heaviest in January and February, and it is not unusual for rain to fall continuously for a week or two. Some areas, such as Nichols and Mandeville canyons turn into veritable muddy torrents. But when the rain stops, suddenly the days are much longer and the sun higher in the sky. This dramatic and refreshing change brings bright skies, lush green landscapes, and gardens and hills adorned with colorful, fragrant flowers.

From June through September both breezes and temperatures rise, and the hills turn tawny. But during July and August smog smudges the views. These seasonal conditions are determined partly by the geography of the Los Angeles Basin. Even the Indians called this the Land of Many Smokes. The ancient Cabrillo Peninsula, now the Santa Monica Mountains, extends one hundred miles east to west, from Griffith Park near downtown Los Angeles, across Hollywood, Beverly Hills, Brentwood, Pacific Palisades, and Malibu, to the Channel Islands, and into the Pacific. This mountainous line meets the San Gabriel Mountains just north of Pasadena. These two mountain ranges coupled with more in the south—the Santa Ana Mountains just east of Anaheim, and the San Jacinto and San Bernardino mountains east of Riverside—form a spacious triangle which opens to the southwest and faces the sea. When there are no strong winds, this basin catches and holds the infamous Los Angeles smog. However, when there are Santa Anas—hot dry winds from the desert—

or ocean breezes, or windy autumn storms from the south, this basin, ringed by four national forests and two island and peninsula complexes, is a glorious natural resource.

The Islands

Eight Channel Islands lie off the Southern California coast. Three of these comprise the Channel Islands National Monument: Anacapa and San Miguel, which are due west of Malibu, and tiny Santa Barbara Island west of Palos Verdes. Once inhabited by the Chumash Indians, who were removed to the missions by the mid-1800s, these islands now serve as wildlife preserves with abundant wildflowers and outdoor attractions. One can explore tidepools, hike, picnic, and swim.

Channel Islands National Monument
1699 Anchors Way Drive
Ventura   (805) 644-8157

Anacapa is the closest to the mainland (eleven miles south of Oxnard) and is separated from it by the Santa Barbara Channel. Its 700 acres are covered by low brush and scrub. The highest point on the island is 930 feet. Anacapa and the other Santa Barbara Channel Islands of Santa Cruz, Santa Rosa, and San Miguel are visible from the mainland. However, on overcast days, the rocky Anacapa seems to hover like a desert mirage, and the name itself derives from the Indian *Anyapah*, "deception" or "mirage."

Anacapa Island
From Oxnard to Santa Barbara

Santa Cruz Island is still privately owned by Dr. Carey Stanton, whose father acquired it in 1936. Twenty-four miles south of Santa Barbara, this rugged and lush island is covered with wildflowers and inhabited by a variety of wildlife, including boar. Santa Cruz is the largest of the Channel Island (twenty-one miles in length) and also has the greatest variety of flora and fauna. The Spanish explorer Juan Cabrillo stopped here in 1542 and found over 2,000 Chumash Indians. To visit you need the permission of Dr. Stanton, who still runs a cattle ranch on the island. The California Historical Society (651-5655) periodically leads tours, and you can also contact the Santa Cruz Island Company, 575 South Flower Street, Los Angeles, 485-4208.

Santa Cruz Island

Santa Rosa is also privately owned. For permission to visit, contact Vail and Vickers, 123 West Padre Street, Suite 1, Santa Barbara 93105. Less rugged than Santa Cruz, Santa Rosa is fifteen miles long, and its highest point is 1,589 feet.

Santa Rosa Island

San Miguel, the most remote of the Santa Barbara Channel Islands, is about eight miles long and four miles wide with elevations of less than 1,000 feet. It has been denuded by draught, sheep ranching, and high winds. Visiting this island is only recommended for the most experienced sailors, with careful guidance from the Coast Guard. An excellent publication which gives detailed information on sailing, topography, anchorages, and history of all eight of the Channel Islands is the *Cruising Guide to the Channel Islands* by Brian M. Fagan and Graham Pomeroy (Capra Press, Santa Barbara).

San Miguel Island

Santa Catalina Island's Casino graces the town of Avalon.

Santa Barbara Island

Santa Barbara Island is a small, 640-acre triangle thirty-eight miles west of San Pedro. Its highest point is 635 feet, but it is surrounded by 500-foot cliffs which give it a very adventuresome and majestic configuration. The vegetation is sparse, but there are abundant sea mammals. For information, contact the Channel Islands National Monument.

Santa Catalina, San Nicolas, and San Clemente Islands

San Nicolas and San Clemente are off limits to the public, but Catalina welcomes visitors. You can get there by boat or airplane. For complete information, contact the Catalina Island Chamber of Commerce, P.O. Box 217, Avalon 90704, 510-1520. Catalina is a year-round delight for viewing undersea life in a glass bottom boat, hiking, horseback riding, fishing, biking, or just relaxing. The world famous Catalina Casino in Avalon celebrated its fiftieth anniversary in 1979; you can still dance there to big band music!

Catalina is twenty-one miles long, eight miles wide and covers forty-eight thousand acres. Its highest points are Mount Orizaba (2,125 feet) and Mount Black Jack (2,010 feet). Cabrillo discovered the island in 1542 and named it San Salvador. In 1892 it was acquired by the Banning brothers who incorporated the Santa Catalina Island Company. Today, the Santa Catalina Conservancy controls seven-eighths of the island to protect the wildlife and wildlands.

Late winter and early spring are migration times for the forty-five-ton California gray whales, which pass close to Anacapa and Catalina. Cruise boats to both these islands offer whale watching as part of their tour during these months. For the Anacapa area, contact the Island Packer Company of Ventura (1695 Anchors Way, Ventura, 805–642-1393), and for Catalina, contact the Catalina Chamber of Commerce. There is also an excellent forty-page booklet, *The Complete Whale Watchers Guide*, by Joe and Robin Valencic available from Quest Marine Research, Box 832, Dana Point 92629.

Whale Watching

Recreation Areas

The Point Vicente Lighthouse, precipitous cliffs, and a magnificent view of the Pacific looking toward Catalina, distinguish this point and the entire Palos Verdes area. What in the 1920s was open farm land has been developed into an exclusive residential community. But the coast along here and the ocean beyond tell another story—of change dictated only by the perpetual movements of wind, ocean, and earth itself.

Point Vicente
Off Palos Verdes Drive, one-half mile south of Hawthorne Boulevard on the Palos Verdes Peninsula

The Cabrillo Marine Museum offers whale watching and winter boat trips, plus many other marine life activities. At the Point Fermin Marine Refuge you can explore rocky tidepools and a small but lovely museum. There's a whale festival each June and grunion nights from March to July.

Cabrillo Marine Museum
638 South Beacon Street
San Pedro   548-7562

The Exposition Park Rose Garden is one of the largest in the nation. Over seven acres contain some 16,000 bushes representing 190 varieties. The garden is adjacent to the Natural History Museum and open daily until 5 p.m.

Exposition Park Rose Garden
900 Exposition Boulevard
Los Angeles

Back in the early 1950s, the city of Long Beach bought eighty-five acres of flat agricultural land. After many years of financial and horticultural planning, the El Dorado Nature Center was opened in 1969. Today visitors can enjoy this forested sanctuary which contains two lakes, hiking and bike trails, and many kinds of plant and animal life. The trees and shrubs here are planted in single species groves, giving a realistic feel for how nature arranges her own garden. The nature center also presents a full program of tours, films, classes, and lectures. Open Wednesday through Sunday. Call to confirm hours.

El Dorado Nature Center
7550 East Spring Street
Long Beach   425-8569

The Descanso Gardens are located on part of the old Rancho San Rafael, first granted by the Spanish governor of California in 1784. The land remained undeveloped until E. Manchester Boddy, owner of the Los Angeles *Daily News*, bought the land in 1937 and began planning the gardens. Best known for its camellia garden, the largest in the world, the gardens contain over 600 varieties of this exquisite flower. The rose garden contains a collection of historical

Descanso Gardens
1418 Descanso Drive
La Cañada   790-5571

roses, some varieties of which date back to the first century. Nature trails, a Japanese garden and tea house, and a bird observation station all add to a many-faceted experience of nature's beauty.

Elysian Park
Harbor Freeway to Pasadena Freeway, exit at Stadium Way; or off the Golden State Freeway
665-5811

Dodger Stadium is located next to Elysian Park. At the stadium you'll find plenty of noise and excitement. But the 575 acres in Elysian Park seem miles away, with their majestic stands of evergreen trees, quiet valleys, forested hills, and miles of hiking trails. You'll find sports facilities here, too, and several picnic areas. Elysian Park also contains Los Angeles' first arboretum, begun in the late nineteenth century. Ask about the ranger guided tours of the rare tree section.

MacArthur Park
2230 West Sixth Street

MacArthur Park is a thirty-two-acre oasis near downtown Los Angeles. Well-landscaped greenery, picnic areas, and a pavilion with frequent band concerts make this a popular retreat for urban dwellers.

Sepulveda Dam Recreation Area
San Diego Freeway north, Ventura Freeway west, to Balboa Boulevard

The Sepulveda Dam Recreational Area in the San Fernando Valley offers a large range of organized sports facilities: three eighteen-hole golf courses and eighty acres of sports fields. Picnickers have twenty additional areas in which to roam. The San Fernando Valley Bike Route winds around and through the park for five miles of traffic-free pedaling. For maps of this and other bike routes in Los Angeles (and there are several) contact the Los Angeles City Recreation and Parks Department, 200 North Main Street, City Hall East, Los Angeles 90012, 485-5571.

South Coast Botanic Garden
26300 Crenshaw Boulevard
Palos Verdes   377-0468

The South Coast Botanic Garden arose not from a historic rancho but from a modern dump. Local volunteers, sanitary engineers, and the Department of Arboreta and Public Gardens all worked together to transform these eighty-seven acres into a lovely garden which contains plants, trees, and shrubs native to Africa, Australia, Mexico, South America, and Asia. The South Coast Botanic Garden Foundation also sponsors workshops and field trips related to horticulture and conservation. A trip to the Palos Verdes Peninsula should include a tour of this admirable reclamation prize.

Los Padres National Forest

Los Padres National Forest is the second largest in California, with 1,724,000 acres under its jurisdiction. This includes some of the wildest and most rugged land in the state. Los Padres is in two sections, the smaller following the Pacific Coast just south of Monterey, and the larger stretching inland from Morro Bay to the San Fernando Valley where it meets the Angeles National Forest. Route 1 will take you to those areas near Santa Barbara, and Interstate 5 to those near the Valley.

Big Caliente Hot Springs

Twenty-six miles northeast of Santa Barbara (directly north of Montecito), via East Camino Cielo, Juncal, Camueso, and Big

Caliente roads, you'll find Big Caliente Hot Springs. The springs are three miles north of the Pendola Guard Station. The curative waters are piped to a concrete pool for bathing. Dressing rooms are also provided. Though we make no promises, the hot springs are said to be therapeutic, so take a plunge, lie back, and relax in nature's own hot tub. Warning: the route to the hot springs includes narrow mountain dirt roads. Don't try them in wet weather, and don't bring a trailer.

Closer to Los Angeles is the Sespe Condor Sanctuary, believed to be the last nesting place of this endangered species. Condors lay but one egg every other year and their survival largely depends on our respect for them and their habitat. The California condor is the largest flying bird in North America, with an average wingspan of nine feet. Remember, all large dark birds are protected by law. The best place to watch for the condors is on the top of Mount Piños, at 8,831 feet, the highest point in the forest. To get there, drive north and west on Interstate 5, Frazier Mountain Park Road, and Cuddy Valley Road. Driving along this route you will be traversing the infamous San Andreas Rift Zone, California's major earthquake-producing fault. Dozens of campgrounds, hundreds of miles of hiking trails, and hundreds of thousands of acres of wilderness make Los Padres National Forest an ideal retreat from life in the city. All campgrounds here are on a first-come, first-served basis. For more information contact the supervisor's office, 42 Aero Camino, Goleta 93017, (805) 968-1578.

Sespe Condor Sanctuary

Mount Piños

San Andreas Fault

Angeles National Forest

The Angeles National Forest, directly north of Los Angeles, is the closest one to the city. Two scenic roads lead into the forest: the Angeles Crest Highway (Route 2), and the San Gabriel Canyon Road (Route 39). Parts of the route may be closed during the snow season, so be sure to check on road conditions before you begin your journey.

The San Gabriel Mountains form much of the Angeles National Forest. Hundreds of miles of rivers, eight natural and artificial lakes, 1,000 miles of roads, and 556 miles of hiking and riding trails accommodate over thirteen million annual visitors. The San Gabriels offer recreation to outdoors lovers all year with summer camping, fishing, and exploring, and winter skiing. Native wildlife includes Nelson bighorn sheep, the endangered California condor, mountain lion, bobcat, coyote, black bear, and Pacific rattlesnake. Fire is an ever-present danger in the national forests and all visitors are reminded of the fire precautions outlined by the Forest Service. For more information and detailed recreation maps contact Angeles National Forest, 150 South Los Robles, Pasadena 91101, 684-0350.

A sun-loving band of stalwart hikers in the Hollywood Hills in the 1930s.

Angeles Crest in the spring, less than forty-five minutes from Pasadena.

Mt. Wilson Observatory
Angeles Crest Highway (Route 2) to
Mount Wilson Road

The Mount Wilson Observatory is located in the mountains above Pasadena just off the Angeles Crest Highway. Ever since mules hauled the equipment for the first solar telescope up the mountain trails in 1904, Mount Wilson has been a world leader in the field of astronomy. In addition to the several solar telescopes, there is a sixty-inch and a hundred-inch telescope in use on Mount Wilson. Visitors are welcome on Saturday and Sunday, 10 a.m. to 5 p.m. The equipment may be viewed at the visitors' galleries, and representative photographs of the heavens are on display in an exhibit hall. Visual observation with the equipment is not permitted. Those wishing to see the stars and planets this way are encouraged to visit the Griffith Park Observatory in Los Angeles, 664-1191.

San Bernardino National Forest

The San Bernardino National Forest meets the Angeles National Forest in the west and continues west and south of Los Angeles. Interstates 10 and 15 will take you to several popular recreation areas here. Arrowhead and Big Bear are among the popular winter sports playgrounds. But year-round outdoor fun is plentiful here. The Pacific Crest National Scenic Trail passes through the Big Bear District of the forest and offers spectacular views of Big Bear Lake to the south and the desert to the north. The numerous creeks and

From Mulholland Drive between Laurel Canyon and the Hollywood Freeway, looking over Universal City.

lakes in the area mean excellent trout fishing. The California Department of Fish and Game periodically stocks many of these waterways.

Reservations are accepted for several of the campgrounds. You may reserve campsites in person or by mail only at Ticketron offices. Requests must be made one week in advance, but not more than sixty days in advance. To reserve in person, go to any Ticketron outlet. By mail, write to Ticketron Reservation Office, P.O. Box 26430, San Francisco 94126. Phone reservations cannot be accepted, and ranger stations and campgrounds cannot reserve campsites. For more information about camping and other facilities write San Bernardino National Forest, 144 North Mountain View Avenue, San Bernardino 92408.

Tourist facilities are available at many of the villages near the forest. The village of Idyllwild, located south of Route 10 and north of Route 74, offers cultural as well as natural delights to its visitors. ISOMATA, the Music and Arts Summer Campus of the University of Southern California is located here and offers courses, concerts, and other cultural activities for children and adults. For more information write USC–Idyllwild, P.O. Box 38, Idyllwild 92349, (714) 659-2171.

Idyllwild

Cleveland National Forest

The Cleveland National Forest is named for President Grover Cleveland, who first designated national forest preserves in 1893. The forest begins five miles north of the Mexican border and extends northwest in three separate sections, up into Orange and Riverside counties. Mountains reach 6,000 feet in this forest and much of it is wilderness covered with dense desert chaparral and cool conifer and hardwood forests. Marine fossils left by a primeval Pacific Ocean, traces of Indian camps, and abandoned mines of nineteenth-century prospectors hint of life here in ages past.

Pacific Crest Trail

The Pacific Crest National Scenic Trail begins in the Cleveland National Forest and starts its northward journey 2,400 miles to the Canadian border. This hiking trail offers breathtaking vistas of canyons, mountains, valley, and desert. Campfire programs and ranger- and self-guided walks give a lively and informative introduction to the history and ecology of the area. Schedules are posted at the campgrounds and ranger stations. For more information write Cleveland National Forest, 880 Front Street, San Diego 92188.

Mount Palomar

Also located in this unspoiled wilderness region is the Mount Palomar Observatory, home of the two-hundred-inch Hale Telescope, largest in the United States. Visitors are welcome at the observatory daily from 9 a.m. to 5 p.m., but direct visual observation is not possible. For this, you are encouraged to visit Griffith Park Observatory in Los Angeles, 664-1191. You can reach the Palomar Observatory via a 2.2-mile trail, or by car on Route S–6. A shorter hike from the observatory to an observation point overlooking Mendenhall Valley gives a grand view of an original homestead area that is still used for cattle grazing.

Lake Elsinore

Lake Elsinore, located east of the Cleveland National Forest off Interstate 15, boasts a fine camping area, speedboat racing, and, at nearby Skylark Airport, the Elsinore Sport Parachuting Center. If you'd rather watch than participate, drive up Route 74, the Ortega Highway, above the lake for a superb view of the parachutists, hang gliders, the Elsinore Valley, and the San Bernardino Mountains.

Idyllwild.

A poster announcing Los Angeles' oldest annual event, the Tournament of Roses.

APPENDIX

Including Transportation, Events,
Twenty-four Hour Restaurants and Services,
the Media, Libraries and Organizations,
and Little Known but Often Useful
Information about Los Angeles.

By Wendy Miller

This chapter is a compendium of information that both visitors and residents will find useful. The first section is Annual Events, special activities around the year. Also included are descriptions of districts where every day is an event, areas that reflect Los Angeles' urban diversity. Advance details of the occasions listed here are published in many newspapers and magazines. These sources are described in the second section, In Print. The third section is Institutions, organizations of public interest and merit. We conclude with Services—emergency aid, transportation, late night places, even how to find a baby sitter at three in the morning when you want to go out on the town.

ANNUAL EVENTS

Tournament of Roses and Rose Bowl Game. Parade of bands, floats, and personalities, then a football game between Big Ten and Pacific Coast Conference Winners. Held on New Year's Day in Pasadena.
L.A. Open Golf Tournament. The first weekend after New Year's Day.
Riverside 500 Stock Car Race.
Whale Watching. Marineland, Point Loma, Cabrillo Marine Museum, Catalina Cruise.

January

Chinese New Year. Dragon parades, fireworks, and festivity in Chinatown; dates vary each year; call Chinatown Chamber of Commerce, 628-1828.
Laguna Beach Winter Festival. Art, theater, and horse shows as well as the annual surfing contest.
Southern California Boat Show. Convention Center, 741-1151.

February

March   *All City Kite Tourney.* Long Beach, 436-9041.
Filmex. International Film Festival.
Return of the Swallows. March 19, San Juan Capistrano, (714) 493-1111.
St. Patrick's Day Parade. Annual parade in Torrance; drowning the shamrock in Irish pubs throughout L.A. We advise those interested in the latter activity to arrive early and start off slow.
Sunrise Service for Easter. Held in either March or April at the Hollywood Bowl.

Los Angeles International Film Exposition (Filmex). A cultural event celebrating film—the art form of the century. Presented by The Filmex Society in association with the City of Los Angeles, the two-week, noncompetitive festival is held each spring (late March or early April) in Hollywood and features contemporary cinema from around the world, retrospectives and tributes, and an exciting variety of special programs. Call FILMEX, 469-9400.

April   *Annual Blessing of the Animals.* Olvera Street.
Custom Car and Motorcycle Show. Held annually at the Sports Arena. Also this month are the City of Hope Motorcycle Rally in Twenty-nine Palms and the Continental Champion Races at Riverside.
Hollywood Park. Thoroughbred racing opens.
Renaissance Pleasure Faire. Agoura.
Riverside Fine Arts Festival. Art exhibits, plays, and entertainment.
UCLA Mardi Gras. 825-4321.

May   *Cinco de Mayo.* Celebrates defeat of the French by Mexico. Call 381-3029.
Hollywood Bowl. Season opens.
Westwood Sidewalk Arts and Crafts Show.

June   *All City Outdoor Arts Festival.*
Annual Bike Day Race. Bicycle race and festival held in Manhattan Beach.
Greek Theatre. Season opens.

July   *Barnsdall Park Art Festival.* Outdoor festivities including art demonstrations, puppet shows, music.
Fireworks. On the Fourth throughout the city, with the largest show at the Coliseum.
Highland Gathering and Games. Scottish festival held annually at Santa Monica Community College.
Laguna Beach Arts Festival.
Los Angeles Shakespeare Festival. Runs all summer at the Pilgrimage Theatre and other Los Angeles locations.
Rancho Days. Annual rodeo held in Torrance.
San Diego and Santa Barbara County Fairs. Held annually at the Del Mar and Santa Maria fairgrounds.

August   *California International Sea Festival.* Swimming, sailing, speedboat races, waterskiing contest over three weeks in Long Beach.

International Surf Festival. Four days of competition at Torrance, Redondo, Hermosa, and Manhattan beaches. Call 545-5313.
Nisei Week Festival. A ten-day festival in Little Tokyo.
Old Miner's Days. Big Bear Lake, (714) 866-4601.
Old Spanish Days. California fiesta in Santa Barbara.
Santa Monica Sports and Arts Festival. Held at the Santa Monica Civic Auditorium, the Santa Monica Mall, and the beach.
Valley Folklorico. Celebrates the founding of the San Fernando Mission with music, crafts, and festivity in Mission Hills.
Watts Summer Festival. 587-7125.

September

Fiesta de la Marina. Labor Day water festival, Ventura.
Night Harness Racing. Hollywood Park.

Los Angeles Bicentennial (1781–1981). Beginning September 4, 1980, a twelve-month celebration—events, activities and permanent projects—throughout the city to commemorate Los Angeles' 200th year. Call Los Angeles 200 Committee, 485-0200.

October

Calabasas Pumpkin Festival. Calabasas.
Los Angeles Boat Show. Held annually at the Sports Arena. Also this month are the International Sail and Powerboat Show in Long Beach and the Lake Elsinore 500 endurance race.

Los Angeles County Fair. At Pomona Fairgrounds, this month-long fair is the second largest in the country.
Oktoberfest. Alpine Village, Torrance, 327-4384.
Ski Show. Los Angeles Convention Center.
Westwood Sidewalk Arts and Crafts Show.

November

Air Show. The largest in the country, held at Point Mugu.
Santa Barbara National Horse Show.
Santa Claus Lane Parade. Including many television and movie personalities, held on Hollywood Boulevard.

December

Las Posadas. Olvera Street fiesta, December 16–24 nightly.
Torchlight Slalom. Big Bear Lake.

Districts

Almost every section of Los Angeles goes by another name—West Hollywood, Mid-Wilshire, Miracle Mile, Silverlake. These sections, each with its own identity and style, are part of the all-inclusive title, Los Angeles. There are, however, several sections or districts in town that are so self-contained, different, or dynamic in some way, we wanted to mention them.

Chinatown
900 block of North Broadway
Downtown

New Chinatown is full of curio shops, markets, and restaurants. Tourist-traps and authentic Chinese places are juxtaposed in this small area of the city. Chinese festivals and processions are frequent. (See Tours, p. 103.)

Chinatown.

Fairfax District
Fairfax Avenue from Sixth Street
to Beverly Boulevard

Los Angeles' Jewish community is widespread, but has its roots here. Fairfax is a great place to walk and browse and a great place to eat. The Farmer's Market and CBS Television City are nearby.

Garment District
Ninth and Los Angeles streets
Downtown

Los Angeles has a large center for the manufacture of clothing. Its showplace, the California Mart at 110 East Ninth Street, features a major exhibition and convention facility with sixty-eight showrooms and meeting rooms catering to the fashion industry. Many quality discount clothing stores fill the neighborhood.

Interior Design District
Melrose Avenue at San Vicente
Boulevard

Most of the major interior design studios are located in this area. The Pacific Design Center, 8687 Melrose Avenue, houses many studios and is the center of Southern California's interior design trade. (See Shopping, p. 000.)

Little Tokyo
First Street east of Main Street
Downtown

Authentic Japanese foods and merchandise are available here. Nisei Week is celebrated every August. Restaurants, businesses, temples, and cultural centers, plus the New Otani Hotel and Japanese Village Plaza make this a downtown gathering place for Los Angeles' large Japanese-American population as well as visitors from the Orient.

Los Angeles Convention Center
Pico Boulevard and Figueroa Street
Downtown   748-8531

A modern center for conventions and exhibitions, offering twenty conference rooms, a huge main exhibit hall, and seating for 6,000.

Westwood
West of the San Diego Freeway
north of Santa Monica Boulevard.

A community in West Los Angeles with a population mix of residents of the West Side and UCLA students. Westwood Village, above Wilshire Boulevard, is a six-block area with shops, restaurants, and movie theaters. It's an excellent spot for a night-time stroll.

IN PRINT

Books on L.A.

California History

John Caughey. *California: A Remarkable State's Life History* (1970).

Carey McWilliams. *Southern California Country* (1946).
Andrew F. Rolle. *California, a History* (1969).

Lynn Bowman. *Los Angeles: Epic of a City* (1974).
John and LaRee Caughey. *Los Angeles: Biography of a City* (1977).
John Anson Ford. *Thirty Explosive Years in Los Angeles* (1961).
Bruce Henstell. *Los Angeles: An Illustrated History* (1980).
Morrow Mayo. *Los Angeles* (1933).
Remi Nadeau. *Los Angeles from Mission to Modern City* (1960).
W.W. Robinson. *Los Angeles, a Profile* (1968).
Max Yavno and Lee Shippey. *The Los Angeles Book* (1950).

Los Angeles History

Richard G. Lillard. *Eden in Jeopardy* (1966).
Jack Smith. *The Big Orange: Jack Smith's Los Angeles* (1976).

Contemporary Los Angeles

Reyner Banham. *Los Angeles, the Architecture of Four Ecologies* (1971).
David Gebhard and Robert Winter. *A Guide to Architecture in Southern California* (1965).

Architecture

Eve Babitz. *Slow Days and Fast Company* (1979).
Raymond Chandler: all of his detective novels acutely examine the author's contemporary L.A.
John Gregory Dunne. *True Confessions* (1977).
F. Scott Fitzgerald. *The Last Tycoon* (1941).
Aldous Huxley. *After Many a Summer Dies the Swan* (1946).
Thomas Pynchon. *The Crying of Lot 49* (1966).
Nathanael West. *The Day of the Locust* (1939).

Fiction

Leigh Charlton and Annette Swanberg. *Glad Rags: L.A. Directory to Discount Fashions* (1979).

Guide Books

George Christy. *The Los Angeles Underground Gourmet* (1970).

Davis Dutton and Tedi Pilgreen. *Where to Take Your Children in Southern California* (1971).

Lois Dwan. *Los Angeles Restaurant Guide* (1970).

Monte Gast. *Getting the Best of L.A.* (1972).

Roni Sue Malin and Judy Ruderman. *Only in L.A.: A Guide to Exceptional Services* (1979).

John Pashdag and Jim Woller. *All Night L.A.* (1978).

Newspapers

Nearly every community in the area has at least one local newspaper; many foreign language and special interest papers are published in Los Angeles. Below we've listed only a few of the larger local publications.

Los Angeles *Times;* published daily, 972-5000.

Los Angeles *Herald-Examiner;* published daily, 748-1212.

Santa Monica *Evening Outlook;* published Monday through Saturday, 829-6811.

Valley News and Green Sheet; published Tuesday through Sunday, 997-4241.

The Recycler. Appearing every Thursday, this is an important advertising paper. To place a free ad, call 626-6622.

Glendale *News-Press;* published Monday through Saturday, 241-4141.

Long Beach *Independent Press-Telegram;* published daily, 436-3676.

Pasadena *Star-News;* published daily, 578-6300.

South Bay Daily Breeze; published daily, 540-5511.

Magazines

Big Valley
World of Communications, Inc.
16161 Roscoe Boulevard, Suite 200
Sepulveda   894-2223

Los Angeles
1888 Century Park East
Century City   552-3399

PSA California Magazine
5900 Wilshire Boulevard, Suite 300
Los Angeles   937-5810

New West
New York Magazine Company, Inc.
9665 Wilshire Boulevard
Beverly Hills   273-7516

San Fernando Valley
Copeland Publishing Company
12345 Ventura Boulevard, Suite A
Studio City   985-2624

Westways
Box 2890 Terminal Annex
Los Angeles   461-4448

Los Angeles *Magazine's* first cover, July 1960.

Small Newspapers and Periodicals

Clouds
1055 Grand Avenue
Long Beach   436-5504

Clouds is published monthly. It is regionally related to Long Beach, but has art, film, music, and theater listings and an art portfolio.

L.A. Weekly
5325 Sunset Boulevard
Hollywood   462-6911

Published weekly. This paper can be picked up free at various locations around town; it features columns on film, music, and art.

The *Reader* is published each Thursday and is free to those who pick it up at various locations throughout the city. It contains a weekly datebook of cultural events in and around Los Angeles.

Reader
P.O. Box 5630
Los Angeles   622-6373

Didn't they ban this in Burbank? Advice to the lovelorn, published twice monthly.

Screw West
1655 North Cherokee Avenue
Hollywood   467-7422

News, feature articles, and photos about Palos Verdes and the South Bay, including restaurant reviews and a calendar of community events.

View
31244 Palos Verdes Drive West
Rancho Palos Verdes   541-3767

World Cinema is free to patrons of advertising theaters. It is published approximately every three weeks and deals exclusively with foreign films.

World Cinema
7520 West Norton Avenue
Los Angeles   385-1323

Rose Garden in Exposition Park.

INSTITUTIONS

Libraries

The ninety-one branches of the L.A. County Library are open to the public, but only California residents may check out library materials. For location of individual branches, call the main office at 974-6505.

Los Angeles County Library

There are sixty-two branches of the L.A. City Library, including the central library in downtown L.A., seven regional libraries and fifty-

Los Angeles City Public Library

four community libraries. Libraries are open to the public, but only L.A. residents may check out materials. For further information and location of branch libraries call 626-7461. Central library: The Rufus B. von Kleinsmid Library, at 630 West Fifth Street, includes over 1,600,000 volumes with excellent research facilities. The library is open 10:00 a.m. to 9:00 p.m. Monday through Saturday. For specific information about the library's holdings, call the main office, above.

UCLA Library System

The UCLA system of libraries includes the University Research Library, the College Library, and sixteen special libraries at UCLA as well as the William Andrews Clark Memorial Library in the West Adams district. Total collections comprise over 4,000,000 volumes. The libraries are open to the public; nonstudents may check out materials after paying an annual fee of $24. For general information call 825-1323. To see if the library has a particular book call 825-7143. The William Andrews Clark Memorial Library, at 2520 Cimarron Street, L.A., houses an extraordinary collection of English literature from 1640–1750, books and manuscripts of Oscar Wilde, Montana history, and modern fine printing. The library is open to the public; materials may not be checked out. 731-8529.

USC Library System

The USC libraries include extensive holdings and excellent research facilities. Libraries are open to the public; to check out materials, nonstudents must pay a fee of $60 per semester or $120 per year. For further information, or to see if the library has a particular book, call 741-5239.

Cal State Northridge Library

Oviatt Library at C.S.U.N. contains extensive collections and fine research facilities. The library is open to the public; to check out materials, nonstudents must join the Bibliographic Society at an annual fee of $20. For specific information call 885-2287.

Huntington Library, Museums, and Art Gallery

The Henry E. Huntington Library at 1151 Oxford Drive, San Marino, houses an extensive collection of rare books and manuscripts. On view in the library museum are a Gutenberg Bible, Shakespeare's First Folio, and the unique Ellesmere Manuscript of Chaucer's *Canterbury Tales*, as well as manuscripts of Washington, Poe, Franklin, and changing exhibits from the library collections. Access to library materials is restricted to scholarly use. For further information call 792-6141. (See Museums, p. 198 .)

Historical Societies

California Historical Society

Historical exhibitions are regularly displayed; members may attend meetings and lectures on California history and receive the society's quarterly journal. 1120 Old Mill Road, San Marino, 449-5450.

Cultural Heritage Board

The board preserves and protects cultural monuments in L.A. and maintains Heritage Square (see Tours, p.192), as well as providing information about local historical monuments, societies, and events. City Hall, room 1500, 485-2433.

Members attend monthly meetings and lectures, receive the society's quarterly journal, and participate in historical tours. The society has offices at the Lummis Home, 200 East Avenue Forty-three, Highland Park, 222-0546.

Historical Society of Southern California

The Conservancy works to save our architectural treasures from destruction. A large part of this effort involves creating public awareness of how much irreplaceable structural richness the area possesses, how much of it is vulnerable to demolition, and how to safeguard it. They give tours of historic buildings and publish walking guides to downtown and Hollywood Boulevard. 849 South Broadway, 623-2489.

Los Angeles Conservancy

Automobile Clubs and Travel Planning

For both members and nonmembers, AAA will provide road and weather information by phone and can issue International Driver's Licenses at any of its eighty-two offices in Southern California. In addition, AAA's World Travel Offices offer complete travel agency services. There are twenty-five such offices in the region. Services for members of AAA include maps and tour books, emergency road service, accommodation and travel reservations, recreation information, and trip planning. 741-4880.

Automobile Club of Southern California (AAA)

With twelve offices in Southern California, National provides services for members similar to those of AAA. For nonmembers National can give road and weather information, issue International Driver's Licenses and provide Traveler's Insurance, Mexican Auto Insurance and Tourist Cards.

National Automobile Club

Resources

The Woman's Building
1727 North Spring Street
Downtown   221-6161

Focusing on women's cultural issues, the Woman's Building also offers referrals for those seeking physicians, lawyers, housing, and a host of other services. They publish a calendar of women's activities, present art exhibits and poetry readings, and give classes in a variety of topics from career planning to video production.

Junior Leagues
6333 West Third Street
Los Angeles   937-5566
1401 South Oak Knoll Avenue
Pasadena   796-0244

The Junior Leagues in the area play a strong role in the community. They sponsor volunteer programs that assist crime victims, educate young people about the dangers of alcohol, provide activities for senior citizens, and preserve the work of native artisans. They work in museums and hospitals and publish a tour guide to the area that gives excellent information on facilities for the physically handicapped.

Chambers of Commerce

Both general information and that concerning special events and attractions can usually be obtained by calling the local Chamber of Commerce. Some of the more important offices in Southern California are given here. Los Angeles, 629-0711; Wilshire Center, 387-1224; Hollywood, 469-8311; Santa Monica, 393-9825; Long Beach, 436-1251; Manhattan Beach, 545-5313; Laguna Beach, (714) 494-1018; San Diego, (714) 232-0124; Santa Barbara, (805) 965-3021; Riverside, (714) 683-7100.

Better Business Bureaus

Los Angeles: Complaints, 382-0917; Inquiries, 383-0992.
Long Beach: Complaints and Inquiries, 435-3741.
Orange County: Complaints, (714) 633-4753; Inquiries, (714) 633-3670.

SERVICES

Information and Emergency Aid

Whether you need emergency aid, personal services, or information, you can generally find it by phone. In addition to the numbers given below, the reference rooms at the larger libraries will often be able to answer your questions. When calling outside of the 213 area, remember to dial "1" before the area code.

Emergency Medical Aid

The Fire Department provides emergency paramedical and ambulance service; they can also help locate the nearest emergency receiving room in your area. Local numbers can be found inside the front cover of your phone book, but if you don't have one when you need it, simply dial "O", say that you have a medical emergency, and the operator will quickly connect you with the nearest paramedic unit.

Poison Information

The Poison Information Center at Children's Hospital will provide information about emergency treatment and the location of the nearest emergency room equipped to deal with a particular case; lines are open twenty-four hours a day. 663-3341.

California Highway Patrol

Emergency: ask operator for Zenith 12000
Road Condition Information: 626-7231

General Information: 736-3001
Watch Officer: 736-2965

Coast Guard Search and Rescue Emergencies: 590-2225

Harbor Patrol 823-4571

Weather 554-1212

Time 853-1212

Telephone Information 411

Transportation

The automobile remains almost a necessity in Los Angeles. Taxis are readily found at the airports and major hotels, but from all other locations must be telephoned. With the long distances commonly traveled in L.A., cabs can become expensive. Although it is possible to get around the city on Southern California Rapid Transit District (RTD) buses, it is neither convenient, comfortable, nor pleasant—and with RTD fares now fifty-five cents, it is not even particularly cheap. On the other hand, judicious use of public transportation can save time, money, and energy. In this way, we recommend bus service when traveling to highly congested areas during rush-hour, or to areas where parking is scarce and expensive.

AIRPORTS

Los Angeles International Airport (LAX)
1 World Way
Los Angeles

Of the five commercial airports in the Los Angeles area, LAX is by far the largest and busiest, incorporating over five square miles and serving some 100,000 passengers each day. During peak travel periods airport traffic conditions become oppressive; we recommend that travelers use either express bus service or the parking lots outside of the terminal area. When driving in the immediate vicinity of LAX, tune your radio to 530 AM for last-minute traffic information.

Parking, traffic, and bus information: AIR-PORT

Additional airport information: 646-5252

Airlines: All major foreign and domestic as well as local and regional airlines.

Commuter Air Service: Golden West Airlines and Aero Commuter helicopters provide service between LAX and outlying airports.

Parking: Inside the airport: 50 cents for the first two hours, $10 per day. Lot C, at the corner of 96th Street and Sepulveda Boulevard: $2 per day. VSP Parking, at the corner of 111th Street and La Cienega Boulevard: $1.50 per day. Free shuttle bus between Lot C and VSP parking areas and the airline terminals operates every ten to fifteen minutes, twenty-four hours a day.

Bus Service: *RTD Airport Express* operates between LAX and Los Angeles, Hollywood, the Wilshire district, Universal City, and Beverly Hills. Specific information can be given by Travelers Information or RTD drivers at the terminals, since it is difficult at best to reach RTD by phone. 626-4455.

Culver City Bus Lines runs a nonstop bus between LAX and the corner of Pico and Westwood boulevards in West Los Angeles. Buses leave from in front of the International, TWA, American, Western, and United terminals every half hour between 5:30 a.m. and 9:30 p.m.; the fare is 35 cents. 559-8310.

Crown Airport Commuter runs from LAX to the Hollywood-Burbank Airport, from there to the Glendale Holiday Inn, with on-call service to La Cañada and the Jet Propulsion Laboratory in Pasadena. Buses depart from the outside islands in front of each terminal at 7:30 and 10:30 a.m., 1:30, 5:30, and 8:30 p.m. The trip takes about forty minutes to Burbank, fifty minutes to Glendale; fare is $4. 750-5439.

Flyaway Bus makes one nonstop trip between LAX and the Van Nuys Airport Bus Terminal, 7610 Woodley Avenue at Saticoy in the San Fernando Valley, every half hour between 7:00 a.m. and midnight, less often between midnight and 5:15 a.m. Passengers may park for up to fifteen days in the Van Nuys lot for $1; the fare is $3 one-way, $5 round-trip. For complete schedule, call 994-5554.

Airport Service operates between LAX and Pasadena, Long Beach, and Orange County. For complete information call 796-9108.

Great American Stage Lines provides bus service between LAX and Thousand Oaks, Oxnard, and Ventura. For complete information call (805) 495-1025.

Hollywood-Burbank Airport
2627 Hollywood Way
Burbank

Light traffic, convenient parking, and superb lemonade make Hollywood-Burbank an attractive alternative to LAX, especially for Pasadena, San Fernando Valley, and Hollywood area air commuters.
General Information: 847-6414
Airlines: Hughes Airwest, PSA, Continental Airlines.
Commuter Air Service: Aero Commuter provides helicopter service between Burbank and other area airports.

Parking: Adjacent to the terminal, $3 per day.

Bus Service: *RTD* provides service from the airport to various locations in the L.A. area. Specific information should be obtained at the terminal (626-4455), since it is difficult to contact RTD by phone.

Crown Airport Commuter provides nonstop service to LAX and the Glendale Holiday Inn, on-call service to La Cañada and the Jet Propulsion Laboratory in Pasadena. Buses depart for LAX at 6:40, 9:25, and 10:20 a.m. and at 12:40, 4:10, 7:40 and 10:10 p.m.; the trip takes about an hour, fare is $4. 750-5439.

Long Beach Municipal Airport
4100 Donald Douglas Drive
Long Beach

For regional flights and a wonderful flavor of the thirties, Long Beach Airport's convenience and pure Art Deco design can't be beat.
Airport Administration: 421-2400

Airlines: PSA, Trans Catalina Airlines, Catalina Airlines.
Commuter Air Service: Aero Commuter provides helicopter service to other area airports.

Parking: Adjacent to the terminal; $3 per day, $15 per week.
Bus Service: *Long Beach Transit* provides local service: 591-2301.

Airport Service provides service to LAX, Orange County, and Pasadena. For specific information, call 596-1662.

Ontario International Airport
Emporia Street and Vineyard Avenue
Ontario

Widely known as the destination of fog-diverted flights to LAX, Ontario actually offers fine facilities and extensive air service in its own right. With ten airlines, it is the second largest airport in the area and a convenient alternative for passengers in the eastern sections of L.A., as well as Orange, Riverside, and San Bernardino counties.
Airport Administration: (714) 984-1207

Airlines: Hughes Airwest, Western Airlines, Trans World Airlines, United Airlines, Continental Airlines, Air California, PSA, American Airlines, Golden West Airlines, and Air Cortez.
Commuter Air Service: Golden West flies from Ontario to other area airports.

Parking: Adjacent to the terminal: $4 per day. Auxiliary parking, behind the Lockheed Building: $2 per day.

Bus Service: *Omni-Trans* provides local bus service: (714) 983-2671.
RTD provides bus service to the L.A. area: (714) 620-1871.

Orange County Airport
19051 Airport Way North
Santa Ana

Airport Administration: (714) 834-2400
Airlines: Hughes Airwest, Air California, Golden West Airlines, Trans Catalina Airlines.

Commuter Air Service: Golden West flies from Orange County to other area airports.
Parking: Adjacent to the terminal, $3.75 per day.

Bus Service: *RTD* provides service to L.A. locations, including direct service to LAX. Specific information should be obtained at the terminal, (714) 620-1871 or (213) 626-4455.

Airport Service provides service to LAX, Long Beach, and Pasadena. For specific information, call (714) 581-5780 or (213) 796-9108.

AMTRAK

Book trains well in advance, especially during peak-travel and fuel-tight periods. Family plans and USA rail discounts are sometimes available. San Diego trains are first-come, first-serve, arrive early, and run fast. Trains depart Los Angeles from Union Station at 800 North Alameda Street. For schedule information and reservations, call 624-0171 or (800) 648-3850.
San Diego passengers now have a choice of six daily trains in each direction, except on Saturdays when there is no 4:30 train. Departure times from L.A. are 7:30 and 10:30 a.m., 1:30, 4:30, 5:30, and 8:30 p.m., with stops in Fullerton, Santa Ana, San Juan Capistrano, San Clemente, Oceanside, and Del Mar. Fare is $18 round-trip.

Amtrak's Coast Starlight, near San Luis Obispo, heads for Los Angeles.

Santa Barbara passengers may take the Coastal train to San Francisco, departing L.A. at 10:00 a.m. and arriving in Santa Barbara at 12:20 p.m., with stops in Glendale and Oxnard. The returning train departs Santa Barbara for L.A. at 4:15 p.m. Round-trip fare is $16.

Bus Service

The Southern California Rapid Transit District (RTD) attempts to provide public transportation throughout the area. The results are extremely variable: along some routes the bus service is more than adequate, but in many areas you can make better time on foot. In downtown L.A. the minibus shuttle service runs along a seven-mile route from 9:00 a.m. to 4:00 p.m. Since it is difficult to reach RTD by phone, information can usually be obtained from drivers and fellow passengers. System Guides are available at the downtown terminal for $1. RTD Downtown Terminal, Sixth and Los Angeles streets, 626-4455.

Individual municipal bus lines, within their limited areas, generally provide somewhat better service; the Santa Monica Municipal Bus Line, which includes a freeway bus to downtown L.A., provides excellent service on the West Side.
Santa Monica Municipal Bus Line: 451-5445
Culver City Municipal Bus Line: 837-5211, 559-8310
Gardena Municipal Bus Line: 324-1304
Long Beach Transit: 591-2301

For long-distance bus travel, both Greyhound and Continental Trailways operate from numerous terminals throughout the area. The main terminals, in downtown L.A., are:
Greyhound Bus Lines, Sixth and Los Angeles streets, 620-1200
Continental Trailways, Sixth and Main streets, 742-1200

Ticket Agencies

Ticketron

Tickets for nearly all theatrical, musical, and sporting events, as well as ski-lift tickets, RTD passes, and travel reservations and tickets may be purchased at any Ticketron outlet. Ticketron has branches throughout Southern California, including most Sears, Ward's, and Broadway stores; for the one nearest you, check the White Pages or Call Ticketron's main office at 642-5700.

Mutual Ticket Agencies

Tickets for most theatrical, musical, and sporting events are available from Mutual, with offices throughout Southern California; for the outlet nearest you, check the White Pages or call Mutual's main office at 627-1248.

Late Night and Twenty-four Hour Places

What to do while waiting for the dawn ... here are a few suggestions and services that are open all night or nearly.

Baby Sitters Guild
6362 Hollywood Boulevard
Hollywood   469-8248

Providing baby sitters on call twenty-four hours a day, the Guild was originally sponsored by Eleanor Roosevelt and artist Jean Harner to provide employment for older women; all sitters are women over forty.

Gas Stations

Most World gas stations are open twenty-four hours. For locations, check the phone book or call 659-8800.

Pharmacies

Thrifty Drug Store, 1533 North Vermont Avenue, L.A., open twenty-four hours; 666-5083.
All Night Pharmacy, 1301 South Garfield Avenue, Alhambra, open 9:00 p.m. to 9:00 a.m., 283-2000.
Horton and Converse Pharmacy, 6625 Van Nuys Boulevard, Van Nuys, open twenty-four hours; 786-8710.
Bel-Air Pharmacy, 820 Moraga Drive, Bel Air, on call twenty-four hours; 472-9593, 472-9594.
Family Pharmacy Service, 8314 Wilshire Boulevard, Beverly Hills, emergency delivery service, on call twenty-four hours; 653-4070.
Knoll's Pharmacy, 16630 Marquez Avenue, Pacific Palisades, on call twenty-four hours; 454-6000.
Mid-Valley Professional Pharmacy, 14140 Ventura Boulevard, Sherman Oaks, on call twenty-four hours; 789-6161.
Modern Apothecary Prescription Pharmacy, 1800 South Robertson Boulevard, L.A., emergency delivery service, on call twenty-four hours; 652-8390.
Robert Burns Pharmacy, 9049 Burton Way, L.A., emergency delivery, on call twenty-four hours; 271-5126.
Warner Plaza Pharmacy, 21809 Ventura Boulevard, Canoga Park, on call twenty-four hours; 883-2455.

Repairs

Residential Services, 1801 Avenue of the Stars, Century City, can provide repair service of all types from its registry of repairmen on call twenty-four hours a day. 277-0770.

Newsstands and Bookstores

Al's Newsstand, 370 North Fairfax Avenue, L.A., 935-8525.

Book Circus, 8230 Santa Monica Boulevard, West Hollywood, open twenty-four hours; offers an adequate selection of books; 656-6854.

World Books and News, 1652 North Cahuenga Boulevard, Hollywood, open twenty-four hours; the best newsstand in town; 465-4352.

General News Agency, 3265 Fifth Street, L.A., open twenty-four hours; 628-3968.

Pico-Robertson Newsstand, 1404 South Robertson Boulevard, L.A., open twenty-four hours; 274-5658.

Republic Newsstand, 660 South Main Street, L.A., open twenty-four hours.

Universal News Agency, 1655 North Las Palmas Avenue, Hollywood, open twenty-four hours; 467-3850.

Markets

Boy's Markets are open twenty-four hours; check phone book for nearest location.

Hollywood Ranch Market, 1248 North Vine Street, Hollywood; open twenty-four hours.

Market Basket, 11766 Wilshire Boulevard, West L.A.; open twenty-four hours.

Mayfair Markets are open twenty-four hours; check phone book for nearest location.

Smith's Food Kings are open twenty-four hours; check phone book for nearest location.

Toluca Mart, 8770 West Pico Boulevard, L.A.; open twenty-four hours.

Twenty-four Hour Market, 601 Atlantic Avenue, Long Beach.

After Hours Clubs

Although liquor is not sold after 2 a.m., these places remain open for dancing and general partying.

Bootleggers
11637 West Pico Boulevard
West Los Angeles   478-7555
Open Friday and Saturday till 4 a.m.
(See Going Out, p. 190 .)

Chippendales
3739 Overland Avenue
West Los Angeles   838-8411
Open Friday and Saturday till 4 a.m.
(See Going Out, p. 190 .)

Dillon's Downtown
1024 South Grand Avenue
Downtown   746-2461
Open till dawn Friday and Saturday

Moody's Disco and Restaurant
321 Santa Monica Boulevard
Santa Monica   451-5003
After hours Friday and Saturday
(See Going Out, p. 191 .)

Odyssey I
8471 Beverly Boulevard
West Hollywood   658-8106
Friday and Saturday to 5 a.m.

Osko's
333 South La Cienega Boulevard
West Hollywood   652-9333
Friday and Saturday to 4 a.m.

Point After
11345 Ventura Boulevard
North Hollywood   769-5555
Friday and Saturday to 4 a.m.

RESTAURANTS

Downtown

The Golden Palace, at 911–914 North Broadway in Chinatown; open until 4:00 a.m.

Vickman's Restaurant and Bakery, 1228 East Eighth Street; open 3:00 a.m. to 3:00 p.m. Monday–Friday, 3:00 a.m. to 1:00 p.m. Saturday.

West Hollywood

Canter's Fairfax Restaurant and Delicatessen, 419 North Fairfax Avenue; open twenty-four hours.

Beverly Hills

Dr. Munchies Grocery and Gathering Place, 9595 Wilshire Boulevard; open until 4:00 a.m.

Ollie Hammond's Steak House, 91 North La Cienega Boulevard; open twenty-four hours.

Westwood and Culver City

Ship's, 10877 Wilshire Boulevard and 10705 Washington Boulevard; open twenty-four hours.

Garden Grove

Belisle's, 12001 Harbor Boulevard; open twenty-four hours.

Long Beach

Hamburger Henry, 4700 East Second Street; open twenty-four hours.

Newport Beach

Howard's, 4001 West Pacific Coast Highway; open twenty-four hours.

Van Nuys

Corkey's Restaurant, 5043 Van Nuys Boulevard; open twenty-four hours.

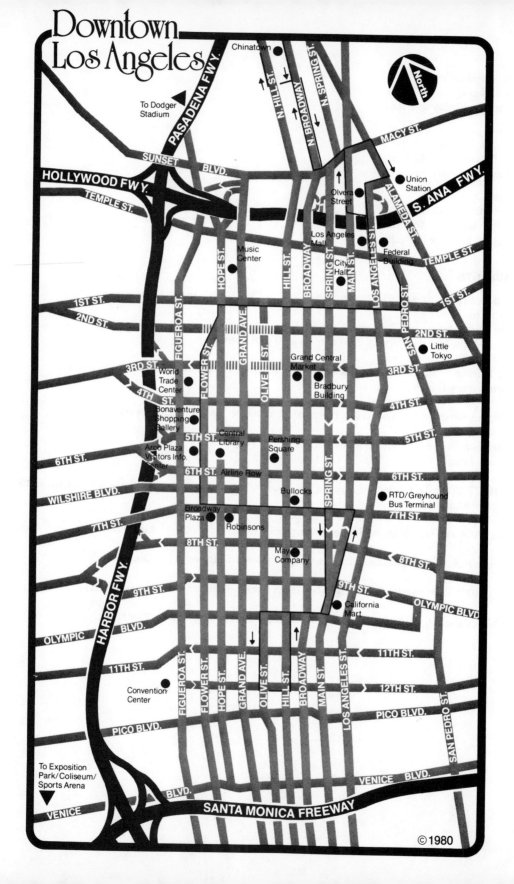

Downtown Los Angeles

North

To Dodger Stadium

Chinatown

PASADENA FWY.

SUNSET BLVD.

HOLLYWOOD FWY.

TEMPLE ST.

MACY ST.

S. ANA FWY.

Union Station

Olvera Street

Los Angeles Mall

City Hall

Federal Building

TEMPLE ST.

Music Center

HOPE ST.
HILL ST.
BROADWAY
SPRING ST.
MAIN ST.
LOS ANGELES ST.

1ST ST.

2ND ST.

FIGUEROA ST.
FLOWER ST.
GRAND AVE.
OLIVE ST.

SAN PEDRO ST.

1ST ST.

2ND ST.

Little Tokyo

Grand Central Market

World Trade Center

3RD ST.

Bradbury Building

3RD ST.

4TH ST.

Bonaventure Shopping Gallery

4TH ST.

Central Library

5TH ST.

Pershing Square

5TH ST.

Arco Plaza Visitors Info. Center

6TH ST.

6TH ST.

Airline Row

SPRING ST.

6TH ST.

WILSHIRE BLVD.

Bullocks

RTD/Greyhound Bus Terminal

Broadway Plaza

Robinsons

7TH ST.

HARBOR FWY.

7TH ST.

8TH ST.

May Company

8TH ST.

9TH ST.

9TH ST.

California Mart

OLYMPIC BLVD.

OLYMPIC BLVD.

11TH ST.

FIGUEROA ST.
FLOWER ST.
HOPE ST.
GRAND AVE.
OLIVE ST.
HILL ST.
BROADWAY
MAIN ST.
LOS ANGELES ST.

11TH ST.

Convention Center

12TH ST.

PICO BLVD.

PICO BLVD.

SAN PEDRO ST.

To Exposition Park/Coliseum/ Sports Arena

VENICE BLVD.

VENICE BLVD.

SANTA MONICA FREEWAY

©1980

360

MAPS

Including the Rosebud Map to the Best of Los Angeles.

The enticing places described in the previous pages are spread out over a vast and varied landscape. However, Los Angeles is more than accessible by automobile, and much of it can be reached by public transportation. And don't forget the walking tours presented in "Tours and Favorite Flings" and in "Architecture and Historic Places."

To assist you in planning your travels, Alex D'Anca has designed a Rosebud map with a legend designating the major points of interest in and around the city. The Greater Los Angeles Visitors and Convention Bureau maps provide a schema of downtown and an overview of Southern California's marvelous freeway system. (A canyon map of a section of the Santa Monica Mountains appears on pages 328–329 in "Scenic and Open-Air Places.") The serious explorer will want a detailed street map to use in conjunction with the maps provided here.

If you spend much time in Los Angeles, most likely you will spend a considerable amount of that time driving. The city has come a long way since 1910 when the speed limit in downtown was twelve miles per hour. L.A. is the city of the automobile, and every effort is made to make that mode of transportation safe and convenient. The drivers here are courteous and efficient, and roads are marked clearly.

So whether you go on foot, by car, by bus, by train, or by boat, do go. Don't hesitate to venture forth—your reward will be well worth the effort.

ABC Entertainment Center
1 Agoura—Renaissance Pleasure Faire
2 ARCO Plaza
Ambassador Hotel
Anaheim Convention Center
Anaheim Statium
3 Angeles Crest Highway
4 Anheuser-Busch Brewery
5 Arboretum
6 Barnsdall Park
7 Beverly Hills Hotel
8 Beverly Wilshire Hotel
9 Biltmore Hotel
10 Bradbury Building
Brown Derby
Burbank Studios
CBS-TV City
11 Cabrillo Marine Museum
12 Cal Tech
13 California Mart
Capitol Records Building
14 Catalina Island
Century Plaza Hotel
15 Central Library
16 Chateau Marmont
Chinatown
City Hall and Mall
17 Coliseum
County Museum of Art
18 DWP Building
Descanso Gardens
Disneyland
Dodger Stadium
19 El Dorado Nature Center
20 El Molino Viejo
21 El Pueblo State Historic Park
22 Examiner Building
Exposition Park
Farmer's Market
23 Fisherman's Village
24 Flower Market
Forum
25 Gamble House
26 J. Paul Getty Museum
Grand Central Market
Greek Theatre
Griffith Observatory/Planetarium
27 Griffith Park
28 Heritage Square

Continued on page 364.

PACIFIC OCEAN

29 Hollyhock House
★ Hollywood Boulevard
Hollywood Bowl
Hollywood/Burbank Airport
30 Hollywood Memorial Cemetary
Hollywood Park
31 Huntington Hartford Theatre
32 Huntington Library, Art Gallery and
Botanical Gardens
Knott's Berry Farm
La Brea Tar Pits
L.A. Convention Center
Times L.A. Times Building
LAX
zoo L.A. Zoo
Lion Country Safari
33 Little Tokyo
Long Beach Convention and Entertainment
Center
34 Los Alamitos Race Course
35 Loyola-Marymount University
36 Lummis House
MacArthur Park
37 Malibu
Mann's Chinese Theatre
Marina Del Rey
Marineland
38 Mayfair Music Hall
39 Mission San Fernando
40 Mission San Gabriel
Mormon Temple
41 Mulholland Drive
Music Center
NBC-TV Studios
42 New Otani Hotel
Norton Simon Museum
43 Occidental College
Olvera Street
44 Olympic Auditorium
45 Otis Art Institute Gallery

Pacific Design Center
46 Pacific Stock Exchange
47 Page Museum
48 Pantages Theatre
49 Pasadena Civic Auditorium
50 Pershing Square
51 Police Station-Downtown
52 Pio Pico State Historic Park
53 Point Fermin
54 Ports O'Call Village
55 Port of Los Angeles and Long Beach
Harbor
Queen Mary
56 Restaurant Row—La Cienega
57 Rodeo Drive
Rose Bowl
San Fernando Mission
San Gabriel Mission
58 Santa Anita Park
59 Santa Monica Beach
60 Santa Monica Mountains
61 Santa Monica Pier
62 Santa Monica Civic Auditorium
63 Shrine Auditorium
64 Shubert Theatre
65 Solari Theatre
66 South Coast Botanic Gardens
67 Sunset Strip
UCLA
USC
Union Station
Universal Studios
68 Venice Canals
Vincent Thomas Bridge
Watts Towers
69 Wayfarer's Chapel
† Westwood Memorial Cemetary
70 Westwood Village
71 Will Rodgers State Historic Park
72 World Trade Center

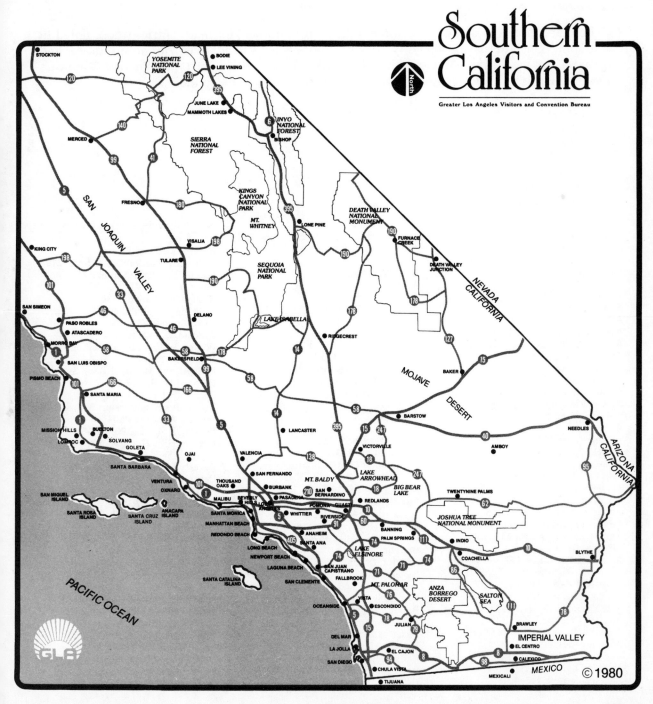

Southern California

North

Greater Los Angeles Visitors and Convention Bureau

PACIFIC OCEAN

© 1980

INDEX

There are three types of entries in the index; page numbers for main entries (those noted in the margins) are listed in bold type; page numbers for secondary entries are in italics; and page numbers indicating photographs and illustrations are in regular type. Where a C appears after an entry, it indicates a photograph in the color section of the guide.

PHOTO CREDITS

Dear Reader:

This Rosebud Publication *The Best of Los Angeles: A Discriminating Guide* will be revised annually to provide you with the most current and useful information on Los Angeles' changing places and events.

If using this guide has helped you enjoy the city, we would like to know. We invite you to share with us your suggestions and comments.

Are you:
☐ a Los Angeles resident?
☐ a visitor? If so, from _____

What did you enjoy most about *The Best of Los Angeles*?

_____

_____

_____

What are your suggestions for the revised edition?

_____

_____

_____

I would like information on other Rosebud Publications:
☐ Rosebud Guides to California and the West
☐ Publications on California and Western history and architecture.

Name _____

Address _____

City _____ State _____ Zip code _____

Phone _____

I would like to order _____ copies of *The Best of Los Angeles.* * Enclosed is $11.95 plus 55¢ postage and handling per copy.

Please cut out and mail to:

— —

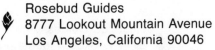

Rosebud Guides
8777 Lookout Mountain Avenue
Los Angeles, California 90046

*To order gift copies, please list names and addresses of recipients on the reverse.

Name _____

Address _____

City _____ State _____ Zip code _____

This gift is sent compliments of _____

Name _____

Address _____

City _____ State _____ Zip code _____

This gift is sent compliments of _____

Name _____

Address _____

City _____ State _____ Zip code _____

This gift is sent compliments of _____

Name _____

Address _____

City _____ State _____ Zip code _____

This gift is sent compliments of _____

- -

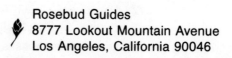

Rosebud Guides
8777 Lookout Mountain Avenue
Los Angeles, California 90046